D1564178

The Publisher
wishes to acknowledge
with gratitude the generous
support of the
LANNAN FOUNDATION
in funding the
Lannan Series of Contemporary Art Criticism,
which is devoted to presenting
the writing of contemporary
critics as well as that of
earlier writers who helped
to shape contemporary
art criticism.

I

Sadakichi Hartmann: Critical Modernist
edited by Jane Calhoun Weaver

II

*The Hydrogen Jukebox: Selected Writings
of Peter Schjeldahl, 1978–1990*
edited by MaLin Wilson

THE
HYDROGEN
JUKEBOX

THE HYDROGEN JUKEBOX

SELECTED WRITINGS
OF PETER SCHJELDAHL
1978–1990

EDITED BY

MALIN WILSON

INTRODUCTION BY ROBERT STORR

UNIVERSITY OF CALIFORNIA PRESS

BERKELEY LOS ANGELES OXFORD

University of California Press
Berkeley and Los Angeles, California
University of California Press, Ltd.
Oxford, England
© 1991 by
The Regents of the University of California
Printed in the United States of America
9 8 7 6 5 4 3 2 1

Library of Congress Cataloging-in-Publication Data

Schjeldahl, Peter.
    The hydrogen jukebox : selected writings of Peter Schjeldahl,
1978–1990 / edited by MaLin Wilson ; introduction by Robert Storr.
    p.   cm. — (Lannan series of contemporary art criticism; 2)
    Includes bibliographical references and index.
    ISBN 0-520-06731-2 (alk. paper)
    1. Art, Modern—19th century.   2. Art, Modern—20th century.
I. Wilson, MaLin.   II. Title.   III. Series.
N6447.S345   1991
709′.04—dc20   90-24311

The paper used in this publication
meets the minimum requirements of American
National Standard for Information Sciences—Permanence
of Paper for Printed Library Materials,
ANSI Z39.48-1984.

CONTENTS

CONTENTS

PREFACE

"I saw the best minds of my generation . . . listening to the crack of doom on the hydrogen jukebox." That's from Allen Ginsberg's "Howl," which I collided with in high school circa 1959 and always emulate for its bedrock American eloquence and an aesthetic disposition that if it were a proverb might go "Make the best of the worst."

I would like my book to be translated into the language of the dead, with copies humbly presented to Charles Baudelaire, D. H. Lawrence, W. H. Auden, Frank O'Hara, and Red Smith. Among the living, the first presentees will be my wife, Brooke Alderson, and my friends Christopher Knight, Gerald Marzorati, and Robert Storr.

This book owes everything to MaLin Wilson, who invented it.

Peter Schjeldahl
July 1989

ACKNOWLEDGMENTS

This book is born of my desire to have at hand the best writings of Peter Schjeldahl, and to be able to locate everything he has written about art. The book includes many of the journalistic art reviews that are his particular forte, but in addition there is a wide-ranging assortment of long and short essays, articles, and book reviews; two poems; and an interview, which itself contains two poems. There were many other pieces we wanted to include, which the reader may find with the assistance of the bibliography that spans Peter Schjeldahl's art writing from his first short reviews in *Art News* in 1965 through the demise of *7 Days* in April 1990.

None of this would have been possible without major support from the Lannan Foundation, to whom I extend my deepest gratitude.

I also wish to thank the University of California Press, especially James Clark and Deborah Kirshman for their extra efforts and Stephanie Fay for her expert editing.

This project has been realized through the combined support, skills, and talents of Greg Powell, my husband, who gave me steady, daily encouragement and spent tedious hours on the computer; Teresa Arellano, who swiftly entered data; Helen Lyons, who provided computer expertise; Sam Peters, who skillfully helped with microfilm; and Neery Melkonian, who assisted with research.

I am grateful to the following publishers and editors for permission to reprint the writings selected for this volume:

SUN press, New York, for "Dear Profession of Art Writing" and "The Artist," in *Since 1964: New and Selected Poems* (1978), 12–20 and 22–23, both reprinted here in "On Art and Artists: Peter Schjeldahl."

Harry N. Abrams, New York, for "To Pico," in *Guacamole Airlines and Other Drawings by Edward Ruscha* (1978), 6–7.

Art in America for "Rothko and Belief," 67 (March–April 1979): 78–85; "[Edvard] Munch: The Missing Master," 67 (May–June 1979): 80–95; "Warhol and Class Content," 68 (May 1980): 111–119; "Cindy

Sherman," published as "Shermanettes," 70 (March 1982): 110–111; "Welcome to Helgaland," 74 (October 1986): 11, 13; "A Visit to the Salon of Autumn 1986," 74 (December 1986): 15–21; "Our Kiefer," 76 (March 1988): 116–126.

The *New York Times Book Review* for "A Book by Larry Rivers," published as "At the Mad Fringes of Art," a review of *Drawings and Digressions*, by Larry Rivers with Carol Brightman (November 18, 1979): 7, 38.

The Pace Gallery, New York, for "Dubuffet, 1980," in the exhibition catalogue *Jean Dubuffet* (1980), 3–10.

The *Village Voice* for "First *Voice* Column," published as "Appraising Passions" (January 7, 1981): 67; "Clement Greenberg," published as "An Inclement Critic" (February 4, 1981): 77; "Exxon Exhibition at the Guggenheim," published as "Stock Options" (February 18–24, 1981): 73; "Julian Schnabel and Susan Rothenberg," published as "Bravery in Action" (April 29–May 5, 1981): 81; "Arshile Gorky," published as "The Great Gorky" (May 13–19, 1981): 101; "L.A. Demystified! Art and Life in the Eternal Present" (June 3–9, 1981): 1, 32–38; "Affairs of the Heat" (July 1–7, 1981): 77; "Disney Animators," published as "American Nightmares" (August 5–11, 1981): 68; "Realism Again," published as "Realism on the Comeback Trail" (November 11–17, 1981): 77; "H. C. Westermann," originally titled "Crimes of the Heartland" (November 25–December 1, 1981): 88; "Only Connect: Bruce Nauman," published as "Only Connect" (January 20–26, 1982): 72; "'Les Drippings' in Paris: The Jackson Pollock Retrospective" (February 10–16, 1982): 94; "David Salle," published as "David Salle's Objects of Disaffection" (March 23, 1982): 84; "Why New French Art Is Lousy" (April 6, 1982): 37–39; "Willem de Kooning," published as "Delights by de Kooning" (April 13, 1982): 79; "Robert Smithson's Writings," published as "A Nose for the Abyss," a review of *The Writings of Robert Smithson*, edited by Nancy Holt (June 1982): 1, 7–8; "Documenta 7," published as "King Curator" (July 20, 1982): 73, and "The Germans' Marshall Arts" (August 3, 1982): 66; "Howard Finster," published as "About Reverence" (August 31, 1982): 73; "Clemente to Marden to Kiefer" (October 12, 1982): 83; "Leon Golub" published as "Red Planet" (October 26, 1982): 96.

Little Caesar Press, Los Angeles, for "I Missed Punk," in *The Brute* (1981), 7–8.

Institute for Art and Urban Resources, P.S. 1, Long Island City, for "Decade of Wonders," in the exhibition catalogue *Abstract Painting, 1960–1969* (1982), 12–13.

Video Data Bank, Art Institute of Chicago, for video interview transcribed as "On Art and Artists: Peter Schjeldahl," *Profile* 3, no. 4 (July 1983).

Mary Boone Gallery, New York, for "The Daemon and Sigmar Polke," in the exhibition catalogue *Sigmar Polke* (1985), 4–5.

The Condé Nast Publications, Inc., and *Vanity Fair* for "The Grant Wood Revival," published as "American Gothic Again: The Grant Wood Revival," 46 (June 1983): 93–99; "Edouard Manet," published as "Love of Manet," 46 (October 1983): 62–68; "In Defense of Artistic Fashion," 47 (April 1984): 97; "Eric Fischl," published as "Bad Boy of Brilliance," 47 (May 1984): 66–72.

Art & Antiques for "Balthus," published as "Pretty Babies," 5 (March 1984): 91–96.

The Saatchi Collection, London, for "Minimalism" and "Philip Guston," in *Art of Our Time: The Saatchi Collection* (London: Lund-Humphries, Inc., 1984), Bk. 1, 28–29, and Bk. 3, 12–14.

Musée Saint Pierre Art Contemporain, Lyon, France, for "Ed Ruscha: Traffic and Laughter," in *Edward Ruscha* (1985): 40–53.

In These Times, Chicago, Illinois, for "The Immigrant Strain," published as "Irony and Agony" (August 20, 1986): 24, 23.

The University of Missouri, Kansas City, Gallery of Art, for "Adrian Saxe and the Smart Pot," published as "The Smart Pot: Adrian Saxe and Post-Everything Ceramics," in the exhibition catalogue *Adrian Saxe* (1986), 13–17.

Hirschl & Adler Galleries, Inc., New York, for "Hopperesque," from the exhibition catalogue *Edward Hopper: Light Years* (1988), 5–12.

7 Days for "Mike Kelley," published as "New Blue Collar" (October 5, 1988): 59–60; "Paintings by Aborigines," published as "Patronizing Primitives" (November 16, 1988): 67–68; "Jeff Koons," published as "Looney Koons" (December 14, 1988): 66; "Courbet," published as "Peep Show" (December 21, 1988): 69–70; "Treason of Clerks" (August 2, 1989): 53; "Velázquez," published as "Mr. Cool" (October 18, 1989): 72; "Baselitz and Kippenberger," published as "Bully Boys" (April 11, 1990): 63–64.

Art Journal for "De Kooning Alone," 48, no. 3 (Fall 1989): 247.

INTRODUCTION

A man of the crowd, he is a direct descendant of the first great modernist poet and critic Charles Baudelaire. An American, he is also a distant cousin to Walt Whitman, Baudelaire's "New World" counterpart. Not, to be sure, the Whitman of egalitarian hymns and bombast, although our protagonist too is the ultimate subject of his texts and a natural democrat. Rather, he possesses in exceptional measure the insatiable avidity that distinguishes the self-made man of taste. In him the febrile curiosity of Baudelaire and the unapologetic omnivorousness of Whitman meet. I am speaking, of course, of Peter Schjeldahl, whose book this is.

You will find Peter among the fans. At times he is a fan himself; at times he is the guilty conscience of his confederates. Always he is the savvy witness of the shotgun marriage of art and spectacle. That aesthetic patricians begrudge him this most of all reflects their hopeless frustration with an expanding art world whose constituents simply will not mind their manners or keep their place. For conservatives of both the Right and the Left, membership in the aesthetic elite depends above all on how one takes one's pleasure. Art, they would have us believe, is the affair of those who dissemble rather than display their enjoyment and their need. It is easy, of course, to bad-rap those who fill the bleachers of culture. It is also pretty late in the day. However much one may wish to cloister art and so preserve it as a strictly contemplative pursuit, artists themselves have long since fled the serene precincts of church and academy. With good reason, since art thrives not only on opportunity but also on sheer flux. By the mid–nineteenth century, Gustave Courbet was pitching his tent on Paris's artistic midway and pitching his reputation in the popular press. The salon became the Salon; the aristocratic drawing room metastasized into a stadium of pictures. Honoré Daumier sketched and recorded the doings and sayings of the masses that flocked to this new entertainment, and if he concentrated on the fools who came to be seen more than to see, we know that somewhere in the crowd his friend Baudelaire was busy talent-scouting.

The nineteenth-century dandy now seems quaint, even risible. Bohemianism ages badly, and the theater of daily life has changed, becoming at once gaudier and chillier. Spotting Whitman's shade in a California supermarket, Allen Ginsberg wrote with whimsical and affectionate sadness, "I saw you, . . . childless, lonely old grubber, poking among the meats in the refrigerator and eyeing the grocery boys." Melancholy by temperament, a dandy can nonetheless ill afford nostalgia. Even if it compares unfavorably with the past, the present is his sole concern. Of necessity, then, he is a man of fashion. And why not? He is not fashion's slave but its watchful scribe. Paradoxically, those who hate fashion are the ones who most zealously believe that "the clothes make the man," forgetting in their ardor that style is human possibility, not a state of nature. Fashion is the promise of identity. Conversely, it is camouflage as well. Careful study of the manners of his time permits the man of crowds to move easily in the variegated mass that is his vital medium. "Dressing the part" and adopting the speech of one's temporary milieu is an act more of empathy than of subterfuge. This chameleonlike willingness to slip into and out of character, like an author's decision to impersonate his subject, is none other than an expression of a deep desire to make contact. Using E. M. Forster's injunction "Only connect" to title a column on Bruce Nauman, an artist with whom he feels special kinship, Peter fully registers the difficulty of that demand and Nauman's ingenuity in meeting it with the mesmerizing fluidity of his persona.

The frequent mention of poets is deliberate. Peter is a poet. Moreover, the archetypal sensibility of which I speak has almost always emerged from the ranks of poets doubling as art critics. Baudelaire is the first in line, Guillaume Apollinaire the second. Paul Eluard, André Breton, and a host of others tried their hand at the job with varying success. The tradition then moved, as vanguard art for the most part did, to New York. There it found its most eager and agile spokesman in Frank O'Hara. "Ah Jean Dubuffet," he wrote, "when you think of him / doing his military service in the Eiffel Tower / as a meteorologist / in 1922 / you know how wonderful the 20th century / can be." Substituting a bright benediction for the murky rhetoric of existentialism and the nervous chatter of symposia, O'Hara saved criticism from the muscle-bound embrace of philosophers and the polite lust of connoisseurs. Waspish cheerleader of the avant-garde and "everyone's" intimate, O'Hara was an exemplary enthusiast, the fan's fan. The mark of his seriousness was the teasing and tender regard he showed for the rough creations of those he admired. Concurring with Baudelaire "that the best criticism is that which is entertaining and poetic, not coldly analytic," O'Hara emended the Frenchman's famous credo that it must also be "partial, passionate, and political" with a bittersweet admonition, "Oh be droll, be jolly, and be temperate! Do not / frighten me more than you have to! I must live forever."

These days, O'Hara's type of criticism has few defenders and still fewer practitioners. In Peter, however, it has a master. For him, as for O'Hara and all the others of their tribe, art writing is a case of pleasure turned to profit. Small profit, mind you; for despite all the glitter that now attaches itself to the art world, even the most visible critics earn little as compared with the artists about whom they write or the curators, dealers, and professors they so easily offend. As free-lancers, they choose a difficult and conditional freedom, surviving as best they can outside or at the margins of the art world's increasingly corporate structures. Since it is widely assumed that no such freedom is possible, that secretly all critics are kept by one or another market or academic faction, preserving independence requires a persistent irritability, a constant willingness to bite the hand that feeds. Taking such writers for granted is a sure-fire provocation.

More than once Peter has fallen out of love with artists as passionately as he took to them in the beginning. He has just as dramatically reversed himself in favor of an artist he has previously found wanting. Consider his change of heart regarding the late work of Philip Guston; in 1981 he was Guston's most articulate detractor, in 1988 among his most eloquent advocates. All of which is to say that Peter is content to be the prisoner neither of his own past opinions nor of the current consensus. Stubbornly exercising the right to disagree with himself, he reminds one that liberty is best guaranteed by a measure of perversity. Indeed, the list of publications for which he has written—and of those for which he no longer writes—attests to the fact that he is not an institutional creature. Without teaching post, editorial sinecure, or private income he belongs to what is fast becoming an endangered species, the critic who writes for a living and whose life is writing.

An amateur of painting like his predecessors, he is, where words are concerned, the consummate professional. As a poet-critic, Peter is moonlighting, not potboiling. Far from disdaining criticism, moreover, he believes, correctly, that it is itself a form of literature. We did not have to wait for "postmodernism" to be certain that it had a dignity of its own. Oscar Wilde, another dandy, said as much—hence the title of his essay "The Critic as Artist." A corollary of this belief is that all judgments of quality must be predicated on a knowledge of the rules pertaining to each genre. A branch of criticism as a whole, art writing in turn comprises many subgenres: the short review, the survey of trends, the portrait, the obituary, the catalogue essay, the "think piece," the rave, the pan. In each the author assumes a distinct responsibility toward the public; each grants a certain license and exacts a certain restraint.

For example, it is hard to be "fair," that is, detailed and measured, in a two-hundred-word review. Reviewers can, however, be precise. To do justice to the work, good or bad, they must be vivid. At the other extreme, a catalogue text, written at an artist's or gallery's behest, is by its very nature an endorsement, but it need not fawn or bore. Praise is the most telling test of critics; few are good at it because it depends less on authority than on self-exposure. More generally, at the same moment frontline critics herald the new, they announce the waning of their infatuation with what preceded it. If they are to account truthfully for that experience, their exuberance will always be mixed with regret; their subject is a romance betrayed as well as a discovery made. Only the callow observer or the market booster rejoices in novelty at the expense of previous obsessions—or attempts to deny the latter. Peter commands all these genres and the complex contrasts of tone they require. Above all a master of the lapidary sentence, he is unmatched at short formats, though recently he revived Baudelaire's discursive staple, the "Salon," describing the typical Soho gallery "space walk" as though he were meandering through imaginatively contiguous rooms of a giant nineteenth-century exhibition. Unique in all of American criticism is Peter's poem-monologue "Dear Profession of Art Writing." A parting shot to a vocation he tried to abandon in 1977, it is the fullest, and funniest, description anyone has made of the cold-sweat nights, chronic self-doubt, and exasperated pride of the deadline critic.

There, as in his work generally, Peter's voice sounds the cadences of everyday usage. For him the mot juste is American speech framed by a prosody that forces us to hear its surreal echoes. Stripped of Gallicism and allied to a street-wise sense of the absurd, that latent surrealism is thus neither more nor less than the giddiness accompanying the recognition that sensations are ideas and that everything is an intoxicant. "The child sees everything as novelty," Baudelaire tells us; "the child is always drunk . . . and genius is no more than childhood recaptured at will, childhood equipped now with a man's physical means to express itself." Peter's preferred "means" is the essay, or more precisely the weekly or monthly column. Although it is the habit of intellectuals to despise journalism, Apollinaire looked to signage for modern poetry and to newspapers for modern prose. He was not mistaken, nor was this merely a cubist conceit. In journalism immediacy is at a premium; literary etiquette counts for little. Although most poets and critics learn their trade in universities, where they read what Apollinaire said remote from the urban chaos in which he did his "research," Peter, a college drop-out and unsuccessful expatriate, began his apprenticeship as a reporter—a sports reporter, in fact. That he feels a strong, and reciprocated, affinity for the *New Yorker* baseball writer Roger Angell is understandable. Quick to follow a lead and versatile in his address, he has more in common with newspaper and magazine writers in other fields than he does with his supposed art-world peers, most of whom he took care to rebuke in "Dear Profession of Art Writing." Impatient with dull hierarchies, he could write in another poem: "The top athlete is sublime / as all things extreme, and perfect in their extremeness, / are sublime, as great poems and paintings are, / and how one can love the one and not the other is beyond me."

Like Angell or any good journalist, Peter writes to be read. The craft of journalism demands much more than a simple desire to be factual; in art criticism, of course, "facts" frequently play a small role. Journalists address a public that scans the printed page on time borrowed from work and routine recreations; the good journalist willing to be plainspoken expresses an innate generosity toward the reader. After all, even though the reader and writer may not share the same information, they are in many ways beset by the same distractions and anxieties. For an essayist, to talk straight to his audience is, therefore, to talk straight to himself as well. Peter's agitated spirit thus inhabits a fluent vernacular prose. Without recourse to Whitman's exhortations or the didacticism of the ideologically "correct," Peter injects a democratic common sense into what is otherwise an exercise in aesthetic discrimination.

Such accessibility is often looked down upon as pandering, just as an inherent avidity for the new is easily judged as modishness and changes in taste as proof of fickleness. Like contempt for the transient, disdain for the vulgar is the intellectual vice of the prematurely wise and the congenitally stolid. "Gloom and solemnity," Ezra Pound once wrote, "are entirely out of place in even the most rigorous study of an art originally intended to make glad the heart of man." Willem de Kooning reminds us that much of the best art is made from "silly ideas," adding, "Spiritually I am wherever my spirit allows me to be. . . . Art never seems to make me peaceful or pure. I always seem to be wrapped in the melodrama of vulgarity."

Not surprisingly, he is in the front rank of Peter's heroes: "Saw de Kooning drunk and saw him sober, dazzling man!" To be sure, genius is hard, if not impossible, to live with and ultimately unknowable. Do not suppose, however, that a critic can fully grasp art's truth or difficulty without some familiarity with artists. For the contemporary art writer, the choices involved represent an imaginative as well as emotional crucible. In the maelstrom of art-world egos, those of writers are not the least vulnerable or vain, further compounding the problem. Throughout Peter's writing, there is evidence of the mutually wounding awkwardness between critic and artist. One of the most intriguing aspects of rereading him is to hear the subtle counterpoint such reciprocal ambivalence adds to his central themes. It has been as much through friendship as through solitary scrutiny, however, that Peter has explored the art of his moment. To the benefit of his audience, he has learned on the job, by confrontation and by osmosis. Lest this method suggest a lack of proper credentials, it is worth recalling that the two critics of the 1950s who now dominate college syllabuses had no formal art-historical training—Clement Greenberg started out his career as a customs official with a literary education, whereas Harold Rosenberg began as a poet and survived as a free-lance pundit and sometime ad man. Neither haunted the stacks, but both had the good sense to hang out in bars.

In truth, all genuine fans are autodidacts. Learning a thing is, after all, the making of its meaning. Close to the action, eavesdropping on those at the heart of it, mingling with rookies and veterans alike after the game is over—although art, like other such "useless" but rigorous contests, recognizes no definite end, only intervals of engagement— Peter still proceeds like the dedicated baseball reporter. His seminars are arguments in the stands, where the rank-and-file enthusiasts and the true and most irreverent experts congregate. Competition is constant on and off the field. In the art world similar exchanges occur at the openings, parties, and Saturday-afternoon rambles that fill the calendar and mark out the progress of the season. At these gatherings, as at the ball park, disagreement is the object.

Peter and I meet in such places, and our friendship is the product of amicable contention, although, as the reader must by now have guessed, this is less a formal introduction than a fan letter from one writer to another. Our acquaintance began with an argument by correspondence over a review Peter had written for the *Village Voice*. We have since become the best of adversaries, and therefore the best of companions. Although I sometimes dispute his estimates of how good a particular artist is—I am inclined to the long view, and he counters with a "fast take" that is often more complex and compelling than the work that inspired it—rarely, if ever, do I dissent from his ideas about who is worth watching. Indeed, he has an uncanny knack for figuring out what is happening or about to happen, in the context of which, predictions about how it will all turn out may simply—and pointlessly—censure delight. He has an even more acute instinct for shifts in popular culture and public sentiment.

As keen an observer of the dynamics of crowds as of the compulsions of the art scene's principal protagonists, Peter takes as his subject not so much the formal course of painting and sculpture as the energy that engenders and envelops them. Sharply focused in its psychic detail, each article contributes to a running chronicle of where that energy accumulates, how it is marshaled, and how it is spent. Without the historian's distance or the luxury of axiomatic theoretical Truths, the working critic must render a vital account of things seen and heard and felt. In the rush of events, being "right" is never having to say you're sorry, and never having to say you're sorry means never saying very much. The rigor and probity of such criticism is, therefore, manifest in the frankness with which it concedes its partiality and examines its ultimate and absolute subjectivity. Wilde again: "There are two ways to dislike art. . . . one is to dislike it, the other to like it rationally[;] . . . criticism is, in its highest development, simply a mood, and . . . we are never more true to ourselves than when we are inconsistent." To read Peter is to follow the sparks thrown off by a mind in constant friction with the world around it, a mind never at rest but fundamentally accepting of the contingency of its thought. Replacing the sociology of context with its poetics, his essays are the complete analogue to the excitement on which they report.

"Then they had this big party and called it the '60s," Peter once wrote. "I was there. Weren't you there, chum? Too bad!" Since then, "they've" had an even bigger party and called it the eighties; in the interim of the seventies, parties were fewer and farther between. Peter was "there" all the while. One must excuse him the teasing arrogance of his rhetorical challenge; he is not the bouncer but rather the reader's inside man. Hence, if you were not there and want to know what it was like, study these texts with care, not forgetting to savor them at the same time. No other critic offers a more accurate or more usefully idiosyncratic record of the anticipation, exhilaration, and exhaustion that register the cycles of the present art world. Combining the desperate alertness of the dandy, the prickly urbanity of the New Yorker, and the skepticism of the midwesterner—imagine a simultaneous utterance of Diaghilev's hopeful demand "Astonish me!" and Missouri's doubtful motto "Show me!"—Peter has made himself the essential critical stylist of our jumpy but incandescent fin de siècle.

Robert Storr

The Hydrogen Jukebox

Terror, Narcissism, and Art

The present widespread disarray and morbidity of the arts in Western civilization represent, it occurs to me, a long-term toxic effect of the atom-bomb terror of the last three decades. This terror, drilled into the world's consciousness, has had the positive result of making the possibility of actual nuclear war remote. But it has also contributed to a progressive devastation of the higher expressions and finer sensibilities of Western cultures.

Most insidious of the terror's by-products is what I'll call the no-future effect. Conditioned to living on the eve of doomsday, we have lost the ability to conceive of a future stretching farther than our own most distant personal goals or responsibilities—our children's educations, say, as the outside limit. The idea of a continuity of civilized existence, let alone of present cultural forms, runs up against the terror and goes to pieces. Only dullards believe in it.

The no-future effect has in its turn another damaging upshot: no past. What possible authority can the preterror past have for us? The past is a place we visit, in books and museums, with a sense of crossing an intervening chasm. It was not always this way. The past once communicated directly with the present in the forms of tradition and stable institutions, such as church and family. Now even the very recent past seems to cold-shoulder us, for reasons I'll get into.

It is hard on artists, on the morale of the creative spirit, to do without the idea of a relevant past. Without the kind of credible tradition that T. S. Eliot rather wishfully celebrated—such tradition being already in decay when in 1919 he wrote "Tradition and the Individual Talent"—the lone artist has nothing but fashion and hunch by which to gauge the value of his or her work. Nor can a usable tradition be reposited or reconstructed. Whatever he said in his criticism, Eliot's poetry—"These fragments I have shored against my ruin"—sounded the proper elegiac note for all such attempts. The more common effort to proceed *as if* a tradition were still alive for one's work leads to the deadliest kind of academicism—art for the cloistered soul.

But the loss of traditional measures of value is the least of the no-past effect's depredations. The prestige of Western cultural tradition took a mortal beating from World War I, but the response of many artists and writers to that disaster was wonderfully rigorous and included buoyant assertions of new, modern values, as if a bigger and better past could be built overnight in place of the old one. Nothing like the lively revulsion, iconoclasm, and new beginnings of artists post–World War I occurred after World War II. The spectacle of civilization gone insane was, in the latter case, at once too familiar and too stupendous, renewed periodically by the atom-bomb terror. The shiny new values, particularly of technological progress, had become unfunny jokes and were cast aside—to be playfully revived in the sixties and cast aside again in the seventies, very badly worn out. Art turned inward after World War II. Its public aspect became the gesture—the kinesthetic expression of an inviolable personal energy and integrity, a last-ditch stand against chaos on the frontier of the self. Every generation of artists and writers since then has been in some sense, often quite consciously, the last, the summing-up or extinguishing, the end-of-the-line generation.

End-of-the-line thinking can give macabre pleasure, lending a satisfying melodramatic air to work and to existence itself. But such thinking doesn't seem supportable anymore. What makes the seventies so eerie is the sneaking conviction we have that this decade wasn't supposed to happen. In a civilization living as if there were no tomorrow, we are the tomorrow. We are inhabiting, in effect, the no-future of the fifties and sixties; and what did those no-past decades leave us with? Rituals of the instantaneous flashing present and protocols of The End. We are doubly, triply bereft—no idea of the past to push off against, no vision of the future to reject, no sense of the present as a moment unique in history. "What history?"

The personality type of our time is the narcissist.

Obsessively self-regarding, self-referential, self-consuming, the narcissistic personality finds authenticity only in the moment-to-moment convincingness of bodily sensations and mental events. The narcissistic artist or poet offers to a shadowy public evidence or dramatizations of these sensations, inviting that public to join in the self-contemplation. Anger, at world or self, alternates with a husky or antic seductiveness, a siren song of love and death or sexy fun, and with abject complaining, the cries of the abandoned baby within. The narcissistic personality is driven by loneliness and braked by fear. Sexually it is fantasy dominated, with a possible tendency to sadomasochism; socially it is anxious, calculating, competitive, aiming to arouse response in others without itself being aroused. Need is its law, outside authority its nemesis.

Of course no one except the autistic child or the out-and-out adult psychotic can be purely narcissistic. Personal survival, not to mention the most rudimentary feelings of personal worth, depend on relations with other people, the formation of friendships, liaisons, deals. We might expect, however, that the social relations favored by the narcissist will be radically different from traditional relations. The exemplary contemporary social unit is the "support group." Hierarchical authority is out; the narcissist won't stand for it. A support group, be it a therapy group or an "alternative" gallery, comes together expressly to advance the individual interests of its members and to get for them what they want, be it health, fame, whatever. The contemporary art world is rife with the phenomenon. It sometimes calls to mind a nest crowded with open-mouthed little birds, all straining for whatever worms chance or machination may bring their way. To speak, in such a context, of the value or meaning or quality of work being done is an indiscretion.

The spectacle of the narcissistic society is horribly sad if not, in the growing respectability of sadomasochistic behavior, horrible period. Deprived of the anchor of a past and the rudder of a future, the new personality is as helpless as a paper boat on the ocean. Narcissism is clinically a natural state in infancy, an arrested state thereafter. It follows that Western societies have lost the ability to help individuals over the hump of infantile narcissism into the state of self-controlled, work-directed, socially adapted adulthood that was formerly the ideal. A lot was wrong with that ideal—the denial of pleasure, for instance—and modern thinkers have subjected it to a withering critique, but without fully reckoning what would replace it, a mode of existence that for many has the overtones of a nightmare.

It would be grotesque to equate psychic suffering in the affluent West with physical suffering in a place like Bangladesh, but in certain areas of our society the comparison carries a hyperbolic truth. A similar dynamic of ever-growing need and ever-diminishing resources is at work. The suffering of the narcissist is no joke, the endlessly craving, endlessly tender self brought daily into contact with an ungiving, wounding world—a world, it sometimes seems, of razor blades and broken glass. (Making matters worse for the narcissist may be the utter indignity of the condition, which seemingly can be described only in pejoratives.) Whence the typical narcissistic defiance, the refusal to grow up. But it's no good. That way lies alcoholism, chronic depression, psychosomatic illness, perhaps violent death. The need for others erodes the defiance. The narcissist with any concern to survive inevitably straggles back into the social sphere.

A complicating factor here is the saturation of the social sphere itself with narcissistic tones and values. I have in mind the peculiarly intense pleasures of the narcissist, pleasures that are polymorphous and continuous and even confused with pain (hence sadomasochism). These pleasures are celebrated everywhere among us, in poems and art and popular music, in the ideology of "lifestyles" (which regards pleasure as a "right" with some amazing political implications—for instance the "right" of the childless to deny housing to those with children, who are the future), in the whole fabric of our culture. That such pleasures are ultimately unfulfilling, are not enough to compensate the inchoate suffering, the loss of meaning, is indisputable, though I'm sure it will be disputed—out of perhaps the deadliest of narcissistic delusions, that *I*, though a million others fail, am going to succeed, am going to beat the game.

So it's no use confronting narcissists with moral exhortation. They are usually hipper about the condition, and better acquainted with its costs in suffering, than the wisest observer. (It's no accident that psychiatry has a lot of trouble with narcissism. Being not a "disease" but an arrested natural state, narcissism can scarcely be "cured." It can only be overcome in the moment of a successful commitment of primary life energies to someone and/or something in the world at large.) And where is the moral authority for any such exhortation to come from? Is there any profession or institution or myth—including religion, state, family, science, and, yes, art—that has not joined in the general debasement, the no-future, no-past debacle?

It does seem that art has suffered less debasement, if only barely less, by its faithful reflection of the debacle itself, its willingness to confront the disagreeable facts, to make do among the ruins. What individual artists and writers have done with the facts is another, case-by-case, matter. In general, the pressures of fragmentation and decline have proved overpowering to even the strongest creative minds, defeating the best individual attempts to do more than synopsize or comment on the situation. The last really prepossessing art movements, pop and minimalism, were essentially synoptic, I believe: pop of the no-past effect, the sensation of everything being simultaneously available and equally meaningful/meaningless, and minimalism of the no-future, the final revelation of the art object's effectiveness, its return to equivalence with all other objects—in entropy, as Robert Smithson poeticized it.

Every subsequent movement, starting with conceptualism (though it might be more accurate to say starting with Duchamp/Warhol), has *embodied* rather than figured forth an aspect of the worsening situation. This triumph of an embedded "process" orientation is in keeping with the rise of narcissism, which can no more allow an objective view of anything than one can objectively view one's own eyes in a mirror. Narcissism floods the world with the projected self. Observation, conception, and execution become a closed circuit, charged by their resonance with the narcissist's own moment-to-moment inner workings. The first and last audience for narcissistically created art is the narcissist who creates it. Only the narcissist's nonart needs—worldly ambition and dread of isolation—carry the work out to others, on whom extraordinary demands for tolerance and complicity are made. And here may be understood the sterility of art discourse in our day. The true creative excitement, the juice, of much contemporary art is hermetically sealed away in the artist. There's nothing essential, *of the essence*, present to talk about, unless the sympathetic narcissism of the talker can generate something on its own.

Which is not to say that narcissistically created art is without impact. Even the mildest of it, with its uncanny, ritual enactments of hidden dramas, can be compulsively fascinating, or even, as in William Wegman's videotapes, very funny. Subject to a classical control, it can even be great, as witness the astounding poetry of John Ashbery. Narcissistically created art is entirely uncompelling only when accompanied by intellectual justifications; these are always and without exception rubbish.

Still, precisely in its present morbid, wasted state, art preserves the creative spark, the seed of a future. If the West avoids a final payoff of terror, if it labors on ten or twenty years under whatever difficulty short of catastrophe, thereby affording the nurturing fiction of a new continuity, a new past, the present era may come to be regarded as a tormented and bizarre time, a historical and cultural low that was nonetheless a turning point, a hinge, a prelude to rejuvenation.

As it is, American culture on practically every level these days is demoralized, degraded, stagnant, its most compelling activity being that of "support structures" far more robust than anything they are supporting. There is no shortage of talent—there is probably as much talent as there ever is—and creative energy. Energy abounds, but like St. Elmo's fire it is a heatless glow, unable to alter what it clings to. I would not suggest that things can't get worse. Things can always get worse. But it seems inconceivable that the present morass will not produce, is not already producing, a spirit of radical dissatisfaction with complacencies, illusions, and tyrannies small and large, a reassertion of the creative individual, a search for meaning beyond the confines of the self, the group, the social game. This will be a movement, if it comes, signaled early on in acts of art.

Admittedly there are only a few positive signs and tendencies in the culture right now. One is the remarkable amount of autobiographical and biographical writing, in both poetry and prose, at its best a public coming-to-grips with the elusive stuff of individual experience. Another is the revival of craft study, plus tough realist and baldly "decorative" painting—developments in rudimentary concerns of mediums following the collapse of modernist pieties (and antipieties) of the art object. Then there is the current saturnalia in popular music. I may be kidding myself, but it strikes me that the hate songs of punk, even with their inverted romanticism of narcissism and violence, signal an impatience with lies, a spasmodic movement toward truth telling. Certainly they are a powerful cleanser of the residual goo of sixties peace-and-love, which incidentally killed more people than punk is likely to do.

I do not include as a positive tendency the rise of "alternative" institutions and media, for although their practical value is multifold and undeniable—one of them provides a forum for this essay, to cite a humble instance—they are entirely too cozy with a multitude of contemporary evils. As responses to the alienation of the creative individual, they are sugar pills for broken legs at best. At worst, they

6

pamper (gently terrorize, really) the artist out of his or her individuality, burying creative development in group process. They flatter the narcissistic delusion that the world owes everybody a living and hearing. They reinforce parochialism, fragmentation, no-fault careerism. Many are extensions of the university cocoon, the intellectual haunted house in which nothing is real except the dread of walking out. The job of running these supposedly democratic entities, since somebody has to, increasingly falls to a new class of professional den-mother types (male and female) whose main qualification is a willingness to dandle the sweet little egos in their charge. One of these types recently promulgated this credo: "Place the artist, not the art." Meaning down with art, up with adult day care. To hell with it.

Perhaps the most insidious aspect of the budding "alternative" establishment is the sense of inevitability it projects. Despite its ideological commitment to impermanence—comical in journals that painstakingly document last week's phenomena on newsprint that will start to disintegrate next week—the new institutionalism is everywhere glossing up its quarters, enlarging its staffs, gobbling more of the funding pie, and, in general, giving every impression of taking up the reins of art culture where museums and commercial interests are supposed to have dropped them. (Actually, the commercial gallery seems to me still the most sensible, flexible, nontyrannical art-world institution. It is only as good as the character of its dealers, of course, but there have been and continue to be a remarkable lot of very good ones, whose profit motivation is tempered by farsightedness and a zeal for the best as they see it. As for the museums, it should be kept in mind how brief—maybe a dozen years, straddling the sixties—was their affair with advanced contemporary art. It ended with artists proving ungrateful, as artists will, and museums simply returning to form.)

The young "alternative" giant will doubtless soon boast a national association that will greatly magnify its ability to command public and corporate patronage. It will also start becoming so oppressive to the independent minded that a counter-alternative criticism will gradually emerge.

Free human creativity in our time is being bought off—with government and corporate money, with enticements to emotional security. The success of the buy-off, the absence of widespread disgust with it, is a consequence of the no-future effect, the atom-bomb terror steadily seeping into every kind and level of civilized endeavor, paralyzing nerve and imagination. This seems a plausible metaphor, in any case; maybe another would do just as well. The fact of general demoralization does not seem arguable. The agency of regeneration, if there is to be one, will be old/new: individual commitment, courage, audacity.

GENERAL NOTE: This essay includes many no doubt received and in-the-air ideas, which I haven't tried to think back to their sources. The thoughts about narcissism are grounded in long personal interest in the subject, given form particularly by recent writing by Christopher Lasch. My sour view of art support structures owes a lot to a three-year hitch on the Visual Arts Services panel of the New York State Council on the Arts. I am indebted for my understanding of the current avant-garde to the work of Edit deAk and Walter Robinson, those wonderfully astringent proponents. This passage in the June–July issue of the *LAICA Journal*, which they edited, really triggered my essay:

> But artists do not want to exclude anyone, especially themselves, from anything, so to have non-competitive cross-pluralism everybody now makes "projects." When you have your project you have finally given a structure, a transient goal, to your gooey perpetual art making.

This is proponency, remember. I ought to include deAk and Robinson in my list of positive signs in the culture.

October–November 1978

Rothko and Belief

A recent article on Mark Rothko by Robert Hughes brings to the consideration of this artist a measured coolness, not to say a cynicism, that seems new in criticism of the major abstract expressionists. It was probably inevitable. How long could the virtual religiosity of the First Generation's own self-image and its opposite pole, the compliment of near-total rejection paid by the pragmatic sixties avant-garde, remain in force? The seventies were unlikely to end without efforts being made to take the confused reputation of the abstract-expressionist masters firmly in hand. Hughes indicates what may well become a dominant view of Rothko, at least for a while: "Rothko, far from being Yahweh's official stenographer . . . was a painter, a maker of visual fictions—better than most, but still prone to repetition and still able to fall victim to his own formulas and reflexive cliches."

Hughes regards Rothko's ambition "to render the patriarchal despair and elevation of the Old Testament" (a caricature, but apt in tone) as misguided, though "very moving," because what he had to work with, "the vocabulary of Symbolism—the fluttering space, the excruciatingly refined, sensuous color, the obsession with nuance"—was simply unequal to "a genuine religious art." Hughes isn't out to debunk Rothko entirely. He praises the "rhapsodic airiness" of "the best of Rothko's paintings in the Fifties" and allows that "perhaps no other American painter had ever devoted himself so whole-heartedly to the cultivation of feeling. On that score alone, Rothko was a major though uneven painter." But he is definitely hostile to the imputation of "the sublime" to Rothko's art, the "awe-inspiring spirituality" claimed for the Rothko Chapel in Houston by Diane Waldman in her introduction to the Guggenheim catalogue. On the ground that such fancy rhetoric is "coercive," Hughes closes his article with what amounts to a blanket ad hominem indictment of Rothko's appreciators:

Sublime, sublime, sublime, the reflexes go clickety-clack, all the way down the Guggenheim ramp. What role does cultural nationalism play in the persistent desire to treat Rothko as an American blend of Turner and Michelangelo? How far are the responses dictated by the uneasy feeling that if verbose obeisances to the Ineffable stopped, the work might suffer? To what extent did Rothko's suicide confer a profundity on the paintings which, had he lived, they might not quite have had? But how can one dare think such things, in the presence of blue-chip masterpieces?

It should be noted that the bulk of Hughes's article is not about Rothko's art but about the horror of his last years ("a tragedy of infantilism") and grisly death, the famous trial ("Victorian melodrama of the fruitiest sort"), and, in particular, the disastrous effects of great wealth and esteem on an artist deeply conditioned to being an outsider. There is also a mordant excursus on financial machination in the art world, seen as "the last refuge for nineteenth-century laissez-faire capitalism." Good journalist that he is, Hughes goes after the Rothko lowdown with "investigative" élan, and his article is invigorating reading. But in his peroration suggesting establishment or market intimidation, or anyway chauvinism, or at least morbid sentimentality as the basis for high estimations of Rothko, he comes close to espousing a populist Philistinism. The issue of "spirituality" in Rothko's work is not so easily disposed of, nor can the testimony of those who believe an elevating experience is to be had there—not least, Rothko himself—be lightly dismissed. On this count, Hughes's corrective stands in need of correction.

Rothko was a Russian Jewish immigrant who grew up in Oregon, started painting only after leaving college (Yale), and settled into New York and the life of art in the gradual, fortuitous way typical of his generation. In the mid- to late twenties he studied briefly with Max Weber, did some imitation John Marin watercolors, fell under the lucky influence of Milton Avery (whose works he later praised, in words that fit his own, for their "poetry and light"), and developed a tentative and nervous realist style, mainly involving vague nudes in uneasy circumstances. As often at retrospectives of the abstract expressionists, one is struck by the unpromising look of the early work, painted at a time when, whatever an artist's individual gifts and sophistication, a debilitating provincialism was still the American climate. Rothko's first really articulated style, in the mid-thirties, was fashionably urban-realist with overtones of social angst. The best of these pictures are of severely attenuated citizens on subway platforms, their tense elongation expressing withdrawal and isolation in a way that brings to mind later Giacometti: the drawing, which has an anguished sprightliness, is some of the most effective of Rothko's career. But he was not to become a poet of the urban scene.

In the late thirties and the forties the rising generation of American artists assimilated European modernism, a process intensified by a sense of world crisis, a collapse of political idealism, and, not least, the presence in exile of important members of the European avant-garde. The Americans picked up the momentum of the Europeans in mid-stride—in late surrealism, with its conviction that the unconscious was the fountainhead, and ideally the director, of all creativity. But the Americans also veered immediately from the European course, which was hedged by rationalistic commitments to Marxism and Freudian psychoanalysis. Rothko, Pollock, Still, Newman, Gottlieb, and nearly all the others tended to the Jungian view of the unconscious as the receptacle of timeless myth. This doctrine sat well with their temperamental individualism and encouraged their belief in art as a medium for profound and practically unlimited inner experience. Much subsequent criticism has seemed embarrassed—as the Europeans were scandalized—by the mingled egocentrism and mysticism of this mind-set, and Hughes is only the latest of many to scoff at its pretensions. But the abstract expressionists' belief in art's access to invisible reality, however grandiose (and one can fairly argue that it proved personally destructive), was the very point of their departure from late surrealist figuration toward a new kind of abstract art—one that promised to yield the reality firsthand. Strictly artistic calculations were also involved, of course; these were painters consciously competing with the old masters. In the happiest instances, like Rothko's, spiritual program and stylistic ambition pulled together.

Diane Waldman writes of Rothko's myth-obsessed surrealist work of the mid-forties, "Contrary to the opinion of some critics, who maintain that Rothko could not draw, and even of the artist himself, the calligraphy of this period is brilliant." Well, I have to join those contrary critics, for Rothko seems an astonishingly mediocre draftsman, as is nowhere more apparent than in the ambitious linear networks and totems of the period Waldman mentions. Rothko at this time is full of ideas about the uses of line; he just can't seem to make a line *do* anything. The attempts at lyrical agitation in a painting like *Slow Swirl at the Edge of the Sea*, 1944, are clear enough in their intention, but they are like diagrams for an engine that simply won't kick over. The spirals don't twirl, the scribbles don't jump, the long curves don't whip, and there is no tautness in the diagonals. Where he seems to want to draw like Miró or Gorky or Klee, he rarely draws even as well as Matta or Baziotes. I found myself thinking with amazement of Dufy, of that facile linear embellishment of color areas. This incapacity is as baffling, as mysterious, as the genius evident in Rothko's quavering, light-drenched gray atmospheres of this period, for he was equally incapable of painting other than beautifully.

If ever the evolution of a radically abstract style seemed absolutely right, the one perfect outcome of an artist's peculiar gifts, it does in Rothko's case to a degree unrivaled except, perhaps, by Mondrian's. With the virtual disappearance of drawn line from Rothko's work around 1947, one feels a nearly physical relief and a sudden exhilaration, as at sighting ahead after a hard journey the marvelous destination one always suspected was there. For as an applier of paint Rothko is Rothko right from the start. Surely viewers have been struck by such early "Rothkoesque" passages as the moody red-streaked sky in a small picture of three seaside nudes dated (dubiously, like all his early work) 1930. An improvisatory chiaroscuro—the washing or scumbling of darker pigments over lighter, or its (infrequent) reverse, the veiling of dark with light, or their alternation in layers—is the fundamental Rothko talent, the ground of his absolute originality.

Great colorists persuade us that in them the eye is somehow more than a merely optical organ, that by itself it can perform the functions, however faintly and indirectly, of touch, taste, smell, or hearing. Rothko, too, was certainly capable of playing the whole synaesthetic keyboard had his temperament inclined that way, but the locus of sensation his colors excite is more internal and, yes, ineffable than that of the senses. It's easy to see how the effect of ineffability is enforced by Rothko's design, with its many studied vaguenesses, its impossible range of subtleties that, going beyond our ability to register them fully, at once ravish and frustrate the eye. The main device is the blurred contour. Part edge and part blend, it appears to knit color shape to color surface when you are looking right at it (which is hard to do, by the way), but when you're peering into the shape, it serves to jiggle the color loose, letting it advance or retreat (the same color can seem to do both in the course of a single viewing) or just hover in the indeterminate overall plane. Such effects multiply with the number of different shapes and colors in a particular painting. Rothko's greatest paintings, which occur mostly between 1949 and roughly 1957, attain a staggering diversity within their deceptively simple format. But it is not the delicate mechanics of the pictures that one notices, except analytically, on purpose; these are only instrumental in delivering the color, which in turn releases a tide of reverie and introspective feeling.

Hughes is undoubtedly correct in relating the interiority of Rothko's color sensation to symbolism. (One thinks of Moreau blacks and yellows, Redon reds and blues.) He is also right that Rothko overestimated the communicating power of his stylistic means; this "mistake," however, was responsible for his major glories. The most important difference between Rothko and the symbolists is the obvious one: they were figurative and he—having worked through late surrealism's elaborate glossaries of myth, which might be seen as the culmination (and extinction) of symbolist metaphor in painting—was abstract. He had gotten rid of everything except color, color relation, light, and atmosphere (and had stressed scale), but, audaciously, he retained the intent to stir particular emotion, an intent not easy even for the symbolists with their literary or hallucinatory subject matter. Rothko proceeded as if sheer color, mediated by a design adjusted to giving it maximum impact and versatility, could convey specific inner experience (in his words, the "basic human emotions—tragedy, ecstasy, doom") and as if this precise linkage of image and emotion could be made without any equation so vulgar as light-happy/dark-sad. "The people who weep before my pictures," Rothko declared in the mid-fifties, with a manic confidence soon to be dashed, "are having the same religious experience I had when I painted them." He plainly failed to make his filmy images bear the weight of anything like a discernible subject matter. However, this failure must be seen as relative to his enormous success, which was to deepen and fortify the connection, the circuit, of color to inner experience. The messages that travel this circuit may be unclear, but they arrive. The emotion that accompanies their arrival is the sublime.

The introduction of the sublime needs, alas, some defense. People besides Hughes are having trouble with the word these days, but while a distrust of high-sounding phrase is commendable, I don't believe that an idea as experientially useful as the sublime is ready for junking. The relevant definition of *sublime* in my dictionary is this: "impressing the mind with a sense of grandeur or power; inspiring awe, veneration, etc." Not an everyday thing, but not so extraordinary, either, for anyone regularly drawn to the stronger sensations of art or nature. (I assume, and hope, that such people are numerous, for it is to them I speak.) The implication is that it's somehow inauthentic or otherwise embarrassing to appeal to this experience by its proper name. But is it even possible, in a willing and receptive state of mind, to visit, say, the Metropolitan Museum—or the Mojave Desert—and not come away with a whiff of the sublime, with at least one instant of riveted, ego-eclipsing attention, of "a sense of grandeur or power," of "awe, veneration, etc."? It *is* a vague word, as the dictionary indicates with that exasperated "etc.," but how precise can one be about an experience that is, in its essence, speechless? There is a distinct arrogance of the rational in Hughes's mockery, as of an old-school mechanist insisting that dreams be explained by sleep position and what one ate for supper.

The proper debate about the sublime should revolve around its relation to particular belief. The Christian's sublime in a cathedral will seem to differ from the aesthete's, though the mental events might register identically on any brain-monitoring apparatus. Neurologically we're similar. It's in what we think and feel about what we sense that variety arises, and it is legitimate for reason to critique this variety and the language in which it's expressed. But reason that is bent on undermining or insulting belief itself is not going to be much help here, for the sublime cannot occur except in a context of belief—belief in something perceptible by the self and greater than the self. (That this something may *be* the self, in its widest comprehension of unconscious and "collective" elements, is the Jungian opinion, which Rothko apparently shared.) There's no need to get oversolemn about all this. The average viewer's "belief system" may come down to simple openness, a suspension of *dis*belief. The fact remains, however, that in the epiphanic moment—which may be either mild and fleeting, the barest ripple in consciousness, or wrenchingly intense—one is, perforce, a *believer*.

That one can experience the sensation of belief, of "confidence in the truth or existence of something not immediately susceptible to rigorous proof" (the dictionary again), without having a mental object or even a word for that belief is a major bet of Rothko's as of much other modern art. It is not, one must add, a feature of much sophisticated art today. The present "era of limits" is nowhere more apparent than in the scaled-down ambitions of our artists. Art as substitute religion—and it was no less than this for Rothko, as for Mondrian—has disappointed us, and there is a general understanding that artistic grandeur is not worth the terrible human investment required to attain it. That's the way things are. It would be more than a shame, however, to let our understandable present cynicism be made retroactive, denigrating great work created at the last high tide of artistic faith, roughly the decade around 1950. It's not piety I'm recommending, just a decent respect for values that, though perhaps we can't share them, are responsible for an extraordinary legacy. For it is the pressure of the values that creates the intensity of the work, and to assume otherwise is to have no comprehension of how art actually happens.

It is also necessary, of course, to look at the paintings. It may be schoolmarmish to say so, and to remind readers of what they undoubtedly well know, that until you see a painting in person you haven't begun to see it at all. But in the case of no other painter is the photograph, including the best color plate, more mendacious than in Rothko's, so perhaps the caveat bears repeating. The exact physical scale of Rothko's paintings and their presence as objects (emphasized by his influential device of painting the edges and leaving them unframed) are as critical as in any art until minimalism fetishized these qualities in the sixties. The felt relation of the painting as a (partially disembodied) body to one's own, the viewer's, body is the very fulcrum of Rothko's art, commented on by his most discerning critics, for instance Brian O'Doherty—who provocatively speculates that the viewer of large abstract-expressionist paintings is the displaced "figure banished (from art) by the imperatives of abstraction," "a figure for which Rothko had the highest regard and regret, a 'picture of the single human figure—alone in a moment of utter immobility.'"

If the word *sublime* has been devalued in our increasingly skeptical age, the word *tragic*, a touchstone for Rothko and his earlier critics, has been practically abolished, except as a synonym for *lamentable*. In a world where, as the pop ethic declares, you're responsible for everything that happens to you, the notion of a special, noble, class of destruction is hardly imaginable. It is elusive in my own mind, and a struggle to conceive exactly what Rothko meant by it. If one could experience Rothko's sense of the tragic, it might be in the severe disembodiment his paintings both represent and evoke. Irving Sandler in his book *The Triumph of American Painting* states the case succinctly: "The passivity and impersonality of Rothko's brush and reductive design . . . suggest a desire on his part that the viewer vacate the active self. This can lead to cosmic identification, but that has a tragic dimension, for it evokes the ultimate loss of self—death." I can't say whether this adds up—it remains unreal to me—but it's true enough that the experience I have with Rothko's art is anything but entirely pleasant. To be shoved back into the febrile jumble of one's semiconscious, half-formed thoughts and feelings—without chemical assistance, and in a public place—can be plenty discomfiting. But I'm unwilling to give the honorific "tragedy" to this discomfiture. The implications, for instance in granting poetic dignity to Rothko's ghastly suicide, are too distasteful.

In any case, Hughes's breezy assurance that Rothko "was [only] a *painter*, a maker of visual fictions" must seem brutally inadequate to the experience of anyone who has intensively contemplated the paintings. There's something more real, even appalling, in Rothko's best work than is touched on by the aridly correct phrase "visual fictions." However, any implication that the paintings are somehow too transcendent for their effects to be analyzed in formal terms would be equally objectionable. Besides scale, there is (until about 1960, at least) the peculiar quality of the color combinations, which might be called atonal. In the most effective paintings, hues harmonize and saturation is more or less consistent, but variations of light and dark, even slight variations, are felt as dissonance. The dissonance, the tonal jump, at once disrupts and intensifies one's sense of the paintings' almost preternatural beauty. It absolutely prevents the work from seeming decorative. It puts the viewer's mind on edge, subtly irritates it into an effort to supply a missing equilibrium, a perfected bliss. This device is the key to the particular subjective involvement one has with Rothko at his best, and its increasing suppression in his work of the 1960s, more than anything else, contributes to the decline of his art.

Rothko's paintings start becoming tonally unified (as they hadn't been since his transitional phase in the late forties) in about 1958, and by 1961 the tendency is dominant, to be significantly reversed only in the very last works. Thereafter, sharp tonal contrasts do occur, but almost invariably they seem calculatedly melodramatic, a flare of red or white in prevailing gloom. Throughout this period his work does indeed flirt with the decorative, a term that holds little terror for present-day painters but which Rothko was bound to regard as an unforgivable sin. His compensation was an almost unrelieved succession of dark and glowering hues and a theatrical hermeticism most striking (and most successful) in his mural projects. To put it cruelly, his only recourse against the decorative was the corny. (Or the almost corny; even at his pompous worst, Rothko, unlike Still, is incapable of being truly vulgar.) He had clearly lost faith in the specific communicability of his emotions, or, perhaps more accurately, in the ability of viewers to comprehend them. His later paintings no longer seek to involve; rather, they preach. The spirituality is still there, but no longer as an open field for artist's and viewer's mutual discovery; now it is more like a set of conclusions. The sublime still occurs, if one is willing to welcome it, but it is a narrowed, darkened, depressing sublime, a connection to consciousness dim and deathly.

Rothko's last paintings—forsaking oils for acrylics, gray with black or brown, usually on paper—miss narrowly but decisively being major works of a new kind for him. They miss literally by a margin, the inexplicable narrow white border defining the image, of two roughly equal rectangles whose abrupt tonal contrast makes for piercing drama along their sensitively brushed common edge. Rothko reportedly fussed about the width of this border, but why? It adds nothing. On the contrary, it devastates the already minimal play of illusion in the matte surface of acrylic paint. Its assertion of the literal surface is unnecessary in painting this inherently flat. Like a graphic mat, it removes the image from the viewer's physical space, isolating it for purely visual contemplation—but this is not a graphic image, it's a painterly (physical) one, on a confrontational scale. (It is the only Rothko motif that looks better in reproduction than in the original.) The procedure of the border seems so self-defeating that it might be read metaphorically as a sign of the compulsive psychological withdrawal that preceded the artist's death. Another possible explanation, less lurid, is vanity—a determination to be different from Ellsworth Kelly and Brice Marden and other painters, in the then crowded field of reductive abstraction, by whom he was obviously being influenced. Whatever the truth, Rothko's lonely ambivalence, at the end, is excruciatingly evident. So, too, is his incredible, unkillable gift for sheerly painting, the like of which we may never see again.

Rothko's art failed to fulfill his spiritual program for it, and both he and his art suffered terribly from this failure. But to attribute the failure to the program itself, as Hughes seems to do, is just too cozy, too self-flattering a conclusion. If belief never had the highest and best human consequences, we could be rid of it in a moment and—"beyond freedom and dignity," in the archbehaviorist's phrase—could pass our lives in untroubled rationality. The fact is that when Rothko's belief faltered, so did his art. If his great works of the fifties lack for us the fullness of a "genuine religious art," that's less the fault of the works than of a world that shifted beneath the artist's feet—as it is continually shifting beneath everybody's—at the moment he gained a footing on it. Rothko's talents and postsymbolist aesthetics were more than equal to a highly developed religious expression—if only the modern world held still long enough for any belief to do more than bud before the frost is on it. Rothko lacked the wisdom of the seventies, which seems to be that belief in anything at all is messy and dangerous, and this does give us an edge on him. But it's a petty edge, as witness the disheartening littleness and shallowness of nearly all new artistic developments of the past few years. Look at our wised-up contemporary art, then look at fifties Rothko. Can we, for survival's sake, learn to prefer the former to the latter?

March–April 1979

Edvard Munch: The Missing Master

The National Gallery's huge Munch show (Symbols and Images, November 11, 1978–February 19, 1979) was one of those museological rarities, a crowd-pleaser that is also a revelation—not just a pleasure or just food for thought but a whole new idea. One is well used to the notion of the "neglected" or "underappreciated" past artist, and to changing one's views of art history in response to enterprising scholarship, but the Munch show went quite off the usual scale of such experiences. The work in it seemed less some unfrequented hinterland than a volcanic eruption in what had seemed the thoroughly charted archipelago of postimpressionist art, where van Gogh, Gauguin, Seurat, and Cézanne command the horizon and Munch has loomed large, if at all, only in the hazy little out islands of symbolism. Compounding the shock is the complacent view, tacitly justifying our ignorance, that many of us have long held of Munch that, as William S. Lieberman wrote in 1957, "like his contemporary, Toulouse-Lautrec, it is in print making rather than in painting that his art reveals its chief significance." This sort of opinion sounds so coolly discriminating that one is lulled into agreement. It is an opinion that on exposure to the National Gallery show seems utterly frivolous.

The dismissive view of Munch's paintings may be sour grapes. There is a pathetically small number of them in this country (and just one masterpiece, Boston's *The Voice*), though the Museum of Modern Art, for instance, possesses a good batch of prints. There are not, in fact, many Munch paintings anywhere outside Norway, where an estimated 90 percent of his work resides, treated there with a proprietary reverence, as the national treasure it is, that has further supported the illusion that this artist is a special, marginal, case in modern art. (He is granted historical importance, usually, as the father of German expressionism, a status that suddenly seems faint praise.) This circumstance stems from several factors, including Munch's disinclination to part with his paintings and the Nazis' sale of German holdings of his work in Occupied Norway, but mainly from reversals in his art and career in the first decade of the century, when he was at the height of a considerable European fame.

Born in 1863, Munch grew up in Oslo (then Christiania) but did his major work largely in Germany and France from about 1892 to about 1902. Mounting personal troubles, not helped by alcoholism, drug use, and compulsive traveling, accompanied a decline in his art and led to his self-commitment to a Copenhagen psychiatric clinic in 1908. Attempts to rejuvenate his work with quasi-fauvist stylistic inventions around this time led to some of his worst paintings. After 1908 he returned more or less permanently to Norway, where, much to his own surprise (if ever an artist had seemed fated to die young, it was Munch), he lived, as a virtual recluse, to age eighty. His work of this long last period, though occasionally great (it included some of his most beautiful paintings), is simply not in a class with what he did in the nineties, and Munch's inconvenient survival, as much as the domination of modern taste by the School of Paris and the sheer unavailability of his paintings, explains his subsequent obscurity. He died in 1944, willing his immense hoard of his own works to the city of Oslo, where most of it is housed in the Munch Museum.

None of all that need bother us today, and the difficulty of placing "the solitary figure of Edvard Munch" in the history of modern art, once routinely averred in American art writing, must surely be at an end. For one thing, the recent revisionist trend in art history, led by Robert Rosenblum, asserts the alternative tradition of northern romanticism "from Friedrich to Rothko," a reading of modern art according to iconographic and emotional values long devalued by "Parisian" aesthetics. But, like most revisionism, this view introduces its own, as it were, counter-distortions, and Rosenblum's treatment of Munch seems unsatisfactory in a number of ways, though rich in novel suggestions. What I hopefully judge our new receptiveness to Munch owes to a more general and more urgent change in historical consciousness—a sense, for instance, that modernism as a system of humane values has become calcified and oppressive—and a consequent anxious search for new bearings. One bellwether of this change, the still rather tentative New Image painting and sculpture movement, has actually reintroduced symbolically tinged (albeit mostly cool) imagery into an art aesthetically continuous with late-modernist abstraction. It would be too much to say that this development signals more than a coincidental relevance of Munch to the concerns of our young artists. (One prominent New Image painter told me she went to the Washington show with excited hopes and came away disappointed.) But Munch's name can only profit from a situation in which the aesthetics-based values that have long consigned him to the second class are in disarray. And it would be a nice irony if Munch, having seemed left behind by art history, should prove all along to have been waiting ahead.

Kierkegaard called anxiety "the dizziness of freedom." It is the perfect phrase for a quality of Munch's great work of the 1890s, a time when he, like many other young Europeans, was undergoing—enjoying, suffering—a moment of vertiginous social, sexual, and artistic liberty. His was a hot imagery, of a historically periodic kind introduced by romantics. It is a recurring project of modern youth—in literature, from the young Goethe and the generation of Byron, Keats, and Shelley to the American Beats—to seize on and interpret the basic experiences of living, particularly love and death, as if they were being experienced for the first time, as if no one ever lived, loved, died before. It usually follows social changes that make its presumptions largely correct: no one ever lived, loved, died in quite this way before. Munch belonged to such a time and such a movement, or complex of movements, artistic and intellectual: for his marginal nationality and questing mind gave him access to the strongest art and ideas of his generation in Europe—and made him a stranger at the feast. From a multitude of sources his art realized an absolutely original synthesis of ideas, style, and technique that it brought to bear on the riddle of human life as experienced by a lonely internationalist of the fin de siècle, a young man gasping in the thin air of an almost intolerable freedom.

How could art-poor Norway have produced such a towering artist? Timing helped. Munch emerged at a moment of both cultural nationalism and new awareness of the Continent; he was also part of a "baby boom." In the early 1880s, when he abandoned an engineering education for art, more than half of Norway was under twenty-three, and radical ideas were touching off combustible sectors of the large young population. A wild and cosmopolitan milieu called Christiania-Bohème—after a novel by its leader, free-love philosopher Hans Jaeger, published and promptly suppressed in 1885—sprang up in the provincial capital city, and some of Munch's early drawings celebrate its smoky, febrile nightlife. A sardonic list of "nine Bohemian Commandments" published in the group's periodical, *The Impressionist*, gives the flavor:

1. Thou shalt write thine own life.
2. Thou shalt sever all family bonds.
3. One cannot treat one's parents badly enough.
4. Thou shalt never soak thy neighbor for less than five kroner.
5. Thou shalt hate and despise all peasants, such as Bjornsterne Bjornson [a leading Norwegian writer].
6. Thou shalt never wear celluloid cuffs.
7. Never fail to create a scandal in the Christiania Theater.
8. Thou shalt never regret.
9. Thou shalt take thine own life.

In this environment Munch had his first affair, with an older, married woman, and got his first taste of the transports and, for him, the inexorable consequences—loss of self, jealousy, despair—of sexual love. Willy-nilly, Munch was accumulating thematic material and developing basic impulses ("Thou shalt write thine own life") for his later work.

The dominant painting style in Scandinavia in the eighties, parallel to Ibsen's then triumphant dramatic style, was naturalism, though with romantic overtones that have been pointed out by Rosenblum. Impressionism was influencing technique without much disturbing the dogma of fidelity to nature. Munch, whose talent was immediately recognized, went to Paris in 1885 on the first of several official scholarship grants. (His country's solicitude for his career was somewhat vitiated by long-lasting, almost complete, incomprehension of his art; thus he was regarded at home as an immature but "promising" talent until well past his peak, when he was installed as a national hero.) The art he saw in Paris was a revelation to him, and back in Norway he labored a year on his first strongly original painting, *The Sick Child*, a reminiscence of the death of a beloved sister, Sophie, when he was thirteen: a horribly frail girl in profile against a pillow, beside her a grieving woman. Munch's heroic struggle to invest a common genre scene ("This was the pillow era," he later acknowledged. "The sickbed era, the bed era and the comforter era") with the very breath of primal emotion and, suppressing everything incidental to the mood, to make death palpable, is apparent in the paint surface—streaked, scraped, clotted, and, one almost feels, punished for its intransigence to the painter's aim, which might be characterized as an attempt to turn naturalism inside out. Munch was still about six years from achieving this yearned-for breakthrough, but if there is such a thing as a great failed painting, *The Sick Child* is it. (Munch, who recycled motifs throughout his career, returned often to this one, most successfully in an exquisite series of prints of just the girl's head.)

On subsequent trips to France in the ensuing years Munch saw and was influenced by the work of van Gogh and Gauguin, to name the most decisive, and also of Manet, Lautrec, Whistler, Puvis de Chavannes, Seurat, and, as art historians have recently guessed, Gustave Caillebotte, whose compressed views of the modern city, its crowds of pedestrians in rushing perspectives, are indeed like daylit bourgeois-optimistic versions of Munch's later, terror-filled urban scenes. (A good article could be written, I think, comparing Munch's *Evening on Karl Johan Street* with Caillebotte's masterpiece in the Chicago Art Institute, *Paris, a Rainy Day*, 1877, two paintings that contain modern urban experience like bookends.) The importance of French painting for Munch can scarcely be exaggerated, and this is my main quarrel with Rosenblum's appropriation of him to the northern romantic tradition. Some iconography aside, Munch stands as a painter with the postimpressionists. Gauguin's flat color areas and sinuous contours were crucial, allowing a frontal composition that escaped the window convention of naturalism and giving the idea of an overtly rhythmic relation of the figure to its surround. And it was of course Gauguin's lead that Munch followed, and extended, in his revitalization of the woodcut.

Munch's relation to van Gogh is subtler and more complex, and may be as much a matter of instinctive affinity as of actual influence. Van Gogh, too, was both participant and outsider in French art. Indeed, if Munch was on the frontier between the northern and French traditions, facing into the French, van Gogh was across the frontier, facing out. That van Gogh was a more integral, more complete painter is no slur on Munch—van Gogh was better than practically anybody— and both artists profit from being seen in each other's company. The stylistic differences between them—between van Gogh's cobbled, impressionism-derived brushstrokes and Munch's longer, freer, more strictly expressionistic ones; between the former's clean, radiant colors and the latter's dissonant, sometimes muddy ones (Munch generally kept a color pure only where it would carry a specific emotional charge)—such differences are more obvious than the similarities, which are, however, dramatic enough when focused on. Mainly there is the subtle dominance of drawing, the way the paint application follows and amplifies an essentially linear order—tight in van Gogh, loose in Munch, but in both the very hook on which they catch, if not our eye, our emotions. In his versatile mastery of the power of line and linear arrangement to spark feeling and convey mood, I think Munch was actually van Gogh's superior. Compared with either of them, in any case, Gauguin's drawing, however sensuous and magisterial, is essentially decorative, freighted with emotion that never comes through, poignantly tongue-tied.

Several other influences, for instance those of such symbolists as Redon, Moreau, Max Klinger, and Félicien Rops, were swallowed by Munch's larger talent almost without a trace.

In 1892 Munch, then twenty-nine, showed a group of paintings in Christiania, the fruit of his subsidized sojourns in France, the record of his self-education. The public reaction, as usual, was bewildered and hostile, but one viewer, a Norwegian agent of the German government, was unaccountably impressed. He arranged that Munch be officially invited to show his work in Berlin, which he did in November. There was a terrific scandal, the show was shut down in a week—and Munch's reputation was made. The resulting publicity spread his name throughout Europe, as a sort of wild man from the North. He immediately signed with a dealer who toured the show in Germany and Denmark. Elated and, for the moment, financially secure, he settled into a Berlin hotel room—he would live mostly in Germany, though with frequent travels elsewhere, until 1908—and was taken up by the city's fervid bohemian circle, the Schwarze Ferkel (Black Piglet), a group of Scandinavian, German, and Polish writers and artists that included the great Swedish playwright August Strindberg, the German poet Richard Dehmel, and an amazing character named Stanisław Przybyszewski, a Polish medical student given to Satanism and sex-drenched, quasi-mystical writings. His vision of sexuality—as "the primal substance of life" and "an unnameable, gruesome power that hurls two souls into each other and seeks to join them in pain and suffering"—resonated closely with the one Munch was developing, and the demon-haunted goateed face in the *Jealousy* pictures and *The Red Vine* is Przybyszewski's.

The theme of jealousy, the worm in the rose of the new sexual freedom, already obsessed Munch from his experiences in the Christiania-Bohème, whose leader, Jaeger, had set a style of arranging triangular sexual affairs in a spirit of almost scientific experiment. One casualty of these *folies à trois*, a man named Jappe Nilssen, became another of Munch's alter egos in his paintings on the theme of love, paintings that by 1893 he was beginning to conceive of as a cycle, a "frieze." Nilssen's is the pain-clenched face in *Melancholy, Yellow Boat*, 1891, which was in the Berlin show and might be seen as Munch's breakthrough painting, if any one canvas deserves that honor. Here the anecdotal drama of the despairing lover shrinking from the sight (or is it only a thought?) of the couple on the distant pier is set in tension with the boldly rendered rhythms of a summer landscape. The view into deep space is checked by the patterning of the black shore and treelines, the dominant blue, the blending of sea and sky at the horizon, the pink of the wavering stripes in the sky echoing in the face, and the bright orange (not yellow) of the little boat is like a stab in the heart.

Sexual jealousy, as it happens, demolished the Schwarze Ferkel, through the agency of a Norwegian music student named Dagny Juell, unwisely introduced to the group by Munch. Bed-hopping deftly around this circle of passionate egotists, she had them in a humiliating competitive frenzy in no time. In a scene of comic horror recounted by Reinhold Heller, "by the end of May [1893], less than two months after Dagny's initial charged materialization in the fraternity's midst, the Schwarze Ferkel's members were all fleeing separately and desperately on trains heading north, south, and east." (All except Przybyszewski, whom Dagny Juell eventually married; she was murdered by a student in Tiflis in 1901.) The breakup was probably all to the good for Munch's art, for, in Norway and back in Berlin, 1893 was one of his miracle years. Indeed, the bulk of his crowning work, *The Frieze of Life*, would be completed in that and the following two years, though it wouldn't come together in its definitive form until 1902, when it comprised twenty-two paintings exhibited in Berlin as *Cycle of Moments from Life* (its final title evidently came in 1918, long after many of its constituents had been sold off). Munch's work of this period was surely one of the most remarkable undertakings in modern, or any, art, a simultaneous unpacking of the artist's own soul and of the zeitgeist, the summary expression of a life and an era in the most advanced pictorial idiom of its time, an idiom that, moreover, kept developing right along with it. It was the fulfillment of a wish, almost a prayer, that Munch had uttered in 1892: "If only one could be the body through which today's thoughts and feelings flow. . . ."

Analyses of the *Frieze* and related works often set up polarities: love and death, life and death, personal and universal, with some (presumably the best) pictures seen to combine the opposites. It would be more clarifying to observe Munch's own divisions of 1902: two sections on love ("Seeds of Love" and "Flowering and Passing of Love"), one on extreme states of anxiety ("Life Anxiety"), one on death—thus three themes, one of them divided in two by a narrative caesura. A tension between personal and general is felt within each theme, and indeed in individual paintings, but is too ambiguous a measure to be critically useful. *Death in the Sickroom*, 1895, is Munch's most explicitly autobiographical death painting, of his family at the moment of his sister Sophie's dying, but the personal reference hardly dilutes its universality as a monumental and theatrical (contemporary critics compared it to Maeterlinck) but absolutely unsentimental presentation of death's devastation of the living. Munch's work is best not where the personal and universal coincide, as they do in *Death in the Sickroom*, but where the tension between them is greatest, as between extremes that meet. *The Scream* and *Madonna*, for example, are at once so intimate and so generalized that they give birth to new ideas, and meanings, unique to them. Rather than apostrophize experience, they create it. But the question of what is "best" in Munch is not, after all, so very compelling. Unlike most modern artists, who when below par can give only lesser versions of themselves, Munch at any level always has a specific content to communicate. He is not an artist to be taken piecemeal (if any great artist is), his work frisked for certifiable masterpieces, but an artist to be studied for what he teaches and shares, for his urgent bearing on the question Matthew Arnold said is the ultimate concern of all culture: "how to live."

How do Munch's paintings communicate? The short answer is: by causing emotional recognitions. The long answer would be an enumeration of a vast assortment of symbolical, formal, and technical devices and tricks, some adapted from other art and some invented. Munch's art is "psychological" in a complicated way; for if his own psyche was the major source of his subject matter, the psychology of the viewer, as Munch could imagine it, was the dictator of his form.

He went after his effects with a degree of fine-tuning calculation unheard of in major (not just eccentric) modern art, a degree practically
Renaissance-Gothic. The broadest class of his devices includes the
ways in which his paintings address viewers personally, making psychological space seem coextensive with the pictorial. The easiest way
of doing this is to have a figure staring out of the picture, as Munch
did frequently, with the effect that a viewer in some cases may feel
involved as an actor in a life-drama (by *The Voice*, as the object of the
woman's seductive expectancy) and in others (*Anxiety*, for instance, or
Evening on Karl Johan Street, where the horror is in stares that go
straight through us, denying our materiality) as the very person who
is experiencing the moment of awful vision. Or an abstracted gaze
(*Melancholy, Yellow Boat*; *The Red Vine*; many others) signals a link
between the background or surround and what the depicted person is
thinking and feeling; the viewer seeing such a gaze has a sense of
becoming that person, taking on his or her momentary fate.

This may be the place to mention Munch's self-portraits—most of
them full face, some employing the abstracted look. (At least one, *Self-
Portrait with Skeleton Arm*, 1895, is stupefyingly both, as one eye takes
in the viewer and the other seems to turn inward—what it sees there
symbolized, one feels, by the skeleton forearm.) The full-face ones are
first-person singular with a vengeance, unnervingly intimate confrontations of the viewer. From the wary purse-lipped youth of the 1880s
to the harsh wintry old man of the 1940s—including *Self-Portrait
between the Clock and the Bed*, 1942, though this complex and astonishing late masterpiece eludes any simple reading—the artist's gaze
carries not only evidence of his mental state but the weight of an
attitude toward the world, which includes the viewer. For what it's
worth, I do not much like the man revealed to me in these pictures—
especially after the period of his breakdown, when his native distrust-
fulness and rigidity, the "character armor" of one braced against the
threats of outer hurt and inner disintegration, take on an edge of
ruthlessness, even cruelty (with an occasional display of inner turmoil
whose nature the artist, pathetically, can no longer communicate). "It
was in quite a brutal way," he declared of his crisis in 1908, "that I
decided to restore myself"—in the process deliberately renouncing his
inner vision and losing, probably, whatever personal charm he may
have had. I don't like this man, but I admire beyond words his courage
and truthfulness.

The most obvious of Munch's compositional devices are those manipulating the relation of foreground to background. There is usually a nearby and a faraway in his pictures, the nearby perhaps a face, often practically crowding out of the frame, the faraway often an infinite plunge. The middle ground may be empty, evoking a poignance Rosenblum identifies as typically romantic; or it may feature a definite break, perhaps a treeline (in at least one of his landscapes, the beautiful *Train Smoke*, 1900, Munch actually changes painting styles at this juncture); or there may be a receding element carrying the eye back, usually diagonally to the left (a diagonal thought at the time, by artists including Seurat, to generate a "sad" mood: a rightward slant was deemed "happy"). (With color, facture, and other means, of course, Munch consistently works against the sense of a rush into space, asserting the paint surface, creating a fierce tension.) The most significant of these elements are the ramplike streets and balustered walks whose sources (van Gogh, for one) are exhaustively examined by Reinhold Heller in his excellent book on *The Scream*, a painting that is a prime example of the motif. Its most telling use, for me, is an almost unbearably sad series of drawings of the artist as a little boy with his young mother, from a memory of her just before her death (when he was five), a day on which the two of them went out walking and looked at the sea. They are emerging from a doorway. The small child tugs awkwardly at his mother's hand; she, quiet and tall, turns stiffly up the fleeing street. The street says *away* and *empty*. It says *gone*.

A full formal and semiotic study of Munch's pictorial means would be very long; I hope I have indicated at least their variety and complexity, as well as why the artist needed so many. The more exact you want a statement to be, the larger must be the language you state it in. Munch had to, and did, master a large and flexible artistic vocabulary before he could achieve even a single painting of unequivocal emotional content. In this he was unlike the expressionists who followed him; he wanted, as Edward Lucie-Smith puts it, "to convey the resonances of feeling, as well as its initial upsurge. With Munch, we get not only the bell-stroke, but its reverberation." And he was also emphatically the opposite of the standard modern artist, steadily reducing means until some tough, definitive aesthetic position has been reached. (This reduction holds even for romantic modernists; Brian O'Doherty writes of Mark Rothko's art as a language reduced to a single Word.) This anomaly—which has kept Munch, in effect, a radical artist—puts him afoul of modern taste, which is bound to regard pejoratively his lack of a style, a consistent, self-informing manner and technique. (His successful paintings have styles—ad hoc styles, as it were—but no very large body of his work does.) Thus even a sympathetic critic, Thomas M. Messer, feels uncomfortable putting Munch in the company of the major postimpressionists: "Munch's departure, unlike those of van Gogh or Gauguin, seems strangely muted, as if those who had so recently preceded him had preempted the most rewarding possibilities and left him an amalgam of recently articulated components." And it's true enough, as I find by trying it, that thinking of Munch's work as a whole, or even a partial whole, produces nothing like the mental sensation—of something strong, dense, and distinct—that the thought of van Gogh's or Gauguin's does. (Or even that of a relatively minor painter: Vuillard, Bonnard.) The whole seems muted, a blur.

But to think of individual paintings is another matter! I can call to mind no image of postimpressionism—not van Gogh's *Starry Night*, not *The Card Players*, not even *The Grande Jatte*—with the vivid particularity of *The Scream, Anxiety, Madonna*, and perhaps a half-dozen other Munchs, and I don't think this is simply an effect of my present closeness to these works. Their very lack of a dominating style puts them in relief to the mind's eye, uninflected by obtrusive common characteristics. (Just try to think *Grande Jatte* without some inner freshman voice chirping "pointillism!") Modernism's bias toward the general over the particular, issues over art works, lurks at the root of Messer's unease—as if the articulation of a new style, a new aesthetic category, were really the only significant intention for a big-time artist. Obviously the argument being broached here is an unmanageably large one, and a digression besides, so I'll be content to leave it unsettled. I would make only the suggestion that there are more ways than one for an artist to be judged great and that one of them may be the simple production of great paintings, however heterogeneous.

Munch's graphic work seems less open to a charge of stylelessness, hence, perhaps, the notion that his prints are better than his paintings. Munch made his first etchings in 1894, his first lithographs and woodcuts the next year, mastering each medium with amazing speed. That most of his graphic work was done in Paris with the celebrated printer Auguste Clot in concentrated periods may account for the impression of relative stylistic unity. Almost invariably the images were reproduced from his paintings, with such changes, concentrations, and refinements as the technical means suggested—incision of the plate, for instance, to produce the delicate hairline skeins of negative space woven into the *Madonna* lithograph (about as close as Munch came to mainstream art nouveau, with which he shared several formal devices, e.g., the "whiplash" line). The tidiness of many of the prints may be attributed to Clot, who did much of the printing without Munch's direct supervision. I love this account by a contemporary, Erich Buttner, of the printing of a series of four-color *Sick Child*s:

> Mr. Munch's coming has been announced. The lithographic stones with the great head were already lying next to one another, neatly lined up, ready to print. Munch arrives, positions himself before the row, closes his eyes firmly and begins to direct blindly with his finger in the air: "Go ahead and print . . . gray, green, blue, brown." Opens his eyes, says to me: "Come, have a Schnapps . . ." and so the printer printed until Munch came back and gave another blind order: "Yellow, rose, red . . ."

(It's possible Munch by this time was bored with *Sick Child* lithos, which the public couldn't get enough of; for some time he lived largely off sales of them.)

Add to all this Munch's brilliant finesses in woodcut—negative drawing (à la Gauguin), virtuosic exploitation of the wood grain, the innovation of sawing up the block to print in different colors—then throw in the best of his etchings and drypoints (e.g., *Two People*, 1895, a riveting picture worth a dozen Ingmar Bergman movies) and surely one of the finest black-and-white lithographs of all time (*Self-Portrait with Skeleton Arm*), and Munch's graphic output does present itself as an altogether sharper and more delectable body of work than his paintings, from which it was in some sense a holiday. The hard work and great discoveries of Munch's art are in the paintings; in printmaking he could freely exercise the facility, stylishness, and decorative flair that in his paintings were instantly expendable. (Another motive for the graphic work was Munch's yearning to reach a wide public, "to bring my art into many homes"; yet another was to make money, enough, he hoped, to avoid having to part with too many of his paintings.) It's a matter of scale: scale of ambition and spirit, of seriousness— the stakes of the game. For Munch, the big game was painting. The idea that the "significance" of his art is to be found in the concise polished print may flatter a connoisseuring sensibility, but Munch's art teaches nothing if not a contempt for mere connoisseurship. Such fastidious discriminations bespeak a mindset that would probably prefer not to deal with Munch at all.

It's true enough that Munch's work, in person and in mass, is hardly ingratiating. One is so used to thinking of him as an image maker, for one thing, that the physical rawness of many of his paintings is jolting. Some are painted on obviously cheap canvas (*The Scream* is on cardboard) or in a peculiarly unappetizing temperalike medium (*Death in the Sickroom*) or bear signs of rough treatment (Munch had the astounding habit in his later years of leaving his pictures outside in all weather, declaring that such exposure would either "kill or cure" them) or of ill-advised later touch-ups, and the technique is often brutal (though rarely crude), alternately negligent and forced, with surfaces as compulsively worked over as those of any de Kooning Women. Some of his paintings have a Matissean mastery and beauty; others look to have been painted, as not a few were, in cheap hotel rooms, under the pressure of an awful nervousness. They evoke an atmosphere rank with smells of turpentine and old cigarette smoke, a life of loose ends, frayed nerves, alcohol and bad food, dirt. This is a redolence that not even the institutional swank of the National Gallery's East Building, and a fancy lighting job featuring spotlighting in overall dimness, could sanitize—thank goodness. It made Munch real to me.

Was Munch crazy? There is a tendency among academically trained critics to shrink from considering overt psychological content; specialization is to blame for this, plus the ideology of modernism that has so effectively enforced a separation of aesthetic from other human values. But a discomfort with psychological matters is going to be a serious handicap for anyone discussing Munch. Deborah Perlberg, writing in praise of the Washington show in *Artforum*, begins: "Veering wildly, as it does, between radical new styles of painting and imagery exaggerated by his own mental illness, Edvard Munch's accomplishment"—which gets the quality of his accomplishment exactly wrong. Style and imagery are at odds—there is a "veer" between them—only in his weakest (mostly pseudo-fauvist) paintings, and as for exaggeration by "mental illness," one can only wonder what, had the artist been a healthier type, his *un*exaggerated images would have been like (*The Sigh*?). What is striking about very nearly all his work of the nineties is precisely how controlled, how undistorted by emotion his images are—images of emotion, of emotional states and visions. The most cursory comparison of his paintings with Ensor's, some of which really are disturbed, or with those of any of the German expressionists, who tend to the histrionic, will suffice to make this clear. *The Scream* may be the all-time definitive painting about hysteria; as a painting, totally realized and integrated, there is absolutely nothing hysterical about it. The blood red sky, the wavering and shooting lines, the informative detail of the two figures walking away (the scream is soundless) are as decisive as hammer blows. It took Munch a year of hard work to evolve the final symbolic and pictorial form for the personal experience *The Scream* represents. He knew what he was doing.

The judgment of insanity is sometimes one with which we evade seeing into ourselves too deeply, an inner hygiene projected outward. No judgment is trickier, or more apt to boomerang. It has been said that there is an insanity of the Left and an insanity of the Right, the latter being by far the more prevalent in postindustrial Western society, in which it passes, indeed, for normality. A cultural devaluation of subjective experience, a quarantine put on strong emotion inside and out, is the work of the rightist madness, in this view. Only the uniquely brave and lucky individual can stand up between that repressive Scylla and its complementing Charybdis, the howling chaos of the madness of the Left (which I certainly don't mean to romanticize). For a time it was given to Munch to be such an individual, most effectively sane when he was contemplating, and by his contemplation making widely comprehensible, the most bewildering and painful experiences of life. He painted, he said, to explain life to himself; he also wanted "to help others make life clearer to themselves"—sane intentions, triumphantly realized. That he had a badly damaged personality is apparent from the record of his life; he was incapable of fully profiting from his own genius for objectifying inner tensions, incapable of finally integrating the experiences his art made visible. Art seems to have been for him a holding action, a series of counter-attacks on a darkness that threatened always to engulf him. What was the nature of this darkness? Where did it come from?

Psychoanalytic readings of artists' minds, reflecting the scientific urge to understand the world by explaining it, naturally irritate artistic sensibilities, which, of whatever stripe, rarely conceive of any meaning divorced from experience. Thus a chemical analysis of water would irk someone mostly aware of being thirsty: it might be correct, but it doesn't matter. But even if we acknowledge that the description of an artist's neurosis is beside the point of his appeal and value, psychoanalytic inquiry is surely not presumptuous when an artist, like Munch, makes thoroughgoing and deliberate use of his own personal history, practically inviting us to observe and comprehend not only his art but also himself, his plight. Focusing on the personal in such a case might even help us measure the transformations of his art, the attainments of the universal that are, after all, what have gotten us interested in him in the first place. It may be especially useful to throw some cold light on Munch's relations with women.

The Bohemian circles that influenced Munch's intellectual development were male dominated, sex obsessed, and misogynist. (Strindberg, in a well-known article on the artist in 1896, spoke of "vermin, microbes, vampires and women.") But it was not until later life, in the aftermath of a particularly nightmarish affair with a marriage-bent woman that ended with a tussle over a gun, which went off, and the loss of part of a finger, that Munch developed the rigid pathology of the misogynist. Before that, for him woman was the subject of reverent awe, irresistible attraction—and terror, a subject his art desperately aimed to objectify. Not having come across any psychoanalysis of Munch in any reading, I'll hazard a brief and amateur one myself.

Munch's mother died when he was five, near the age of the Oedipal crisis, and his sister Sophie when he was thirteen, near that of puberty, a time of natural incestuous feelings. It seems likely that the sensitive child and adolescent, lacking any consoling explanation for these catastrophes (his father, a military doctor, and other relatives could offer only their stilted and bathetic Lutheranism, which repelled him), would associate them with his own awakening sexual urges in a terribly hurtful way. The guilt, rage, and fear thus irrevocably linked to these urges made them a threat to his stability, but they were too strong to be repressed. (Moreover, such repression was scorned by the fin-de-siècle avant-garde.) They had to go somewhere, so they were projected outward onto women, in effect amplifying feminine seductiveness with an overlay of the young man's own desires, which he then experienced not as stirring within him but as coming from without, an awful magnetism, almost literally a death-ray. The association, at times the absolute blending, of sex and death is the deepest and most potent mystery in Munch's work, from the macabre comedy of *The Maiden and Death* (a voluptuous nude in erotically explicit embrace with a skeleton) to his *Madonna*, surely one of the most sublime male visions of female sexuality in all of Western art.

Madonna is no less than the picture of a woman in orgasm from the point of view of her lover. She is almost life-size, her body cut off by the bottom of the picture just above the crotch. Her arms are behind her, indistinct as if in a swirl of movement. Her breasts fall slightly to the sides—this is almost certainly a view from above. Her head swoons back and to one side. Her hair is alive. Her closed (but somehow all-seeing) eyes, their sockets in the skull emphatically outlined, are like the wells or whirlpools typical in Munch's women, exerting a sucking tug. She has a scarlet halo. She is surrounded by abstract emanations, undulating to her movement. For the rest, Munch spelled it out in one of his prose poems, addressing his creation:

> The pause when the entire world halted in its orbit. Your face em-
> bodies all the world's beauty. Your lips, crimson red like the coming
> fruit, glide apart as if in pain. The smile of a corpse. Now life and
> death join hands. The chain is joined that links the thousands of past
> generations to the thousands of generations to come.

In other words, the woman is conceiving a child—a moment of triumph for her and for the human race, human continuity. It is also a moment of deathlike loss for the lover, henceforth of no more biological significance than the drone ant after mating with a queen.

The differences between the *Madonna* and traditional Western erotic art—pictures, that is, of women, painted or taken by men—are dramatic. This is not woman as object, for instance: this is woman as *subject*, orchestrator not only of the sexual encounter but of all humanity. The male's place in the scheme of things is poignantly conveyed by the border of spermatozoa and the skeletal fetus in the lithographs (motifs carved into a frame, now lost, for the original painting—there are several painted versions). I don't mean to make this picture out to be in any sense "feminist"; I doubt that many women would accept the world on the narrow, violent terms on which Munch is willing to grant it to them. Still it is rare in art to see the sexual act itself as the fulfillment of the woman's desires rather than the man's— unless she is a whore, of course, as this woman certainly is not. (Munch's clearest whore image, *Sin*, 1901, shows a used-looking red-haired nude of cowlike stupidity, no femme fatale but rather a born victim.) *Madonna* is an image of integral woman at the apex of her biological function and nature, an image of universal fatality that admits of no qualification, beyond good and evil, Munch's best deduction, from his own tumultuous experience, of what the secret of life, if one could see it, would look like.

That the *Madonna* dramatizes, to the fullest extent, the central mental disturbance of Munch's life does not render it a neurotic or eccentric picture. Anyone who could think so in the presence of the painting would have the sensibilities of a vending machine. Like all of Munch's greatest works, and to a greater degree than any other modern art I can readily think of, the *Madonna* demonstrates the seemingly miraculous transformation, through art, of private obsession into universal meaning. It holds up a mirror, albeit a distorting (or, better, a selecting, stylizing) mirror, to the mind; it offers itself as a permanent human reference. (And, unlike knowledge gained by scientific psychology, it stands in no danger of being invalidated by future discoveries.) The miracle is only seeming, of course. It is the ordinary miracle of art, brought off occasionally by even very pragmatic artists whose "obsession" may be no more than an interest in good design and whose "meaning" may be no more than the realization of an aesthetic novelty. (Munch's is an alternative use of art, not an adversary one.) It is achieved with craft and style.

The *Madonna* represents the highest point of generality Munch attained without betraying the felt truth of his personal experience— without, that is, sheering off into a mere headiness. (It is thus automatically the single greatest symbolist image, because Munch had no peer among the symbolists; no one was even close.) He could generalize too fecklessly, following that philosophical itch that accounts for most of what later generations have found silly in symbolist art and literature, all those glamorized conventional ideas. His occasional efforts to make an upbeat synthesis of his views of life and death, in drawings of plants sprouting from corpses and the like, are Munch at his weakest, full of earnestness and deserted by his inspiration. (The late work—heralded by the vast and, judging from reproductions, achingly banal murals he did for Oslo University between 1909 and 1916—doggedly pursued the theme of reconciliation, mainly in pictures of workers and Norwegian nature.) He was, however, heroically resistant to the itch throughout the first two decades of his work, riveted to the particular experience, the particular feeling, as if he were a naturalist of the psychic interior. And there is a sense in which Munch never abandoned naturalism, which hung on invisibly, as a nagging conscience, long after exterior reality had been lost to sight.

His was indeed a naturalism turned inside out, and Munch pursued its logic relentlessly. "If one sees double [when drunk] one must for example paint two noses," he told his diary in 1890 or 1891, with no detectable irony. The displacement of objectivity went even further, out of present time: "I paint not what I see," goes his most famous quote, "but what I saw." And yet the sense of the objective, of something actual being made visible, persists throughout his art. It's as if the artist's seeing, measuring eye retreated inward from his face, his "I" retracting with it, leaving more and more of the mind in a state of being "out there"—until finally the eye seems to peer up from the brainstem, taking in with aesthetic detachment, and recording in a language constructed from art and memory, the whole wild landscape of the self. Nothing could be more unlike the sentimentalized ideas typical of symbolism or the sentimentalized chaos (anti-ideas) of surrealism. The integrity, in both senses, of Munch's vision more than its poetic content is what awes us, what makes us feel that he is uniquely great. The best, most accurate, encomium to Munch may still be that of one of his earliest critics, the German Karl Scheffler, in 1902. Munch, said Scheffler, is "a Romantic who cannot lie."

May–June 1979

I Missed Punk

I missed punk
because my record player was broken
because I was suddenly older
because I can stand only so much distraction
only so much excitement and elation
but mainly because my record player was broken
and none of my friends cared much about new music

(Back in the '60s the thought that I'd missed something
would depress me terribly
Now it's one of those things that happen)

Who are we anyway
any of us
who care about new music or anything?
We are ones who care about their own skins, certainly
about saving them
and not being totally crazy and alone, in pain
We will go through a lot of incidental pain
as long as it keeps us in company
even ridiculous company, which most company is
We certainly don't want to be alone
and this makes us ridiculous

What I want to be is virtuous and noticed
What good is virtue if no one notices?
You don't know it's virtuous unless someone says so

I missed punk
but it brushed past me in the cultural bazaar
and seemed to drop a hint about virtue

being what I'd always thought:
a readiness to lose, to let go
because only in loss is one not ridiculous
(if anyone notices)

Never resist an idea
Never say no to a contradiction
They have come to help you
smash the ego
which always reconstitutes
(and if it doesn't, well,
your worries are over)

1979

A Book by Larry Rivers

Drawings and Digressions
(New York: Clarkson N. Potter, 1979)

Larry Rivers is one of the great personalities of the last thirty years in art, and if you would like to get to know him here's your chance. Besides over three hundred reproductions, this sumptuous volume features an autobiographical text, edited from tapes by Carol Brightman, which is as revealing and entertaining as any in the literature of artists talking. It is a document, full of slightly scandalous anecdote, that tells of survival in the New York art world—and at its maddest edges, where artistic and personal ambition, aesthetics and career tactics, art and life mingle in a hall of distorting mirrors. The terrible human costs of persistence in such a world, where ego is the only dependable reality (if you have a weak one, forget it), are implicit in the book, but so are the great fun and sense of spiritual election, of being a gang member in the boiler room of modern culture.

Rivers's element was always chaos. From the Bronx, the son of Ukrainian Jewish immigrants, he received a medical discharge from the wartime air force (for a "hand tremor"), studied music at Juilliard, began painting, was quickly married and divorced (two sons), was a touring jazz musician, changed his name (from Grossberg), began his recurrent flirtation with heroin, found his way to Hans Hofmann's class in Provincetown, Massachusetts, started showing, was hailed in print by the art critic Clement Greenberg (who would change his mind), traveled in Europe, received an art degree from New York University—and all this takes us only to 1951, when Rivers, twenty-seven, was a fledgling presence on a New York scene exalted by the triumphs of abstract expressionism. It was about this time that he met Frank O'Hara, forming a symbiotic friendship with the poet that would be one of the chief events in both men's lives. O'Hara later described Rivers's initial effect as that of "a demented telephone. Nobody knew whether they wanted it in the library, the kitchen or the toilet, but it was electric."

Rivers was haunted, then as always, by feelings of inauthenticity. He considered himself "a fake American—sort of American by mistake. After all . . . I spoke Yiddish till I was six years old." Nor would there be ultimate relief from this homeless feeling in the international religion of modern art. "I produce art, I make art. Is it out of some overall interest in art, or is it just a constant concern with myself as an artist, having been identified as an artist, and continuing the identity?" But he threw himself into painting to the depth of his anxiety, with a commitment to prove himself, to be the real thing. Not content to compete with the abstract expressionists in their arena of ambiguous freedom, he took as his heroes the old and modern masters, from Rembrandt to Bonnard, whose legitimacy seemed to him beyond doubt. And he would take on these masters in the most masterly of mediums, the one Ingres called "the probity of art": he would draw.

He drew and painted (his paintings being largely drawing by other means) friends and nudes and friendly nudes, female and male. As he tells in *Drawings and Digressions*, one of the first of his "notorious" works was a full-length portrait of O'Hara, modeled after a painting of Géricault's plus combat boots and erection. He did many images, sometimes several to a canvas, of his mother-in-law Berdie Burger, a huge mild woman who lived with him in Southampton (during a period when he had fled the city) and looked after his sons. Then in 1953, the year O'Hara wrote the "action" poem "Second Avenue" and dedicated it to Rivers, Rivers painted the "literary" history painting *George Washington Crossing the Delaware*—an inspired provocation in the then overwhelming climate of abstraction. The painting was snapped up by the Museum of Modern Art and made his reputation.

Rivers undertook *George Washington* after reading *War and Peace*: "I wanted to make a work of art that included some aspect of national life. . . . It was like getting in the ring with Tolstoy." The Mailerism is not fortuitous; the painter has a lot in common with the author. If as a figurative artist Rivers was something of an odd man out in the fifties art world, he had the wit to see that the oddity was itself a distinction, to be cultivated zestfully.

Artistic parody, artistic nostalgia, sassy sexuality, classical lift and elevation: Rivers's work at its best, which it often was into the early sixties, is a high-wire act, or teetering jazz solo, that is gorgeous and exciting. His style may have been all mannerism—he languidly and accurately describes his "thing" in drawing at the time as "a little line, a little erasure, a little heavy, a little gray"—but the mannerisms are fine-tuned to the whine of the artist's exacerbated nerves, his "impossible" position. His life, meanwhile, was often a howling mess. He refers in passing in this book to "a long period of homosexuality, a little bestiality, a little of this and that and drugs." Indeed, the life chaos seemed necessary to feed and balance the ordering in art, informed by O'Hara's ethic of incessant attention, incessant openness, "Grace / to be born and live as variously as possible." As grueling as the relationship with O'Hara sometimes was for both men, it produced probably the most sparkling poet-painter collaborations ever: the *Stones* lithographs of 1958. Still, it was all, in one of Rivers's favorite ambiguously loaded usages, "insane." There is a limit to human stamina, and Rivers was bound to find it.

Several misfortunes befell Rivers in the sixties. First the art world changed, suddenly and drastically, as a vast wave of ambitious, pragmatic young artists, fired by the achievements of abstract expressionism but having none of its romanticism, hit and took over. Rivers's enfant terrible position—perfectly genuine in the pious fifties—was outflanked by the cool newcomers, whose rejection of him would be a permanent hurt. He married again, had two daughters, was divorced again. In 1966 Frank O'Hara died, at age forty, after a hideous, ridiculous auto accident on the beach at Fire Island. And Rivers got involved, through a Dr. Feelgood, with the one drug that, by counterfeiting inspiration, could disorient his muse: amphetamine, by daily injection. There followed a period of wildly gimmicky, tinselly three-dimensional work, all manic carpentry and plastic and light and airbrush and Day-Glo, that was simply not very good. Rivers had always perversely strained his connection to his actual feelings; the speed obliterated it.

Rivers in his life has entertained a set of romantic susceptibilities guaranteed to kill or burn out most people at an early age. It's a set heavily weighted to the dark end of modern enticements: sex, drugs, art heroism, hipsterism, White Negroism, hysteria. At best, he keeps these demonisms in tension with a high, poetic, daredevil humor, a humor worked out by Rivers and O'Hara between themselves (see their "How to Proceed in the Arts"). Thus Rivers's existential torments are discharged in a series of dandyish poses: young old master, connoisseur of American cliché, clinical sex fiend, Jewish prodigal son, painter among the poets, good bad boy of art. In each pose there is true desperate romantic sincerity. Back away far enough and facetiousness threatens to engulf everything, and in Rivers's amphetamine period, with O'Hara no longer around to kid him back to himself, that's exactly what happened.

Today Rivers pronounces himself off drugs—scared off by health problems—and his art is better. He has never returned to the direct painting and drawing attack of his halcyon work. He works with carbon transfers and an opaque projector and admits, though defiantly, that "lost nerve" is a factor: "This [mechanical] way of working . . . gives me less anxiety. . . . Why should I have to struggle?" The new paintings and drawings are rather pale and brittle presences, with only occasional flickers of the old dashing humor and sensuality. Rivers comforts himself with the thought that painting may be, after all, "an old man's art." What was once a four-alarm fire is down to embers, but these are being banked to last the winter. Meanwhile, there is nothing wrong with Rivers's gift of gab or with his memory—a completely nonanalytical, immediate, intimate memory—of what the people and events in his life have felt like. There's the giddy mixture of tones, from guttural laconic to high parodic, that was his great natural gift to the poetry of Frank O'Hara. He can make a confession of his commercial propensities sound like a recitative:

> I was your artist willing to make deals. I didn't have any guilt about it. It was the money and the action. You make something, a dealer buys it, puts it up for sale, someone else buys it; the dealer makes money, comes back for more—I'm in the world hanging on someone's wall. What else was I about? What else would give me pleasure?

Just try tinkering with the phrasing of that. It's as perfect as Keats or Charlie Parker.

It would be poor manners to repeat here Rivers's passionate gossip about the famous and the less well known people in his life. But sweet and pungent things do get said about John Ashbery, Leonard Bernstein, Gregory Corso, Willem de Kooning, Edwin Denby, Jane Freilicher, Grace Hartigan, Imamu Amiri Baraka (Le Roi Jones), Howard Kanovitz, Kenneth Koch, Norman Mailer, John Bernard Myers, O'Hara, Jackson Pollock, Terry Southern, and Jean Tinguely, among others, including wives and girlfriends. (There could have been many more, had the talk not been limited to people of whom Rivers has drawn portraits.) And we get anecdotes, as of Jackson Pollock, who so hated a Rivers sculpture owned by Leo Castelli that, leaving a party, he tried to run it down with his car. In 1957 Rivers won $32,000 answering art questions on the television quiz show "The $64,000 Question." He went straight to the Cedar Bar in Greenwich Village and ordered drinks all around. The check was snatched from him and passed—enviously? reverently?—from hand to hand, until all had looked their fill.

Little that Rivers says of the 1970s in the book touches on the art world proper. His estrangement from that world began in the early sixties and was fairly complete by the end of the decade; his social milieu had become one of diverse friends, and his reputation had eddied out into the general celebrity culture. One wag recently called him "Channel 13's idea of a great artist." He remains, however, a true artist, with a chronic integrity. His few apparent attempts at fashionable sell-out imagery have never made it over into real slickness; he is incorruptible despite himself. It is probable that had he died when O'Hara did, Rivers would be much more highly regarded than he is today, but our century has more than enough young martyrs to art and excess. Rivers's survival gives us a more practical and agreeable hero, the recklessly honest man who, in this exhilarating funny-tragic book, shows his wares and unfolds his tale.

November 18, 1979

Warhol and Class Content

Andy Warhol's Portraits of the '70s at the Whitney Museum (November 20, 1979–January 27, 1980) was received by the big-media reviewers with vehement distaste. Hilton Kramer more or less threw up his hands in horror. *Newsweek*'s critic seemed upset and descended to calling Warhol's brushwork "swish." Robert Hughes, lately our most provocative critic, was in top spleen in *Time*, getting off culinary zingers like "pistachio-and-strawberry glop" and "autistic cake icing." I was puzzled by the hostility, because for me the show was delightful and seemed perfect in its way. It had the old sixties virtue—which Warhol, like Frank Stella, seems never to lose—of a big, splashy stylistic idea brought off in a big, splashy, completely self-confident manner. I don't know if I'd argue with Hughes's haughty remark that the portraits "can hardly be said to exist within the sphere of aesthetic debate"—wherever that is these days. But I do think they are a solid, typically Warholian coup, an unexpected use of painting that is right on the pulse of certain changes in the culture. The critical revulsion just makes them all the more interesting. It seems to indicate that with his "social icons"—as David Bourdon incisively called the portraits five years ago—Warhol has, once again, hit a nerve.

Aesthetically, the portraits can scarcely be called derivative or unrealized. They are robustly themselves, full of pictorial savvy, and often beautiful. Their beauty is admittedly most apparent in small doses, at living-room scale. Hughes called their composite effect at the Whitney "coarse and repetitive." There was, indeed, nothing delicate about the impact of fifty-some double portraits ranked in triple tiers on walls painted a fudgy brown. But "repetitive" is wrong; the range of idea and effect within the portraits' mechanical premises was impressive. Just about every portrait held its own in the melee of images; there were few wallflowers at this party. And though no one acknowledged it, a firm physical command of the Whitney's fourth-floor cavern is a noteworthy achievement for any painter. A lot of people are going to judge the portraits from reproductions, which is a pity. Reproduction effaces textures and the paintings' sheer objectness, the way they hold and seem to "ride" the wall. They do this by a number of mutually reinforcing means that mediate between the scale and space of the room and the scale and space of the viewer: architectural placement; blocky projecting stretchers; identical size of image and support; hot "advancing" color; big brushstrokes; the simple rivetingness of the outsize human face. This is sixties aesthetic high tech, as in Stella or Judd—cold, efficient, bedazzling.

The reviewers don't deny Warhol's resourcefulness—how could they?—but they manage to suggest that there is something reprehensible about it. Every hostile review I read, for instance, used the phrase "decorator colors" with maximum scorn. Now, it would be more interesting to relate Warhol's endlessly variegated palette of aggressively "odd" flavorful hues and tints to the chromatic cuisine of late color-field painting, to which it assumes an impudent relation. But if the arcane research of professional decorators is also evoked, why is that not a plus? Is there a moral order of colors? (I smell a treatise here.) What is inherently unserious about, say, the excruciation of a saturated cocoa brown next to a saturated pale denim blue? On what basis should we judge such pleasures unworthy of us? As for Warhol's brushwork, is that to be condemned for its efficiency? If Warhol coolly mimics de Kooning's way of yanking the visual field apart with wet-in-wet strokes, that procedure surely signifies something different and more deeply gripping for de Kooning than for Warhol. But if Warhol's use of it makes pictorial sense and fits the overall strategy of his art, what's the beef? (Do we like painting or don't we?)

There is no sense of pastiche about Warhol's portraits. Their form evolved from his silk-screened multiple images of the sixties, with the important addition of a technique, derived from certain dime-store fine-art reproductions, that involves printing the image on a prepared irregular surface, giving the illusion of "original" facture. Warhol transforms the technique by using it very broadly, for a variety of ends; there is no Lichtenstein-like satirical acknowledgment of its source. Still, a lot of people, *Newsweek*'s art critic among them, fall for the commonsense illusion that the acrylic paint is applied on rather than under—or is perhaps identical with—the silk-screen enamel. The fact is that nearly all color, including that of eyes, lips, and hair, is laid down before the screening; only occasionally and sparingly does Warhol add important touches with a brush, adjusting the balance of photo and paint in paint's favor. The wet-in-wet handling (where it is thick; often it is flat, posterlike) dries before receiving the image, which gets its "painterly" look from being distorted by the topography. Warhol had developed the aesthetic and expressive possibilities of this technique in nonportrait paintings for years, notably in a series of large, mysterious near abstractions called *Shadows*. His ability to improvise with it has reached such a point of casual assurance that one can easily miss its virtuosity.

It should be apparent that if there is a difficulty with Warhol's portraits, it must be external rather than internal. Not to put too fine a point on it, the portraits are social artifacts, mostly of rich people (a few are fellow artists and art-world types), whose homes they are meant to adorn and whose pretensions to cultural eminence they are meant to ratify. I think this is what exercises Warhol's detractors, and what they fail to distinguish from matters of aesthetic performance and taste. Both offense and confusion are readily seen in Hughes's antic eloquence: "Warhol's admirers . . . are given to claiming that Warhol has 'revived' the social portrait as a form. It would be nearer the truth to say that he has zipped it into a Halston, painted its eyelids and propped it in the back of a limo, where it moves but cannot speak."

Bourdon's elegant characterization of Warhol's portraits as "social icons"—*icon* conveying the almost Byzantine timelessness with which they invest their subjects—anticipates the gist of Hughes's sarcasm and puts it in a positive light. From another direction, Robert Rosenblum's introduction to the Whitney catalogue, a model of bravura scholarship, sweetens Warhol's infatuation with high society by invoking the tradition of social portraiture that flourished in the fin de siècle, with J. S. Sargent, Giovanni Boldini, and others. (Hughes himself brackets Warhol with Sargent only to conclude that Warhol "lacks Sargent's ability to realize and construct a painting"—a judgment I would probably disagree with if I understood it, an impossibility in view of the apples-and-oranges aesthetic differences involved.) But even the most useful shifts in terminology and category, like Bourdon's and Rosenblum's here, make no answer to the source of Hughes's ire, which seems outside the sphere of art altogether—and very much of the essence. To take social portraiture seriously, as we are certainly not used to doing, is to give at least as much attention to its social as to its aesthetic meanings. However tentatively and clumsily, the art critic must follow where art leads, even onto sociological—and potentially political—ground.

Warhol in the seventies emerged as something he was once prematurely accused of being: a servant of the rich. The charge was premature in the sixties because, though a willing darling of the moneyed, he persisted in working out artistic inspirations from "classless" and other-class sources; only gradually did the relationship become a closed circuit that included the meaning of his art. The central question for us—an open-and-shut case for Hughes—is whether to view this status with benignity. To do so would mean accepting at least two propositions: (1) art as service is okay, and (2) the rich—the rich in general and Warhol's rich in particular—are okay. Putting it another way: (1) can art today be important though it advances interests other than its own? and (2) is the legitimacy of today's social elite an acceptable fiction? Before trying to confront these uncomfortably large questions, it would be well to ask how Andy Warhol got in a position to raise them.

The awesome match of cultural trend and personal idiosyncrasy that made Warhol the man of the hour in the early-sixties avant-garde is part of our mythology. Certainly no arrival in art history was better timed—though, if stories are to be believed, Warhol was almost too late. One tale has him, in early 1962, frantically casting about for an image to secure his place on the already careering bandwagon of pop art. Warhol quickly discovered that what he had ready to hand, in his own sensibility and experience, his own worldview, was the trump card of the whole movement.

The son of an immigrant Czechoslovak laborer, Warhol is one of the very few modern artists from an authentically working-class background. A lot of what has seemed miraculous, angelic oddity about him is explicable in light of the modern American working class's avidity for the products and values of capitalist popular culture; ambivalence about these things usually has been the province of a middle class able to take their availability for granted from birth. Warhol's enthusiastic view of the commodity and celebrity culture, shaded by his vicarious intimacy with that culture's social underside (its lower-class ways of death, by car crash or electric chair), gave him the edge in the race to valorize the commonplace. By comparison with his still galvanically powerful Marilyns and electric chairs of 1962–66, the work of the other pop artists seems distanced, even debilitated, by middle-class irony. What was for them "material" was for him subject matter, form, and content. The occasional imputation of naïveté (or cynicism, for that matter) to Warhol is itself a species of middle-class naïveté (or cynicism), the failure to imagine that our culture presents a radically different face when seen from its periphery.

The rewards for Warhol's talent and timeliness did not, of course, stop at art-world success. The easy social mobility toward the upper levels that accompanied the upheavals of the sixties shuffled people from show business, art, government, crime (drug pushing), fashion, and the whole circle of infectious celebrity connoted by "jet set" and "beautiful people" into the deck of inherited, corporate, and professional wealth. This mini-revolution plucked Warhol from the bottom of the heap and plopped him without ceremony or initiation at the top. A sort of arriviste's arriviste, he set a new style for the new rich, a style that might be called democratic decadence—a facetious refurbishing of the seven deadly sins for people uneasy with their sudden opportunity to indulge them and lacking anything better to do. The model of the style was set by the unblinking, unjudging camera eye of Warhol's great early films (especially *The Chelsea Girls*). One might behave very badly, but as long as Andy Warhol, the disembodied genius of the People, was there to look on, it was somehow all right.

What Warhol had to offer his new-rich patrons, at the outset, was more than surface flash; it was a moral alchemy by which a dronelike social role was made to resemble the historic role of the avant-garde. This had never happened before in America because never before had a generation of American wealth been so young, so cosmopolitan, and so deprived of social function, including even the function of regulating its own existence, "maintaining standards." This was a sixties generation, remember, imbued with liberal/anarchistic values; Warhol said recently that Gerald Ford's son Jack is the only Republican he knows. Welfare-state ideology foreclosed philanthropy, the traditional face-saver of the idle rich, and there was nothing left but the aura of spiritual election that in our time art alone has seemed able to confer. And in Warhol the new rich got not just any artist but an artist who personified democracy, sexual liberation, and liberal permissiveness generally, an angelic innocence that said oh and yes to everything, even to boredom, the worm in the apple of the misspent life.

That Warhol's moral magic has drastically diminished will be apparent, I think, to anyone who dips into *Andy Warhol's Exposures*, his recent book of photos and breathless verbal accounts of the aging new rich. His world has caught up to (and onto) him; now his passionate avarice, fame-love, and workaholism merely reflect his surround. (In the eighties it seems that the thing for everyone is to have a job, or at least to look busy.) Where he once certified "celebrities," now he hob-nobs only with the certified McCoy. His once hypnotically succinct way with words has gone from oracular to almost orotund. Even his aphorisms are lame, as when he proposes to supplant his most quoted quip with "In fifteen minutes everyone will be famous." One realizes with a start how crucially Warhol's hothouse of social nomads and street people, the laboratory of his social creativity, contributed to his cultural authority. That strange authority is long gone now, consumed by the anxiety of the rich to think well of themselves. For Warhol, it seems anything but a bad bargain. His conspicuous contentment, at a time of disillusionment with the powers and promises of art, may be part of what makes his middle-class critics so testy. In any case, with the dissipation of his aura Warhol emerges in the surprising role of mere working artist.

What interests us is the *kind* of working artist Warhol is: an artist working for a particular class. It is not a role he takes lightly, nor is its performance confined to portrait commissions. Two of his nonportrait themes of the seventies seem apropos: Mao and the hammer and sickle. Rosenblum suggests that the imposing Mao portraits, some fully fifteen feet high, are an investigation of "the frighteningly severe and remote authority of the leader of a modern totalitarian state." This seems correct as far as it goes—the big Maos distill an emotion that might be called the totalitarian sublime—but it's just too somber to fit Andy Warhol, whose intention almost always includes an element of audi-ence complicity, of titillation. For me, the Maos and hammers and sickles relate to the electric chairs and car crashes of the early sixties—the difference being one of class content. The shock value of the earlier paintings was in images of plebeian catastrophe; that of the recent paintings is in images of historic menace to the ruling class. Warhol offers his patrons both a delicious horror and a promise of emotional mastery over it: they can hang it on their walls.

Turning revolution into an upper-crust consumable would seem automatic grounds for condemnation to many critics today, but I don't think this reaction is inevitable. Whatever attitude one takes toward the commodity-based logic of current capitalism, it ought to be possible to view Warhol's extreme and subtle extension of it positively, as art that says something about a culture and an era—and does so with impressive detachment, derived from the artist's tranquil acceptance of cultural entropy, of decadence. We admire the artistic expression of past cultures whose citizens we would have hated to be, and I don't see any bad faith in granting the same discrimination to our own. Art with conscious, fully integrated social content is arguably a category transcending political lines, evoking a standard as good for the goose of the Right as for the gander of the Left. And by such a standard Warhol must be judged to rank high—at least as high as the best socialist realism, for instance. I don't suppose he's as good as Bertolt Brecht, but I don't think the comparison is unthinkable.

A Warhol portrait starts with a deliberately conventional "characteristic" photo of someone. High-contrast printing and screening onto a rough colored ground partially destroy the photo's informational content in the interest of an idealization. Color and paint-handling fill in the ravaged images with a mood, a set of pictorial cues presumably tailored to the aura of the person. It's not flattery in the usual sense, but rather flattering inclusion in a timeless privileged realm of art—art here practically identical with social prominence, which in turn is practically identical with money or celebrity (usually both). The iconic character of the portraits as much as says that the contemporary social order is eternal. There is nothing sentimental or even particularly rhetorical about this idealization, which is straightforward, an automatic feature of the artist's attentiveness. And there is such adeptness and insouciance in the performance, such a distilled painting pleasure (as in Fragonard), that the elevation of the subject can't get portentous. It might all be a joke. But if so, it's a benign, smiling joke. Warhol convinces us that he really does like people and painting—in his own grasping way, by which the people he paints are more likable for being rich and for parting with some of their riches for a portrait (the fee was $25,000 per panel five years ago). His idealization does not drip sweetness and light, but it's no harsher than the temper of our times.

Are the rich different from you and me only because they have more money? The famous anecdote tells us that this was Ernest Hemingway's answer, a doctrinaire American-democratic answer, to F. Scott Fitzgerald, who knew better. The rich may start out as regular Joes in the chips, but given a little time, wealth changes everything, including basic humanity. It does this by taking on a life of its own, in power and precious timeless possessions, that dwarfs the simple human lives in its vicinity. *Ars longa vita brevis* is rich people's thinking. Anyone can name exceptions, but rich people almost inevitably lack an accurate sense of the grind and frustration of life as most people experience it. They may not think they do, but they do. And although few may be the monsters of "carelessness" that Tom and Daisy Buchanan are in *The Great Gatsby*, from the viewpoint of the harassed, scruple-ridden middle class even the best of them may look a little monstrous. They just don't get it—don't get the struggle, the ups and downs, the tight emotional cost accounting of trying for a better life in the vast American ordinariness. So naturally they are resented, and the complaining tone of Warhol's detractors in the great media organs of the middle class seems to me the tone of exactly this resentment. In a way, the Whitney Museum was just asking for this. The self-satisfaction of the well-off, flagrant in the gala portrait show, can hardly have been less guardedly expressed since Fitzgerald's pre-Depression twenties.

The Whitney, once an institution relatively open to (and at times beleaguered by) the creative and critical legions of the art world, threatens under its current director Tom Armstrong to become a stockade for new-patrician sensibilities. Armstrong's catalogue foreword invokes "Andy Warhol—this quiet, omnipresent being who commands our respect and asks for nothing but receives all" and concludes, "I have never wavered from the mark with Monsieur Warhola . . . when the lifeboat is launched I want old Blondie at the oars." There is so much social Freudian-slipping going on here that one hardly knows where to start, or end. I'll point only to that jolly prognostication of Warhol and Armstrong escaping the *Titanic* together, a fun image of the Revolution worthy of Marie Antoinette. It can only leave non-identifying readers wondering where they fit in: trapped in steerage, or part of the iceberg?

How one stands on Warhol's patron class is not, after all, incidental to a full response to his portraits. I would urge only that the connection be seen as the truly interesting thing it is, a historic bonus added on to the experience of works that are good in their own right, as paintings. Unless we are going to accept ideology—in this case, middle-class ideology—as the determiner of value in art, I don't see how we can avoid concluding that Warhol has created something of lasting value. Has there ever been an artist who so coolly and faithfully, with such awful intimacy and candor, registered important changes in a society? Like a great reporter, Warhol has stayed on the story of what Marxists hopefully term "late-capitalist" America since that story broke in the early sixties. His underclass childhood somehow left him amoral as a man and incorruptible, because profoundly indifferent, as an observer. It is not necessary to like him to appreciate what he gives us with his art—and may continue to give us as his big story develops further. He has the terrible virtue of not caring particularly what happens, even as, with camera and tape recorder, he is present at every happening in his significant social microcosm. Watching him watch the rich, one knows somehow that whatever may befall us in the rest of this century, there aren't going to be any lifeboats for anybody.

May 1980

Dubuffet, 1980

Pace Gallery, October 31–November 29, 1980

Late flourishings in the careers of great artists are among the most heartening pleasures of attending to the course of art. Matisse in his cut-paper decorations was one such case; de Kooning in his vertiginous "landscape" abstractions has been another. Still another, given the mounting evidence of his recent collage-paintings, is Jean Dubuffet.

> Ah Jean Dubuffet
> when you think of him
> doing his military service in the Eiffel Tower
> as a meteorologist
> in 1922
> you know how wonderful the 20th Century
> can be

The lyric note of familiar awe that begins Frank O'Hara's 1959 poem "Naphtha" seems more than ever appropriate to the contemplation of a career that in 1980 is yielding works of such friendliness and force. That this career really began in 1942, during one of the worst moments of what has been, on balance, a horrible century—and that Dubuffet's new work revivifies many of the feelings of his earlier periods—somehow makes the present moment more wonderful, a reminder that nothing good is ever lost and that redemption is one of life's undying possibilities.

It is a mark of Dubuffet's peculiar originality that one hesitates to call this latest of many changes in his art a development. As always, notions of evolution and progress are alien to his achievement, which was born in response to the devastating cultural crisis of postwar Europe. When the headquarters of modernism shifted from Paris to New York after World War II, so did the sense of contemporary art as having, and being, a history. "School of Paris" stopped signifying an international crossroads and fount of innovation and started signifying mere taste, a delectation becalmed in time. Dubuffet's greatness, in this regard, owed precisely to his acceptance—with zest rather than anxiety—of the newly ahistorical condition of European art and his rejection of the frail and decorous gestures of his contemporaries. Nor did he waste energy beating a tradition that was already dead, though few seemed to realize it. His famous apprenticeship to the art of primitives and the mentally disturbed, those denizens of ahistorical time, showed his understanding of the new situation. Like Robinson Crusoe, he was improvising ways to live, and to live well, on a desert island. Great artists wrest opportunities from catastrophes.

Except for one thing, Dubuffet's sensibility bore little resemblance to the sensibilities of post–World War II New York artists. That one thing was a taste for the extreme, which early on won him the affection, albeit sometimes puzzled and exasperated, of artists here. The low point of his reputation in New York probably came in the 1960s, when American art resembled a cyclotron of hypercharged historical particles. The "synthetic" emphasis on the linear in his then predominant *Hourloupe* series looked, to an avant-garde obsessed with radical color, scale, and structure, as irrelevant as the similar emphasis in late Picasso. And the anarchic ironies of Dubuffet, by which an art object declares unallegiance to all artistic ideals, seemed tame compared with the strident facetiousness of pop art. But the historical preoccupations of American art peaked in the late sixties and came a cropper in the seventies—one prophet of the change was Robert Smithson, with his romance of entropy—issuing in a mood of exhaustion, bewilderment, and injury. (The Vietnam War and other political and social events had a lot to do with this, of course.) As the trauma wears off, it reveals its positive effect in a newly tender, almost elegiac, curiosity about past ideas and attitudes of modern art that once seemed so disposable.

The very title of Dubuffet's series of the late seventies—*Theaters of Memory*—seems perfect to describe the mood of American high culture in this year when people flocked almost penitentially, like prodigals come home, to the great Picasso exhibition. It is a new and unsettling experience for Americans to sense how the past grows simultaneously more remote and more available, more uniformly spread before the eye of the present. Whom should we, feeling thus expelled from history, find East of Eden? Jean Dubuffet. Ever shifting but unchanging, because anchored in a bedrock understanding of human creativity, Dubuffet has all along inhabited the homeless sense of life that is only now becoming general. That this vast international orphanage is in fact habitable would seem a reassurance beyond hoping for, except that it is the very reassurance that Dubuffet, by his example, offers. By resurrecting his past—not returning to it, because nothing in Dubuffet is ever really left behind—he shows change to be harmless and superficial in relation to the irrepressible fact of human subjective vitality that only death can alter. Far from being another of the fabulous heroes of the receding modern epoch, like Picasso, Matisse, and Pollock, he emerges as a tutelary genius and vagabond companion, a Walt Whitman of art. He is on our side, and we are increasingly on his.

One of the poignant aspects of Dubuffet's sudden closeness to us—poignant because adventitious and probably fleeting—is stylistic. In its near-decorative alloverness, his work has rarely looked more modernist, at least in the shallow sense by which that term is used nowadays to denote little more than certain figure-ground relations in painting. (It is also used to connote a sort of aesthetic Anglicanism, the established church of high culture, and in this sense Dubuffet is as much the outsider as ever.) But if his practice somewhat resembles that of present American painters, most of the resemblance goes the other way. The tendencies called New Image and New Wave, by which young painters have been experimenting with flat evocative imagery in their flat fields, bring American art by an exhausting historical route into intersection with Dubuffet's amoebic and embedded figuration. Judging from things I hear some of our most interesting young artists saying, this deeper level of Dubuffet's example may be stirring or at least linking up with a new identification, a determination to base future art on foundations more primordial and expressionistic, less style-bound.

The technique of Dubuffet's recent collage-paintings—including his current series, *Brefs exercices d'école journalière*—is simple, but its formal workings are complex. Dubuffet makes a huge variety of abstract patterns in acrylic on paper, cuts them up, and glues the pieces in an irregular quilt. Barbara Rose (in *Arts*, April 1979) has given a valuable formal account of the "brilliant use of scale disjunctions, provoking spatial discontinuities that impede any reading of the painting as literally flat"—"a spatial illusion that is incomplete and abbreviated." To appreciate the formal disjunctiveness of these pictures, imagine them without the figurative images that are applied last, like stamps on a package. Without the figures, the fields would be totally chaotic. There is something essential here about the peculiar feeling Dubuffet gives us, a feeling of joy in our humanity that might seem strange in being occasioned by human images so distorted, crazy, isolated, and oppressed. The aesthetic fact is that they organize and make expressive the abstract dynamic of the field, which seems, in fact, to have been made as wild as possible so that its taming by the images may be as dramatic as possible: coherence, withheld, arrives at the end all at once, with a bang. One might regard this as a trick, and in a way it is—a trick grounded in the artificiality of painting. There is no miracle in the fact that it works, only in the existence of an artist who should have such an authentic and, above all, such an encouraging use for it. To concentrate overmuch on Dubuffet's formal achievement would be like reading a love letter for its spelling.

Barbara Rose's essay is useful in saying what can be said about the formal and stylistic ideas Dubuffet derived from dada, German expressionism, and Paul Klee and the reciprocal influence (or anyway the points of mutual concern) between him and the abstract expressionists. Dubuffet's major influence on American art, as Rose confirms, came in Chicago, where he delivered a legendary lecture titled "Anticultural Positions" in 1951. What might be called his aesthetic anthropology remains a defining characteristic of Chicago art. His disappointment with the New York scene was thorough. "I came to America believing I would find non-conformism," he told Rose in 1979, "but I was mistaken." While being, as Rose notes, "the *only* major European artist to keep pace" with formal innovations in New York in the fifties and sixties, he was preoccupied with the sources and ends of art, not just its means. He thus emphatically parted company with the formalism that increasingly prevailed in the United States. Innovations that American artists viewed as artistic monuments, he regarded as artistic tools, and if sophisticated American taste still has trouble with his work, it may be because he exploited such things as, in Rose's words, "the redefinition of figure-ground relationships in post-cubist three-dimensional constructions" so casually and irreverently, like someone eating lunch on an altar.

Only by a process of projection and association, not as an art lover but as a person, can one make ultimate sense of Dubuffet's pictures.

56

This is not the same as saying that they are literary, a dread epithet that he eludes as neatly as he does "merely decorative." Early on Dubuffet confronted the implications of using figurative imagery in quasi-narrative ways and decided that what it involved was not an illustrative process but a faithful medium for the reality of the mind, a "language" alternative to verbal language. In his Chicago lecture he declared that "painting, especially much better than words, allows one to express the various stages of thought, including the deeper levels, the underground stages of mental processes." Obviously he would reject the implication, once widespread, that there is something inherently more basic and original about abstraction than about figuration. And indeed, is it possible, in introspection, to find a level of the imagination—not just a peculiar state of mind—that does not entail visual imagery? Art for Dubuffet is a question of truth to experience, including the largest one—that of being human. It would certainly be wrong to use his example to denigrate the majestic achievements of abstract expressionism, which was decisively conditioned by an American yearning for a pictorial tradition in the grand style. But it is important to understand that a more, rather than a less, comprehensive ambition for art led Dubuffet to shrug off the imperatives of American abstraction.

Dubuffet's figures are little mirrors for the mind; they put the viewer in the picture. The question What is going on here? is transformed into What is happening to me? Of course, this process is attended by irony. It is a game located somewhere between an outright joke and a magical charm—one cannot locate it exactly, because it is its own location. For all his ferocious rejection of School of Paris tradition, Dubuffet profited from the way in which that tradition normalized the occupation of the modern artist, making possible the sublimely ironic pose of the artist as an ordinary person doing an ordinary job—a kind of bricklayer of the marvelous. Dubuffet never had to heft the burden of existential seriousness, the do-or-die ethos of the abstract expressionists, who were obliged to create in a cultural vacuum and to be heroes or nothing. Thus his figures have never had to declare a meaning, a relation to any particular content or to any iconographic tradition. (One is of course free to make any linkages one pleases, but these must be tentative and partial, because the figures are, above all, emblems of the inarticulate.) Dubuffet's figures have no rational reference and no "inner life." Their cartoony eyes, even in full-face, are always abstracted, averted, or otherwise oriented to a space other than the literal space of the painting and the psychological space of the viewer. They never meet the viewer's gaze.

Dubuffet's figures are psychological foundlings, discovered on the artist's mental doorstep, belonging to everyone and no one. The crucial difference between these figures in Dubuffet and similar personages in the art of children, primitives, and the mentally disturbed is precisely their absence of intention. One knows or suspects that the child, primitive, and disturbed person have particular private understandings of their work (the child sees a perfectly reasonable likeness of her mother, the disturbed person sees God); what they lack is not intention but style, considered as a consistent way of making intentions manifest to an audience. Thus one justly feels a little supercilious, a little beside the (unknowable) point, in one's enthusiasm for naive productions. (We are alert these days to nationalist and sexist chauvinism in artistic judgment; might there not be "sanist" and "adultist" insensitivities as well?) The element in which Dubuffet's figures exist is the suspended intention of a sane, sophisticated man. This suspension is necessarily ironic because necessarily intentional itself, but Dubuffet's will—a good, trust-inspiring will—is sufficiently strong to carry beyond the irony to the public level of participation that he wants art to serve. His figures are wide open to the viewer's emotional projection because he has seen to their emotional neutrality. They are proof alike against sentimentality and cynicism.

My own most informative encounter with Dubuffet's work was the installation, in 1975, of his *Milord la chamarre* (Milord of the fancy vest) on the Seagram Plaza in New York. Everyone knows the wonderful *Group of Four Trees* at the Chase Manhattan Plaza near Wall Street, but for me the *Milord*, a twenty-four-foot sculpture of polished steel petals painted with a wriggling network of thick black lines, was even better—in fact, quite the most successful installation of modern public sculpture I've ever seen. (This is not as large a compliment as it ought to be.) As its analogue to the patterned or crusted field of a Dubuffet painting, the sculpture had nothing less than the Seagram Building, that masterpiece and talisman of modernist architecture. By being figurative and kinesthetically charming, the insouciant, deracinated *Milord* held scale in its surround as no abstract or formally self-contained sculpture could. (Are we ready yet to face the fact that abstract sculpture has failed as public art?) And by appealing to levels and states of mind suppressed in the ambience of the neighborhood, it made common cause with sheer human vitality beyond architecture, beyond politics and sociology, and even beyond art. In my mind's eye I can still see it standing there, indomitably alive amid that bleak grandeur, and this memory makes me happy.

A lesson of the coup pulled off by *Milord la chamarre* on Park Avenue is that Dubuffet's figuration realizes its effect in dependence on its surroundings and on the contrasts thus evoked in the viewer's mind. Another steel-petal sculpture, *La chiffonnière*, looked fine but wasn't nearly as effective last year when set against the trees of Central Park. (The setting subverted the image, a rag woman, by pointing up the artificiality of the steel at the expense of the "natural" forms.) And the tendency of figure to merge absolutely with ground in some of Dubuffet's work has seemed a weakness—sensationally remedied when the surface burst into three dimensions and assumed an architectural scale, thereby assigning the viewer, in actual body, the role of figure in the composition. The *Theaters of Memory*, with the teeming resonance of their multipatterned fields, give Dubuffet's figuration perhaps the most efficient foil it has ever had.

Dubuffet's art is expressionist in cultivating a deliberate vulgarity, or at least a deliberate excess. (There are exquisite things and qualities in Dubuffet, but he seemingly takes pains to assure that there will be too much of them. At the same time, his evident deliberation puts an ironic distance between his excess and the horror vacui of the primitive and disturbed, which it resembles.) The dadaist notion of subverting tradition is all too easily and complacently understood, but what does it mean when an enormously gifted and ambitious artist applies it to practical ends? What does it mean to want to make an art for the comfort, not of the exacerbated aesthete or even of Matisse's tired businessman, but of a shopkeeper or a blue-collar worker? It means, to begin with, ruthlessly expunging the significance (not the existence) of all aesthetic refinements not immediately comprehensible to the untutored. For a pipe fitter, say, to be drawn by fascination with the work into contemplation and study, thence to an illumination of the work's higher meaning and appeal, would in this context be a dirty trick—a treacherous confirmation of the upward-mobility principle in culture and society, another proof of the superiority of the leisure class. There must be no higher meaning and appeal. Dubuffet observes the existence of good taste, as of industrial capitalism, without any mission to destroy it; he is intent only to avoid contamination of the faith he is bound to keep with the lumpen both in society and in the individual unconscious.

The complete absence of any refinement viewed as an end in itself makes an aesthetically trained and sensitive person's encounter with Dubuffet's work a little jarring, if not downright grueling. Thus the frequent tendency of art writers to treat him in the "master-at-work" genre, attending to calculations and nuances in his supposed creative process as if these were somehow of the essence. It's like standing behind a cannon admiring the trajectory of its fire, the better to evade the knowledge that the target is oneself. I find that a certain coarsening of my own responsiveness, an ironic willingness to be as "dumb" as the work, is necessary for me to register and test the effect and significance of Dubuffet's art. This is not something exclusive to Dubuffet or even to art. In a culture deeply (and, it seems, increasingly) uncomfortable with direct emotion, any expressive content that is unmediated by conventional forms feels barbarous. (There is even a backup convention for mediating this feeling: the exotic.) But Dubuffet is probably the only major postwar Western artist who has both consistently and successfully challenged our fear of feeling, striving with relentless goodness of heart to wean us toward joy. He may also be our only major artist unsullied by one of this century's great illusions, that art can somehow replace religion. He understands that no religion means no religion, period. He understands further that art is more important than taste, and that life is more important than art.

I would like to bring my reflections on Dubuffet's recent work, and on what it suggests about art and culture in 1980, to some neat conclusion. But if Dubuffet teaches anything, it is that there are no conclusions, and no true beginnings, either. There is only the middle, the presentness of life. Every attempt at art or discourse, no matter how ambitious or intelligent, properly ends only in rejoining an incomprehensible flow, invisible and silent. Beyond that, his great gift is to make the reality of this all-consuming torrent palpable, and to make it seem a cause of joy rather than terror—release from the tyranny of ego rather than the ego's panic-stricken disintegration. So much of our art tacitly preaches the opposite, policing consciousness, counseling fear. The separation of art from life that is enforced by modernism— and dialectically reinforced by avant-garde attempts to bridge it—is simply ignored by Dubuffet. We best enjoy his work, not in an elevated or especially acute frame of mind, but just as ourselves, full of the anxieties with which our world invests selfhood. These anxieties become the rhythm of our response, inflected with anger or glee. To imagine this, think of a person with a bad limp, distressing to watch. Gradually, as one watches, the limp is subtly transformed, becoming articulated, purposeful, inspired—a dance! The person is dancing! For the surprising consolation of such moments we are inclined to thank and salute Dubuffet, and to leave him, at age seventy-eight, where he has always been, in mid-career.

June 1980

First *Voice* Column

More is happening in American art right now than ever before. There is more of everything and of everybody, including critics. There is more public interest and much more money—not necessarily in that order. There is also a lot of confusion, fatigue, hysteria, cynicism, and paranoia. Sometimes I wonder how anyone stays sane. There is something faintly unwholesome—heavily made-up and neon lit—about the scene, but it is very exciting.

Today anything, though of course not everybody, sells, and the effect on our experience of art is retroactive. Laid out and organized by the scholars and curators, the modern canon has become a vast and teeming bazaar. The recent succession of historical exhibitions has been wonderful. Picasso, postimpressionism, the Russian avant-garde of 1910–1930, expressionism, Hopper, on and on. We have the effects of a frantic art market to thank for much of this revivalism. Thanks, market.

Modern art history has ceased to represent a road traveled, and has come to seem an encircling panorama. All of it is available, ripe, ours. (There is a tendency to feel a little overwhelmed and guilty, a little unworthy of it, hence resentful, flip.) The term *postmodern*, which everyone hates and uses compulsively, expresses the almost metaphysical strangeness of our time. It connotes "postpresent." If something travels faster than light, where is it? Or, rather, when is it? The feeling today is a bit like that. We have this inkling of a historical momentum that at some point—whoops!—outdistanced history.

The writings of Robert Smithson, who died in a plane crash at age thirty-five in 1973 on the site of one of his earthworks, are indispensable in trying to think about all this. Polemicist for minimalism, science-fiction addict, mystifier, and prophet, he used the word *postmodernism* in the late sixties and rhapsodized about pluralism and cosmic entropy, "crystalline" as opposed to "linear" history, and an aesthetic of waste, sediment, and ruin. He had already made himself deliriously at home in the posthistorical house of mirrors we have all come to inhabit, trying not to fall down out of sheer disorientation.

As corporate capitalism becomes more enveloping, rationalized, and sterile, art is increasingly charged with representing the repressed, factored-out, amputated life of the emotions, the thwarted—and dangerous when thwarted—sum of the sexual and survival instincts that Freud called Eros. Mere evidence of the human hand, a mere brush stroke, glows today with talismanic intensity. All sorts of people respond reflexively to such things, corporate capitalists no less than anyone else. The art that holds this charge is speedily bought and sold, plunged into the originally offending medium of money like hot metal into ice water. No wonder our vision gets steamed over.

Dealers run the show today. There are more good dealers and they are more influential, as well as richer, than ever before. Dispensers to artists of the erotic warmth of acceptance and, figuratively, love money, and dispensers to the world of the commodity that is Eros objectified, dealers are smack at the crossroads of contradiction. To think of them is to imagine a flicker of images—angel and monster, the best and the worst. To think too long and hard is to risk throwing up.

Beneath hip veneers, many journalistic art critics today are testy, defensive, and carping. This may be because they are beset from without by hordes of the recognition-starved (one's mail some mornings is like a nest of open-mouthed baby birds) and from within by a haunted sense of their own powerlessness. Such purposeful power as critics used to have disappeared with the time lag between the appearance of something new and its acceptance, a transition that dealers manage now seemingly in a matter of hours. The art-worldly function of critics has become largely ceremonial: after-dinner speakers at the victory party. Thus critics tend to dig in their heels.

The average piece of bad criticism a decade ago cozied up to some rising artist or art idea and implied that anyone who couldn't see the critic's jargon as a form of higher common sense was an idiot. The average piece of bad criticism today reads like something from *Consumer Reports*. The art is tested; its tires are kicked. Pretensions to importance are attributed, inspected, and dismissed. The critic glories in remaining unmoved: "Ha, you missed me!" More artists hate— really hate—more critics today than ever before.

I'm talking about relatively young critics, in the same generation as today's emerging artists. They are filling a vacuum left by art writers of my generation (I'm thirty-eight) and the preceding one, many of whom have quit journalism, victims of the rate and directions of change—heartsick at the eclipse of much they cared about and the triumph of much they despise. The newer critics are the progeny of a semieducated middle-class audience that repels the older critics. This audience has some virtues, including an influential appreciation of clarity and style in writing. Its vices, faithfully mirrored by many critics, include laziness, voyeurism, cynicism, and envy.

This has been coming for a long time. In 1975 I left the Sunday *Times* Arts and Leisure section after years of regular contributing because, as the new editor explained to me, "heavy criticism" was being de-emphasized. I still had a job if I wanted it. "There's a big future in this business," my amazed ears heard him saying, "for a young man who will be an investigative reporter in the art world." Maybe with the same speech the editor got someone else to write a prying but toothless piece on Castelli, which I believe exhausted the idea. At about the same time, Tom Wolfe's ill-informed *The Painted Word* was a best-seller.

The art world, with its traditions of personal dealing and secrecy, its intimidating spaces, and its dizzying mixture of ineffable values and effable bucks, rouses anxieties that are allayed by suspicions of cabal. The main fact missed by "outsiders" is not that the "inside" is an assembly of angels, but that the inside does not exist. The art world is a balkanized anarchy, with lots of little insides, lots of little games, better and worse people, hierophants and hustlers. Meanwhile there is art, available to anyone who has a personal use for it. Love of art and hope for it are the only solid ground in this swampy, fecund craziness.

Nothing in today's torrent of art seems great and epochal, but how could it? The historical sense that underlay avant-garde greatness, replacing the social agreements of pre-"modern" times, is gone, and nothing replaces it. We are obliged to remake from scratch the foundations of our taste, as of our politics and our very lives. Old ways of judging linger as unexamined habits, comforting defenses against the recognition of our common lostness. Thus defended, one is deprived of the compensatory joy of current liberty and profusion. I want to affirm these values, so costly to everyone's peace of mind, and to encourage others who affirm them too.

January 7, 1981

Clement Greenberg

Sometimes I forget about Clement Greenberg for months at a time; then suddenly I'm thinking about him again—mostly useless, compulsive, tongue-exploring-a-cavity thoughts. As the avatar of Authority in the art of the sixties—that parricidal decade—he was the enemy, and most critics who were not his progeny (and some who were) had it in for him. He had anathematized almost everything in new art, and to claim one's own experience it was necessary to battle his ideas. My own aptness for the fray was limited, since Greenberg's rhetoric so intimidated and infuriated me that I could barely read him.

So I kept on obsessing about him intermittently through the seventies, when his visibility and influence waned drastically in New York. People knew about the informal network of his adherent curators, dealers, and academics nationwide. There were rumors of his do-this/do-that intervention in the work of his favored artists (Noland, Olitski, Poons, Bannard, et al.) and of his unique traveling salesmanship for them—Tupperware parties of collectors in Houston, Denver, Seattle, Toronto, and other countryseats. But it became increasingly hard to work up polemical enthusiasm over the tasty painterly cuisine of the color-fielders, and his own writing became a routine of preachings to the converted, carpet bombings of current trends, and assaultive letters-to-the-editor. It all seemed long-ago and faraway.

But not for me, somehow. At last I studied Greenberg's only book of general criticism, *Art and Culture* (Beacon, 1961), and both the wonderful and the fishy aspects of his triumphal march through modern art came into focus. I still wanted to bust him one for his damned arrogance and presumption—his total depreciation of other viewpoints—but just when I might have tried, I became aware of something else: that almost nobody reads him anymore. Anti-Greenberg rhetoric deteriorated through the seventies to a level of carefree ignorance. A whole generation of art people is emerging that is dumber than it strictly has to be because it is convinced that it can safely discount his writing.

A couple of weeks ago, for the first time, I heard Greenberg lecture—at the Nassau County Museum of Fine Arts in Roslyn, where there is a show called The Abstract Expressionists and Their Precursors. The museum is a new one, in the renovated mansion of an old estate; like much of the overflow lecture audience that night, it oozes suburban affluence and culture appetite. It's a good setting for Greenberg, whose incessant talk of "quality" often reverberates with that word's antique social usage (and with snob-appeal advertising in general). However, the question period revealed general incredulity about his critical stance.

It is pretty incredible. Radically positivist and formalist at base— "art in a vacuum," as he complacently allows—his approach brushes aside content, subject matter, psychology, semiotics, politics, biography, artists' statements, everything except the discrimination of the practiced eye. The result is a quasi-religion of "quality"—"quality" down through the ages, observing an inexorable agenda of formal development—with the critic as hierophant. (When he talks about the "good" in art, his voice is liable to take on an evangelical tremolo.) The audience wasn't asked to think. Quite the contrary. Greenberg repeatedly referred conceptual questions to "better minds than mine," mainly Immanuel Kant's. He concerned himself with demolishing other critics' "misconceptions" and with jumping his tigerish taste through hoops of fire—denying "quality" to Willem de Kooning after about 1948 and to Franz Kline after the mid-fifties and so on.

A young seventy-two, his bulgy, rather cute features often rearranged by grins, smoking Camels, gesturing brightly, Greenberg in person is completely disarming—a personable little man behind the Wizard-of-Oz display of his prose. Seeing him makes it easier to grasp his intellectual terror tactics as *tactics* and to start imagining why someone would want to employ them. I picture a man who loves his own response to art so extravagantly, so beyond all reason, that reason in his hands is just a device to project and generalize that love. No mere Bernard Berenson–style King Connoisseur or even a T. S. Eliot–like Voice of High Culture, Greenberg historicized his love and rolled it into the present—art for art's sake on tank tracks. Almost incidentally, he organized the unruly data of modern art more persuasively than anyone else.

Greenberg carries himself with a slightly ceremonial courtesy that I associate with adepts of Eastern religions, but he's nobody's bodhi-sattva. Nothing perturbs him, including the vexation his own arrogance provokes. In argument he goes gaily and mockingly for the throat. His somewhat hypersensitive Roslyn audience reacted with nervous titters and little shouts of alarm when he let fly pungent personal opinions of Still, Newman, and Motherwell. Grinning into the genteel clamor, he remarked, "As St. John says, 'The truth will make you free.'"

For Greenberg, there is only one use for art—the pure and intense arousal of what might be called the art emotion—and really only two categories of high art: the best—and everything else. No one gets into Valhalla entire, not even his paragon Jackson Pollock. Asked about Pollock's *Blue Poles* (the painting Australia paid $2 million for in 1974), he dismissed it as a "failure." The audience swooned again, and his response was almost plaintive: "*Pollock* knew *Blue Poles* was a failure. He knew he had lost his stuff after [nineteen] fifty-two. *He* didn't take umbrage." Other artists took umbrage aplenty. De Kooning likes to tell about ejecting Greenberg from his studio when told that painting figures (the Women) wouldn't do. De Kooning was right, no doubt, as a teacher of manners. But the genre of artist-knight versus critic-dragon is no answer to Greenberg's cogency.

Judging Greenberg the way Greenberg judges artists—summarily, in career phases, and taking no prisoners—one can say that after the late fifties his sense, already calcified, of the "culture" in its relation to art parted ways with lived reality, and his taste sheered off into mandarin eccentricity. One can say that with justice and still not shake the challenge of his unnerving fundamentalism, his insistent identification of art value with aesthetic feeling in the teeth of every other appeal. The big subtle rhetorical machinery of *Art and Culture*, with its vast comprehension of art history in sync with the artist's simplest formal decisions, remains unrivaled to this day. It is as important to American criticism as the abstract expressionists are to American art. It is a book not so much about its period as of it, in the best way—as narrow in its means and ambitious in its ends as, say, Barnett Newman's paintings.

One cannot do with Greenberg's work what one can with that of his eloquent but outclassed major antagonist, Harold Rosenberg—pick the choice insights and throw the rest away. In opposing him one must do him the honor of opposing utterly. He is a system maker, and his thought is all of a piece and tinker proof. Periodic attempts by others to retool his historicism—adding a little Freud or a little Duchamp or Wittgenstein or Derrida—don't last long. The option to Greenberg's system is no system, a willingly suffered climate of uncertainty with our permanent desire for "standards" and "criteria" part of the weather—always turbulent, always unallayed. Reading vintage Greenberg can be depressing because its cocksure lilt contrasts so painfully with one's own usual lack of conviction. Still, it is in just such grinding extremes of discomfort that creativity may find work to do.

February 4, 1981

Exxon Exhibition at the Guggenheim

Special Notice

TO CRITICS, EDITORS, ASSIGNMENT EDITORS From [Guggenheim Museum] Public Affairs Officer

Grants from corporations and government agencies are vitally important in maintaining the continuing strength of programs offered by cultural institutions throughout this country.

. . . We believe that both government agencies and corporations are encouraged to continue [their support] if they receive acknowledgement in the press . . .

When reviewing or mentioning the exhibition, we therefore ask that you give public recognition to those who have helped make it possible.

Nothing simpler. The corporation that helped make possible the Guggenheim's current show (January 30–April 5, 1981), 19 Artists— Emergent Americans: 1981 Exxon National Exhibition, is Exxon. Exxon is a corporation which, art lovers will rejoice to learn, turned record profits in 1980, though with a fourth-quarter slump of ominous import for civilization as we know it. Just so we won't forget that name, it's Exxon. (Exxon, take note.)

The show looks it. It looks like that mixture of sentimentality and self-consciousness that characterizes a certain kind of bad sex and most kinds of governmental and corporate support for the arts. (The sentiment here is the indefensible notion that art is good for you.) One's first impression is of frisky, even puppyish, ingratiation; this is in line with the present ethos that sees art as a form for the delivery of (interpersonal, community) services. The ethos is "pluralism," which has amounted to democracy as social hygiene. It is democracy adapted to the needs of organizations, a matter not of individuals but of handy unit groupings.

This may be a lot to bring down on a show that purports only to spotlight nineteen artists of, in Guggenheim director Thomas M. Messer's elegant phrase, "less established but conspicuous talent." However, apart from the half-dozen or so interesting artists among those spotlit and its virtuous intent, the event is just asking for it. From its corporate sponsorship to its completely catholic, self-abnegating taste, it is a very seventies-style affair served up to the increasingly (thank goodness) less sanguine regard of the eighties. This makes it as good an occasion as any for precipitating lingering dissatisfactions.

W. H. Auden made a wonderful discrimination about the early work of poets. Such work, he said, is neither good nor bad; rather, it is imaginary. It is written by adolescents who, though intoxicated by poetry, have yet to discover personal reasons for writing. In the seventies—which will go down in history as the period of the baby boom's extended adolescence—imaginary poetry, imaginary art, imaginary criticism, and imaginary politics flourished, as often as not with the aid of imaginary (governmental and corporate) money. (Psychoeconomic principle: money is imaginary that does not belong to the people who spend it.) Thus: more and more "culture" to less and less effect.

Emergent Americans was curated, in a year of Exxon-funded travel, by Peter Frank, absolutely a seventies art person, though better than most. Frank is a tireless cross-pollinator in the art world. He is abrim with good will and good intentions and, as far as I can tell, generous and without cynicism—virtues that will seem minor only to the mean and cynical. But he wouldn't know the difference between a ringer and a real artist if it fell on him, which it just has.

A real artist—I'm going to jump into this with both feet—has temperament, which may be defined as any satisfying answer to the question, why would someone, someone in particular, want to make this particular work? (The ringer answers with abstract generalities that once had reference to aesthetic problem solving; now they are more likely to be appeals to "sensibility.") The real artist is independent not only—in some cases, not even—in approach and style, but right to the core. His or her work has the same mysterious integrity of being that a mature person has, the same resistance to expectation and categorical understanding. It has nothing to do with high seriousness or opposition to fashion. Mark Rothko was a real artist, but so is Andy Warhol. Nor is it necessarily a question of quality. Perhaps only real artists can be (really) bad. It might help to distinguish between a sense of vocation that is self-generated and one that is taken on.

Pluralism views art as it views society, as a large but finite deck continually being reshuffled and redealt. Frank more or less explicitly proposes his selection of Emergent Americans as a set of helpful suggestions for the next hand. It's all dutiful and joyless, as it always is when political anxiety—in this case, "fairness"—invades the realm of the pleasure principle. Real art stands out as something essentially uncalled-for and existing for itself, whatever its relation to other realities. It is no coded demand for a piece of the pie of recognition. It is its own whole pie, take it or leave it.

Applied to the Exxon show, this homemade criterion narrows the field drastically. Most of Frank's artists are exemplars of various academicisms, reordered codes, and wishful finesses. It's a case of pluralism as, to bend a Marcuse phrase, depressive tolerance, a mild nightmare of art styles proliferating and miscegenating across the land independent of human need, will, and predilection. How a sixties ideal of freedom for all got taken hostage by corporate power is a story for the eighties to tell.

February 18–24, 1981

Julian Schnabel and Susan Rothenberg

Not long ago a line was going around that in the fifties American art had heroes, in the sixties it had stars, and in the seventies it had hits. This was a good line. Anyone who lived through much of it had to note the degenerative process, the way meaning and value leaked from the figure of the individual artist to the aggrandizement of the sur- rounding commercial, social, and institutional structures, both estab- lishment and "alternative." Art increasingly seemed to exist not be- cause someone needed to make it, but as a hit parade, so that these structures would have something to sell, discuss, and "support."

This is rapidly changing. Heroism, even, may be returning to art. If so, it won't be because art-world structures, especially the commer- cial, have faltered but precisely because they have fattened and accel- erated beyond sanity. Money has no meaning today in that branch of the commodity-futures business called the art market. There is a pre- 1929 feel in the air, an intimation not just of downturn but of good old-fashioned catastrophe. In a weird way, this situation in which everything succeeds begins to resemble the one of thirty years ago in which nothing did. That, too, was a situation that could not last.

Heroes are born of extreme situations. A hero deals with a threat- ening reality—be it a common enemy, a condition of suffering or injustice, or "fear itself"—in a way that affirms shared values. The current anxiety and anomie of our culture are realities that put most sensibilities on the fritz. Not Julian Schnabel's sensibility. That Schna- bel is a hero for our time may not be exactly a compliment to either him or us. But his present two-gallery show (Mary Boone Gallery, April 4–May 7, and Leo Castelli Gallery, April 4–May 2, 1981) both sizes up some prevailing torments of art and life and turns them to account in a way that must be called, with only a little irony, heroic.

Schnabel would be the Francis Ford Coppola of art if one could picture Coppola with all the studio heads, distributors, and other mo- guls on his side. He is in a state of total success. Everything in the show is presold, for up to $40,000. (Were young Schnabel's paintings to appreciate on the pattern of Jasper Johns's *Three Flags*—$900 in 1959, $1 million last year—one would go for not quite $45 million in 2002. Don't bet on it.) With a waiting list stretching to the horizon, everything he sloshes with paint for as long as this madness lasts will be minted money. Some people grumble about "hype." But with momentum like Schnabel's, who needs hype? Time to paint, yes. A team of crack accountants, yes. Any promotion is just trimming.

Schnabel has an attitude toward success that is either Byronic or naive. He welcomes it, he has said, because it enables him to do what he wants. That's a heroic switch on the more usual notion of success as a reward for doing what someone else wants. Like a holy fool, he takes the world's ritual piety—in his case, the value of individual creative liberty—absolutely at its word. "You think you like painting," his art seems to say. "Well, here!" If Schnabel is technically less radical than many other artists (he makes paintings), that's because liberty can be demonstrated seriously only in a context of conventions. The stuff of convention—fractured, heaped, turned upside down and inside out—is his artistic material, as if history were his studio assistant.

The quality of Schnabel's work, which will matter in the long run, in the short run is impossible to assess, partly because our standards are so much in flux. It seems clear that at his best, as in many of his "plate paintings," he is very good and that at his worst, as in most of his works on paper, he is lame. Any nicer judgment is temporarily beggared by the brashness of the answer he gives to a standard modern question, what is painting about? His reply might be paraphrased: everything I think up, improvise, and steal. It's that atavistic, Picassoid/ Duchampian/de Kooningesque "I" that stops one dead, in admiration or in fury.

The classic test of a real hero is the possibility of a tragedy. Those who are cynically embittered by Schnabel's triumph forget what the Greeks knew, which is that hubris is a self-punishing offense. The hectic, up-in-the-air, hysterically ambitious aura of Schnabel's show— its sense of massive preparation for something, some conquest or revelation, that is not yet and may never be—is none too reassuring. He is not so much tempting fate as actively razzing it. Look out below.

Another tale of heroism in the era of art success gets another chapter with Susan Rothenberg's new show (Willard Gallery, April 1981). She is certainly a hero of mine. The comparison of Rothenberg with Schnabel could be given a binary neatness: her "personal" with his "cultural" content, her "closed" with his "open" form, introvert with extrovert, and so forth. ("Female" with "male" suggests itself, but I think I'll leave that mine field for another day.) But they have in common ferocious individualism, talent, a grasp on the possibilities of major art now, and waiting lists.

Six years older than Schnabel (who turns thirty this year), Rothenberg, with her essentially abstract paintings using outlines of horses, pioneered the New Image aesthetic and came as close as anyone to being a solid star in the hit-happy late seventies. She captivated me with her last New York show in 1979, when she broke the mold of her popularity with an all but vengeful group of paintings featuring expressionistically dismembered and distended horses. It was an emotionally clenched, even grueling show, fantastically well painted—in her usual gritty repertoire of tempera lines and shapes, mostly black, embedded in furiously active white gesso grounds—but as cold as death. It was like a great malevolent joke in a year of solemn cuteness.

Schnabel, too, has been assaulting the convention of "trademark art," retooling his style from picture to picture and even from one end to another of a single canvas. But Rothenberg's iconographic evolution, culminating in her elimination of horse motifs, is more dramatic because it has been conducted on a symbolic down elevator. For all their charm, her earlier horses bore a psychological charge as projections of an "animal" self. Her subsequent dismemberments, which abolished charm, had a feel of violent psychological upheaval whose issue, positive or negative, was in doubt. Her huge new paintings—outlined faces (featureless but for almond-shaped eyes) superimposed on outlines of fists or splayed hands—suggest images from the very forebrain depths.

That may sound corny, but it isn't. There have never been paintings like these. What distinguishes them from other expressionist art is the uncanny disembodied control that rules their flurried strokes, the minute adjustments and impactions of their violence—as if hysteria could be fine-tuned. Furthermore, the crude, glowering, panicky images are dumped right in the viewer's face. No message, no storytelling, no empathy, no pathos, no mysticism, no coyness. It's all there in the paint—the dense red or black or white or blue outlines smoking in the dirty white or black grounds. (The surface often evokes a choking atmosphere, full of flying ash and pumice.) Thus—again, and to a new

74

extreme of shivery force—the hint of a diabolical sense of humor, a strange, cold joy. In the belly of the art boom, Rothenberg is getting away with symbolic murder.

I could imagine Julian Schnabel as a pop-Napoleonic eagle riding the thermals of an overheated time. I could imagine Rothenberg as a rogue mole, if moles were also predators. What red meat are they after? Power certainly, but power of what kind? I would say the power to confront the world, to make a difference, to command meaning in an age when meaninglessness is like an engulfing storm. Their heroism is a ratio of our feeling of impotence. I love Schnabel for making the transfixing of chaos look easy. I love Rothenberg for hauling up images from chaos that do not so much suspend as crush disbelief. It's all grand, high, grim, hilarious sport—playing high-stakes games with paint as the market roars and the sky darkens.

April 29–May 5, 1981

Arshile Gorky

Arshile Gorky made some of the greatest paintings of his time. He also came up with some of the greatest titles, and his Guggenheim retrospective (April 24–July 19, 1981) is fun to read as well as look at. *Garden in Sochi*; *Love of the New Gun*; *Anatomical Blackboard*; *Good Afternoon, Mrs. Lincoln*; *Water of the Flowery Mill*; *One Year the Milkweed*; *Diary of a Seducer*; *Scent of Apricots*; and *Charred Beloved* are among my favorites—funny-elegant, permanently haunting. Then there is the wrenching *How My Mother's Embroidered Apron Unfolds in My Life*.

Gorky's mother starved to death before his eyes in 1919, when he was fourteen. They were Armenians, fleeing the Turks. In 1920 Gorky arrived in the United States, where he saw his father—briefly—for the first time in twelve years. He started to paint. Gorky (real name Vosdanik Adoian) was softly handsome, big-eyed, shy, and fantastical. He amused and irritated contemporaries with his great-artist airs. They considered his studious imitation of Picasso, Miró, and Kandinsky slavish. We can see now that much of his supposedly derivative work of the late 1930s was better than the stylistic inventions of anyone his age in the country, if not the world.

Few artists of any time have set about more determinedly—with such a mixture of extreme humility and extreme ambition—to be "great." He worked at modern painting as others may once have worked at sainthood. (Fascinated, the young Willem de Kooning became a close friend.) Through the Depression, Gorky always made sure he had more canvas, more paint, and more brushes than anyone else, even if it meant going hungry. He was an odd figure in that time of egalitarian poverty. He preached Ingres at left-wing political meetings. Out of sheer exasperation with Gorky's arrogance, David Smith once chased him down a street, trying to hit him.

Gorky's end was so terrible as to be nearly black-comical. In the course of two years, he had a bowel-cancer operation, a studio fire in which he lost large stores of work, and an auto accident that broke his neck and paralyzed his painting arm. Then his wife took their daughters and ran away with one of his best friends. In July 1948 he scrawled "Goodbye My Loveds" on a crate and hanged himself.

Is any of this important? Isn't it just gossip? We probably ought to feel ashamed at taking the voyeuristic, van Gogh's–ear interest in artists' lives that we do. But such interest needn't be entirely frivolous, especially at a time like the present when the questions of what an artist is and what an artist does have taken on renewed mystery and urgency. The dignified textbook stories of Gorky and early abstract expressionism—formalist à la Clement Greenberg, "heroic" à la Harold Rosenberg and others—have paled. Now we need *our* Gorky.

Everyone agrees that Gorky was a "transitional" figure in the transplanting of major modern art to America. Rosenberg emphasized the forward edge of the transition—Gorky as pathfinder. More persuasively, Greenberg put Gorky at the end of modernism's European phase, "a votary of French taste and an orthodox easel-painter, a virtuoso of line and a tinter rather than a colorist." The issue is important, but I suspect that many of us—maybe because the present itself feels so transitional—will be moved less by whence Gorky was coming or going than by those moments when his work was most in flux. In fact, that was exactly when he was best.

Conventional wisdom has it that Gorky's career was a process of triumphal growth, each phase better than the last. Had he lived longer, the wisdom runs, he would have achieved much greater things. Having accepted this, I was startled to find myself disappointed with many of the paintings after 1944, when Gorky nailed down his most distinctive style: surrealistic linear networks (done with a thin "liner" brush) floating on melting, indeterminate grounds. The real heat of the show is in roughly the years 1936–44, the thick of his struggle to make a "museum art" of abstract surrealism.

Gorky's shapes throughout are "biomorphic"—nonspecific evocations of biological organisms, from microscopic life to landscape. The formal development is from modified synthetic-cubist arrangements of what look like pieces of Picasso women to the cobwebby linear figures that André Breton dubbed "hybrids." When he came to New York during World War II, Breton, the surrealist pope, claimed Gorky for the movement. Gorky was influenced by literary surrealism to the extent of wildly sexualizing his images—all those feelers, holes, and trembling nodes. (The influence also showed up in his wonderful titles and, more furtively, in love letters he wrote plagiarizing the poet Paul Eluard.) Reinforced by patches of hot color like bodily inflammations, his later biomorphism produces an intense intimacy—that scratchy, crawly, under-the-skin feel that would be ghastly but for the artist's unmistakable sweetness. He comes through as the most tender of demon lovers.

For the virtuoso he was, Gorky had regular trouble making interesting things happen in depth illusion. His figurative work—including his sentimentally overrated pictures of himself as a child with his mother—is often indecisive and inert. (De Kooning's figure paintings of the thirties, with their stunning exchanges of presence between figure and ground, run rings around Gorky's.) His constant battle to make his pictorial space cohere—with lines cutting through thick, nubbly surfaces in the late thirties, then bleeding into washy, misty ones in the early forties—is the formal drama of his art. The more pitched the battle—and, in general, the flatter the result—the better. What's wrong with his late work may be that by too neatly disengaging drawing from painting, it causes this tension to go slack.

I think it unlikely that had he lived, Gorky could have topped himself. His gift was for discovering unsuspected possibilities of eloquence in modern art, not ultimately for putting those possibilities to work in a purposeful way. Diane Waldman makes an apt comparison of Gorky to Cézanne in her catalogue introduction. Cézanne, too, revealed enormous artistic potentials that he had no final way of applying. In both cases, the applications were quickly made by younger artists.

What is the significance of Gorky's biography for his art? In a familiar way—promulgated by T. S. Eliot as the "dissociation" of "the man who suffers" from "the mind that creates"—there is none. Even in as explicit a painting as Gorky's *Agony*, it is the mind's joy in creation, not the dreadful suffering of the man, that we mainly feel. In another way, though, Gorky's horrible personal insecurity, locked in tension with his aesthetic idealism, is what grips our artistic as well as human interest. No detached problem-solving spirit motivates someone to undergo first the abject self-effacements and then the huge risks that Gorky embraced.

What does an artist do? Gorky seems to answer: the impossible. A displaced, poor, and traumatized Armenian in provincial New York, he could think of no more tractable project for himself than to join the seraphic ranks of the masters. Did he make it? We're not the ones to say, because our view of what constitutes greatness in art or anything else is so vexed. But Gorky's best art shows us the miracles that belief in it can work. And we are just the ones to appreciate his self-inventing, reckless grace. The attainment of individuality against ridiculous odds is right up our alley.

What I love about Gorky's titles is their redolence of serene exaltation. Each gestures from a secure height—that of a successful art work—toward the emotion of "the man who suffers," momentarily left behind. They celebrate the seemingly effortless lift-off of great art. The water of the flowery mill may be a liquid that one drinks in order to be as free as God. Years ago, I tried several times to write a poem titled "Water of the Flowery Mill"—I wanted to get in on that. No go. The price of being that high is everything you are and everything you've got.

May 13–19, 1981

L.A. Demystified!
Art and Life in the Eternal Present

Los Angeles—My fate keeps bringing me here, and I never get used to it. It starts when I step off the plane—World Airways usually, down the stairs and onto the tarmac like an aviation pioneer. There is the familiar shock of the soft dead air and fierce milky brightness, the instant and afterward incessant feeling of being a sugar cube dissolving in warm fluid. Even on the rare glycerine-clear winter day, the atmosphere is more real than anything that occupies it, including one's own body. In the right frame of mind, one's consequent feeling of shapelessness can be an immense baby pleasure.

I never get used to the driving. Too much driving is not good for you, I've decided. It concentrates you too much, ruining the diffuse attentiveness that is the mind's optimum state. I can see it in L.A. eyes, that flicker of habitual greed for far-off destinations, plus the gemlike life wish ("No crashes today for baby!"). Half the town's mental energy is mixed and burned with gasoline. Still, even the driving can be strange pleasure.

The lack of surprise—the unending "anonymous chunks of stuff," in the approving words of Bruce Nauman, probably the best artist who ever lived here for long—is like an endless surprise. One's eye gets tuned to make fine discriminations among types of the dumb, the gaudy, and the forlorn. And the freeway interchanges really are something. No two alike. I imagine lucky engineers, at drawing boards, manipulating the sinuous templates called "French curves" in aesthetic ecstasy. Entered from any direction, the classic San Diego–Santa Monica traffic-churn in West Los Angeles takes the breath away with its low, subtle, sweeping forms—Mona-Lisa smiles in concrete.

I never get used to it. Writing this, I'm sitting in the cute old bungalow ("old": about 1940) my wife and I have rented temporarily in Hancock Park near the County Museum ("near": one mile). My wife is an actress doing pretty well in Hollywood, that company town—like an Appalachian mining village—a few miles to the north. It's lovely here. Our roses are blooming. Birds are singing. There is the background whoosh of traffic on Olympic Boulevard. And here comes the definitive L.A. sound: a hovering police helicopter. At night they buzz the neighborhood with searchlights, seeking criminals. I wonder if they catch any.

I'm happy to be writing, happy to have something that needs doing. L.A. "survivors" are people who work hard. Parties of the successful don't wind down; they vanish in a twinkling well before midnight. Long day tomorrow. The work does not do wonders for people's personalities. Like the driving, it concentrates them too much, at the expense of curiosity and variety. Conversation tends to be homogenized and flat, produced with half a mind to be heard with half an ear. But the parties too can be sensuous pleasures. Almost everybody looks beautiful and dresses beautifully. Healthy limbs transporting handsome heads, with whispers of light fabric, through sliding doors.

Will they get it about visual art? Whether they like art or not— and by "they" I mean most of the social, institutional, and commercial art people, plus a lot of the artists—I can't decide. What do they see in it? What do they want with it? Maybe relief from the concentrations of work and driving, wordless relief from the toil of dull conversation. But so much of the dull conversation centers on it. An obsessive subject is the future and how culturally rich and bright it will be here. What will most probably happen will be a continuation of the eternal L.A. present, the eternal conversation about the future.

Only Hollywood matters. What it doesn't overshadow it infects. This is what they don't get about art, that it's the opposite of the movies. In Hollywood you make a deal, then you make a movie. In the art business, you make a work, then you make a deal. Thus in art they're always starting from the wrong end. The upcoming downtown Museum of Contemporary Art (MOCA) is perfect L.A.—one huge exhilarating deal, one cloud castle of pure futurity. Meanwhile, few notice how little important art gets made or can get made here. Bruce Nauman lives in New Mexico now, as does Ken Price. So many good ones move on.

Other good ones stay. Today I will have lunch with Ed Ruscha ("Roo-shay"), who may be the best regional artist in modern history. I think I owe my sanity to Ed Ruscha. When I first came here for a long spell, and before I met him, I thought constantly in my lonely distress of Ruscha's images and one-liners, his totally indigenous style of seeing and joking, his way of maintaining a civilized diffuse attentiveness in this glutted, deracinated atmosphere. (I also thought constantly of Raymond Chandler, still the only major poet of L.A.) It helped. Ruscha makes the place seem possible. You have only to regard it the way he did in his great foldout book of photographs of every building on Sunset Strip. The book is titled *Every Building on the Sunset Strip*. With that phrase looping in your mind, you are ready for L.A.

Ruscha has studios in a vaguely Spanish-Moorish court of defunct shops, circa 1920s, that is straight out of Chandler. Ruscha dates starlets, always has. Once when I went to lunch with him at a restaurant near the Paramount lot, various angelic forms seemed to throw themselves at him out of the air. "Oh, Ed!" Bashful, smiling, folksy (from Oklahoma), Ruscha wears soft, casual, terrific clothes and, always, terrific shoes. (Once, seated between two of the town's top veteran artists at a dinner party, I heard absolutely nothing all evening but cars and shoes. Were they trying to drive me crazy?) It is a joy and a relief to be with Ed Ruscha.

Next day. Over margaritas and enchiladas at Lucy's . . . Why go on! Why clutter up, with details of my chitchat with Ruscha, the timeless charm of "over margaritas and enchiladas at Lucy's"? Eating at any of the innumerable great Mexican restaurants here brings a self-satisfied sense that you, for one, know your way around L.A. and around life. The opposite feeling—panicky realization of what an incurable idiot you are— comes with dining at any Italian restaurant here.

Why am I digressing from the subject of art in Los Angeles? Because that subject, narrowly considered, is cheerless at the moment. Apart from all the visionary frenzy about MOCA and the mammoth loft and gallery boom in the downtown area—thousands of artists flooding the available space, property values going bananas—little is happening. There are many good artists, all doing what they do, but most could be doing it anywhere, in New York or on the moon. What would be called in Hollywood the "creative end" of the art world is torpid.

Whatever befell the new regionalism of the late seventies? With New York addled and enfeebled, it seemed possible for other places to pick up the slack and move art in unique directions. There seemed to exist, briefly, a "window" for outland assertions. But nobody took advantage of it (if, indeed, it wasn't an illusion). At best, there was an overall rise in the level of mediocrity. The scene here continued its long, slow subsidence from the mythical heights of the sixties technique-y minimalism known as the L.A. Look and the oh-wow sublimities of installational Space and Light.

In that prepluralism era, Los Angeles was home base for a few truly international artists—Nauman, Robert Irwin, Larry Bell, others now and then. (Bell, also, has moved to New Mexico: Irwin, the Space-and-Light guru, is enmeshed in the politics of the Artists Advisory Committee of MOCA, whose board he and Sam Francis are on.) According to Nauman, they didn't see each other much here. They met on the road in New York and Europe. Except in little spurts, there has never been a true L.A. scene. The paradigmatic local artist of the sixties may have been John McCracken, a relatively isolated master of the "finish fetish" who with single bright-colored, glossy-surfaced leaning plank shapes hit on a sensational wrinkle in late-minimalist aesthetics. Those things were popping eyes around the world for a season or two. And that was about that for McCracken.

It's weird thinking about the past of this place. It does have a good bit of past by now. Expansion continues, but the balance is tipping toward entropy. Still, there is the overpowering present tense of the light and air, the unremitting swoon of the senses. I know it's Thursday because I hear the "gardener" blowing vegetable matter around in my driveway with one of those silly deafening backpack blowers. (The merest hovel in L.A. comes with a once-a-week "gardener.") But the word *Thursday* seems ridiculously abstract as a designation for this luminous Xerox-copy morning.

What am I doing here? Writing about art! What is L.A. to art or art to L.A.?

It's a status game of a complex sort, for one thing. The other night I was at a party of art people, mostly collectors, at a TV producer's mountainside palace in Bel Air. In this current spell of blessedly clear conditions (somehow I can't bring myself to dignify what happens in the air here as "weather"), the L.A. basin below glistened away to the horizon. The catering was sumptuous. Everyone looked swell. And the rooms were full of collectors nattering about their acquisitions— a Frankenthaler, a David Salle. The tone was giddily competitive.

"You'll soon be getting up in our league, Doug." Collecting as indoor tennis.

Art is selling as if there were no tomorrow (and who knows?). The buyers include more and more movie and TV people, the resident aristocracy. Most of both the goods and the taste are imported from New York. Norman Lear and Bud Yorkin are among the wholesale consumers, as are heavyweight execs Barry Lowen, Dan Melnick, and David Begelman. I don't doubt that some of them love the stuff, but a lot of the action looks like sheer narcissism. The new elite service industry in Hollywood—following psychiatry, accountancy, and massage—is art consulting. Consultants have been witnessed hawking art works on TV sound stages between takes. And it seems that half the people I see in the galleries (which are generally deserted, by the way) are consultants asking for slides.

Consulted collecting extends to local corporations, which have gone for the investment-plus-prestige line in a big way. (Bank billboard on Wilshire, with image by Ron Davis: "Where Banking Is a Fine Art.") A few L.A. artists reputedly sell well, among them the ineffable Billy Al Bengston, who has parlayed a flair for hedonistic, slightly nasty decorative effects and personal salesmanship into a light-manufacturing mini-empire. (The regulation first purchase for young marrieds here, it is said, is a Bengston watercolor.) Ed Moses seems to be doing all right, too, without ceasing to be an underappreciated, if very odd, abstract painter. At the low end of the market is a middle-class taste for sweet, somewhat scuffed-up semiabstract stuff à la Richard Diebenkorn, what Clement Greenberg calls "luxury painting"—modernism without tears.

Then there is Chris Burden. Remember Chris Burden, who years ago gave the postconceptual avant-garde a shot in the arm—his own, winged by an assistant with a .22? The last of the L.A. internationalists, he has never sold well here, but he has commanded a certain mixture of awe and pride. Now he commands another emotion: fear. Burden has always been a gun freak, and lately he's taken to carting his artillery, plus ammo, around with him in public and acting sinister. Compactly fleshy-muscular in the Robert Blake mode, Burden all but sputters with nervous intensity. He lives in a garage off an alley near Pico Boulevard, western L.A.'s most woebegone strip. I had some jumpy, disjointed conversation with him there. Then he produced a living machine gun, which he commenced to wave around, snickering.

I calculated within a millimeter the distance to the door, which I was soon through, taking large gulps of Southern California air.

Burden brings up another thing about L.A.—the inveterate spectatorship or, to put it less politely, voyeurism. Only an incredible insensibility to personal implication explains how people could stomach those halcyon Burden performances in which he put himself in grave physical danger. In effect, Burden created a double bind of two behavioral conventions: the citizen's injunction to do something in a perilous emergency and the gallery taboo against touching the art work. There is a lot of power in such manipulations, but what does it take to undergo them without throwing up?

Pert Molly Barnes, dealer and consultant to the stars, is an ever-flowing source of social lowdown. She shows the paintings of Martin Mull. She is living proof that kitsch fictions like *Scruples* have points of contact with reality. She is bullish on art. Why? Why, because Los Angeles collectors "used to be social misfits, looking for identity. Now very glamorous people are doing it." In other words, the lawyers and doctors are out, and the moguls are in. Picture Monroe Stahr, Fitzgerald's *Last Tycoon*, watching with his wonderful eyes as new Ellsworth Kellys are presented for his approval by Molly Barnes. "Molly," Stahr murmurs, "what would I do without you."

Mollyism is not absent from the conversation of supposedly more serious people. You often run into the subliminal self-flattery that there is a classy audience here, which there isn't. There is nowhere to learn about art except superficially in this town. So far, MOCA and the new modern wing planned for the elephantine, crashingly undistinguished County Museum confirm a cultural neurosis termed by Peter Plagens, the only truly national art critic L.A. ever had (he lives in North Carolina now), an "edifice complex." More pretentious wall space with nothing to hang on it. The one impressive museum collection here is that of Norton Simon, built on the ruins of the late lamented Pasadena Museum (which he continues to dismember by deacquisition). The city's greatest private collection of modern art belongs to Simon's sister Marcia Weisman in Beverly Hills; she is a force behind MOCA.

I'm putting it all very harshly, I see. Actually, MOCA, scheduled to open in 1984 just before the Olympics, seems bound to be something grand. People are rightfully enraptured about the director-curator team they've hired—Pontus Hulten and Richard Koshalek, the Butch Cassidy and Sundance Kid of museology. Both are at once internationalists and populists with worlds of flair. Still, it's hard to see what, besides itself, MOCA is going to bring. The expectations of the deal-first mentality are to laugh. *Images and Issues*, a slick new art magazine notable for frantic boosterism, editorialized last year, "Our history begins with 1980. I can imagine no better spot on which to stand, at this moment, than the edge of a miracle spread out on paper—the end of a vacuum." I flash to Aimee Thanatogenos in *The Loved One*, on a swing attached to a teetering cliffside house, gaily soaring out over the abyss.

The great psychological craving of America, perhaps stronger in L.A. than anywhere else, is for family. This is a cliché, but it covers a hunger so widespread and gnawing that it can scare you to death. In a place where most relationships seem to be mediated by money and/or fantasy, people want so much to count on somebody that they fall into wish-fulfilling megafantasy, if not into cults. Every second artist and dealer and corporate hotshot seems to have a long-winded global-village rap, patiently explaining in futurese how the energy crisis or a spiritual force or increased air travel or what have you is leading to whatever Utopia, with Los Angeles the Capital of Sweetness. I'm not exaggerating. You can't believe the things people here will say to you with a straight face. A line of Shelley haunts me: "Pinnacled dim in the intense inane."

The wishfulness of L.A.'s citizens is simply explained as the effect of a life that enforces independence to the point of autism. Try to lean on anything or anyone and you'll fall down, if you can find anything or anyone in the first place. Los Angeles is a city without public spaces. There are only private spaces—fenced haciendas of self-maintenance and self-invention—surrounded by the soft, dreamy, zinging-with-light nowhere in particular. Lacking the habit of social discourse, people here when they try it are naturally a bit fluttery and overblown. And a visitor had better not feel superior. The place gets to you fast. Here I am again at my Olivetti, and there are the birds again; and the breeze through the window is like the touch of the world's most considerate lover. My nearest friends are miles away; in fact, they don't exist. Nothing exists but this moment of sensation. (Get me out of here!)

Back to Chris Burden for a moment. Nervous-making as he is, Burden richly reflects another aspect of the local spiritual economy—a lack of social abrasion in gradient steps between concord and actual violence. A sacred monster, he displays, and aestheticizes, a pathology—much as Forest Lawn aestheticizes death—at the opposite pole from the culture's self-involved pleasures. The effect may be somehow to reinforce and ratify those pleasures. His is a mad social poetry that has its genuinely moving moments. Last year Burden invited a group one afternoon to the palisades in Santa Monica overlooking the Pacific. There a powerful telescope was set up, directed by an assistant. Looking through it, they saw, far out at sea, someone (Burden) paddling a kayak in a dazzle of light from the declining sun, a lone, tiny, laboring silhouette appearing and disappearing in the sparkle. This went on for exactly two hours. Then the telescope was whisked away and everybody went home.

Among suppliers of blue-chip art to the upper crust, the most visible is Doug Christmas, who runs the hyper-glossy Ace Gallery in Venice, with a branch in West Hollywood. His visibility owes to his New York wares and spendthrift advertising; he regularly buys the back covers of *Art in America* and *Artforum*. His lavishness does not always extend to paying artists what he owes them. From the extraordinary horror stories one hears—and it takes a lot to make a dealer horror story extraordinary—it is a marvel that he stays in business. Still, between bouncing checks and fielding lawsuits, he carries on in high style. Christmas also has one of the gaudier utopian patters around, centrally featuring Europeans and Asians flying direct to L.A. on vastly improved supersonic airliners while New York presumably languishes in its grime.

A sleek new blue-chipper is Larry Gagosian, who has a David Salle show up as I write this. He has a gallery space and office that, without being in the least ostentatious, breathe the cold excitements of money—whites and grays with carefully gauged amounts of Southern California light. The air in the office is like vaporized stainless steel. Steely himself, aftershave-ad handsome, Gagosian told me he figures to give the business two years to prove itself. "If I weren't doing this, I'd probably be in real estate." On the wall behind him hung a beautiful black-and-white Kelly, and, thinking about it now, I wonder how the square-foot price of that canvas compares with condominium rates in Century City. Selling paintings, Gagosian may be in real estate after all—vertical real estate, flat condos, prestige addresses for the eye.

If it sometimes seems that the only values in Southern California are real estate values, that's because it's hard to imagine what other kind of values there might be. There is, it's true, a pervasive big, soft, mystical spiritualism that seems to precipitate in people's brains out of the radiant Pacific emptiness. Space-and-Light aesthetics—Irwin, James Turrell, Doug Wheeler—get charges from it. But everything comes back to real estate, as in the atmospheric effects in Gagosian's office. Oddly, the upshot is not so much to cheapen the spiritual as to spiritualize the material. Nowhere else is the aura of money so cleanly magical. It's fascinating, like a cobra.

Speaking of empty, another of my frequent stops here is the Los Angeles Institute of Contemporary Art (LAICA), with its nifty museum near Beverly Hills. The museum mounts some interesting and challenging shows. Some days no one—no one!—comes in. Does this discourage LAICA's staff? Not really, somehow. They plug away at documenting and communicating, putting out the often sharp *LAICA Journal* and generally maintaining standards like shipwrecked Englishmen observing teatime. Well, standards are about to bend. With perhaps a touch of lonesome hysteria, LAICA is planning a show for this fall of sports pictures by Andy Warhol and (deep breath) Le Roy Neiman. Let us change the subject.

Sex. There isn't much explicit sex in L.A. art, though sex is as monotonous a feature of the basin as the temperature inversion that keeps the smog locked in. The massed legions of beautiful, lightly clad, self-conscious bodies collectively generate such explosive force that sometimes you think the place will just combust, going up in one gruesome fireball. Out here this time without the protection of my wife, who is in New York, I find it terrifying. (For a less shadowed view, consult my collaborator Mr. James Hamilton, bachelor photographer.) What makes it weird is how languid and, well, static the sexuality is, as if it were an impersonal power that had nothing to do with desire. In New York it is tenser and more behavioral—people get silly or hostile or sheepish, more themselves. Here people's bodies broadcast delirious animal messages, and their eyes are bland, almost defeated. Every attraction has the same subtext: "Here we go again."

I see that I have made my first overt comparison of Los Angeles and New York, something I swore not to do. Comparisonitis, relentlessly malicious, is something every New Yorker comes down with here, like the flu. Recovery is possible. It comes with the realization of just how peculiar a place L.A. is, and what a radical sense of the human it breeds. A central mystery is how L.A., with none of the characteristics of even a small traditional city, can nonetheless be, and feel like, the great world city it is. Just how little engagement can a city give its citizens and still be a city? Damn little indeed, answers L.A. It suffices that the citizens perceive each other and themselves as people marked by a difference, a way of being in the world that is their own. The L.A. way, cutting across every social division, is in a haze of pleasure.

This is never going to be a real art center unless, in the process, it ceases to be L.A. The very word *center* is a solecism here. Downtown L.A. may sprout skyscrapers and institutions forever, as some anticipate, yet it will never feel like the center of anything. Downtown is a neighborhood distinguished by difficult parking. A realistic hope, voiced to me by Koshalek, is that apartment construction will bring enough people there to constitute a neighborhood-as-city, a land-island metropolis. MOCA will then function as the cultural corner store. Meanwhile the real estate god will long since have expelled the current artist settlers from the cement Eden. Where will they go? It hardly matters in "scene" terms. In every compass direction from the clustered loft buildings of downtown lies the limitless, energy-swallowing sprawl that is L.A.'s definition and fate. There, all sense of difference is homogenized in the even spread of sunlit privacies—across which falls a common shadow.

What is the flip side of the love of pleasure? Fear of pain, here the pain of crime. Burglary is epidemic. Violent crime is widespread, often horror-movie vicious, and—in the basin's blanketing anonymity— somehow much scarier than elsewhere. Ever topical, Chris Burden drives around the city for hours a day with his machine guns and pistols in his new black Buick sedan. A hit man's car. If Burden himself weren't so frightening, one could get an odd, poetic reassurance from the knowledge—the thought that out there at this moment, cruising some boulevard (a moving red indicator on a fantasized street map), is this heavily armed artistic concrescence of the city's faceless dread. (As it is, the image just heightens a suspicion of engulfing madness.) Fear keeps people in private, apart from each other; being apart feeds their paranoia, so their apartness grows. It can make chance encounters disconcertingly poignant.

I will conclude with a culture event: a car crash. Two years ago my wife and I were first on the scene of an accident in West Los Angeles.

A Volkswagen had flipped off the Santa Monica Freeway and rolled to the edge of an exit ramp. It was 2 A.M. Brooke rescued a girl wandering dazed and bleeding on the freeway; I tended to a stunned boy sitting beside the wreck. They were miraculously little hurt. (Forget the Volkswagen.) Other cars stopped. People helped or, too late to help, stood around and chatted pleasantly. A huge Mexican family showed up from a nearby house with water and towels; evidently this happened a lot. The mood was elated, even exalted. The girl looked down at her stained white slacks and said, laughing, that she knew she should have worn her red ones. Others laughed too—a sweet sound in the dark. Presently the L.A. police arrived, strutting and bullying in their best mercenaries-in-Africa style, and reluctantly we all returned to our cars.

It's an old joke here that people have crashes for the company. To move up in the world, go to Wilshire and Doheny and ram the first Porsche that comes by. (In fact, I've seen people after fender benders exchanging information and smiling—smiling!) For some reason I am remembering about that night how, in the illumination of headlights and smoggy sky glow, everyone—Anglos, blacks, Mexicans—looked simply terrific: handsome, pretty, dressed just right, and relaxed. Now I'm not sure whether I'm remembering or imagining, but it seems to me that their voices, which included my own, were like those of happy children. I mean children who know that they are lovable and that the world is kind.

What a terrible city. It's Sunday, and today's big cultural event (to which a local art critic will devote two lead paragraphs in the newspaper tomorrow) is the beginning of daylight saving time. Late-afternoon sunshine fills our yard like incandescent melted butter, setting the oranges on (yes) our orange tree aglow. Soon the sun will go down—that sudden, lights-out, neon-on Southern California sunset. A police siren goes by, making all the neighborhood dogs howl. You would think they'd get used to it. I will never get used to any of it. Tomorrow I will take a cab to the airport, climb the World Airways boarding stairs, and go home.

June 3–9, 1981

Affairs of the Heat

It's full summer in Manhattan, and I wonder who, if anyone, is reading this column. The compulsion to stay abreast of things that makes people column readers evaporates in the heat. Some of us who have summered on this island enough times to get the hang of it—in my case, fifteen of the last eighteen years—know the feeling of quiet liberation, the voluptuous calm and lonesomeness that the solstice can bring. I wouldn't dream of disrupting this semisweet and secret mood for myself or anyone else.

So let's all go to the Frick. The Frick Collection in the summer. Nothing is more perfect. Do you truly like art? If you don't like the Frick Collection in the summer, your aesthetic sensibility is dead. A neo–eighteenth-century mansion built in 1914 and filled with European masterpieces—bequeathed by the steel baron Henry Clay Frick to the citizenry as a monument to himself—it is a Temple of the Muse, American style. In intimate, muttering New York summer, one attends it to refresh an old irrational attachment and to gauge the changes of a year. What has a season of unremitting presentness done to the classic past and to oneself? But never mind the pensive stuff. Let's just go.

Some people visit the Frick to pay a call on just one picture. The picture will be different for each person, and will differ for the same person over the years. The Frick is a place for the selection of personal touchstones, a site of love affairs with art. It reminds one of what is easily forgotten in the chill museums, that taste is erotic at base. Frank O'Hara wrote, "Sometimes I think I am 'in love' with art." That sentence should be engraved over the Frick's entrance.

I think of Frank O'Hara because my enthusiasm for his poetry determined my first Frick picture love: Rembrandt's *Polish Rider*, that wildly atypical (for Rembrandt, and for equestrian painting) vision of a youthful armed-to-the-teeth warrior on his sinewy, rather doglike steed. Gustily romantic and sexy, it was a talisman for O'Hara at his most rhapsodic and perverse. I still think of O'Hara whenever I look

91

at it, which may explain why my ardor for the painting has waned. It was, after all, a ricochet romance.

My first untutored infatuation—in my autodidact, inventing-the-wheel naïveté—was the *Comtesse d'Haussonville* (1845) of Ingres. For years I kept a postcard reproduction of it tacked up, adoring the image with the totally inarticulate zeal of obsession. I would visit this painting only, heading straight for it without looking left or right. I can't say why exactly. Maybe I was simply gazing at it on a day when the concept "masterpiece" suddenly sank way in. Ingres made pictures that scream "masterpiece!" loud enough to wake the dead. The gross anatomical improbability of the comtesse's right shoulder, perhaps because I noticed it without being told, was a secondary jolt that tumbled me into doting.

I may never love another painting the way I loved that Ingres, which is just as well. In the typical aftermath of such things, it is faintly repellent to me now. (To be rid of it, I mailed the postcard.) My subsequent Frick affairs have been flirtations or discreet arrangements by which I've gotten cozy with artists whose charms had previously eluded me. Thus, largely thanks to the Frick, I've entered into occasional intimacy with Fragonard (though not Boucher), Cuyp, Hobbema, de La Tour, the English portraitists (who go so well with the Thomas Hastings architecture), and Whistler.

My most recent, and continuing, fixation is on *The Village of Becquigny* (1857–64), by the Barbizon landscapist Théodore Rousseau. Not until being riveted by this smallish canvas last year had I ever given Rousseau, or Barbizon in general, more than a passing glance. It is a view into a forest village. It has an enameled, vaguely candy-box look at first, but the fanatical rendering of light and texture gradually mesmerizes, communicating an effort of attention verging on meditation verging on ecstasy. There is a strange lumpiness or pebbly effect to the modeling of surfaces, as if the scene veiled some swelling, polypy organisms or plasmic energy. Am I crazy to see this? The picture is descriptive, Dutch-conventional, static. No other Rousseau I've seen since has gripped me this way. Only at the Frick.

For all it matters, the Frick has a special exhibition on until August 9: eight Houdon busts from 1777–91, arrayed in the oval room of big Whistler portraits. They are very white, very convincing, and—to eyes lately delighted by John Ahearn's portrait sculptures of Bronx proletarians—quite snappy. Especially captivating is the one of Thomas

Jefferson, looking as personable, and as fantastically intelligent, as any Founding-Father fan could wish. But whoever needs an occasion to visit the Frick is not right spirited.

What else? Well, where else, outside the numbing profusion of the great museums (and notably the hilarious re-creation at the Met of Robert Lehman's claustrophobic pack-rat digs), can you find such perfect treasures of fourteenth-century Siena as the Frick's little Duccio and Barna da Siena? The rarity of Piero della Francesca sanctifies his panel here but also makes it too self-conscious for real Frick dalliance. (Beware, as Oscar Wilde said, relationships entered on one's knees.) Velázquez, Goya, Vermeer, Giovanni Bellini, Titian, Holbein, Veronese, Bronzino, Chardin, Hals, Van Dyck, and El Greco hang glamorously at ease, self-confidently irresistible. The grandiose Claude Lorrain and Turners look dubious of their own seductive powers in the late twentieth century—all the more reason to cherish them if one can. And oh yes. The Frick is the one place where I've actively enjoyed, rather than dutifully admired, rooms of old furniture.

In all of this, I'm uncomfortably aware of heaping indirect praise on old Mr. Frick, who embodied the Satanic as well as the Promethean values of the laissez-faire era. (He had strikers shot.) His mansion is a place for reflecting on this discomfort—this American anxiety of fundamental illegitimacy, of wealth and culture as theft—amid well-loved beauty. But the anxiety is somehow marginally more bearable in the New York summer, when human sadness feels so vast and unalterable. In the sadness, such aesthetic consolations as the Frick echo with distant joy.

July 1–7, 1981

Disney Animators

Apart from its regularly sold-out screenings, Disney Animations and Animators (the Whitney Museum of American Art, June 24–September 6, 1981) is badly calculated as a crowd-pleasing summer show. It is a confusing archival jumble, murked up by a worshipful presentation. But the fault is not all the Whitney's. There is bewilderment and a certain anxiety just in thinking about Disney—the man, the genius, and the corporate phenomenon. A lot of it is inherent in his work, which is so often disquieting on purpose. He played anxiety like a piano.

The paradox about Disney as an entertainer of children is that he was—and, in his still-lurching robotized spirit, is—not friendly or even particularly nice. I speak as a member of a generation given psychic wounds by *Bambi* that remain tender to the touch. And I regret to say that my daughter recently shared a theater with a hundred or so other wailing youngsters enduring *The Fox and the Hound*, a new Disney Studios feature that sports another murdered mother. This odd penchant for the grim has to be factored into any assessment of the late king of popular culture.

First it must be registered that Disney at his best was as good as popular art ever gets—not as cherishable as Chaplin, Astaire, and the Beatles, but fully as dominating and innovative. He approached cartoon animation as an engineering problem—for instance, how to mechanically translate and extend acting techniques—at a time when the daring and pride of American engineering were Promethean, or Frankensteinian. The strategic problem was to astonish, charm, tickle, and scare the bejabbers out of kids of all ages in vast numbers, simultaneously, everywhere. The solution was know-how apotheosized. Another master of manipulative cinema, Eisenstein, was a Disney fan.

Disney's first audiences were largely adult. His early short cartoons tend to be smutty, and his great early features—until *Fantasia*, whose box-office failure trimmed his creative sails—are full of mildly highbrow stuff. A lot of high-art types in the late thirties were crazy about him. Others, like Clement Greenberg in his justly famous jeremiad "Avant-Garde and Kitsch," were not. It takes imagination today to believe how awesome Disney animation and the whole popular-culture technocracy then gearing up appeared, and how monstrous they looked to European-oriented intellectuals.

It's interesting to see the way Disney did it—or to glimpse, rather, because prolonged attention tends to sicken. He hired remarkably gifted artist-draftsmen and technicians, encouraged them to fantasize and invent, then squeezed their fantasies and inventions through the mesh of an anonymous corporate style. All the work of individual animators at the Whitney looks alike; looking closer, one sees evidence of individuality, like bumps under a blanket.

Probably the animators didn't mind. For the ethos, or romance, of the operation was that of exalted teamwork engineering, today as old hat in America as the cult of Lucky Lindy. (The Japanese have cheerfully inherited it.) I still feel the tug of this old technocratic optimism, among other nostalgias. My wife and I have routinely hauled our daughter to Disney revivals, which she enjoys only intermittently (not nearly as much as Tom and Jerry). The unforgivable *Fox and the Hound* tears it once and for all.

Popular culture isn't the problem for us today that it was for, say, Greenberg, who didn't hesitate in 1939 to lump Hollywood movies as an art form with socialist realism and fascist propaganda. We've been brought up on popular culture and imagine, at least, that we see straight through it even as we enjoy it. The have-your-cake-and-eat-it aesthetic too narrowly called camp is our cultural common sense, a benign national cynicism. For a while there in the sixties it looked as if the division between high and popular art might disappear, to the detriment of neither. This hasn't happened. There is a difference, and it makes a lot of us squirm.

What makes Disney antique now is his hubristic ambition to forge animated cartoons into a complete dramatic art. Except in *Snow White*, with its very funny dwarfs, the usual upshot is humor insufficient to the preponderant sentimentality and terror. (There is more unalloyed joy in almost any Mel Blanc–voiced Warner Brothers cartoon than in anything by Disney.) Disney's historic feat, like Henry Luce's, was to make ingesting popular culture feel like going to church. He made it sacrilegious to question whether you were having fun.

Is Disneyland fun? Not really, though it is stirring and even moving in an inchoate way. When I was there, I got lost in wonder at the multitude of superlatively engineered devices—each object and machine invented or reinvented from scratch and each a prototype, one of a kind. Mass consumption of the non-mass-produced. The talent, effort, and expense are so magnificent you'd be an ingrate not to love the place. The result is a pleasure admixed with something heavy, something a bit solemn and grueling.

The same might be said about most people's experience of high art. "Mass consumption of the non-mass-produced" could describe the Louvre. Disney had a flair for sublimating the terrible dutifulness of American devotion to "culture." (The kind of thing you get in all its direct dreariness on Channel 13.) The secret irony here, known to a relative few, is that real high art scorns solemnization. It lightens and liberates. It invites a unique consumption of the inexhaustible. It differs from popular art in demanding one spiritual prerequisite: the ability to be alone.

God knows most of us Americans hate being alone. This may explain why our popular culture is the best in the universe. We keep pouring the cream of our genius and love into producing the antiloneliness serums that are movies, pop songs, and television shows. We take nothing more seriously than our fun. Well, all of this has been said many times before, often by pundits displaying that other familiar compulsion, to make people feel bad about what makes them human and sociable in whatever way their world allows. Loneliness is no sin. It is "an infinitely gentle, infinitely suffering thing" in need of infinite consolation.

August 5–11, 1981

Realism Again

Realism? Did I hear someone say "realism"? I did indeed. In recent months, there has been a din of exhibitions and publications centered on modern realist art—realism being defined, in the inclusive sense everyone seems to prefer, simply as representation of the visible world. The latest noise is Contemporary American Realism since 1960, a show of 101 artists at the Pennsylvania Academy of the Fine Arts in Philadelphia (September 18–December 13, 1981). In the New York art world, all the clamor has a barbarian ring. With the partial exception of realists with impeccable modernist manners, like Alex Katz, Philip Pearlstein, and Chuck Close, realism is invariably condescended to, when noticed at all, in the precincts of "serious" art.

What has happened? Not, certainly, any new theory (new New Realism) or major qualitative leap in practice. The short list of famous and really notable American realist painters today is, amazingly, almost identical with the list of ten years ago, when there was loud talk of a realist revival. Indisputably on both lists—of non-photo-realists—are Pearlstein, Katz, Neil Welliver, Al Leslie, and Jack Beal; the death of Fairfield Porter marks one major loss, the maturation of Rackstraw Downes one major addition. Among photo-realists, nothing has occurred to awaken anyone from a ten-year sleep: Close, Richard Estes, and Robert Bechtle still look strong, and the rest still look interchangeable. So the current realist furor is a function of interest, not production.

Many things determine the flow of interest in a culture. In American culture it usually has something to do with money. The new prominence of realism gets a boost from the hungry, expanding market, augmenting an already sizable demand. Despite art-world snootiness, realism has always found collectors—collectors now in a position to want their tastes ratified. That golden glow around realism is partly an emanation, but also partly a reflection of nearby lucre. Witness the title of a present show at the Guggenheim: Seven Photorealists

97

from New York Collections. It's a show that smacks of appeasing the wealthy. Today money doesn't only talk; it may also criticize and curate.

There is nothing especially new in this except blatancy. Nor could it have a decisive influence, were it not that modernist taste, though still in command of art-world institutions, has lost drive and conviction. Mocked by its own latest avant-garde—the young cannibals of neo-expressionism—establishment modernism has no ready squelch for the new feistiness of realism. People have always liked realism in art. Such liking, armed with a little economic clout, may be enough nowadays to sweep the field. To hold and consolidate the field could prove to be another matter, however.

Supporters of current realism will have to do better than the pluralist mishmash of the Philadelphia show. A compulsion to educate, combined with a genteel dread of intruding anything so gauche as an idea or discrimination, produces a show replete with pompous catalogue, verbose wall labels, and perky slide show, all as softheaded as the day is long. The selection of works, moreover, seems perfunctory, as if mainly ceremonial. Nearly all the 101 artists are represented—often at less than their best—by only one or two examples.

A show so heterogeneous—doggedly ranging from photo-realist motorcycles to academic nudes and archacademic allegories—defies straight criticism. To review it, one would have to re-curate it in one's head. As it was, I found myself pondering the unasked and unanswered question why in this day and age anyone would want to paint realistically. What motives, energies, and values are involved? I noted a few that seemed to recur:

Appropriation. Realism as a way of taking command of the outside world is very American, as witness the forays into the wilderness of nineteenth-century painters like Church and Bierstadt. Welliver, stunningly well represented here, seems firmly in this tradition, dominating nature in the very act of confronting and detailing its wildness. In a way, the photo-realists do the same thing to the urban and mechanized American scene, and Chuck Close does it with the wilderness of the human face. To paint the wild world is to control it; then to buy the painting is to own the wild world and to own "culture," as well.

Cultivation. Much realism exalts a refined, middling-sensual, alert-to-nuance sensibility that reflects the values of an ideal upper-middle class. The painterly "intimism" of Bonnard and Vuillard, as brilliantly revived by Porter with input from abstract expressionism, projects a cultivated, attentive enjoyment of both nature and culture. Jane Freilicher, represented by a beautiful big Hamptons landscape, is a faithful exemplar of this spirit. The aim is not to appropriate but to express civilized harmony with an environment already appropriated, already one's own.

Eroticism. Naked women galore, many imbued or regarded with a sexuality that is hostile, sometimes sadistic, at least sullen. This is true mainly, but not exclusively, of work by men. It is most emphatic in work that tends to the academic. (This is interesting as a sign of the times: most academic nudes used to be sentimental, rather than nasty, in their sexism.) The apparent neutrality of Pearlstein intrigues in this context. His nudes, clinically observed at close range, exist not only in the closed space of paintings keyed to abstract aesthetics but also in the special social situation of the studio, where people sell, by the hour, the right to view their naked bodies as objects. Now, this is a situation with an obvious erotic charge, but one protected and, as it were, purified by cultural agreement. Pearlstein both heightens and rigidifies this tension, which may be why he appeals to both relatively modernist and distinctly conservative taste: the former admires his unflinchingness, the latter his demonstration of the sturdiness of convention. Both aspects signify "professionalism."

Social fantasy. Appropriation, cultivation, and eroticism mark approaches to the world as it exists. Fantasy authenticates a world that doesn't exist. (It can do this compellingly in art because of our penchant for reading any painting as a "world" in itself, therefore an equivalent to the whole real world.) Alex Katz is a good example, on a grand scale. His pictures present a world of perfect dinner guests— graceful, untroubled, irresistibly attractive. It's a beguiling fiction, which suits the modernist high artifice of his painting style: New York aesthetics, New York fantasy.

Art fantasy. Painters like Leslie and Beal regret the loss of ancient artistic powers, like allegory and moral statement, to modern self-consciousness. They try to recover these powers by will and in the process enact a fantasy of time travel, of history as a two-way street. There is something hysterical in the enterprise, but something moving, too. It is beyond academicism, because it involves the wholesale resurrection of a past artistic role, the artist as narrator and preacher to society, in an age with no apparent use for that. It is ambitious in relation to the world, but its ambitions are contained within the world of art. It is a fiesta of contradictions, but it's alive.

The above are five sample answers to the question, why paint realistically? All are indirect. None says simply: to be realistic. The absence of a foursquare, capital-R realism, in the line of Courbet, accounts for the feeling of suburban sprawl among current representational styles. If anyone today raises the possibility of an unconditional realism, it is probably Rackstraw Downes, with his small, riveting panoramic landscapes—rural scenes where nature is interlaced with evidence of human use. The one little Downes landscape in the Philadelphia show made a big impression on me. Rigorous, cool, passionately absorbed in its subject matter, it was practically alone in making me think more of the world—of reality, whatever that is—than of art. In the stylistic Babel of that show, I kept returning to the Downes, as to an island of silence. Tactfulness like Downes's is so rare today it's exotic.

November 11–17, 1981

H. C. Westermann

H. C. Westermann died of a heart attack November 3, six days after attending the opening of his current show (Xavier Fourcade Gallery, October 28–November 28, 1981). He was fifty-eight. I never met him. I enjoyed his art, but I never quite lost a resistance to its frequent corniness and constant craftsiness. I wonder, then, why news of his death hit me hard, leaving such an ache.

Maybe it has something to do with the Midwest, which is where I'm from and where Westermann, during thirteen years in Chicago, came into his vocation. Though he was born and raised in Los Angeles and lived in Connecticut after 1961, he seems to me simply the premier "midwestern" artist of this era, if only because he doesn't quite belong anywhere else. Nothing quite belongs or doesn't belong in the Midwest. People there put themselves together from spare parts (or else flee to the identity of one or the other coast). Westermann's aesthetic of surreal/expressionistic assemblage happens to be a typical visual expression—or perhaps reaction formation—of creative individuality in the Midwest, that zone of fragmentary, mismatched, and oddly twisted cultural imperatives, that vast center that is all periphery.

There are artists in almost every midwestern city somewhat like Westermann, working with a similar combination of romantic autobiography and folkish atavism, but I've never seen one as good as he. For one thing, few people are put together from such an interesting set of parts, or put together with such existential wit. His roustabout youth, culminating in a war experience of kamikaze attacks, was full of macabre romance out of Jack London and B. Traven, but with irrepressibly goofball overtones. Call him Ishmael/Popeye, this tattooed he-man who "became a fucking coward" after seeing the corpses of shipmates stacked like cordwood on the deck of the U.S.S. *Enterprise* and who reenlisted for the Korean War because "I wanted to see if I was still a coward—I was!"

He had been ailing for years, an especially sad fate for a man—

the former Marine and professional acrobat—who so valued physical vigor. (When he lived in a boiler room in Chicago in the 1950s, Westermann daily carried a boulder up and down stairs to stay in shape.) A sense of desperate vulnerability and insecurity, continually undermining great personal strength and resource, is a thematic engine of Westermann's art and perhaps the basis of his shamanistic appeal. It has special resonance in the landlocked, sheltered, righteous Midwest, where moralistic and pragmatic suspicion of raw personal experience heightens both the seductiveness and the terror of such experience. To have actually undergone some elemental height or depth of life is vaguely shameful there, where to have secrets is not nice and to share them is alarming. The comic possibilities in all this avoidance are obvious. They are the stuff of Second City humor and much Chicago art. Perhaps in America generally, but in the Midwest particularly, "being crazy in public" is a priestly function.

Of course, Westermann's holy craziness was conveyed in works of the most fanatically painstaking craftsmanship, which calls incessant attention to itself. This is admirable and charming; there is both virtue and pleasure in it. But Westermann's compulsive craft does not often fit snugly with his subject matter or humor. A joke loses something, or gains something extraneous, when it is built like a Fabergé egg. Westermann's craft and content (unlike Joseph Cornell's) have a multiple-choice feel; a viewer gets to respond to one or the other alternately, but rarely to both at once. This unresolved stylistic problem makes demands on the viewer's good will, which fortunately is rewarded in ways other than the aesthetic.

What does Westermann's work speak about? Perhaps "how to be a man" in a world that is out to get you. His passion for the well-made—the well-made for its own sake—seems a form of masculine protest against modern society, as does, in another way, his strident insistence on remembering, recounting, and memorializing, in his armada of *Death Ships*, the horrors he witnessed in America's most popular war. What makes the protest poignant rather than overbearing—what makes *macho* the wrong word for it—is that Westermann's prevailing desire seems to have been for security, not domination. Living with his wife, the painter Joanna Beall, in the Connecticut house they built themselves, he hatched images of insanity and terror as if to keep reminding himself just how blessed with luck he was: the wanderer safe in port, home from the sea. It's hard to find a photograph of him not delightedly smiling.

Westermann is such a necessary figure in American art—as an upholder of large compelling values not accommodated by mainstream modern art—that if he hadn't existed, he would have been invented. A law of our cultural economy dictates that there be artists' artists for every constituency and historical pass. In New York, Lucas Samaras, more sophisticated and vastly less reassuring, has functioned this way, as the almost universally respected "outsider." Westermann did it for the heartland.

Westermann was very successful. The present show at Fourcade, comprising almost everything he created after his retrospective at the Whitney in 1978, was almost entirely sold out long before the opening. There are major Westermann collectors on both coasts and, of course, in Chicago. His influence on younger artists was deep and decisive in Chicago and also in the San Francisco Bay area, places where his combination of the craftsmanly and the quirky became an important model of how to "do art" outside the cosmopolitan nexus. Less measurable is the quantity of comfort and cheer his work has brought to people who share, at whatever level of intensity, the sense of anxious individuality that drove him. He always seems to bring out the best in reviewers of his shows—a festive rhetorical lilt, a holiday feeling. He was an artist people loved to love.

Not me, though. My appreciation of Westermann was ambivalent; I felt better contemplating what was wrong than what was right with him. Thus his death becomes, for me, the ironic occasion of a belated self-recognition. Now I find it useful to see in my grudging attitude a discomfort with my own midwesternness—which long ago I fled at a dead run, with no intention of ever looking back. (This is an old American story, which is why I feel only a little embarrassed to be telling it on myself.) Westermann stayed with his share of the culture's contradictions. He fought fire with fire—Middle America's shoddiness and hypocrisy and dumb patriotism with Middle America's values of pleasure in work and modesty and table-turning humor.

Looking at the teeming inventions in the show, I find it difficult to believe that there won't be any more like them. It doesn't seem fair. Westermann's work is so lively when about death—as in several new funny coffins, including a bent one for a bent baseball bat—and is so permanent looking, built to last, that actual death in his case seems more than usual an indecency, a lack of respect, a failure of humor. Westermann was brave, buoyant, and endlessly self-regenerating. He seemed to approach each new piece the way another artist might approach a whole career, starting from scratch and finishing with an air of utter finality, of having had the last word on everything. And the last word is invariably insouciant, the light, triumphant gesture of the escape artist who has done it again. Suddenly this gesture, no more to be repeated, seems important and cherishable—as if, after all, Westermann wasn't making jokes about something serious. He was making serious jokes.

November 25–December 1, 1981

Only Connect:
Bruce Nauman

For a while there in the late sixties Bruce Nauman was one of the most abundantly inventive artists anyone had ever seen. It is interesting to remember this—on the occasion of Nauman's current two-gallery show (January 9–January 30, 1982) at Castelli's 142 Greene Street space and, upstairs, at Sperone Westwater Fischer—because the late sixties are squarely in the blind spot of present art consciousness. During those years the force of earlier "big styles"—abstract expressionism, pop, minimalism—was beginning to spread itself, deltalike, toward the tranquil gulf of the seventies, but it still had momentum. More to the point, there was still, at least in principle, a readiness in the art audience to value the "difficult" in new work, especially work by artists perceived to be pushing the frontiers of aesthetic possibility. In today's eager but negligent atmosphere that time seems long ago.

Artists in the late sixties were optimistic about the aesthetic potential of technologies and systems, and Nauman played with most of them—video, film, photography, light, sound, language, mathematics, holography, and more—to memorable effect. His work was Duchampian in its wit and insolence, in its teeming paradoxes, puns, and other forms of mental short-circuitry. It reminded some people also of Jasper Johns for the way it invested brainy art gestures with a psychological charge—an air of withdrawn, self-involved emotion only obliquely revealed in each piece. Like Duchamp and Johns, Nauman seemed to spin art out of sheer self-consciousness. An adept sculptor, craftsman, and all-around showman, he was a Barnum of introversion, embodying anxious or hostile states in broad jokes and spectacular displays. Typical of his bottomless facetiousness was a spiral of writing in neon that read, "The true artist helps the world by revealing mystic truths." Typical of his capacity to unnerve was an empty room in which a recorded voice hectored, "Get out of my mind! Get out of this room!"

What was really inconveniencing about Nauman, however, was his work's skewed relation to the various dialectics that defined "advanced art" in the late sixties. He seemed always to be entering the scene from some informed but eccentric angle, and living mostly in California had something to do with it. It cost him critically. Robert Pincus-Witten, who invented the term *postminimalism* and used it as a procrustean bed for many artists (with consequent amputation of the odd limb and meaning), taxed Nauman with "narcissism," then still a dirty word. And Nauman ran into definite trouble with New York audiences when he started showing austere "behaviorist" environments—a corridor so narrow it could be passed through only sideways, a suspended "room" whose walls stopped at mid–shin level—that induced physical self-consciousness and mild sensory deprivation. Nervous urbanites (including me) found such work conducive less to mind expansion than to anxiety attack.

Nauman's disconcerting presence wasn't the only thing that felt marginal in the art world of the seventies. After a last burst of artifice and hysteria in conceptualism and so-called body art—most of whose practitioners owed something to Nauman—the idea of an avant-garde mainstream dissolved. Art in general started to feel marginal to the commercial, professional, governmental, and alternative institutions that "supported" it not wisely but too well. A new audience appeared whose attention span could be measured in milliseconds, and a new consumer criticism emerged to serve it. Though slow in registering, these changes inexorably affected the reputations of many art stars whose work had been geared to the tight, centered situation of the sixties. They weren't dropped from prominence—in the new art world nothing actually failed—so much as defused, their impact deadened by incurious acceptance.

Nauman's fate through all this was at once harder, in terms of worldly success (he lacked regular patronage, except to some extent in Europe), and less undermining, because he had always been a lone wolf. In a way, Nauman's work since the late sixties—forbidding, puzzling, and tentative as some of it is—has revealed, to those few continuing to care, an artist more significant and valuable than the modernist cowboy of the late sixties. He has kept alive the avant-garde "antiart" impulse not as an ideological program or art-cultural game but as a personal predilection, a mode of conscientiously being in the world. If his relation to the changing art audience and market has become ever more attenuated, his commitment to his own peculiar slant of vision has correspondingly deepened. Both the emotional content and the open-ended, almost oriental, detachment in the presentation of his work have intensified.

The lovely, vaguely haikulike, title of Nauman's double show—Violins. Violence. Silence.—is a reminder that unlike many artists who toy with language, he has a poet's ear. "Violins" is an obscure reference to a late-sixties videotape in which Nauman, untutored in the instrument, played a violin whose strings were tuned D, E, A, and D. This morbid musical pun recurs in one of his new sculptures, called *Diamond Africa*, in which the legs of a suspended cast-iron chair sound the same notes when struck. "Violence" is a political allusion, to torture in South America. The three sculptures at Sperone—cast-iron chairs suspended within circular, triangular, and square eye-level corrals of steel bands, each roughly fourteen feet across—are collectively titled *South America*. "Silence" might be an injunction or a piece of advice on how to encounter these pieces—these shaped columns of space containing chairs, tilted at unsittable angles, that seem mute testimony to some anonymous catastrophe. In context, "Silence" suggests no rhetoric, no sentiment, no conclusion—and no evasion.

"Silence" also jibes with the effect of two new sculptures—crude plaster elements roughly wedged and braced together on Castelli's floor in configurations, one circular and one indescribably irregular, respectively about twenty-three and twelve feet across—from Nauman's series called *Models for Tunnels*. The concept is of vast underground tunnel networks (going nowhere) for which these sculptures are rough sketches. The coarseness of execution appears intended to direct attention away from the pieces toward the imaginary, though scarcely imaginable, projects they prefigure. It doesn't seem to matter much to Nauman whether any such project is eventually realized. These homely metaphors of subterranean grandeur are self-sufficing—generating, with some effort of the viewer's imagination, a psychological state of isolation, refuge, silence.

Trying to explain for myself the uncanniness of Bruce Nauman's recent work, I think again of Duchamp and Johns. All three are artists of self-contradicting, radical skepticism directed against assumptions of art experience and even of experience generally. They make self-canceling signs—like the dumb public emblem given intense subjectivity by color and brushwork in Johns's *Flag* paintings or, vice versa, derisively objective models of subjectivity, as in any of Duchamp's works involving the erotic. But to say all this is to say very little about the impact of such artists; it is merely to describe thought structures easily analyzed and aped by others.

Less comprehensible about Duchamp, Johns, and Nauman is the personal drive that keeps running them into the brick wall of their own intelligence, as if, with some mixture of amusement and despair, they never cease to be amazed by the futility of it all. For the integrity of these artists—their ironic, lonely dignity—consists in observing and being true to a "failure to communicate" built into every language, every style. Such artists haunt the mind with a sensation like that of being in a remote, supposedly secret, place and suddenly feeling that someone else is there, too. This presence, a small pressure somewhere in consciousness, feels neither friendly nor unfriendly, neither "good" nor "bad." It is intimate without being in the least personal. Trying to confront it is like trying to bite your own back.

In the late sixties there was a fleeting notion that this sensation could be made the basis for a conscious "criticality," an ideology of change. But, as Nauman seems instinctively to understand, the sensation signifies an irony of existence that cannot be directed or contained and certainly cannot be handed down as a tradition. Each true instance of it is terminal. D, E, A, D. It can be tracked only by a solitary individual, and its track can be registered only by another solitary individual. This recognition made Nauman rather a spoilsport then. In the frenzied sociability and revived political fantasies of today, he is doubly an unwelcome guest. But his work and example, like the fact of human solitude they apostrophize, can afford to be patient. Time is on their side. Time *is* their side.

January 20–26, 1982

"Les Drippings" in Paris

The Jackson Pollock Retrospective

Until late last week I was one of very few people who had seen the Jackson Pollock retrospective that was supposed to have opened January 21 in the giant's toy of a museum at the Pompidou Center, better known as Beaubourg, in Paris (February 4–April 19, 1982). The museum was closed to the public by a strike of cleaning workers, its cavernous spaces, cluttered with mustn't-touch litter, evoking a city hours before the arrival of an invading army. The union had agreed to the admittance of foreign journalists on assignment, but for appearance' sake my access was through back corridors and elevators and a staff entrance in the middle of the exhibition. Thus I entered first the show's climactic room, a high-ceilinged space 79 by 66 feet, lined with eighteen drip paintings from 1947 to 1950, fully installed and lighted, perfectly deserted. The hairs on the back of my neck saluted. I didn't breathe much.

Even after the show completes its run, I will be among only a few Americans who saw it. This knowledge makes me feel almost guilty, plus a little angry. Paris is the show's first and last stop; it will not come here. Moreover, as everyone who comments on it takes a certain shuddery enjoyment in noting, there may never be another major exhibition of these widely dispersed, increasingly fragile, hard-to-insure paintings. There is something crazy about it: that anything as important as Jackson Pollock's art should remain, for most of us, known only in glimpses and rumors. You don't "get" Pollock one, two, or three paintings—masterpieces, even—at a time. There should be a Pollock Museum, but there won't be one. So I looked hard, trying to forge my impressions into durable memories. It's so easy to forget what a Pollock—what any painting, but somehow particularly a Pollock drip— is really like. Reproductions are dry bones.

As it happens, this show does not lend itself readily to close contemplative looking. It doesn't have the immersive quality I remember from the Pollock retrospective at the Museum of Modern Art in 1967. It is didactic, masterpiece oriented, and almost coldly theatrical. One reason is the absence of works on paper—which were seen in a show that toured Europe and ended at MOMA in 1979–80. Another reason is the schematic installation, in five rooms: works of the thirties, works of the early to middle forties, the fireworks of 1947–50, the black-on-raw-canvas figurative drip paintings of 1951–52, and finally the heterogeneous last paintings. (Pollock died in 1956, at age forty-four.) Actually, there is one other room, very French: an anteroom of photographs, catalogues, and other memorabilia, with Hans Namuth's famous films of Pollock in action projected continuously on one wall. I was told that many people in cinemaniacal France know—and revere—Pollock almost strictly on the basis of these films, as a peculiar sort of movie star.

Considering the selection overall, one might miss a painting or two—especially Australia's great snarling *Blue Poles*, 1953—but for its size the show feels close to definitive. *Blue Poles* apart, Pollock's most important canvases (all from 1950) are on hand—*Autumn Rhythm* gazing across at MOMA's *One*, and *Lavender Mist* at a fifteen-footer of branching black skeins from Düsseldorf, *Number 32, 1950*. One after another, the finest Pollocks, big and less big, answer an inaudible roll call, "present" in more ways than one. Can it be their last reunion? I keep returning, with a sinking feeling, to this thought. They belong together.

Pollock thought so. He left a letter asking Lee Krasner, as his executor, to "keep the paintings as intact as possible." She hasn't, of course. Standard art-world practice being what it is, there is no surprise in the estate's lucrative dispersal; any other policy on the part of Krasner and her several advisers down through the years would have been astonishing. Gratitude is due Krasner, moreover, for the monumental catalogue raisonné of Pollock's works issued in 1979, an arduous labor of love. But some dumb, stubborn thing in me keeps insisting, against all reason, that Pollock's work belongs not only together, but also somehow *to* some entity—nation, culture, civilization, I'm not sure what—beyond the sum of its legal owners, including museums. Strangely, I do not feel anything similar about the work of any other artist. Why?

The incredible thing that happened when Pollock broke contact with the canvas, making a drawing stroke in midair that created the painting, that caused the painting to occur, has been felt and expressed in numerous ways. It was widely taken, before Vietnam-era embarrassment descended, as a nationalistic event, keynoting "the triumph of American painting." This was vulgar, feeding a national mood of imperial entitlement (born of America's domination of a war-smashed world) that has a lot to answer for. The Greenbergian idealism that explained Pollock's success in march-of-time deterministic fashion was also vulgar and also has a lot to answer for—solemn coercion to go with the solemn inanity of Harold Rosenberg's competing rhetorical fantasy, "action" painting. Then there was and is the Babel of various myth-mongers and plain gossips, from busy-bee Jungians to moralizing journalists. So much noise!

I would like Pollock's work to stay together and on constant view to make, or help, everybody shut up. Not that everybody would, but it's not so simple to be glib in the zone of silence that each truly assured Pollock generates—a zone dramatically enhanced by each additional painting. There can be little good-faith generalizing in that zone, which is defined by the precipitation of general ideas and inchoate urges into very specific form. It's not a matter of overwhelming perfection. Pollock was no Matisse, effortlessly right, and no Picasso, playing godlike with the elements of art. In bulk, you get what a close thing his greatness is, how hedged with conflicts and chances and limitations even in his moments of profligate beauty and celerity, when heart-stopping graces fall like loose change. You get, in a word, how radical he is, radically interrogating art, restlessly nagging and pushing and nudging, trying to force art to make good its promise, never made good, of some mothering absolute. Without rhetoric or irony, almost without style (or with style broken down, crudely materialized, literally flattened), he tried to call art's hand, to make it finally what the twentieth century has repeatedly demanded, in vain, that it be: secular salvation.

How do you get all that from paintings? You get it by looking, carefully and calmly, and by noticing what isn't there. I've made a list of some things that aren't there.

Gesture. The marks in a Pollock drip painting result from the movement of his hand. The marks and the movement are different things, without connection: this is what makes the marks so specific, matter-of-fact, real. It is important to sense how the marks were made, immaterial what Pollock was "feeling" when he made them.

Expressionism or mysticism. Pollock's paintings never, early or late, function as commentaries on anything or as embodiments of emotional attitude, at least not in a way that can be experienced with any direct- ness. Sincerity is never an issue. The one unvarying emotional pressure is naked ambition. As for the mythic and magic figures in Pollock's paintings before and after 1947–50, Lawrence Alloway, with that spoilsport sensibility of his that is rarely taken enough to heart, once noted what they are: clichés, fashionable commonplaces of the time's surrealist and psychoanalytic iconography. They may have been excit- ing and liberating for Pollock, but that's neither here nor there in the paintings, where they function instrumentally and neutrally.

Decoration. It seems incredible, looking at Pollock's paintings in 1982, that they could ever have been confused with decorative design, except semantically. (Wall-sized allover motifs: wallpaper.) Decoration involves spaces that are filled. A Pollock is built, an accumulation of specific decisions. Decoration doesn't engage you in thinking how it was done. A Pollock lets you think about nothing else.

Color. The only colors in Pollock that feel like themselves to me, that resonate with my remembered experience of those colors, are black and silver (aluminum). The others are just "color" of a certain tone and saturation. I include the lavender of Pollock's most sump- tuous painting, *Lavender Mist* (though undeniably something won- derful is added when you think of the name for it: "lavender"). This does not make a Pollock more drawinglike than paintinglike. Paint, not color, makes painting. Specificity again: the way the color is ex- perienced so thoroughly in terms of *how it works in the picture* that all its associations are scraped off.

Transcendence. The idealism of psycho-spiritual lift-off is, in its many forms, the fountainhead of endless modern cant. It embodies a desire that is real enough, a desire that Pollock plainly shared. But he never claimed that any such thing is made actual in his work. It isn't, and it isn't in any art work. What is actual in Pollock's best work is the closest, fiercest, most honest asking: asking for transcendence, ask- ing why transcendence cannot be. The silence of Pollock is a silence of listening for an answer, listening down into the self, out into history, everywhere. There isn't an answer. But there is the listening.

They're just paintings. This is what's so hard to get over about Pollock's work, what can make you shut up suddenly, confounded. The radical materiality, the almost stupid factuality of it—both in and beyond the felicity and the mastery—can stop you dead because of what it's about. It is the factuality of sheer human limitation, the dead end of the romantic, of desire. It's like getting to the place where the gods are supposed to be and finding nothing. A discovery like that should kill you, but it doesn't. The painting keeps being a painting, beautiful and lively and forlorn. You feel—I feel—that this might be something worth remembering and worth being true to. It gives a taste of truth that, with courage and luck, might just become a predilection, a habit of being true. It would be nice to have this art always accessible, for recovering the taste in its original sharpness, as sharp and unmistakable as tears on the tongue.

February 10–16, 1982

Cindy Sherman

Cindy Sherman's recent show of ten 2-by-4-foot color photographs (Metro Pictures, November 7–28, 1981)—of herself in the roles of various withdrawn (anxious or dreamy or stupefied) women—is the sleeper hit of the season so far, and the movie jargon is not strained. This is photography as one-frame moviemaking. The pictures feature wide-screen proportions, high-angle midshot compositions, "classy" cinematographic lighting, punched-up color, and the look of Method acting. The subtlest and most effectively cinematic element is framing that does not crop expressively, as is usual in photographs, but functions as the passive container of a complete fictionalized reality (or real fiction), a world-in-a-rectangle that addresses itself directly to the imagination. Film aesthetics seem to me far more about this kind of charged containment than about, say, motion. I have never seen anything like these pictures—including Sherman's earlier work in a similar vein, which they surpass by a wide margin.

Sherman is one of several young photographic artists who have been credited with an ideological approach to picture making, a deliberate manipulation of semiotic codes supposedly intended to reveal and undercut conventional responses. The smart skeptical line about these artists has been that they are all very well but too much the prisoners of their premises to sustain interest. As Thomas Lawson wrote in *Artforum* (October 1981), "What ambiguity there exists in the work is a given of its own inner workings, and can do little to stimulate the growth of a really troubling doubt."

That made sense to me until I saw Sherman's new pictures, which knock it into a cocked hat. Not only does this work generate "really troubling doubt" (about the way pictures affect and mean, among many other things), but it does so with beauty, wit, sensuality, and intensity—with style. There can be no getting around or explaining away such plenitude.

Part of what's prepossessing about these pictures is what they aren't: narcissistic or exhibitionistic, for instance. Much in and about them suggests both syndromes, but it is filtered through the work's stylistic intelligence. Sherman the performer is wholly obedient to Sherman the director. In herself, she has an extraordinary actress—selfless and undemanding, game for unflattering angles—and she knows how to use her acting talents as she knows how to employ those of Sherman the lighting technician, costumer, and makeup artist. The sense of, as it were, team discipline is exhilarating, incidentally making me realize how seldom this sense is met with even in superior movies. Only iron-willed auteurs like Hitchcock and Kubrick regularly have it. It's what makes the difference between entertainment value or star quality and quality, period.

Like Hitchcock or Kubrick, Sherman appears to understand that the success of a technological art, after the stage of conception, is a technical affair: realizing the idea to the practical limits of the medium. Her special insight is that this rule applies even to would-be deconstructors, unless they are content merely to signal their ideological probity to each other. Her special gift is to have a profound subject—selfhood, identity—that gives to her rivaling (and implicit criticism) of state-of-the-art moviemaking a sharp emotional focus. This is serious art because it is about something serious.

Very much unlike Hitchcock or Kubrick, Sherman takes the movie fiction of a character observed in vulnerable solitude as the departure point for an exploration, in depth, of vulnerability itself. (In the movies it's usually a narrative setup, as with Hitchcock's oblivious females: the trustingness of Teresa Wright or Janet Leigh or Tippi Hedren like a soft bull's-eye for violence.) To say that Sherman gets inside her characters is to state the simple truth. In each case, the "outside"—costume, wig, makeup, props—is a concise set of informational cues for a performance that is interior, the dream of a whole, specific life registering in a bodily and facial expression so right and eloquent—albeit blank, vacant, and absentminded—as to trigger a shock of deep recognition.

The experience is not altogether agreeable. In Sherman's new pictures the universal state of daydream or reverie is instantly recognizable, the moments of harmless, necessary psychosis that are a recurring mechanism in anyone's mental economy. These are moments when consciousness dissolves back into itself, when wish and reality, personal and collective memory are one and the physical world ceases to exist. This loss of self does not cause panic only because it is unconscious, an interlude of vagueness automatically forgotten. Sherman makes it concrete. She shows it occurring to particular women, women whose nationality, social class, lifestyle, sexual tastes, and general circumstances feel tantalizingly guessable.

The drama is in the abyss between matter and mind, object and subject. Presented with detailed evidence of both—Sherman's superb acting makes the content of her characters' heads seem almost specifiable, too—the viewer can in no way integrate them. The result may be (is for me) a disquieting sense of just how rickety and contingent a structure personality is.

So. From movie-ness to intimate, crazy recesses of the self, Sherman casts a wide net of implication. She has developed a way of using codes and techniques from popular culture to tell complex truths, which resonate back to her sources. Hers is an intensely satisfying kind of deconstruction as salvage. She builds new local structures of components scavenged from existing general ones. It is an approach that yields seemingly effortless access, for thought and feeling, to realms of cultural and individual experience usually impenetrable and intimidating and just about never addressed simultaneously. Its success depends on such an exotically idiosyncratic combination of talents that its stylistic influence is likely to be slight. If her work is rather a hybrid growth in art's garden, however, the current speed and luxuriance of that growth should quiet any doubts about its future possibilities. Sherman is onto something.

March 1982

David Salle

And now David Salle. The West Broadway three-gallery parlay—
Mary Boone I, Mary Boone II, and Castelli (March 6–31, 1982)—
hereby becomes an institution of the eighties, though it's unlikely to
be reactivated soon for anyone besides Salle or Julian Schnabel (for
whom it was inaugurated a year ago). No one else these days so dominates, at once, market demand, critical debate, and public imagination.
The opening of the Salle show was suitably auspicious. Attractive
crowds came through cold and rain to swell the occasion, and cham-
pagne came in stemware on silver trays. *People* magazine was present.
The twenty paintings were all large and spectacular, and had long
since been sold (except for two retained by the artist). Since a lot of
people are made justifiably uneasy by the self-hyping of such art-world
Events, it may be useful to establish at the outset that this show would
be an Event if catered with a box of Chiclets and held in a subway
toilet.

Salle is my personal favorite among current younger artists (he's
thirty); and that, for me, is saying a lot, because I think this is a time
of extraordinary younger artists. I like him for many reasons, some of
them so idiosyncratic, so close to my heart, that I feel obliged to mis-
trust them. For instance, Salle's unabashedly literary intelligence and
playfulness—his way of pushing around the meanings of images much
as poets push around those of words—appeal to me mightily. He
reawakens a naive, literature-drunk dream of what painting is about
that got largely chastened out of me in the formalist sixties. Not that
the poetic analogy comes close to defining his art. Omnivorous digester
of modes and styles, Salle is also a neo- or ironic formalist. In brief,
he is an artist who evokes virtual Rorschach readings of critics' pet
tendencies. Part of addressing such work is to take careful account of
one's own position among the other blind men touching the elephant.

Salle combines elements—techniques, formal devices, styles, images—from high, low, and middling pictorial sources. In this he is like

many artists today, mining both gold and dross—and structuralisti-
cally emphasizing their common features—from the mountainously
heaped remnants of modern culture, a culture which (even if, like me,
you think the term *postmodern* is gibberish) has begun to feel distanced, historical, dead. What makes a Salle show uniquely an Event
right now may be only that he combines more information more effectively than anyone else, thus threatening to gather the authority of
the whole field to himself. If just temporarily, he is a symbol of art's
future, celebrated by some and vociferously rejected by others.

Salle had a lot of academic art training as a child in Wichita,
Kansas. He went to Cal Arts in the early seventies and in the course
of getting his M.F.A. became, like almost everyone else there and
then, a conceptual artist making elegantly self-referential art gestures
in the form of videotapes, environments, and so on. He moved to New
York in 1975 and gradually worked back into painting via drawings
on canvas of academically rendered nudes and, for instance, ambiguous images from old news photographs. The principle was presentation, a cold-blooded, subversive distancing of images, revealing and
undermining the way they hook us. His innovation was to use the
formal repertoire of recent abstract painting, notably stained color
fields and diptychs, as a container-image, an image of itself, within
which his borrowed "hot" figurative images were presented like butter-
flies chloroformed and pinned in space. He complicated things further
by overlaying sharp contour drawings on fuzzy tonal ones, thus piggy-
backing images and activating contradictory types of pictorial space
simultaneously.

When I first encountered Salle's work, two or three years ago, its
vertiginous mix of blatancy ("storytelling" pictures) and elusiveness
(the "story" was impossible to figure out) made me a little sick. I was
also rattled by the frequent use of pornographically posed female
nudes. It now seems to me hardly conceivable that in his determined
excavation of the culture's most charged pictorial matter, Salle would
not have availed himself of these ritualized vehicles of male fantasy.
But it made me so nervous that I rather comically felt a surge of relief
when in last year's show Salle presented a male nude. What may have
been even more shocking was Salle's cavalierly offhand exploitation of
classically modernist pictorial devices, those sacred signs. He was using
them like cheap tools, without even the upside-down respect accorded
by satirical irony (as in Lichtenstein). I itched to dislike this stuff.

Then it started to get me. It was like a welling, congested, sentimental weepiness without an object, as emotions triggered by images
of, say, a depressed-looking girl smoking in bed and some unspecific
tragedy in a crowded street sought cathartic resolution, in vain. It was
an abstracted sensation of dislocation, yearning, and loss that started
resonating with my sense of what both art and life are like here in the
late twentieth century. Suddenly Salle's harsh artifice seemed heroic,
an earnest of authenticity—without ceasing to seem perverse, against
the grain. From talking to Salle, I conclude that the perversity arises
from his caring for his subject matter, feeling the seductive or poignant
tug of its associations. Thus the relentless objectification he practices
has a certain masochism. Fortunately, we do not require our artists to
be models of wholesome adjustment, only to give access to otherwise
inaccessible realities; and this Salle does, for me at least, in spades.

Has success affected Salle's work? Inevitably so. It wouldn't say
much for his honesty if at this point he maintained a posture of forlorn
alienation. His new work is less inward and melancholy, more calculatedly provocative and antic, than the stuff I at first resisted. The
tender qualities of his earlier painting have burned off, with the compensation of increased virtuosity, wit, and showmanship. The nearly
absolute (no-two-alike) variety of the twenty paintings here bespeaks
incredible fecundity. Salle's image scan reaches both higher and lower
than before, from particular styles of modernist abstraction—in brilliant Kelly/Albers/Noland pastiches—to creepy old sci-fi comic books.
Included are quotations from depression-era social realism (Reginald
Marsh a specialty), some frenzied "action" painting, more life-class
nudes (female and male), and schematic furniture and interiors (from
what Salle calls "the lexicon of popular good taste"). There appears to
be nothing he can't make work in a self-canceling, startling, exactly
off way. Here and there he even goes all out for sheer sensuous, glis-
tening beauty, and he gets it effortlessly, without the slightest loss of
sardonic aplomb. As usual, his titles add another layer of unassimilable
meaning, eagerly suggestive and no help at all—for example, *The Old,
the New, and the Different*.

The two main areas of the exhibition, Castelli's and the larger of
Boone's, differ distinctly in feeling. Castelli predictably favored more
elegant, subdued, relatively brooding pictures; Boone shows mostly
up-tempo, hectic, even garish ones. The former section seems a valedictory reprise of Salle's earlier manner; the latter indicates an inex-

orable development driven by what Salle knows about what he has done and how it has been received by the world. There is game playing in this development, but the game has desperate overtones. How can Salle maintain a critical, subversive edge on art conventions while enthusiastically embraced by art's conventional infrastructure? The short answer is that ultimately he can't. (The long answer is a lot of qualifications ending in the same place.) The process that will recontextualize his most violently ripped-from-context material as "Salle-ana" is in full chase. At the moment he appears to have enough energy and contrariness to stay ahead. A lazy popular opinion was that the Castelli stuff was much superior to the Boone stuff. If Salle is lucky and determined, the Boone stuff will be judged better than whatever outrages he unclenches next year. But he can't keep it up forever.

Does it matter? Can anyone, once committed, be radical indefinitely in any effective way? Every effective radical strategy may have a conservative component that emerges in time. In Salle's case, withering hyperconsciousness of painting's historically deadened condition, made manifest with painting's own tools, ends up giving painting a vitality and conviction it hasn't enjoyed in many years. Is Salle, along with other artists working in analogous ways, managing to heal the catastrophic split between painting and the avant-garde impulse that dates from the late sixties? Maybe the apparent reconciliation is a hybrid that will droop overnight. Then again, maybe time will reveal that my question is irrelevant.

March 23, 1982

Why New French Art Is Lousy

Isn't Paris the city of the self? It sure isn't the city of art anymore, or the city of liberated living or anything else that once made everybody in the world want to be an honorary Parisian. But it's still the capital of the culture of Montaigne and Rousseau, culture of practically compulsory self-absorption—self-consciousness fine-tuned and humming. Take the prettiness, the subtle playing up, the impersonal flattery of Parisian manners, so embarrassing to democratically down-mannered Americans. Never bad-mannered, Parisians when you don't count have *no* manners; you don't exist for them. To see the pretty manners, which one never wanted, pointedly withheld is the exquisite torture of Americans. We hate it. A woman I know, her serviceable French patronized all day, finally asked a snotty saleswoman, "Do you speak English?" "Why, yes." "Good. Fuck you!" Paris is still Paris.

The next to the last time I saw Paris, it was 1965 and I was a young poet and dropout ending an aimless, unhappy year there. The last time was two months ago, and I was a considerably older poet and an art critic on assignment. The city, though faster and more prosperous, seemed little changed: Paris is Paris. I felt unchanged, too—as regressive as at a family reunion on Christmas Day, the same haltingly self-conscious midwestern refugee. Only this time I had a job. I reviewed the Jackson Pollock retrospective at the Beaubourg and researched the Parisian art world, trying to keep my professional mask straight as I reeled through the beautiful, intimidating city: "Hello, I'm an art critic from New York . . ." (Start right out in English, and all educated French will answer in English automatically, before they know what they're doing.) That's worth something, not much but something, in Paris, where art people are testily but distinctly aware of their international marginality to Manhattan Island. So I met dealers, museum people, critics, and artists and saw what I could see.

The art galleries of Paris are scattered among the narrow streets near Beaubourg and the narrow streets of the Left Bank. They tend to be small and to lurk on second floors and in grim little courts, poor relations of the bookstores, restaurants, and cinemas that teem along the sidewalks. To be French is to read, eat, and go to the movies. I doubt that I saw more than three dozen viewers, total, in the twenty or so galleries I attended—photography galleries excluded, photography being catnip to the French. The relative desolation was heightened for me by the throngs in the Louvre and, for a magnificent show of French Gothic art, in the Grand Palais. It was crushing at the municipal Museum of Modern Art near the Palais de Chaillot. The major attraction there was a show of photographs of the poet Jacques Prévert and his friends. In a simultaneous exhibition of young French artists, you could hear dust settle.

The contemporary art market in Paris is a beggar. If in the United States new money tends to buy new things, in France it almost invariably buys old: School of David drawings, antiques. In visual art, to the extent that there is interest in visual art, France is an incredibly conservative country. Nobody makes any bones about this, or about the utter bias of French sensibility toward the literary. For someone formed by visually oriented New York, this tyranny of the word is as impossible to get used to as, say, the tyranny of sensation in Los Angeles. I felt it as a nagging oppression, evident as a subconscious resignation among even those whose life is art. A well-connected artist gave me his funny impression of the weekly planning meeting of critics and cultural reporters at *L'Express*. First come film and literature, and the discussion is animated and general. Philosophy follows, tossed around with slightly less intensity. Then, with fewer participants at each stage, there is talk of theater, dance, and music. Finally, in an atmosphere of snoring disregard, art is quietly discussed by the two staff critics. The one thing that gets shorter shrift is architecture, brought up only when there is to be the periodic article wondering why contemporary French architecture is so bad.

For the Parisian intelligentsia art is a sideshow or minor province of the mind. Every French writer seems to write about art at some point, but usually with high-handed presumption, as a tour de force. When not journalistic plodding, art criticism is philosophical tap dancing. Subtle, dazzling, and inexhaustible, French discourse may be the envy and model of intellectuals everywhere, but, from the standpoint of one of its occasional, minor subjects, there is something monstrous about it, like locusts. Two French art magazines, *L'Artiste* and *Art*

Press, though subject to literary deliriums, take a relatively dedicated and chastened approach. The latter's current cover, reflecting the intellectual vogue of theology in Paris these days, juxtaposes a photo of the pope delivering a blessing with one of Jackson Pollock painting, his arms spread in an analogous gesture. Cute.

Is all this ironic, given a culture that for well over a century, until World War II, harbored the most glorious painting tradition on the planet? I ventured the question to some people, and was scoffed at. The French have never liked art, I was repeatedly assured. Why do nearly all the legendary scandalized responses to modern art involve French audiences? And, of course, the twentieth-century School of Paris is in large part a foreigners' club, waning for lack of new members since foreigners started redirecting themselves across the Atlantic. Yes, but until, say, Gauguin, the genius was almost entirely native. It's obvious enough, in any case, that since the early 1940s, with the exception of Jean Dubuffet, Yves Klein, and some brief group efflorescences, Paris has been a visual-arts tank town. Parisians don't deny it—how could they?—nor do they make boosterish claims for the local product. If anything they regard their own artists with familiar condescension, which can't be too inspiring to those artists. I got plenty of chance to sample this attitude, because everybody was talking about the upcoming "French invasion" of New York.

This display of twenty-one French artists, representing twelve Parisian galleries, at fifteen New York galleries, was officially dubbed Statements New York '82. In one way just the latest in a current series (or blight) of nationalistic art manifestations, the Gallic version had some bizarre aspects, especially in view of its sponsorship by the ever-surprising Socialist government. It was funded by the ministry of foreign affairs—originally budgeted at $100,000, a figure quickly exceeded—with all sales proceeds (which would be pure profit) going to the galleries and, after their commissions, to the artists. I was especially intrigued by the extravagant gossip that attended the affair in its formative stages. This was and is my closest firsthand experience of Parisians among and about themselves, an anthropological field trip slightly beyond the pretty manners and arrogant obliviousness. Reflecting on it now, I see in my mind's eye what I want to call the look, the typical expression of my Parisian interlocutors. The look is cocked, guarded, assessing—mental wheels turning almost audibly—laced with a certain ironic avidity, an almost impersonal curiosity and casual malice. No match for that intensity of consciousness, I blinked into the birdlike brightness and sharpness of the look and scribbled in my notebook the carefully phrased dirt these people were sprinkling on each other. And on New York.

In the Parisian art world, the famous, almost voluptuous, chauvinism of the French comes out in provincial paranoia about New York, as with people telling you, a New Yorker come to look at their art, how chauvinistic—"protectionist" is the going buzzword—New York is. They speak knowingly of the Manhattan art "mafia," about which they have some startling ideas. Everybody wanted to know from me how the "German invasion" of the fall had gone over. Not very well in critical opinion, I answered. To which a prominent artist and a dealer separately said something like: "Ah yes. The Jews wouldn't stand for it." More than one Parisian art person also hazarded that New York dealers were taking a welcoming attitude toward the French with the cunning intention of justifying their prior neglect: "They want it shown," said a dealer confidingly, through his cigarette smoke, "so they can say it's all shit."

Everyone smokes, of course, seemingly two or three cigarettes at a time. I had forgotten that. As a heavy smoker, I loved it, liberated from the guilt that goes with the habit here these days. Smoking and smoking until the room stinks, everybody hurrying to light everybody else's cigarette. That and the food are two things I like about Paris, the city where the self has things its way. The self and its whims rule, and the more specific the whim, the more a matter of particular senses, the more imperious, not to be interfered with. Could this have something to do with the French coolness toward visual art? There is something stubbornly, dumbly resistant, some inhuman integrity, about a serious painting or sculpture that frustrates the usages of the self—the delectations of the decorative, the erotic, the intellectually abstruse. What the French can't enjoyably process, can't process as enjoyment, falls into a gulf of indifference. Or so it seemed to wildly generalizing, Protestant-puritan me, forlornly observing those atheist Catholics so stretched and flexed with keen indulgence. Smoking or eating, I could feel of the same species; when it came to art, as to most other things, I felt like a little green extraterrestrial.

At the rear of a dismal court near Beaubourg is the gallery of Daniel Templon, the storm center of Statements New York. Templon is a natty, tirelessly hustling little man with quick eyes behind thick glasses, a cigarette holder, and a level of raw ambition that earns him the indignant scorn of nearly everyone else in the art world. He hatched the idea of the New York adventure in the first place and exercised major sub-rosa control through close relations with Leo Castelli, opener of doors on the New York end. More than a third of the artists involved were his. The critic deemed necessary to present the shows—the *commissaire*—had originally been his ex-wife, Catherine Millet, but that hadn't worked out. The critic then chosen, Otto Hahn of *L'Express*, so detests Templon that he fastidiously avoids mentioning him by name—referring in his catalogue introduction to "a certain Parisian gallery which . . . enjoys the friendly support of a powerful colleague." The "powerful colleague" is Castelli, and in conversation with me Hahn refrained from naming him, too, calling him simply "the head of the Mafia."

I talked to Hahn, a gentle, charming man, in his house out near the end of a Metro line. His small art collection features neo-dadaist works from France's last internationally popular movement, the early sixties new realists. At one point, unprompted, he handed me a telegram I had heard rumors about, the main mini-scandal of the French invasion. It was addressed to him from Castelli and his fellow New York heavyweight Andre Emmerich, and it concluded: "UNDER CIRCUMSTANCES WE BOTH WISH TO DISASSOCIATE OURSELVES FROM THIS PROJECT UNLESS REMEDIAL ACTION TAKEN PROMPTLY." The circumstances were that late in the planning an artist named François Martin had been rather offhandedly included by a foreign affairs ministry official, and a little-known New York gallery, Schlesinger-Boisanté, had been added to accommodate him—all without consulting Castelli. The remedial action, taken promptly, was the ousting of this artist and gallery. The peremptory knuckle-rapping telegram seemed to traumatize Hahn and others in Paris. Already beholden to the New York commercial establishment—as to their one-man local equivalent, Templon—they were now being bullied by it, and they had no choice except to cave in.

Castelli's brand of hardball—justified from his point of view by a desire to protect the luster of an event to which he had lent his name, influence, and three gallery spaces—was an exotic experience for Parisians, who do not countenance backchat from their own cultural tradesmen. Anti-commercialism is a settled first principle of French ideologies of both the Right and the Left. Indeed, the same person can seem to harbor animus against the commercial from contradictory impulses: reflexive leftist abhorrence of capitalist self-interest plus reflexive aristocratic disdain for capitalist presumption. You needn't visit France to know all this, but it takes on a peculiar perspective there, far from the Mammon-dominated American art world. There, where dealers are low on the totem pole (and collectors practically don't exist), the voice of distaste for the power of money is, as often as not, the voice of power. Cultural power in France is almost strictly institutional, creating an atmosphere as culture-shocking to me as Castelli's telegram was to Otto Hahn.

I ate a wonderful dinner in Paris with Daniel Buren and a mutual friend. Buren, France's one current international art star, is known for his temporary installations of vertical-stripe designs. He was not in Statements New York. He said he would have participated if given a nongallery space, but this was refused. Happy, prosperous, and shrewd, Buren surprised me. I guess I was expecting a hard-bitten ideologue, Marxist critics having made a lot of his particular anticommercial stance. But in fact Buren has made an excellent career of introducing his mildly disruptive stripes into museums and other institutions in Europe and America. If anything, he is a supremely adapted realist in a culture where the significant money and opportunity for art are public rather than private. To oppose the ragamuffin commercial art scene in France is hardly to be at the barricades. On the contrary, such opposition is establishmentarian. Buren's "subversion" of "object art" is made-to-order for curators and other functionaries for whom any relation to the market is a bad smell.

I failed to reach Jack Lang, Mitterrand's minister of culture, in Paris but caught up to him in New York at a cheerful, fulsomely high-minded press conference he gave in connection with Statements New York. We American reporters were interested in dollar breakdowns of France's stupefying billion-dollar budget for culture (due to go even higher next year). Lang, a dashing regional-theater man, waved off these questions: numbers are "too boring," he protested. As if interminable hot air about the "role of spirit, imagination, and intelligence" in resolving the "general crisis" were *That's Entertainment III*. Lang's vision for civilization might be called bureaucracy with a happy face. His afflatus knew no bounds, including those of political plausibility. Asked why a Socialist government was supporting private galleries, he pronounced: "We believe in competition, the spirit of creation, and enterprise. The state now reassumes its traditional role in supporting the arts. We say the private sector should, too." Meaning that the private sector has been malingering? Lang repeatedly seemed to suggest that if all the butchers, bakers, and candlestick makers could share the crusading enlightenment of Mitterrand, Renaissance would be now. Disconcertingly, he also repeatedly slipped into the language of a hard-bargaining trade minister. "If you welcome our artists," he concluded with veiled threat, "we'll welcome yours."

He is talking about art here. Or is he? What with the tyrannies of self, word, and ideology, art is rarely at the center of discourses that bandy its name in France. Art generally feels beside the point. This was certainly the case when the French invasion landed in New York. The point of Statements New York—the very title reeks of it—was heavy, smarmy diplomacy. An air of unreality sprang from its all-around, interest-serving pragmatism: for the French government, flogging the national culture; for the Parisian galleries, trying to open up their stagnant market; for the New York galleries, getting the free ride of all-expense-paid shows; for an enterprising distributor of an unfamiliar French cognac, the promotion of donating cases of the stuff to the openings; for the artists . . . One younger painter spoke of showing in New York as "a consecration." Good luck. Others, paranoically braced for hostility, were ecstatic about the social warmth of their reception; I could have told them that this was not necessarily a favorable sign of their art's impact, but I didn't. The older and wiser were stoical. Martial Raysse, unshown in New York since 1970, shrugged: "I had no choice."

This was indeed a party no French artist could afford to miss. Some inevitably did, but based on what I saw in the galleries of Paris, the twenty-one exported artists were pretty much the cream of French artists in mid-career—not, as some New York critics charitably assumed, a cross section. The test being more than fair, the results were all the more disheartening. Even with contextual distractions factored out, I found about a half-dozen of the artists interesting and just one strongly to my liking: Raysse, who showed at Janis. A proponent of the delectable, rather chichi, French variant of pop art in the sixties, Raysse evidently underwent a career crisis at the end of that decade. He ended up in his native south of France, where he has developed an eccentric but peculiarly satisfying kind of small painting—imaginary landscapes floating like clouds or thought balloons in white grounds—that has straightforward mythic content; sweet, intense color; and a calm, melancholy eroticism that I want to call Mediterranean, meaning some mysterious emulsion of Grecian timelessness and Riviera pleasures. The modest concentration of Raysse's new work makes me aware of how crippled much other French art is by an arch straining for effects dictated by tyrant word or tyrant tastefulness.

Through the mid-seventies, French painting was dominated by the theoretical activity of the so-called Support/Surface school, a come-lately version of reductive formalism with structuralist and (somehow) Marxist elements. Led by the critic Marcelin Pleynet, who has since gone Lacanian, this coterie poured out enormous dense texts about simple, generally agreeable abstract paintings. It seems to have been about how to make a painting that was historically justified après Mondrian, Pollock, et al. The emphasis on procedure made a hero of, for instance, Simon Hantai, who crumples canvas, paints on it, then stretches it back out. What I saw of his work in Paris and at Emmerich here struck me as resoundingly feeble. Better was Claude Viallat, who spreads allover patterns of sensitively brushed lozenge shapes, in ardent colors, on various surfaces. His show at Castelli's Greene Street space included works on pieces of tent canvas and on one whole huge tent. It has stayed with me as an instance of what's most lovable in post–School of Paris French art—the aesthetic delirium of Dubuffet and Klein, that kind of cover-the-earth expansion of the art-making gesture. (It's as if only crazy compulsiveness can throttle nattering French rationality.) Viallat's style is one-note, however—like Buren's stripes.

Then there were the youngsters, in their early twenties, of a budding little French New Wave shepherded by Bernard Lamarche-Vadel, the editor of *L'Artiste*. The most prominent are Robert Combas and Rémy Blanchard, who, with adjustments made for the provincial scale of Paris, might be called the French Schnabel and Salle. Like the latter, they are new-figurative painters who upset conventional applecarts and make fruit salads of the spillage, willfully combining techniques and images from various cultural sources. Though still drastically limited in both reach and grasp, Combas's insolent big-scale cartooning and Blanchard's shiny, drippy, coarsely framed versions of German hunting-lodge motifs are lively, open to international suggestion, and, in context, refreshingly controversial. (More traditional avant-gardists in Paris despise them.) They and their young friends were fun at their

Holly Solomon opening, mildly punky looking, dazzled by New York, and bursting with pride. At a French embassy party later, Holly, giggling, was introducing them as "my boys": "Say hello, boys"; "Say goodnight, boys." They grinned. However, they showed a depressing and ominous alacrity, when asked about their work, in reeling off stale theoretical justifications and lists of influences they were supposedly synthesizing. The tyranny of the word, again. Coming from those fresh young faces, it sounded horrible. Shut up, boys.

Even had the art in it been far better than it was, Statements New York would have left behind what it did: an impression of leaden dutifulness. I conclude, with hope of being contradicted by future developments, that between Jesuitical ideology and smother-loving bureaucracy, blind word and blinkered self, art doesn't stand a chance in that country. Not that it should. Why should anyone care either way? Artistic anemia may even be a price paid for a kind of perfection: Paris the city of surfaces, manners, styles; of all sorts of exclusions; of perfected "outsides"—city of walls. When I close my eyes and think "Paris"—recalling the disembodied, hallucinated state I get into there—I see the walls and the colors of the walls. How many gradations of gray and brown and gray-brown are possible in a three-cornered matrix of nearly yellow, nearly pearl gray, and nearly black? How many more are there when you factor in the variable sunlight filtered by clouds and moist atmosphere, on a scale from crepuscular murk to yellow-white fire? Lost and dissipated—evaporated—in the alien state, I seem to get myself back through my eyes, condensed in the light-soaked, infinite subtleties of those surfaces. Well, you can get mentally fucked up anywhere, I suppose, but only in Paris is there the spiritual safety net of those old, old walls.

The ritualized cant of nationalist or otherwise provincial pretension makes a lack of art painful, by denying it. It's as if having art, like having a nuclear strike force, were indispensable to collective self-love, but art doesn't come to order in that way. You may have to care much, much more about art than about, say, your nation if your art is going to amount to anything. Art that works, that makes a difference, is still and always a matter of the alien, the exception, the not easily assimilated, the alternative reality. The more I travel, the more I'm struck by what a fluke, almost a freak, New York is, as a place where a significant number of people simply happen to care about art—art for, yes, art's sake—at once seriously and sociably, as a matter of course.

It doesn't make them politically or intellectually or in any other way reliable or admirable; it doesn't make them good citizens. Maybe the contrary. In Paris or Los Angeles, in what can be called with complete accuracy the art provinces, I know I feel a little foolish for caring so much, a little decidedly uncool. And I can't wait to be home again among my brother and sister art fools.

April 6, 1982

Willem de Kooning

In 1968, Willem de Kooning had a retrospective at the Museum of Modern Art that confirmed both his greatness and, it appeared at the time, his marginality to contemporary art. Even fervent de Kooning fans like me had to concede the latter. The show followed by one year a Jackson Pollock retrospective that didn't look a bit marginal, seeming full of links and challenges to contemporary developments in minimal, postminimal, and color-field art. Compared with Pollock's radical materiality and alloverness, de Kooning's attachment to virtuosic brushwork and cubist space looked conservative; and the cult of his creative personality, which had enfevered a whole generation of artists in the late fifties, seemed corny. Finally, there was evidence that in the preceding eight or so years de Kooning's inspiration had faltered, adding few ornaments to his established glory.

However, there were some little-noted suggestions of newly stirring energies, especially in de Kooning's drawings—which he was doing in large numbers, often with his eyes closed, in a determined attack on his own signature habits. There was also a concurrent show of new "abstract landscapes" at Knoedler that carried some of the anarchic energy of the drawings over into singing flesh-colored painting. But the fashion of the time had its cap set in another direction, and there was an unspoken sense that de Kooning could safely be pensioned off with the other surviving abstract expressionists, as a genius emeritus. So no one was prepared for the amazing, almost embarrassingly grand, development of his work since then, each succeeding show as flustering as that of a hot young newcomer. De Kooning, who will be seventy-eight this month, has steadily been turning out—as if it were easy or as if he had nothing better to do with his sunset years—some of the freshest, wildest paintings anyone ever saw.

De Kooning's new show at Fourcade (March 17–May 1, 1982) of nine paintings from 1980 to 1981 seems even more than usually a magnificent affront to reasonable expectations. It has given me more concentrated aesthetic pleasure than any other gallery show this season, and this has been a season of terrific gallery shows. The paintings are complicated, violently self-contradictory, mockingly perverse. At first glance, they may look, repellently, both harsh and muffled. The harshness is an effect of evil color and seasick composition; the muffle results from a general scraping off of paint in the pictures' final stages, reducing many layers of work to a thin, often glossy film. (De Kooning has always scraped his paintings down while working on them, to keep the surface manageable; rarely before has he left them that way.) Flattened, his repertoire of brushstrokes becomes a graphic image of itself, queasily disembodied.

Unlike other recent de Koonings, these don't appear caught in the act of tearing themselves apart. Even the big seven-foot ones feel a bit like drawings waiting for mats. But this static, contained quality has nothing to do with tameness or serenity. The drama may be muted, but it is thereby all the more intimate and insinuating. The paintings start working for the viewer when the viewer starts working with them: getting close-up information, backing up to integrate it, getting more close-up information, and so forth. Once that process is begun, it's off to the races.

What does it mean to work in "cubist space"? It means maintaining an illusion of continuous shallow depth which each pictorial element appears to bite into or poke out of. This commonly entails keeping all elements fairly similar in scale, touch, and so on. De Kooning has always played fast and loose with such canons of orderliness, but over the past fifteen years, and preeminently in this show, he has smashed every formal consistency except overall surface texture. Thus tiny things presume to "balance" huge things, amorphous to offset sharp, wide-open to answer dense—and somehow in the consequent chaos, the composition by hand grenade, this comes to pass. Everything looks eager to fly off, to be free of its unspeakable neighbors, but the canvas is a sealed arena. There is a spiraling energy as the parties to this pictorial brawl, without losing their irritability, gradually reveal themselves to be dancing.

The secret, if that's what it is, seems to be the utter aggressive particularity of each element, each piece, of the picture. There are isolated passages, set off in the pictorial equivalent of quotation marks, that have a stylistic emphasis found only in really terrible painting— in the Washington Square Art Show, in Paul Jenkins. These include palette-knife rainbows, little brush frenzies, all manner of things yearning to be called sensitive or sensual or otherwise meaningful. The paintings take time because it takes time to make emotional connection to these poignant and clownish components—then to see how they work in the rioting whole, which starts rioting only after you've been looking for a while.

Kenneth Clark has opined that you can't enjoy a pure aesthetic sensation for longer than you can enjoy the smell of an orange. Maybe so, but when art is as technically and formally inexhaustible, as multivalent, as these new de Koonings, the sensation keeps renewing itself like a self-winding watch and enjoyment goes on and on. This can spark an unsettling conflict between one's values, which may uphold such pleasures in principle, and one's habitual uses for art—like being in an orgy and suddenly suspecting that all you really wanted was a nice friendly hug. There is nothing friendly about these paintings and their grueling ecstasies.

As usual with de Kooning, the handling is wet-in-wet—high-keyed color worked with lots of white paint, which keeps things lively and advancing. There are screechy yellows, electric blues, boudoir pinks, and—as painter friends assure me—two of the most ungovernable hues in the painter's kit: alizarin crimson and thallo green. These are dyelike synthetic pigments, transparent like nail polish and viciously intense. They affect other colors the way garbage cans kicked downstairs would affect chamber music. They give the Dutchman no great difficulty. Two paintings on Fourcade's ground floor could be called "Who's Afraid of Alizarin Crimson and Thallo Green?" One employs heaps of the crimson in a primary triad with more ordinary yellow and blue, the other uses the green with its secondary mates, orange and purple. The supporting colors are present in such sparing quantities that you may overlook them. But they make for subliminal chords, wisps of harmony threaded into the barbaric clangor.

The paintings on Fourcade's second floor are like palimpsests of de Kooning's career, representing simultaneously the full variety of his famous stroke, from thinnest line to broadest smear. He has reached back to his own work of thirty-five and forty years ago—and to that of Arshile Gorky and Matta (who else? Jean Hélion?)—for some of the shapes and overlaid or scored linear figures that appear in these stilled maelstroms. (Two startling very recent paintings I got to see in the gallery's back room take the archaeology even farther, suggesting revamped, late-thirties hybrids of synthetic cubism and biomorphic surrealism.) But the incredibly fluid stroking of his post-sixties work dominates. There are great droopy swaths, like clothes blowing on a line; abruptly wobbling ones, as if something had bumped his arm in mid-gesture; bodiless contours, hinting at absent Women; and rushing blurs that wittily stop or start on a dime.

I've been harping on the necessity of cooperating with these pictures because we live in a quick-take era. Most of us have lost, if we ever had, the habit of delectation, for the good reason that so little today either demands or merits it. We may have trouble crediting the very possibility of such pleasure as de Kooning offers, the pleasure of a contemplative journey that has been anticipated—that is met with a Cheshire smile—at every turn. Again, the experience is not cozy. It's almost insulting how smart these paintings are. Like master criminals tweaking an addled detective, they hide in plain sight.

A sign of our culture's embarrassment about old age is that we go all gooey when an old person does something with spunk. It's a way of protecting ourselves from the knowledge that we and the old are the same species, alive in the same instant of time, responsible to the same gods. I love de Kooning for making any such sentimentality inconceivable in his case. Aging has touched his art with, if anything, even greater audacity and more resonant defiance, giving new edges to a mastery of painting's resources that remains a wonder of the world.

April 13, 1982

Robert Smithson's Writings

The Writings of Robert Smithson (Edited by Nancy Holt. New York: New York University Press, 1979) is the most significant book of American contemporary art writing in twenty years. It was published in 1979 and soon sold out its edition. In the glacial way of university presses, NYU has gotten around to a reprinting, but the book was gone from the shelves for what seemed like forever. The hiatus was vexing yet eerily characteristic—Smithsonesque. It produced a sense of dislocation, of mild disaster, in the art-cultural mindscape that the poet of entropy, time-death, and universal forgetfulness might even have enjoyed. Be that as it may, we must, now that it's back, try to keep this darkly dazzling book from again slipping away. Oblivion can wait.

Robert Smithson died at age thirty-five in a 1973 plane crash while directing aerial photography of his last earthwork, *Amarillo Ramp*. How much had been lost was unclear at the time. Smithson's visual art was just getting on track, becoming strong and satisfying after years of purposeful but wildly problematic experiment. Recent museum and gallery retrospectives have confirmed that as a sculptor Smithson lagged behind his own conceptual and poetic powers, creating eclectic, awkward work that seemed more overwhelmed than informed by his ideas. Only in some marvelously suggestive drawings—and ultimately in his two or three best earthworks—did his grasp begin to match his reach. But that reach, apparent in the trajectories and swirling figures of his prose, already constituted an achievement of real grandeur, though few people knew it until this book brought together his scattered writings.

I didn't know it. A dazed newcomer to the art world of the late sixties, I couldn't make head or tail of Smithson's dense, sarcastic, rapturous articles in *Artforum* and *Arts* magazines. I failed to understand the arcane ideological jousting in which Smithson was the Black Knight of minimalism—polemicist for Judd, LeWitt, Morris, Flavin, and Andre, among others—versus the forces of Greenbergian formalism, whose champion was Michael Fried. (In his introduction to the book, former *Artforum* editor Philip Leider puts Smithson in the context of this historic gang war.) Smithson in person intimidated me, and I resented it. I would see him at his front table in Max's and reflect defensively that there was something seedy and dubious—something reminiscent of the guys in high school who carried slide rules—about him, with his bad skin, glasses, and nervous smirk. He would be talking and talking, and I never went near enough to hear the words. So his words, when finally I encountered them in book form, were a big retroactive shock.

It is not possible to summarize Smithson's thought, because his thinking was determinedly "dialectical," self-contradictory, kaleidoscopic. He was fascinated not so much by ideas as by the way ideas break down in the vicinity of ultimate questions, cosmic perspectives, sublimities of doubt. With awful satisfaction, he contemplated the operations of the "death principle"—entropy, the inexorable slide toward energy extinction spelled out in the second law of thermodynamics—everywhere, in everything. He was an unflinching metaphysical dandy, an avatar of Baudelairean "terror and delight" in the age of the hydrogen bomb and the suburbs. He made "archaeological expeditions into the recent past" in the suburbs, where, he wrote, "reality dissolves into leaden and incessant lattices of solid diminution." He loved construction sites: "ruins in reverse." His favorite museum was the Museum of Natural History. He hated the "life-forcing" cant of liberal humanism. But to say these things, to say anything, about Smithson is to be aware of something opposite. Weirdly interlaced with his near nihilism, for instance, was an unkillable democratic American optimism.

Whitmanesque, slightly. (Or Whitman heavily laced with Poe.) Like Whitman, Smithson was a New Jersey boy and a self-willed, self-sophisticated ragamuffin. He was born in Passaic and grew up in Rutherford and Clifton. William Carlos Williams was his baby doctor. He was an isolated only child, given to collecting fossils and live reptiles. He did not attend college but got an education on the road, which took him to Mexico, and in the New York art world. He was a hipster-polymath, imbiber of high-proof cultural potions: Anglo-American modernism (Eliot, Pound, Lewis, Hulme), the Beats (including his friend Hubert Selby, Jr.), Freud and Jung, ancient civilizations, skimmings of science and philosophy, science-fiction novels and movies, *Mad* magazine, and the conversational academy of the 10th Street, Cedar Bar scene. Was he, at times, a bullshitter? That came with the territory. By the mid-sixties he knew the ins and outs of New York weltanschauung, New York zeitgeist, as rats know sewer systems. In brief, he was cut out for a brilliant career.

He was a member of and the spokesman for a fitfully brilliant generation, the hard-nosed, hubristic wave of (male) artists who took over the vanguard—or the "paradigmatic," to use a buzzword typical of Smithson at his most tendentious—in the newly expanded and savagely competitive sixties art world. A great intuition of this generation, with which they roared past the genteel followers of Greenberg, was to combine modernist high seriousness and rigor with demotic impulses, with a redolence of the wider culture and a protopolitical response to it. In Smithson's stunning 1966 survey/send-off of his peers, "Entropy and the New Monuments" (monuments that instead "of causing us to remember the past . . . seem to cause us to forget the future"), they appear as a race of dangerous electric-brained midnight rebels less likely to be found at a museum opening than in a 42nd Street movie theater:

> The movies give a ritual pattern to the lives of many artists, and this induces a kind of "low-budget" mysticism, which keeps them in a perpetual trance. The "blood and guts" of horror movies provides for their "organic needs," while the "cold steel" of Sci-fic movies provides for their "inorganic needs." Serious movies are too heavy on "values," and so are dismissed by the more perceptive artists. Such artists have X-ray eyes, and can see through all of that cloddish substance that passes for "the deep and profound" these days.

In hindsight it is easy to say that few of the artists Smithson thus heralded (a couple of dozen in the essay at hand) were up to the mythic scale he evoked, as it is easy to say that his writing at the time was better than his sculpture. But then, Smithson's writing at its best was better—more inspiring—than practically anything. Later in this roller coaster of an essay, he arrives by way of Buckminster Fuller and Lewis Carroll at a practical way of relating geometric sculpture to the fourth dimension (defined as "ha-ha") in terms of "laughter and crystal-structure":

the ordinary laugh is cubic or square (Isometric), the chuckle is a triangle or pyramid (Tetragonal), the giggle is a hexagon or rhomboid (Hexagonal), the titter is prismatic (Orthorhombic), the snicker is oblique (Monoclinic), the guffaw is asymmetric (Triclinic). To be sure this definition only scratches the surface.

That passage is typical of Smithson's humor, a humor-about-humor not so much funny as ecstatically cracked—a "mournful giddiness" (in his phrase) that acts as a safety valve for his irritability.

Smithson was irritable because so ambitious. Ambition for art and artists (only incidentally including himself) was behind his intellectual destructiveness, his pulverizing attack on existing values. Only the sufficiently wrecked or debased seemed to strike him as ready for transformation into a complete new art, an art that would necessarily disregard the confining structures of the art world and the museum and would engage all space and time. Earthworks resulted: instant sacred sites of a quasi-religion based in calm, rapt meditation on the direct implications of modern science and philosophy. As Carter Ratcliff has noted, the sighting of this horizon of possibility seemed to free something in Smithson, something positive and visionary. He got practical, not only in engineering his own earthworks but in sketching a whole new approach to the modern problems of landscape and ecology—for instance, a nonnostalgic aesthetic for the reclamation of strip mines. In a wonderful and tantalizing late essay, "Frederick Law Olmsted and the Dialectical Landscape," he set off on a train of thought that seems certain to have led to great things, had he lived.

I must confess that the maturing, public-spirited Smithson excites my imagination less than the younger, demonic Smithson, maybe because the cultural despair that drove the latter has proved more durable than the cultural hopes that drew the former on. The disintegration of values that Smithson at first identified with and even celebrated—trying thereby to bring it under the control of sensibility—continues apace, with no end (except The End) in sight. By contrast, the notion that artists, given sufficient independence and authority, can ameliorate the human lot has grown emptier and emptier since Smithson's death, providing a new roost for conventional sentiments and a virtuous sideshow for governmental and corporate bureaucracies, the Mothers Bountiful of so-called public art. To Smithson as a partly reconciled consultant of mining firms, I thus prefer Smithson the author of "A

Tour of the Monuments of Passaic, New Jersey" (1967), his wittiest essay. The "monuments" include a parking lot and a sandbox, viewed as concretions and extinctions of infinity and eternity. "Time turns metaphors into things, and stacks them up in cold rooms, or places them in the celestial playgrounds of the suburbs." Smithson had, you could say, a nose for the abyss.

Nothing in this book is to be confused with "good writing," except by way of conscious parody. Smithson was fantastically talented with words, but his use of them is high-handed and self-subverting:

> In the illusory babels of language, an artist might advance specifically to get lost, and to intoxicate himself in dizzying syntaxes, seeking odd intersections of meaning, strange corridors of history, unexpected echoes, unknown humors, or voids of knowledge . . . at the end, if there is an end, are perhaps only meaningless reverberations.

Language as a hallucinogenic drug. Smithson's style or antistyle obviously has a pedigree in modernist literature, in Nabokov and Borges, Joyce and Burroughs. What makes his writing unique—almost freeing it from the whammy of being "literature" at all—is the specific matrix of art works and art criticism that contains it and gives it bite. There is something remarkably unalienated about Smithson even at his most sardonic, because his coruscating skepticism leads always into the practice of art, into the world.

Smithson was prophetic. He was already using the word *postmodern* in the early seventies. Furthermore, he seemed to know what it meant, to have a theoretical grip on it—in his concept of time as a "crystalline" structure (where "remote futures meet remote pasts"), as opposed to the old (modern) "organic" structure (linear history). He more or less predicted the movement toward pluralism in art—whether as a wholesome growth of democracy or as entropic dedifferentiation isn't clear. That he did not anticipate the recent resurgence of painting and figurative imagery should be enough to make supporters of that resurgence, like me, nervous. Smithson had such a convincing sense of the future that even someone inhabiting that future hesitates to disagree with him. (Greenberg used to have this effect, too.) If he missed anything important, thus leaving the future something to play with, it was the erotic, which he never addressed except in occasional equivocal allusions to sadomasochism (horror movies as satisfiers of "organic needs"!).

The strangest flavor in Smithson is a Keatsian passivity, a voluptuous exhaustion, entropy at the scale of the emotions. "At this stage," he could write, "lethargy is elevated to the most glorious magnitude." He loved the mirror, which "contains everything." There are passages of his writing where you can almost believe that he is sinking through reverie toward sleep, muttering. His ideas have the dream quality of being at once forthright and irresponsible, meaning unfazed—untouched, really—by any rational objection. In a man of such intellectual energy and tenacity, this incessant mental swooning unnerves and exhilarates. It is also incredibly seductive: a disembodied voice insinuating blissful rest in "tired distances." The movement of Smithson's imagination, like the favorite shape of his sculpture, is a spiral: indirectly but inexorably in. The movement is rapturous, abandoned, hilarious: laughter in a void that begins to feel like paradise.

The Writings of Robert Smithson is a book of, at least, art criticism, poetry, autobiography (it includes several informative interviews), aesthetics, social theory, and religion. Its oddness and complexity make it slippery, so special that I can't imagine anybody ever assigning it to a class: what could they possibly "discuss"? I keep expecting, fearfully, to see it disappear from the bookstores again, lost through the cracks in our categorical thinking. Even unread, however, it may be a book that exerts an incessant subliminal pressure on the collective imagination. Fashions may rise to cover it, as the Great Salt Lake reportedly has risen to cover *The Spiral Jetty*, but like *The Spiral Jetty* it is there. And because it is there, nothing else can ever be the same.

June 1982

Documenta 7

Documenta, the world's mightiest contemporary art show, comes but once every five years. Funded to the tune of $3 million by the regional government of its host city, Kassel, West Germany, the newly opened seventh Documenta (Summer 1982) features over a thousand art works by about 180 artists from 21 countries, mainly the U.S. (52), Germany (41), and Italy (26). (There are just 25 women, 10 of them American.) It is mounted in three big rebuilt (because destroyed during World War II) eighteenth- and nineteenth-century buildings and on the surrounding grounds. At the two-day press opening, a thousand press passes were in use, and artists, dealers, museum folk, and other interested parties were everywhere. The scale of the thing is awesome.

The tenor of the thing is truculently modernist-conservative this year. The American and European minimal/conceptual generations of the late sixties and early seventies are favored, as is, to a lesser extent, the older group of prominent German painters (Baselitz, Lupertz, Penck, Polke, Richter). Younger painters are largely shoved to the peripheries. "Tradition" is approvingly, even fulsomely, evoked; the huge catalogue even leads off with T. S. Eliot's war-horse modernist tract of 1919, "Tradition and the Individual Talent." Site-specific extravagances by institutional favorites Joseph Beuys, Daniel Buren, and Lawrence Weiner dominate the grounds of the show's main building. You quickly grasp that youth and change are not to be the bywords here.

Briefly put, Documenta 7 is about the muscle-flexing and self-congratulation of a curatorial elite. In Europe, unlike the market-influenced U.S., publicly funded institutions have the mediation of art culture in their pocket. Curators there are not kingmakers but kings; and in Documenta director Rudi Fuchs, a forty-year-old staggeringly arrogant Dutchman, this system has a perfect little Metternich. Fuchs seems intent on stabilizing the international art situation for the security of its reigning heads, versus the bugbears of commercialism, nationalism, populism, feminism, and other barbaric forces (euphemized by him as "diverse pressures and social perversions"). This determination has involved him in an approach that could be called disciplinary in the punitive as well as the professional sense. To spend some days exploring this show is to get a lesson in the workings and uses of majesty.

The relation between words and deeds in Documenta is so slippery that it takes time to register. In his catalogue introduction, Fuchs promises "order," "dignity," and "tranquility"; in an earlier, notoriously self-dramatizing, letter to the invited artists, he rhapsodized about "the soft sounds of Apollo's lyre. Art is gentle and discreet, she aims for depth and passion, clarity and warmth." So that art's frail sweetness might prevail, Fuchs decreed "that the structure of the exhibition must be one of combination and encounter," meaning that works by individual artists are spotted throughout the show in combination with those of other artists. Far from letting the art speak for itself, of course, this tactic promotes a melee of abrasions, non sequiturs, and rebuslike puzzles. The result is utter coercive subordination of "individual talent" to fantasized "traditions" and a curatorial whim of iron.

Only a few artists come off at all well, usually by dint of a relatively compact and isolated hanging. Most are simply mugged by the installation of their work. This is certainly true for the younger American painters represented—all six of them, including Brett de Palma and Judy Rifka but not including Susan Rothenberg and Julian Schnabel, who incredibly were not invited (in protest, it was said, against their commercial success). The echoing absence of Schnabel in particular is one of the two big individual stories of this Documenta. The other is the triumph of Anselm Kiefer, the best painter in Germany and maybe the best, period. Kiefer's vast encrusted, mythologically resonant landscapes effortlessly survive internecine "combination and encounter" with, among others, Richard Long and Andy Warhol, projecting a mastery and a power of reference that make them, for me, the show's emotional hub.

New U.S. art is generally limited to the semiotical picture making and media manipulation that can most readily be accommodated to a continuing minimal/conceptual "tradition." Thus Dara Birnbaum, Troy Brauntuch, Jack Goldstein, Keith Haring, Jenny Holzer, Barbara Kruger, Sherrie Levine, Robert Longo, Matt Mullican, Cindy Sherman, and Jeff Wall are on hand—often to strong effect, considering the withering circumstances. As she has been doing with monotonous regularity lately, Sherman makes the biggest splash, with some new confrontational, grimly unglamorous color photos of herself that yield roughly the experience of a live wire grasped bare-handed.

The exclusion or belittling of Italian and American painters—the works of Sandro Chia and Francesco Clemente are wretchedly displayed, as are David Salle's—contributes to an impression of thorough German dominance in the category. Kiefer, of course, needs no such deck stacking in his favor, and Sigmar Polke, Gerhard Richter, and A. R. Penck require only decent installation—which they get—to establish their excellence. Many of the other Germans would at least hold their own in a fairer match. So this aspect of the show came across less as defensive than as just petty.

As for the installational (i.e., "traditional") work that constitutes the official court art of Fuch's peaceable kingdom—Andre, Beuys, Buren, Graham, Haacke, Kosuth, Kounellis, Le Va, LeWitt, Long, Merz, Nauman, Oldenburg, Orr, Penone, Pistoletto, Ryman, Serra, Tuttle, Weiner, the familiar names reel on and on—much of it is good, but the cumulative effect is self-canceling and stupefying. What is this stuff about? What is it for? Locked in an institutional embrace, can it express anything significant anymore except that embrace? What possibilities of development remain for it that are not mere academic frills and finesses? For all the grandeur of its presentation in Kassel, Fuchs's "tradition" appears vulnerable from any distance: the cruiser *Belgrano* of late twentieth-century culture.

The real juice of Documenta 7, becoming stronger in my memory as my visit recedes (and the dramatically displayed minimal/conceptual big names mostly fade into grayness), is its evidence of the new vitality of German culture, particularly in painting but with a percolation of energies not to be contained in any one area. I'm not talking about lots of Germans here. The main figure is that man from the Black Forest, Anselm Kiefer, with his historical/poetic landscapes, supported (in my fantasy credit reel) by ironic abstractionists Sigmar Polke and Gerhard Richter. A host of Germans do fill walk-on and spear-carrier roles. Costarring Joseph Beuys as Yorick's Skull.

Kiefer, thirty-seven, may be the first artist since the years of the great darkness to make being German seem like a good idea. It is precisely from wells of old German darkness that he hoists his bucket, and the fluids are rich and pungent. His themes are history, myth, and landscape, coexisting in a medium of encrusted shit-colored heart-grabbing painting with attached objects and scribbled words. "The Earth still trembles from the footsteps of fleeing giants," goes (in translation) a tag from Victor Hugo he often uses; and standing in front of the work, I feel it to be true, as if the reverberation of ancient catastrophe were coming right up through the floor.

Kiefer seems to expect trust. If he is a humanist—and I think he is, in some lost capacious sense of the term—it is without any reassuring sentiment or piety, even without the lifeline of irony. A twenty-foot painting in oil and sand features the German names of places that don't have those names anymore, having been annexed to Poland after World War II. Is the artist affirming or mourning that well-deserved national loss? Neither, or both. In whatever case, he is springing the locks on one after another historical and archetypal yearning and terror, reawakening a dream of art's ability to redeem the unbearableness of the world and even, like Margarete's golden hair (yellow straw in his paintings), to hold out last-ditch personal salvations.

Kiefer is, shall we say, heavy. Lighter and more comfortingly civilized in their sardonic ways, Polke and Richter are virtuosos whose abstractions-as-images-of-themselves strike a transatlantic chord with the best New York stylists (a connection that the show suppresses). Thematically heavy while given to flimsy hysterical postures, the feckless young degenerates of mostly Berlin-based "Wild Painting" provide a lively, screechy background din. Add filmmaker Hans Jürgen Syberberg, represented by the screening of his version of Wagner's *Parsifal* (which I missed) and by a stunning, wildly theatrical, basement grotto of Teutonic props, including the derisive Hitler puppet from *Our Hitler*, and the complicated smokiness of Germanic revival becomes unmistakable.

It's startling without being, for me anyway, disquieting. (I was spooked only by the Frenchman Daniel Buren's vaguely martial outdoor environment of fluttering pennants, with loudspeakers emitting classical music; to hear Wagner over loudspeakers in Germany is to have something icy and mad toy with your vitals.) One element of reassurance is the omnipresent Beuys, an immensely effective clown-shaman in German politics and culture. He is a licensed baiter of authority—upstaging the bigwigs at the opening press conference in elegant slapstick fashion by extolling an ornate crown as a symbol of power and placing it before Fuchs and others on the dais (well, you had to be there)—and an insister on connections between art and public life that this Documenta seems designed to neutralize. However, in his court-jester role, Beuys is really part of the establishment matrix, thus at a distance in time and spirit from the crisis points of today.

Documenta 7 is classy but sluggish with its imploded vision of an art of—in Fuchs's words—"order," "dignity," and "tranquility": art in a hospital zone, resting comfortably after being pulled from the wreck of the avant-garde. This is a vision demanded by the present institution-intensive situation of art, a situation with terrific inertial force (especially in Europe) that can be expected to pertain into the foreseeable future. This being so, the practical yardstick of energy and significance in new art will be the extent to which it violates the vision, however modestly—bursting through it, *Alien*-fashion, with meanings unassimilable to the institutional host. Certain Germans show how in Kassel.

July 20 and August 3, 1982

Howard Finster

Nothing in the art-loving life is as sweetly fascinating as first exposure to a "naive" talent. Sophisticated art yields itself with difficulty; "primitive" tribal art is intimidating in its unknowableness; and "folk art" worthy of the name has long since been wiped out by mass culture (though the urge strangely survives in, for instance, subway graffiti). But the woodnotes wild of the untutored art crank, be it Henri Rousseau or Grandma Moses or any of America's innumerable small-town *bricoleurs*, are instantly accessible and adorable. There's one catch: the enchantment is hard to sustain or renew. The main exception I can think of, aside from Rousseau, is Sam Rodia, whose Watts Towers I find permanently beguiling.

The Reverend Howard Finster, a sixty-six-year-old retired Southern Baptist preacher now showing at the New Museum (August 7–September 22, 1982), is not an exception. My first response to his various, antic, apocalyptic work was astonishment and delight. On subsequent visits, my enthusiasm cooled. Why? What chords of wish and identification does strong naive art touch, and what causes the ensuing disappointment? Not that everyone is touched or, having been, is disappointed, but I don't think my experience is unique.

Finster's story has elements true to the pattern of many another modern naïf. Though with some background in carpentry and handicraft, he came late to art after a life filled with energetic purposes (eight congregations, many tent revivals). He has been painting for just six years, turning out 2,500 or so works in that time. His home in Sommerville, Georgia, reportedly is a total environment of created objects and inscriptions. Most of his pictures incorporate verbal matter: biblical quotations and original poems, epigrams, jeremiads, and so forth. He is distinctly an eccentric, apparently regarded with bemused tolerance by his community. (Naive art, as opposed to folk art, is individualistic, even alienated—an eruptive singularity.) His art could be termed a hobby that got out of control or came under the control of extraordinary motives and powers.

Finster advertises himself as a "man of visions," divinely inspired. He paints what he "sees": hell, heaven, and extraterrestrials are specialties. He also paints historical scenes and figures, cultural idols (e.g., Elvis), and himself (an ever-grinning Bible beater). He spouts lurid social prophesy: a young woman clamped in "THE DEVILS VICE" (a vise—Finster spells very badly, often to lucky effect) cries "TO LATE NOW," and the same picture warns that "DRUGS CAN PEARLISE THE GREATEST NATION ON EARTH AND CAUSE IT TO LOOSE THE LAST WAR" (he means "lose," I think). He makes sumptuous assemblages of wood, mirror, electric light, and, among lots of other things, pieces of TV sets that he has melted down in a homemade furnace. Some pieces reflect on their own making: "YOU LOOK AT THE SCRAP AND DESIDE WHERE TO MARK OUT FOR THE BEST EMEGES . . . YOU CAN TURN MOST ANYTHING INTO ART."

Finster's talent is essentially eidetic, meaning reliant on the capacity that makes us see faces in clouds and cracked walls. He evolves images and ideas from accidental properties of his materials and from dreams, visions, and irrational associations. He trusts in chance and the unconscious, and they reward him with wonderful things. At the same time, his preacher's instinct impels him to spell out meanings and point morals, and his ebullient self-satisfaction spatters his work with personal brags. Interlaced with his endlessly surprising inventiveness is a terrible hectic garrulousness. Gradually it becomes clear that this mind, despite its robustness and access to splendors, is a prison.

Is every mind a prison? We would not like to believe that, and a yearning for proof of spontaneous connection to the real may be part of a taste for naive art. Thus the excitement of discovering an innocent genius, and thus the grinding letdown when the slavish structures of this genius become unmistakable. Jesse Murry, who curated this show, argues in his catalogue introduction that Finster's art "moves beyond a personal vision to be concerned with the disposition of humanity facing the world," but I don't see it that way. I see it as an exitless labyrinth.

I simply cannot imagine a proper use for art like the Georgia reverend's. Resisting sentimentality, nostalgia, "charm," and other forms of condescension, I'm at a loss how to value Finster's amazing gabble of received content and inspired forms. (I haven't mentioned medieval angels and devils, Albert Einstein gazing into a sky full of UFOs, the Mona Lisa, mirror-encrusted heavenly mansions, THE TRELLACE OF THE SUPERBRAIN, a paean to the virtues of Coca-Cola, and a social demonology featuring a "YOUNG DRUG ATTIC," a "HIPLECRITT," and a "MEDLING BITCH"—Finster is a man of peeves as well as visions.) To the extent that I take him seriously, I feel sick to my stomach.

Which is the measure of a certain power, perhaps. Finster's work radiates individual strength and optimism—chipper even when evoking "FIRE AND BRIMESTONE"—in defiance of a godless society. It devours and regurgitates the world's junked objects and beliefs. But it does so without consciousness, and only consciousness, in all its frailty, avails against the meaningless. Well, I suppose faith avails too, but it must be a faith permeable by the actual world, not hermetic and hallucinatory. However lush, the domain of the contemporary naïf is a paranoid's garden, finally yielding just more evidence of present futility.

August 31, 1982

Clemente to Marden to Kiefer

Art lovers in New York and baseball fans everywhere get weird in
October. For the former, it is the season of undulled appetite, when
an unleashed flood of new objects and images temporarily scintillates
with interest and promise. For the latter, it is the ferociously acceler-
ating climax to long, languorous months of foreplay. What, then, of
those of us for whom both art and baseball are chronic passions? Pity
us! Each addiction being in its own way total, we are beside ourselves.

A tendency is noted around dinner tables to discuss the aesthetics
of baseball at very great length, as the sane and the innocent tiptoe
from the room.

Another tendency suggests itself as a heretofore neglected possibility: view the world of October art through the lambent October
mists of baseball. A method for such madness happens to be ready-
made in a brilliant little book of several years back by poet Charles
North, *Lineups* (reprinted in his *Leap Year*, Kulchur Foundation,
1978). North proved by example that any quantitative category of
qualitatively diverse units—movies, colors, diseases, and so forth—
can be subjected to the subtle yet ineluctable analysis of talent and
temperament that determines a baseball player's optimum position in
the field and place in the batting order. For instance:

> San Francisco ss
> Munich cf
> Paris lf
> Rome c
> Madrid 3b
> London rf
> Athens 1b
> Istanbul 2b
> New York p

Isn't that great? My only trouble with this lineup is North's National League purism, which deprives him of the wild card of the designated hitter. (Havana, batting seventh.)

So. With collaboration from art journalist and hardball fancier Gerald Marzorati, I recently set about compiling a roster of present art stars according to the Northian paradigm. Carried away, I have embellished it with analytic descriptions in that important American folk-poetic form, the scouting report. Marzorati and I set rules—for example, that all named artists should be roughly of baseball-playing age and should be coming off hot seasons—and broke them repeatedly. For the relative absence of abstract painters, performance artists, realists, sculptors, and women I have no defense. For the presence of Europeans, presumably good only for belaboring balls with their feet, I have no explanation. This is just the way, in the frenzy of free association, it turned out.

Please note that a batting order is not an order of preference. Actually, if you can't interpret one, don't guess; ask a friend who can. With that, the lineup:

Francesco Clemente, shortstop: smooth, great range and hands, great off-balance arm . . . switch hitter, weak bat but outstanding on-base knack, good eye, will bunt for hit . . . threat to steal.

Cindy Sherman, third base: middling range but super quickness, Gold Glove, hasn't missed a ball hit her way in two seasons . . . disciplined hitter, pulls inside pitch for distance . . . selfless player, cinch to sac bunt or hit behind runner.

David Salle, center field: uncanny range and glove, fluid speed, (Roberto) Clemente type, makes it look easy . . . line-drive hitter all fields, league-leader doubles and triples, rally maker . . . temperamental, injury prone.

Anselm Kiefer, first base: two-ton Teuton, just adequate at position, can be bunted on . . . fearsome slugger, aggressive, bad-ball hitter, can take anything downtown . . . slow but intimidating on bases, catcher advised not to block plate.

Julian Schnabel, right field: Reggie Jackson clone . . . erratic glove, grandstand catches may follow initial misjudgment, arm strong but wild . . . picture swing, strikeouts and homers in bunches, scary in clutch . . . Mr. October.

Ken Price, designated hitter: pure hitter, great bat control, strokes the ball, consistent .300 . . . no threat on bases.

Brice Marden, second base: keystone pro, range limited but good jump, unreal pivot . . . tough out, sometime power . . . knows the game, team captain.

Susan Rothenberg, left field: medium glove, unstylish but determined, body-blocks short hop . . . strict pull hitter, streak power . . . consistent effort, hometown favorite.

Joel Shapiro, catcher: solid, smart, calls a good game, good arm but release has lost snap . . . contact hitter, rarely strikes out, longball infrequent . . . slow but wily on bases.

And on the mound:

Frank Stella, starting pitcher: ageless vet, owns the ball . . . heat diminished but sneaky with awesome pitch assortment, super control, mixes speeds, throws changeup for strike . . . competitor, will brushback.

Ed Ruscha, short relief: submarine delivery . . . indifferent heat but slider and screwball sparkle, keeps everything low.

Jonathan Borofsky, long relief: every kind of slow, junk exclusively . . . jug-handle curve, great knuckler, confusing windup . . . control doubtful.

Keith Haring, pinch runner: rabbit speed, incautious but known to outrun pickoff, first to third on anything.

So there's the team, a formidable one (with a payroll to match). Will I stop here? Would you?

General Managers: Willem de Kooning, Jasper Johns.

Manager: Leo Castelli.

Coaching Staff: Louise Bourgeois, Ellsworth Kelly, Malcolm Morley, Richard Serra, Cy Twombly, Andy Warhol.

Batboy: Scott Burton.

Trainer: Chris Burden.

Grounds Crew: Walter de Maria, Michael Heizer.

Statistician: Lawrence Alloway.

Umpiring Crew: Rosalind Krauss, Douglas Crimp, Craig Owens, Benjamin H. D. Buchloh. (Krauss, Crimp, Owens, Buchloh—they even sound like umpires.) Rule-book deconstructionists, they tend to award first base on foul balls and to throw everybody out of the game.

National Anthem: Laurie Anderson.

Bird Mascot: Rene Ricard.

Howard Cosell: Hilton Kramer.

Some might object to the above on the grounds that art is not a game. But then, neither is baseball.

October 12, 1982

Leon Golub

It's Leon Golub's time.

A fringe figure for most of his long career—one of those artists who, though not unknown, might be termed famous for being ignored—Golub has rather suddenly become a leading artist of our cultural moment, which he is helping to define. As usual when such things happen, the reasons are chicken-and-egg, a meshing of achievement and happenstance. Golub's new big paintings on unstretched canvas, at the Susan Caldwell Gallery (October 9–November 6, 1982), continue a remarkable sharpening of his powers. They are also right on the button of present issues in art and the world, including aesthetics of the best new figuration and shocks of the evening news. It's as if Golub were an alarm clock set to go off in the early eighties and wake everybody up.

Golub, sixty, is from Chicago, where thirty years ago he was the leading light in a figurative expressionist movement which contributed to that city's stylistic independence from New York, though it didn't cut much ice elsewhere. (New Images of Man, a 1959 Museum of Modern Art show that featured it, sank like a stone.) With his wife, artist Nancy Spero, Golub spent most of the years 1956–64 in Europe, then settled in Manhattan. His work entered a phase of heroic battling male figures inspired by late Roman art; it then became overtly political in reaction to the Vietnam War. Huge paintings on torn canvas of American soldiers shooting civilians recalled Picasso's 1951 *Massacre in Korea* and had a similar flaw: the misfit of general outrage and specific circumstance, the futility of indicting a nation by showing some anonymous soldiers engaged in standard atrocities.

In the late seventies Golub retreated from the ambition of his Vietnam paintings. He painted an unprepossessing series of about a hundred small portraits from photos of world leaders, including Nelson Rockefeller, Mao, Franco, and Ho Chi Minh. These crude, bland little pictures, their paint scraped down into the tooth of the canvas, suggested no political intent but rather a simple mindless fascination with the "look" of powerful men. They did nothing for most viewers, but it is now apparent that they did worlds for Golub. When he returned to big formats, in his *Mercenaries* and *Interrogations* series, it was with an idea for political art stunning in its sophistication and courage: give the political criminal, not the victim, full and particular humanity. Get inside criminality: what is it like?

Golub's is indeed a political art, brilliantly so. Shunning the inauthenticity, for a superpower citizen, of presuming to speak for victims of power, he projects himself into the most distant tips of power's tentacles—its obscurest wielding and wielders. He confronts power where it is both dark and vulnerable, in dirty work done out of sight and out of mind. He does so with his own painstakingly evolved version of the New Yorkish big-scale frontal post-Pollock perceptual machine. The main thing about the Big Picture for him is the way it locates and affirms the presence of the viewer, who "completes" the work by looking at it. Not coincidentally, his mastery of this powerful formal mode has brought with it the ultimate spelling out of his lifelong subject matter: violence.

The most horribly intimate form of violence is torture, practiced or condoned by many countries, agencies, and militant causes but admitted by none. Unheard and unseen, torture is a nation—a planet—coextensive with our own, but apart, an antiplace. This antiplace is populated by two classes: torturers and victims. No third parties link the torture planet and planet Earth. Unlike terrorism, which is an evil that brutalizes and demoralizes theatrically, torture is toxic precisely in its secrecy, its unreality even to those who know it is real. It may take place at the dusky edges of civilization, but it rots the core.

Golub employs the metaphysical antiplace of Pollock and Newman, a site of new meanings also for many younger artists today, to make torture real. He doesn't "rub our noses in it," in the common self-defeating way of political artists. He simply and almost courteously includes us in the peculiar social situation of torture—or in the fellowship of richly individualized torturers and mercenaries, the guys who make a living in this line. By dint of scale, framing, frontality, eye contact, and so on, Golub's images are less on the wall than in the room—with us. Our noses may be involved, after all. These are toiling, sweaty men, who smell (you can tell by the scraped, rubbed grunge of their clothes). But then the victims probably smell worse.

Time in the pictures is alternately relaxed and intensified, slow and fast, the way it feels as you live it. In *White Squad II* it feels one way to the torturer standing nonchalant in a posture pulled askew by the heavy revolver he is holding to the head of his victim on the floor. As it appears, the torturer knows that he is not going to fire; for him, time is poking along in a workaday way, ever so slightly enlivened by sadistic enjoyment. Meanwhile, he evidently has managed to convince his victim, writhing in some access of agony beyond panic, that death is imminent. The victim has a very different sense of time. Looking at—participating in—the picture, we register both senses and add our own, from the rhythms of our own heartbeats, nervous systems, lives.

The torturer in *White Squad II* is pretty slimy looking. Most of Golub's mercenaries and torturers—whose originals he finds in soldier-of-fortune magazines, among other photographic sources—are raunchy but personable. The young soldier or cop in *White Squad III* who eyes the viewer while making an ambiguous movement—reaching for his gun?!—is almost attractive, with part-Indian South American good looks. (Behind him a colleague seems about to put a bullet in the head of an emaciated victim.) Golub's vignettes transpire in an abstracted Africa or South America—"at the peripheries," as he has said, where "governments or agencies are reluctant to use the central or public organs of control."

Golub has no firsthand experience of these irregulars of power, but I feel—believe—that he has them down to a fare-thee-well. "There's the lumpen type of mercenary," he says,

> who takes on these jobs for five hundred bucks a month and enjoys the fun and games, and the interrogator, who is more civil, brutal as they are, because this guy has to report to someone else and has to know the forms of social discourse. . . . Ultimately they're manipulated, also raw material for the machine, but for the moment they have their privileges.

And you can bet they get a kick out of them, in a spirit that seems to say: "Wouldn't you?"

Identification flows to the torturers, not the victims. Golub shows how natural this is. Partly it's the phenomenon of evil's superior fascination: as in *Paradise Lost*, Satan gets all the best lines. More important, it's the nature of torture, which is to dedifferentiate its victims, to reduce them to a point beneath possible empathy, to make them things. In those bare, stale basements and back rooms only the victimizers are fully personal functioning beings. We look at the victims. We get to know the criminals, at work and play.

Mercenaries at play, posing as if for snapshots with sexually ambiguous whores (women or men?), inhabit two pictures that are my favorite Golub paintings, ever. They are unusual for him in being vertical (ten feet high) and in dispensing with the flat, oxide red background that has assured the frontality of his other images, at the cost of a certain stiffness and stridency. Here the backgrounds are as heavily worked as the figures, with an energy and suavity vaguely reminiscent of Richard Diebenkorn. The colors run to warm pastels, with delicious red and blue-green passages. Totally assured now in what he has to say, Golub is painting as never before.

Golub's hard-won mastery ramifies his message without in the least softening it. Increased tactility, sensuousness, and liveliness make the viewer's participation really irresistible. To look at these pictures is more than ever to get and be gotten by them. The raffish mercenaries—sandy-haired goof and dark-haired, finger-snapping dude—have an infectious familiarity somewhere between that of TV actors (*The Dukes of Honduras?*) and neighborhood Joes. Their vitality buoys the heart—and is an abomination to the mind, which knows what's going on. It's party time on the planet of torture, and we are there.

Thereness, hereness—specificities—are the weather of Golub's new work, which explores and manifests what ordinary political art merely, with contempt or frenzy, gestures toward. One has to go a long way back for a suitable precedent: Manet's *Execution of Maximilian* comes to mind, as practically a template for *White Squad III*. Manet put the lethal fusillade in the middle ground and in the foreground a young, winsome soldier calmly facing front. It is about a horror of the actual: this is happening and nobody is stopping it. And because it is painted, and thus permanent, it will go on happening just this way forever, a wound in consciousness that will never heal.

Golub's working methods being arduous and slow, his paintings are properly expensive. This fact, plus their presence in a glossy corporate-looking gallery, is not an irony exactly, but an extra, external twist to the work's drama of complicity. The paintings can handle it, keeping their moral penetration even as they take their place in the commercial panoply of contemporary art. They belong in major museums, which I hope will take a deep breath and buy them. They present evil—evil that implicates us—but on another level their existence represents something better about us and even, we can wish, more lasting.

While I was viewing the show, a bunch of college-aged girls breezed in. One of them immediately said, "Now, talk about making a *statement*," and another said, "Gosh, just *look* at them"—which they did for about twenty seconds. But they were impressed. The paintings were impressive to them, grabbed into memory in the quick no-thought-needed way of young minds, which never know what they will have a use for. It cheered me up, making me think of what human energy might eventually find to do in a world still complex and terrifying but more truly known.

October 26, 1982

Decade of Wonders

Now down the narrow streets it swiftly came,
And, widely opening, did on both sides prey.
This benefit we sadly owe the flame,
If onely ruine must enlarge our way.

John Dryden, "Annus Mirabilis"

Being asked to "reminisce" about the sixties makes me feel suddenly old and at the same time hot to oblige. The sixties were such a richness and a Rubicon—in art and in absolutely everything else—that first-hand reflecting on them is sure to become a growth industry as the hangover of the seventies wears off and the sources of the strange new present start being excavated. I feel defined by that time—a "sixties person," even "very sixties"—though in ways far from clear to me, since they have to do not with any deeds or big ideas of mine but with shocks and impressions I received passively and have scarcely begun to sort out. The subject is still smoldering, like the ruins of London in John Dryden's "Annus Mirabilis: The Year of Wonders, 1666"—a basically celebratory poem about war, disaster, and a crisis of authority during another century's swinging sixties. It is a terrific metaphor for our own sixties, when more or less everything fell or flew apart and a feckless optimism reigned. For a while there, anything seemed possible, and everyone was a holy fool.

Going to art shows in the sixties was a magical practice, like divining entrails or, as in Dryden's poem, trying to make out the prophetic implications of two comets that appeared over London. (It seems that way again today, doesn't it?) One went to see the work of a new artist, or the new work of an old artist, in hope of a revelation, a "paradigm." It was an era mad for definitions and definitive forms, thus titillated by demonstrations that no such things were possible—by the utter relativities of Andy Warhol, say. Artists of the time can be divided into those who made definitions, those who undermined definitions, and those who found seams of individual expression in the shifting, grinding fault zone between. This show (Abstract Painting, 1960–1969, P.S. 1, January 16–March 18, 1982) of fifteen abstract painters—including Jo Baer, James Bishop, Ralph Humphrey, Robert Mangold, Brice Marden, Agnes Martin, Doug Ohlson, and Robert Ryman—is devoted to the third contingent. There still seemed to be some connection between the order of art and the order of life, as if by getting the art just right we could straighten out—or smash, because who needed it?—the world. I remember my glee in 1967 when Frank Stella's irregular-polygon paintings appeared to signal the destruction of tyrant formalism, then my consternation at critic Michael Fried's ingenious recuperation of these works to the regime. It all seems insane in retrospect, and maybe it was.

Naturally painting of the sixties was abstract—or "essentially abstract," if it happened to have images. Abstraction, in thought and feeling as much as style, was an orthodoxy so deep that no one noticed it, including the antiauthoritarian many of us who saw and decried "orthodoxy" everywhere. It was an era of projection in which the utmost generality—the blankest, most all-accepting silver screen—was only common sense. Try to find a single artist in the present show whose work contradicts what I'm saying. You can't. (And I would bet that all these artists were praised at some point for being heterodox. Ha ha.) Well, as the sixties drew to a close, there was a little shift, an inflection toward "meaning" (specific, particular) that some of us found, I can't remember how exactly, in the work of, among others, Brice Marden and Agnes Martin. But by that time the paradigm game was over (not won or lost) and could not resume without a fundamental change in the rules. (Has that happened now?) Suddenly, wishing didn't make anything so anymore. Suddenly nothing worked.

What does it mean to look for the stuff of your life in the productions of art? Nothing very good, probably. But it is absolutely modern, isn't it, and has characterized other amazing moments beside the sixties. (Maybe including the present.) I'm talking about aesthetic preference as spiritual autobiography. I recognize this show as someone's story—not mine, though most of the artists here represent at least one-night stands in the diary of my polymorphous appreciation, my art love. With a couple of exceptions, these artists are characterized by a certain tact and equilibrium, by theoretical givens infused with what we critics despairingly call the personal. (No one knows what it means, but mentioning it always soothes, like a letter from home.) My own list of main squeezes from the sixties would highlight more extreme qualities, including extremes of fame and obscurity (Warhol and Stella and some people you never heard of) that equally lent themselves to intoxication. I was young and vicarious. I could dream, couldn't I. Art love as a storyboard pinned with throbbing scraps of second-hand life. It's all still there in my emotional attic, and someday I must tell it. You should tell yours, too.

Stories. We walked into galleries, and stories spontaneously formed in our heads, and they knocked us out. The stories were so exciting that we tended to babble—"we" meaning me and whoever knows what I'm talking about and isn't gnashing teeth at my presumption. (There will be time and occasion to be careful, modest, accurate, and fair.) Art criticism then was mainly babble, because the emphasis was on the stories as magic charms: getting the art to be what you said it was. (Criticism of the sixties becomes very funny when you try seriously to imagine the audience critics were writing for: sensitive monsters arise in the mind's eye.) It seemed that with the right words in the right order you could conjure history and steer it like a toboggan. (Then the slope ended and everything slowed down and slowed down, and stopped.) You can't say it wasn't glorious. You can't say it wasn't crackers. It was a time of fire that shouldered through narrow streets and left them broad boulevards. On those consequent thoroughfares, which lead nowhere, we have wandered in a daze. Now we are aware of new traffic and the sounds of new construction and deconstruction. It's an anxious moment. Will there be uses for us? Will they want to hear our old, unlikely stories?

November 1982

The Grant Wood Revival

Why now—really, why ever?—a revival for the painter of *American Gothic*? The very idea of a Grant Wood retrospective (Whitney Museum of American Art, June 16–September 4, 1983) this year—the last one flopped resoundingly in 1942—induces something like vertigo. Revisionist art history has shown a formidable capacity for reanimating old war-horses and putting dead letters back into circulation, but there is supposed to be a limit to everything. Is nothing sacred or, better, irredeemably profane? If we can't count on Wood and what he stood for—the cracker-barrel nationalism that flourished briefly in American art during the Depression—to stay entombed, what can we count on?

It seems we can always count on the wonderful responsiveness of cultural appetite to political mood. The mood now is of course conservative, full of longing for values hazy in every respect except that they are absent. It is a mood, perhaps, of wanting to miss something in preference to feeling empty. This puts us in touch with the bereft and frightened public that took Wood and the other American Scene painters—Thomas Hart Benton and John Steuart Curry—to its heart in the early 1930s.

Is there more to the art of Grant Wood than *American Gothic*? A little. Not very much. He was a modestly talented artist who painted a number of striking pictures, one of which became preposterously renowned. As is not always true in such cases (think of the Mona Lisa and Whistler's Mother), this picture is also the artist's best, a work that says very well just about everything that Wood had to say. To have created such a work can be anything but a blessing for its creator. Wood never recovered from the triumph of *American Gothic*. It was the tail that wagged the dog of his career.

American Gothic was painted in 1930, when the late-blooming Wood, thirty-nine years old and fresh from a revelatory exposure to Flemish and German old masters in Munich, was entering his peak artistic period. The period lasted all of about three years, long enough for him to become more famous than any other American artist before Andy Warhol and long enough for his fame to start doing him in. A self-involved, hypersensitive man—"strange, mild, and somehow defenseless," in the words of a biographer—he was ill equipped to distinguish himself from his public image: first as a hero of American cultural independence, then, when rising internationalist sentiment eclipsed the American Scene, as a crypto-fascist villain of reaction. When he died of liver cancer in 1942, predeceased by his reputation, he was an anguished, baffled soul.

He was an Iowa farm boy who spent most of his life in Cedar Rapids, a city that nurtured his career (a local mortician was his long-time patron) and still jealously guards his legend as a homespun genius. Wood always intended to be an artist. The ambition took him three times to Paris, where by all accounts he was completely unaffected by modern art. Indeed, until almost accidentally picking up on Memling and Holbein, he seems not to have been influenced by any particular artists of any time, his notion of art being a generalized sentimental one of late nineteenth-century provenance. His most solid inspiration was literary, based on the strong movement in midwestern writing from Hamlin Garland to Sinclair Lewis. It provided both subject matter and tone for instant communication with people who knew nothing about contemporary art.

That was just about everybody in America in 1930. European modernism still caused uneasiness where it was not an object of xenophobic resentment, and even the smart sets of New York and Hollywood were primed to embrace an art product that had heartland bona fides. (Wood's collectors included Cole Porter, Alexander Woollcott, John P. Marquand, Edward G. Robinson, and King Vidor.) If ever "the age demanded" a flavor in art, it was what the age got in American Scene painting: the distillate of a national self-preoccupation that also informed, though in less overwhelming quantities, the work of Edward Hopper, Stuart Davis, Reginald Marsh, Charles Burchfield, and other distinctly superior (and therefore spoilsport) American painters.

Wood failed, tragically, to understand that the American Scene's appeal to mass taste succeeded because the Depression-era masses desperately wanted to be appealed to, not because they had any profound identification with his Iowa farmers—or Benton's crapshooters or Curry's John Brown. These images were the fashionable signs of an emotional need for rootedness that turned to revulsion once allayed by returning confidence. STICKS NIX HICK PIX, *Variety*'s immortal 1935 headline announcing the ingratitude of rural audiences for movies aimed at them, could have been an apt crack of doom for folk-pandering oils as well as celluloid. By then, Americans were ready for headier stuff than the branch water of rustic nostalgia. The next artist with an impact comparable to Wood's was Salvador Dalí.

As the world moved into war, the American Scene was widely stigmatized as a native equivalent of socialist realism and Nazi art. This cheap analogy ignored the deep-dyed liberalism of the artists and their work—though some of their supporters were another matter. (These included the notably loathsome Thomas Craven, a New York critic whose campaign against modernism included such tactics as calling Alfred Stieglitz "a Hoboken Jew.") Wood, who headed the New Deal's Public Works of Art Project in Iowa and rebuffed overtures from rightist groups, was devastated by the criticism. But it was no more exaggerated in one way than the earlier adulation had been in another.

Unlike *American Gothic*, most of Wood's paintings have had a good long rest in obscurity, and the first impression they make is likely to be one of considerable freshness. The brilliance and transparency of old-masterish multiple-glaze techniques and the sprightliness of rhythmic, firmly organized compositions give immediate pleasure. Most arresting of all is Wood's gift as a dramatist of personality. He may have dealt in regional types, but he had the sense to know that the typical is a subtle grain or admixture, not a physiognomy. The people in his paintings have the deep humor that good character actors bring to their roles, a quality of mysterious anarchic life beneath caricatured surfaces. Even the broadest and dimmest of them might be capable of doing something surprising.

Wood's major flaw is an irresolution about his enterprise overcompensated by compulsive, ultimately fatiguing, mannerisms. The orderliness of his paintings is imposed, not organic. There is absolutely no reciprocity between artist and nature in Wood's tidy heaving landscapes, which, far from communing with the good midwestern earth, are wackily surreal in the manner of a Warner Brothers cartoon. (As the art historian Matthew Baigell observed, "One almost expects Porky Pig to bounce out of the shrubbery.") Even Wood's winning way with local color was to be bettered in popular culture by the films of Preston Sturges.

Mention of popular forms points up just how untenable Wood's position was. In effect, he was competing in the name of fine art with the monstrous efficiencies of Hollywood and Norman Rockwell—that great unpretentious entertainer whose pictorial sugar had addicted the nation. Wood aspired to squeeze serious painting in among the "lively arts," a feat later performed by Warhol with the diabolical irony and calculation it required. Wood's naive sincerity briefly flattered a democratic fantasy of the artist as a "man of the people," but the people's actual taste, then as now, was for impersonally manipulated images.

To the extent that Wood remained true to his notion of "high" artistic values, he shot himself in the foot. The great wrong turn in a career that must have looked promising to anyone in 1930 was his failure to understand the popular and also the aesthetic success of *American Gothic*. This was a picture with a clear economy of subject, technique, and design, relatively devoid of pointless elaboration. Having pulled it off, however, Wood backtracked from the laconic realism that made it work. He so dreaded being dismissed as "photographic"—thus "inartistic"—that he missed his best chance of a sustained vocation: to be a Norman Rockwell with dignity and brains.

Picking through Wood's small body of mature work—kept small by a self-consciousness that paralyzed his imagination for months and years at a time—one can find a few pictures that support more than fleeting interest, usually because they have a strong conceptual component, literary or otherwise. *Death on the Ridge Road*—high-speed catastrophe about to occur amid bucolic, indifferent fields—is a stylized scream against mechanization that still rivets. (The painting is also the artist's single confrontation with a rural reality later than 1910 or so.) *Daughters of Revolution* packs at least a memory of the political punch it delivered in 1932, when old-line forces like the D.A.R. still threatened to frustrate reform. *Woman with Plants* remains an affecting painting and *Dinner for Threshers* an impressive one. A bizarre late work, *January*, raises the artist's faults of rigidity and whimsy to a hallucinatory pitch that very nearly redeems them. But it is for *American Gothic* that Wood will continue to be remembered.

A magnificent fluke, *American Gothic* has been devoured, without being digested, by the popular imagination for more than fifty years now. The painting has, perhaps, just the right minimum touch of vulgarity to make it immune to vulgarization, as purer works of art are not. It has belonged to demotic culture from the start. Claiming no special elevation, it cannot be pulled down. Though popped out of the context of other art into wild, vague realms of secondary meaning, it maintains a primary existence, an identity with itself.

With some effort, in the physical presence of the picture, one can change it from a full-scale reproduction back into a painting—something one can be alone with. As a painting, it is a bit too labored and finicky, with parts that don't so much hang as cling together. (The distant trees fall right out of the frame: Wood would have been far ahead as an artist if he had never tried to paint a tree.) The painting works well enough, however, for the image to take hold as a touchstone for complicated thoughts and feelings comparable to those evoked by a great short story—which in some ways *American Gothic* is, as a visual fulfillment of the spirit of Lewis and Sherwood Anderson (with a dash of H. L. Mencken for spice). It tells a story about what people can get to be like in America.

You probably don't need to have grown up in midwestern small towns (as I did) to feel the bite of *American Gothic*'s ambivalence, but it helps. For one thing, such a childhood gives you perspective on the old silly question that has turned this painting into a national Rorschach test: does it satirize or celebrate rural America? Clearly—to me—it does both and neither. Most significant, it manages to objectify, in the dour but alert characters portrayed, the definitively midwestern compulsion to polarize everything in moralistic good-or-bad terms that makes such disheartening questions come up in the first place.

Evidently Wood's sister and his dentist, the sitters for *American Gothic*, never ceased to be nervous about what they had been party to, and Wood himself, rather pathetically, agonized about what the picture meant. (He kept changing his story.) They were no more comfortable than anyone else with the unexpected spiritual nakedness that makes this otherwise funny, charming image permanently absorbing. They were also less able to avail themselves of the national knack for banishing unwelcome ambiguities by imposing one or another interpretation on the painting.

On his deathbed, the heartsick Wood told his friend Benton that "when he got well he was going to change his name, go where nobody knew him, and start all over again with a new style of painting." So: a sad end, though with a fantasy as impeccably American as everything else about "one of America's favorite artists," as a current press release inevitably calls him. His story is a cautionary tale, as if we needed yet another, about what it may mean to be favored by Americans.

June 1983

On Art and Artists:
Peter Schjeldahl

This is an edited transcript from a videotaped interview
produced by Lyn Blumenthal and Kate Horsfield in 1982.
Robert Storr interviewed Peter Schjeldahl.

I guess I would like to start with some autobiographical things. What prompted you to come to New York in the first place?

Growing up in small towns in Minnesota, I knew I was going to go someplace. There is a tendency for bright misfits in the Midwest to slide off either to the West Coast or the East Coast. Coming to New York was almost pure chance for me, a roll of the dice. I dropped out of college and was a newspaper reporter in Iowa. I applied to small newspapers near big cities on both coasts. The only letter I got back was from a paper in Jersey City—right across the Hudson—and I came out and spent a year here in the early 1960s. Then I became involved with the poetry scene.

Were you writing poetry of your own?

Yes. From early on.

So you took the newspaper job to survive, or did it represent a separate ambition?

I don't know. I always had a penchant for journalism. I was a terrible reporter, so if I had any ambition in that direction it didn't last very long. I was much too self-conscious to be a good reporter. But starting out as a sports writer for my high school paper, I've since done most of the things that you can do in journalism, at one time or another.

Did art criticism come directly? Was it something you already had in your mind to do?

Starting to write art criticism was an accident, too. In 1964 I dropped out of college once and for all and went to Paris for a year and then settled in New York and the Lower East Side poetry world. It was a New York tradition for poets to write art criticism, mostly for *Art News*. And in my case it just took. It was one thing leading to another in the way things do when you're in your twenties. In a way, I date my serious art critical work from just the last few years. In the mid-1970s I decided to quit criticism, and I spent a couple years not doing it, at the end of which I decided that I missed it and also that there was nothing else that I did very well that they pay you for. I had that attitude that poets and artists have—that you are doing this to support yourself in your real work—and that seems to me often defensive and not the case. I mean, do you save energy by being second-rate at what you do to support yourself? Maybe quite the contrary. So when I got back into it, it was with a more committed feeling.

Was there something in particular about the work being done in the fifties and early sixties that accounts for so many poets' deciding to write about art?

I think it was sociological. The survival of the bohemian scene and atmosphere. Certainly in the 1930s and 1940s the art world was small and it overlapped with the poets—there were always poets around. Poets at the Cedar Bar. The generation of important poets when I came to New York included John Ashbery and Frank O'Hara, who were heroes to me. Ashbery is a critic and O'Hara was a curator at the Museum of Modern Art. Tom Hess, the editor of *Art News*, was very receptive to poets as critics. I do think poets who can accept the discipline or humiliation of critical work tend to have an advantage in writing about painting.

In what respect?

There are similarities between poetry and painting. Both are conventionally framed, endlessly ambiguous mediums, capable of highly nuanced meaning and very solitary in execution. Something like that. But there is nothing new about this. It goes back to Diderot and Baudelaire and Apollinaire. The French tradition of writers and artists being together was very much alive in New York in the 1950s and going into the 1960s. It is less true now because artists tend to enter the art world not in the odd ragamuffin ways they used to but straight from art schools. So there is specialization. And poets go through writing workshops, if they don't watch out. But it still exists. I think right now if writers and artists get together, their meeting is probably mediated by some other scene, like the performance scene or the rock scene.

You wrote recently in a review of David Salle's work that you were interested in him partly because you felt that you shared a similarity of imaginative process. Have there been times when the art being made seemed to come from a sensibility radically different from yours—and were those difficult times?

Well, yes. The late 1960s. Minimalism and even pop art, with its studied dumbness, and certainly color-field painting seemed to demand a purely descriptive approach and didn't lend themselves to a verbal elaboration. And then the effect of the growing specialization hit. You got all these sort of two-noun arts. Noun-as-adjective arts. Video art, performance art, concept art, narrative art. And you had artists doing their own writing. That deteriorated rather quickly. Well, I mean it deteriorated into the great seedbed of the 1970s, which becomes a more and more peculiar time as it starts to recede—and more important too, probably.

Is that to say that to write criticism in the seventies it was necessary to take a theoretical position of some kind?

I think criticism had a nervous breakdown in the 1970s. I hope I am not projecting unduly from my own experience, but the critic of the 1970s for me was Lawrence Alloway. He was the only first-rate critic who embraced pluralism. Somehow he had the nervous system that could stand it. It drove everybody else crazy. Criticism in the 1970s became a matter of just keeping track of things, making taxonomical systems—all these artists who were sort of equally worthy and how do we keep them all in mind. It was a time of marking time in which a lot of things happened, though, the consequences of which we are seeing now.

A lot of the writing of the seventies leaned heavily on books by intellectual heroes like Wittgenstein. Did that create problems for some who avoided such critical references or rhetoric?

There certainly is a crisis of audience; I mean, who are you writing for? By the 1970s, the art world had reached a point where it had expanded beyond all previous boundaries. It was like a nova that explodes and then condenses into a neutron star. I mean, as the edges keep exploding out, the center condenses—and boy what a wonderful metaphor. You get mini-scenes in which people play intimidating games. And are territorial. I think obscure writing is a form of territorial behavior that can be compared to the behavior of monkeys in close circumstances.

Well, who is criticism written for? Who do you write for?

I have always written for general audiences of one size or another. I guess I have never lost my sense of myself as a journalist, which was a fairly low form of life in the 1960s and into the 1970s. But it became more important as the 1970s went on because in fact there was a large audience, and toward the end of the 1970s you get a lot of young critics coming along writing very clearly, writing good journalistic prose. Some of them not as smart and as informed as they ought to be. But the idea that somebody should have to crawl over broken glass to get to art fell into disfavor. There was the puritanical hysteria of the late 1960s and early 1970s when artists were trying to adjust to the "commodity fetish," as it was then talked about and still is to some extent. The flight from the commodified art work and the art industry and the art business finally collapsed. There was just no escaping it. Which means that the younger generation now, depending on your point of view, is either corrupt or realistic.

If at one extreme you are uncomfortable writing for a very narrow group of art "specialists," are you ever worried at the other extreme about writing for too large or general an audience?

I think that the limit of the audience is pretty much the limit of the interest or difficulty of the subject. And I try to increase my range. If you are writing an article about van Gogh for a glossy magazine, you should be able to reach anyone who has been to high school because van Gogh does. But if you are writing an article on the influences of suprematism on industrial production in the early 1920s in Russia, then it seems to me that you could be just as clear in your approach but anticipate a certain level of information in anyone that would be reading that.

I want to ask about the choices you make of who to write for and what kind of freedom that gives you. You have written for the art magazines—

for all of them really—and also for the "New York Times" as well as for the wide circulation "glossies." I was wondering how the decision to write for one or another came about?

Usually I was asked in the first place. In a way, as a writer, I don't feel that I work for publications so much as I work for editors. I write a lot for *Art in America*, when I do write for the magazines, because Betsy Baker is the editor. And when I wrote for the *Times*, I was very lucky because the editor of the Arts and Leisure section then was Seymour Peck, who I think a lot of New York writers will pay homage to. I once figured out my two criteria for an editor. One is that he let me do anything I want and two that he not let me make a fool of myself *unwittingly*. And also that he be a very good word craftsman, who is openly thrilled by good writing. I'll knock myself out to please an editor like that.

How do you understand your relationship to a particular artist about whom you are writing? Say you are reviewing an artist favorably, do you set limits for yourself, do you feel in any way responsible to your subject?

I once made a chart of what goes on in criticism—just tried to diagram what is going on in an act of criticism. I made two vectors. These are preexisting. One is between the artist and the art work. And then there is the critic and a line that crosses the first one to the reader. And then there are dotted lines on all four corners. Isn't this cute? That is the critic's only direct relation: to the reader. And his first responsibility. You are giving somebody something to read. Then there is the critic's relation with the art work and with the artist, and then the reader's relation to the art work and the artist. And the critic can address any of these relations. I've found in trying to explain this—I used it for a workshop once—that I finally had to erase the dotted line between the critic and the artist because it was so mysterious that it probably wouldn't be a line. It would be a snarl. Can I read a poem? This was written in the early 1970s and it was sort of a composite of the successful pop and minimal artists I was observing from the sidelines. I was far removed from the center of things, but I would hang out and gape. For my kind of personality, I think getting involved in the art world was a matter of wanting some of that manna or magic that the artist is presumed to have. And then with the disillusionment of discovering that it is not there, at least not there in any personally accessible way, the romance wears off and you are either a professional or you have moved on to something else. I don't know if this will illuminate anything, but you asked me to bring it along so I am going to read it.

The Artist

The artist does not want to deal with the world.
He wants the world to deal with him.
He realizes that, to this end, he needs the help of others.
Gaining this help involves him in a series of accommodations for which he despises himself and those who help him.
But his original artistic vision remains uncompromised.
It is formidably mysterious, even to him.
Then one day he is a success, and it seems to be exactly what he had imagined it would be.
Money, of course, but also the sense that an unlimited number of possibilities for experience await his leisure.
His former friends and supporters now hate him, but even among themselves they pay tribute to his talent.
His work proceeds satisfactorily.
He cultivates what he regards as a rich gamut of eccentricities.
At some parties he is taciturn, at others garrulous.
He finds it increasingly easy to satisfy his limited, if mildly irregular, sexual appetites.
He collects Art Deco one year, Navajo blankets the next—or, rather, he has assistants collect for him.
He is appalled to realize that he has a drinking problem.
He is bothered by a feeling that his progress in life has somehow fallen behind schedule.
He becomes obsessed with the thought that he must create one monumental, devastatingly original work.
After a period of intense application, he does so.
The public reaction is favorable, but no one seems devastated.
This throws him into a lengthy depression.
He is surprised by the thought that his reputation has gotten out of hand.
Every month or two he reads a new article by some idiot, praising him.
The occasional intelligent article—which he often has trouble understanding—fills him with a vague uneasiness.

Surrounded by assistants and dealers and involved in endless
    projects, he feels like an industry.
He finds that he can do without parties.
He manages to quit drinking for weeks at a time.
He worries about his health, which is perfect.
He reminds himself continually that he can do whatever he wants.
But all he can think to do is work.

1972

Now, I think that there is a degree of malice in there. Partly disappointment, I suppose, in discovering the feet of clay. And also a certain
degree of envy. I mean, the artist is a very complicated kind of hero
in modern times. The hero of "possibility," I guess, is what gets to us.
The idea of being able to make things as God makes things, and have
them change the world.

How is that different from the position of the poet as you see things?
    The position of the poet is nowhere. Poetry has no standing in the
world. There are plenty of myths of the poet, but they are all inherited
and they are all empty now. There is nobody inside them. Simply
because the world doesn't pay enough attention. Without attention
there is just no way the myth is going to kick over. It doesn't happen
in isolation. The act of an individual artist can engage the structures
of the culture. But there has to be some reciprocity, there has to be
some back and forth.

*But this is a time when some people lament the fact that there is so much
public attention being paid to the visual arts, while the poet's alienation is
something like the alienation that people . . .*
    See, I don't think that too much attention can be paid. Not to say
that it's fun. It is fun but it is also incredibly nerve-racking and anxiety
provoking. A lot of people would like things to be nice and cozy and
unpressured. And they don't come to New York to be artists, or they
shouldn't.

*I am asking about poetry, though, and it seems that the poet's position as
you described it is akin to the artist's in previous periods, periods for which
some now profess nostalgia. I wonder if you think the predicament of poets
is likely to change and if their scene is likely to develop as that of visual
artists has?*

I think that that kind of alienation is overrated. It is a great waste. Maybe in the days before World War II, when everyone was expected to grow up very quickly and extended adolescence was not a value, there was something to that. Learning through suffering—when you didn't go into the family business and had to live like a gypsy. I don't know that suffering has the same value anymore. It tends to lead to very self-muffling behaviors. Little tribal groupings and cottage industry. I don't know. Those are values, but not when you are talking about ambitious art. Anyway, many years ago I turned my back on the poetry world. I just find being around artists much more bracing and inspiring, and I guess my creative inspiration comes from artists more than from poets.

Was that connected with your decision both to stop and then to start writing criticism again?

I think every few years I experiment with some kind of radical rejection of everything and then come limping back with my tail between my legs. In the mid-1970s I wasn't writing for the *Times* anymore and the idea of going someplace else just seemed pointless. Actually, I spent two years working on a biography of the poet Frank O'Hara that fell apart because of problems with the estate. And then I tagged along with my wife, who is an actress, to Hollywood and I spent a lot of time in Los Angeles. And I discovered for one thing that not writing criticism didn't in the least increase my productiveness as a poet. And I got interested in seeing how well I could do criticism. Then when the *Voice* job came up about a year and a quarter ago, it just seemed right. I have been having a lot of fun with it.

You described ambition, here and also in the review of Schnabel, as being a key thing to a certain kind of art now. Could you expand on that?

I guess there is a certain kind of irreplaceable force of will that is required, a drivenness or creative craziness that just has to be there. Of course, there are many uses of art. There is a way and an obligation to give the appropriate value to everything. The idea that there is only "the great" is crazy to me. But there is in fact the great. There is in fact the possibility of an art that brings together—it can only be talked about in big generalizations—maximum information of the moment. That quality of being the answer to a question that nobody knew was being asked, but that in fact is *the* question in some way. And the only people who are going to find that are people who have thrown themselves off a cliff. I don't know.

What about the relation of people like Schnabel, who seem to have that kind of ambition but are very young, and people who have that kind of ambition but where the experience of it, for people who look at art, is over a very protracted period of time? I'm thinking of somebody like Westermann or de Kooning.

Well, Westermann would be a much different case to me. He is a very peculiar and eccentric artist of a type who might be seen in opposition to what I was just talking about. But in competitive opposition. He was gonna do it his way and what he did was not "it"; he did something else. Which makes him very cherishable. A lot of artists really love him. And I'm not sure why. De Kooning is of course a perfect example of the titanically ambitious artist . . . with the requisite sense of humor, maybe a gallows humor about staking so much on art. There is something ridiculous to begin with about dirtying up a piece of cloth and expecting people to leave their homes to go see it. You know, it's all rather silly.

During the seventies art was often involved with irony, and I am curious to know if you think circumstances . . .

Irony isn't new. It's the modern condition.

Well, what I was getting at is whether the kind of ambitiousness that one sees now is different. Take the Germans, for instance. Their "seriousness" or "expressionism" is not qualified by self-referential irony in the same way. Has there been a change of context . . .

You are talking about a change in style and attitude, but I don't think that this bears on ambition. I don't know. It's all so general. If anything I am saying about ambition is true, then it has always been true. The only reason I find for talking about it now, because it is sort of dumbly obvious and true, is that it is in opposition to the bad implications of pluralism—and the politeness that grew up around art in the 1970s, when a career became kind of a right that you had. It was understood that if you didn't want too much and didn't behave too badly, you would have your niche. There is that trivializing aspect of it. Art is very silly and it is very free. The freedom is there to be used. It takes somebody with a lot of ambition and stamina to use it. The immediate effect is that everybody else gets nervous.

Do you see pluralism as having had good aspects to it as well?

Well, it was necessary I suppose. Yes. It was a period in which I wasn't very happy because I like things to come to heads. I like things to have edges and be exciting and have high stakes and be dramatic. That is my own personality, but certainly everything we see that is good now profited from that time. It was certainly necessary for the hierarchical arrangements of the late 1960s to break down. Because they had just become clubs for the successful, who then were in a position to administer homeopathic doses of humiliation to those coming up, to preserve that situation, which couldn't be preserved. Do you want me to rephrase what was just said? It's about the idea of what art can do—turn the corner of the culture, make a difference in the culture. It seems to me that a good artist necessarily would have to have more reasons than that. If that's your only reason, then you probably should be in Hollywood or television or something that really has an effect. I guess it is simply that art requires a taste for being in an area of unknown possibilities. And a tolerance for not knowing. There are all kinds of other reasons. It's a matter of temperament. Some people tell me I'm a rugged individualist. I guess it's true. I come from Nordic stock from North Dakota, and I don't understand people who don't have the value of self-reliance. I don't think I'm moralistic about it. Or I try not to be moralistic about it.

I mean, as a critic you have certain things you can say or are given to say by your makeup. The happiness of a critic may be when it's your turn, when the one thing that you have always had on the tip of your tongue seems to be the one thing everybody needs to hear. And then you give it everything you've got. You can't worry about being absolutely right because then you would never say anything.

Does one have a conscious sense of power? Is it a comfortable or uncomfortable position to be in?

Well, the idea of power is very uncomfortable for most Americans who came through the (for the lack of a better word) counter-culture, isn't it? It seems to me that most critics will immediately say when they are asked how it feels to have power, "Oh, I don't have power. The dealers have power. The collectors have power." I think that is an evasion. For myself, I guess I would like to put it more in terms of influence. I mean, if I have influence, good. One of the deepest motivations of all critics is to try to make the world more comfortable for themselves. I think at the root of the critical impulse is some kind of adolescent outrage at growing up and discovering that the world is not nearly what you hoped or thought it might be. Criticism is then a career of trying to move the world over and make it more habitable for your own sensibility. But it is a process that revolutionizes you if you undertake it. You come over a lot more than you bring things over. But there is still that thought of changing things. If that has the effect of raising somebody's prices or getting somebody a position of some kind, that's not what you meant.

The situation for critics you are talking about sounds a lot like the one that confronts painters, like Schnabel, who "want it all" . . .

Well, art has a critical side. All artists are critical, whether they know it or not. I mean, different values light up at different times, often because they have been repressed by previous generations. So the practice of naked ambition becomes a critical act, a critique of the sensibilities and the structures of the previous generation. Or the current generation. There is a real overlap right now. That's what's exciting. New values are existing side by side with old values which are still very strong. So that there is a real struggle and a lot of clash. And a lot of people are breaking out in hives. Including me on occasion. But I just think that there is so much more good about that than bad.

You once wrote in a review that "it is nonsense to say that modernism is somehow dead but it is obvious that modernism is old." Could you expand on that?

Well, modernism can't be dead because to be dead something had to kill you. And there is nothing to kill modernism. I mean, what would it be? Postmodernism? That's a bit of nonsense. But I think that there is definitely a sense that we have seen all the moves. All the basic moves. The change right now is one of attitudes toward them. In a certain way what is happening now is a very revolutionary change. But it is one that is almost like X rays. They are passing through every part of everything without changing its structure. But the picture sure is different.

How is it a revolutionary change?

Well, I don't know. *Revolutionary* is a dead word really. But the change is quite violent, I think. It is sort of a draining of juices out of old values. Somebody like Salle is interesting in that he treats in this very evenhanded, cold-blooded way all kinds of images and techniques that carry a lot of myth and value—used in such a way as to objectify all those things. It is quite violent, and also extremely liberating. Inherited values are a burden. Modernism says that it is a good idea to throw out burdens. I think maybe now one of our burdens is the idea of throwing out burdens. So it gets very complicated. It spirals back on itself. I wish I could be clear about it. One of the disadvantages about being a frontline critic is that your theory is ad hoc and patched together from week to week. But then there are plenty of critics being theoretical, and I read them.

What is your reaction to the Marxist or sociological critique of the present situation that says in effect if there is a "revolution" afoot, it is a palace revolution in that it is happening in a fairly stable art-world structure and signals a new and expansive phase of that structure?

I think that there is a lot to be said for that. I don't think that's wrong. But of course the penchant of that kind of critic is to think that once you have said something like that you have closed the case and you are permitted to stop thinking. Certainly we are in a period right now where the larger structures of the society in the culture and the economy are locked. It is the opposite of the 1960s, when all these structures were very fluid. There was a lot of social mobility, a lot of political ferment. I think they are very much locked right now. I am going to say something that will probably be taken wrong or maybe will be taken right, and in any case will make me unpopular, but it seems to me that any real artist is going to prefer a situation like this one. The way any real artist would love to have been in a Renaissance court or in seventeenth-century Holland—moments when money and power are locked up by a certain class. It's because of the leverage, of having something to push off against. And a certain kind of security and a certain kind of continuity. To say that is to name a major anxiety because—what am I saying?—that I prefer the poor to get poorer and the rich to get richer? No. The citizen and the political animal in me hate that. So part of me likes it and part of me hates it. And that's an anxiety that with irony and humor and gum and hairpins I have to maintain. But it is a dynamism which makes the future seem like an interesting proposition. One way or another.

Do you see the alternative scene—alternative spaces, critical publications, and so forth—as being in any way a challenge to the current art system, as anything to push off against?

No. It has been said by other people that the robustness of the commercial market right now, and this sort of confidence it has, owes tremendously to the work that the alternative spaces did in the 1970s. As a farm system and as a presorting, staging area. That isn't what the alternative spaces set out to do, but that is what happened. Certainly the alternative spaces now, with a couple of exceptions I can think of, are more over against the museums, the way the galleries are, than they are over against both, or over against galleries, certainly. No, you don't change big structures by tinkering with little ones. There may be good little ones. There may be good reasons for tinkering with little structures, and immediate benefits. But the critical act of an individual or a small group works only on a small scale. Being clear about the state of the larger structures is as much as you can do. To that extent Marxist criticism has been important. It certainly has been important to me, although it makes me grind my teeth sometimes. It is so necessary not to be naive about what is going on. But what I hate about a lot of the Marxist critics is the morality they attach to every work. To see something as being implicated in the present structure is to disqualify it. But that ends up disqualifying everything except something so perfect that it doesn't exist.

What determines the life expectancy of the radical element in work that is done within the gallery system, the locked-in structure?

I don't know. It is up to the people coming up, I guess. When I am talking about the radical nature of someone like Salle, I don't want to fall into the trap of saying that this is his value.

To what extent do you think art is legitimately a matter of pleasure? Almost as the primary value.

I would say about 100 percent. I don't see how you can get around that. I don't know, is there an opposition between pleasure and criticality? Criticality is a pleasure for people who like it. I have been writing something about Robert Smithson lately, thinking about the late 1960s and the opposition between minimal and color-field criticism. Color-field meaning the late Greenbergian sort of gentrified pleasure. They made pleasure very much the whole point. But they made it flabby. There is no edge to it and no engagement of the culture.

And the minimalists sort of went the other way. They completely repressed the idea of pleasure and made the art all edges. And I was very confused then because my intellect was absolutely lined up with the minimalists. But damn it, I would look at some of those paintings and they were so pretty. And that is not nothing. I became friends with a lot of the people who became known as lyrical abstractionists— sort of the non-Greenbergian color-field painting, more eclectic color-field painting. And they were murdered. They were killed. Between the deep blue sea and the devil it was just forget it. And that was a real lesson. The possibility is always limited. I mean, sometimes they just won't let you do something. They have no use for it.

I wrote this poem in 1976. This was my valedictory to art criticism when I decided I would never write it anymore. It has lots of indiscretions in it which made things a little touchy when I started getting back into criticism. I wrote it to read in place of a lecture at the Art Institute of Chicago for the Friends of Modern Art, who hated it a lot. Anyway, that's enough.

Dear Profession of Art Writing

My crummy benefactor, how can I not be grateful?
For 12 years fount of my sustenance, social identity, claim to fame,
without you where would I be today?
Teaching?
Teaching what? I don't know anything
but you, Profession of Art Writing.
Would I be more a poet than I've become?
Maybe, but at what cost? That much closer
to complete physical and psychic collapse, or beyond it already,
an unhappy memory, another scalp
on the belt of drug abuse and cultural devastation,
gibbering in some Rocky Mountain ashram,
understood to have had a good mind, some adventures,
a wad of lyrics poignant and obscure . . .
I would not at any rate be sitting here
snugly, at this desk, this typewriter,
as baby daughter capers in next room

and cat suns on daybed. A picture of total contentment.
I must be a jerk not to regard you more highly,
Profession of Art Writing, my lucky charm.

Or perhaps like a teenage suitor shocked
to have conquered, I find you hard to "respect."
You did favor me awfully readily.
A rhetorical knack—what else did I bring to you?
Abysmal ignorance, slovenly habits of thought, star-struck
narcissism, a starved and sneaky ego . . .
Yet success came my way in cozy degree.
I get top dollar when I'm nervy enough to demand it.
I get frequent opportunities to decline,
with secret glee, offers to write or speak.
Still, I have craved in vain the approval of my betters,
the ambitious toilers, the scholars, the committed,
from whose difficult harvests I gleaned at random
whatever I've provided of food to the mind.
Not that I lose any sleep over that. What's ghastly
is that on occasion I mistook my hand-me-down taste
for the light of election, and poured ink on the worthy.
I still blush, hotly, for those occasions,
yearning for a large bomb to fall directly on my head.
Like that supercilious dismissal of William Baziotes—horrible!
And László Moholy-Nagy, for God's sake, I patronized your
venerable ghost! And Susan Crile, estimable painter,
what full moon was shining when I sat down to review you?
Also Stanford University, and redoubtable scholar Albert Elsen,
I sneered at your splendid museum,
behaving just like a paranoid's dream of a New York chauvinist,
oh shame! James Brooks, you didn't complain
those years ago, but even today you could flay me with a look.
Jim Dine, how could I, and Joan Snyder, how could I
denigrate your indubitable value in the (unpronounced) name
of (nonexistent) standards of acceptability?
Richard Hamilton, where did I get off
welcoming you to America in that disgraceful fashion?
And Gio Pomodoro, though you never will be to my taste,
that was no excuse for behaving like a fat-mouthed provincial!
All these atrocities in the Sunday *Times*, each in a million copies
just whizzing off the presses, fanning out over the land,

alighting in libraries—microfilm, oh God!!—
unkillable and infamous words! Just let me
take this knife and . . .

But no. (Puts knife back in drawer and closes it.)
Already I feel a little better . . .

So back to you, Profession of Art Writing
whose fool I've been: who needs you anyhow?
What loosens the purse strings of the journalism business
to finance the bad conscience of louts like me?
The imperatives of commerce, is it?
Capitalism? The art-buck megalith and entertainment combine?
Are we all just lackeys?
Seemingly so. But then who isn't, here and now?
(If we aren't bourgeois, then what the hell are we?
as James Schuyler once said something like.)
But is the artist, for instance, a lackey,
upon whose peculiar habits this whole industry turns?
The artist, our dream god or goddess of freedom,
free to act crazy in public, free to send his craziness forth
in the tidy receptacles of his work
which, though inexorably they reach the iron museum,
stirs souls on the way—don't they?
(FUCK!!!
You see, I can do that because I'm a poet.
Poet, n: a currently negligible species of artist,
an atavistic survival, like painters.)
Many art writers, as I did, hopefully start out
expecting to be the friends and peers of artists,
participants, even, in grandiloquent studio illuminations—
this before we encounter the artist's reticence,
artist's pettiness, desperation, gloom,
the artist's uncanny resemblance to just about anybody
nine-tenths of the time, and in the tenth tenth
the artist is off somewhere, unavailable, working.

In the meantime one has written a number of things
embarrassingly adulatory, partaking of the second kind of sin:
the fawning rave.
(Not as bad as the first, because all that gets hurt
is the sensibilities of the sensible;
these heal in time.)

The other sin, disgruntled and malicious,
follows as night to day,
or at least it did in my own impulse-ridden zodiac.
Then for some of the driven and bright ones (not me, need I say)
comes the tabernacle chorus of formalism,
of solicitude only for the work, which suddenly starts behaving
with a small, humorless but pertinacious mind of its own—
like a set of well-trained lab assistants in this old favorite
of mine: "Frank Stella's new paintings investigate
the problem of shape as such." Ouch!
Strung out between such crystalline insanities
and the utter murk of creative reality, art writers
commence to be furtive, neurotic, displaying
by their tics and funks and struts, their introvert theatrics
what might be the superfluous disorder of an artist's mind.
The sleep of art produces reason,
vague and excited mental movements in the night
before the deadline. Even as we meet here
an art writer somewhere is in heat,
smoking, spilling coffee, squinting at illegible notes,
studying for the 20th time a slide irritatingly too red in which
he sees, or did yesterday, a late spasm
of constructivism. "Bullshit, bullshit," whispers
his most hated and reliable inner voice,
leitmotif in a fevered subjective babble, e.g.,
"What is this work? Who made it? What did he or she intend,
portend? What influences, contexts, matrices apply?
What does this work do to my cherished notions?
What to my enemy's cherished notions?
Is it any good?
If I like this, how can I like what I liked last week?
I guess I really am a lightweight, what the heck.
I'm also in a rut: second time this month I've reviewed this gallery.
Well, can I help it if Leo Castelli is a genius?
On top of everything else, I'm supposed to be *fair*?
Hmm, do I have to insert a definition of suprematism?
Probably. Gotta think of the amateur audience,
bringing it up to my own midget educational level.
Drink deep, or taste not . . .
Fortunately I love art, or I'd be a real phony after all.
I'm not just a Lipton Tea Taster, I'm a Lipton Tea Lover!
But do I love the art here at hand?

Do I want to persuade others that they ought to love it, too?
Don't people have enough guilt without feeling responsible to some
     paint-spattered sheet metal?
Well, that's their lookout, this stuff is terrific,
and I'm making such analogies!
So pretty, they can't help but be wrong.
If the footnote critics ever read me, which I doubt,
they'll start snorting with disgust just about here.
Poetic drivel! they think, I think.
But can only art be beautiful?
Can't I be a little beautiful, too?
The cookies were lousy, but the box was delicious.
Jeez, I sure hope somebody is going to read this.
It is an eventuality one would do well to anticipate.
Let's see, how many s's are there in Lissitzky?"

And so he taps on into the perfervid night,
ending at last in a daze of self-satisfaction—
after retyping, the best part,
that's where he puts in the jokes and finesses,
chuckling to himself (heh heh, you smart aleck!),
making the paragraphs shapely, the transitions neat—
then a number of stiff drinks, then sleep.
We will pass over in silence, draw
a merciful curtain on, the subsequent second thoughts,
sudden doubts, the cold sweat over an inapt
or impolitic phrase now irretrievable, inconsolable fits
of self-loathing; then later the scream of anguish over editorial
meddling, followed shortly by a taste of ashes:
another product of his sweat and blood come and gone
like spit on a griddle, unremarked,
no feedback, useless, as if it never happened;
then the check in the mail, a sigh, and on to the next.
Peace to all that. We won't even mention it . . .

Profession of Art Writing, you were not always thus.
When before, for one thing, has your seedy self
so long held the exquisite attentions of a poem?
(Wow, I'm even original!)
Once strictly a gentleman's or partisan's occupation,
or the busman's holiday of an academic,
except in France, of course, whence sprang the poet-critic

tradition:
Baudelaire and Apollinaire inspiriting Frank O'Hara
inspiriting me, a tradition
that is today justly, alas, in disrepute.
A poet who insists on behaving like one
is good about art mainly when everybody else is determined
to be extremely excited.
The license poetry gives to feeling, not to mention the mean streak
nourished by a career of deprivations,
does not make the poet a dependable wide-ranging thinker—
except in France, of course, where everyone is doomed
to be smart about everything, I hate them!

Anyway, then came the postwar American ebullition—
"crashing waves of paint," as Schuyler put it—and greatness
out walking in the street and drinking at the Cedar,
and Rosenberg and Greenberg, and world leadership,
and secretly CIA-funded exhibitions, and journals, symposia,
The Club! "the Irascibles"—*Life* Magazine, unbelievable!
who's in, who's out? the color this year is purple!
did you hear what de Kooning did to Joe Hirshhorn?
and Hirshhorn collecting, and people actually collecting,
and Ad Reinhardt warning of corruption—isn't he cute?—
and Katie-bar-the-door here comes Nelson Rockefeller!
Money! veritable long green, not right away but soon,
and gosh everyone wants to be there
if not to field at least to spectate—and the parties!
Then they had this big party and called it the '60s.
I was there. Weren't you there, chum? Too bad!
So anyway, art writing no longer seemed such a tacky job.
It was practically compulsory. And me,
what with my dynamite way with words, y'know,
I got into it, and then it wouldn't let me go,
though it gradually became not nearly so glamorous again
and here I am fit for nearly nothing else. Hello.
Hello 1970s, as dramatic as an overexposed photograph.
Hello, have you heard photography's the thing now?
(Jesus, I don't know an f-stop from a flapjack eraser.)
Fading fast here, folks. Fading fast, Profession
of Art Writing, you really have been incredibly good to me.
I've traveled—around town, and once to Chicago—

and met so many interesting people!
I have elicited monosyllables from Andy Warhol
and been stared at like I was some kind of moron
by Robert Motherwell. Been in a videotape by Les Levine.
Alex Katz cut me out of aluminum.
Portrait painted by George Schneeman and by Peter Dean.
A noted critic gave me heartfelt counsel:
"It's all public relations," she said nonchalantly.
(Speak for yourself! I've wished ever since I'd replied;
boy did I hate that! though it was truer of me at the time
than not true, I'll allow.)
Thomas B. Hess asked me the best question, truly,
that can ever be asked of an art reviewer—
like all great questions, unanswerable.
Saw de Kooning drunk and saw him sober, dazzling man!
Delighted in the friendship of, besides those
already mentioned, artists Bill Barrell, Jennifer Bartlett,
Lynda Benglis, Joe Brainard, Rudy Burckhardt, Scott Burton,
Robert Dash, Donna Dennis, Martha Diamond, Rafael Ferrer,
Jane Freilicher, Mike Goldberg, Frank Owen, Yvonne Jacquette,
Tom Kovachevich, Doug Ohlson, Larry Rivers, James Rosenquist,
Herb Schiffrin, John Seery, Michael Singer, Arlene Slavin,
Jim Sullivan, Neil Welliver, Nina Yankowitz
and others too numerous, etc.
The art world drew me insensibly away from poetry
and the company of poets—not a bad event.
I could not have lived long, what with my vertigo,
on that precipitous slope. (Here I direct your attention
to the present-day mountaineers, my heroes,
whose feats make non-boring poetry conceivable:
Ginsberg, Koch, Ashbery, Schuyler, Padgett. Up there, hello!)

Since we seem to be into the credits now, reeling,
let us turn to the career critics, your captains
and minions, Profession, without whom . . .
But here they come in dancing array!
Inspiration, let us call them by their qualities:
Lucy R. Lippard of the portable moral authority;
Hilton Kramer the abhorrent, who makes art sound as appealing
as a deodorant enema; nice-making John Russell;
Harold Rosenberg, honey-tongued blowhard (but great, why not?);

charmingly repellent John Coplans; David Bourdon, cub reporter;
Robert Rosenblum, hosanna king; Donald Kuspit, avid bore;
Peter Plagens, aging whiz; Brian O'Doherty, or
can you whiz forever?; Carter Ratcliff the cornucopiate,
from whom I steal all my ideas; schizzy and impeccable
Michael Fried; inexplicably diffident Irving Sandler;
Leo Steinberg, a bit too smart to be Kenneth Clark,
and regrettably in the wrong country; Clement
Greenberg, worm-eaten colossus, our Father,
who taught us that art is not virtue, but power;
egregious claque-flack Kenworth Moffet;
William Rubin claque-flack of undeniable gifts;
Linda Nochlin, lead on!; anxiety-prone Amy Goldin who
   rejoices my
heart; Diane Waldman, sedatives in prose;
absurdly talented Sanford Schwartz, so mellifluous sometimes
I want to beat him up; honorably obsessive Joseph Masheck
and earnest Roberta Smith, to your bright futures I would tip
   my hat
if I had one; excruciatingly mild James Mellow;
Gregory Battcock, 'nuff said, and 'nuff-said Mario Amaya;
John Perreault John Perreault; Peter Frank—Peter Frank?!;
Walter Darby Bannard of the chronically misdirected energies;
Barbara Rose, educator and discourager; Robert Pincus-Witten,
lunatic savant of St. Theresa and tautology;
Dore Ashton, enthusiast; Hayden Herrera of the kind heart;
Elizabeth C. Baker—hi Betsy!; Phyllis Derfner kindly shape up!;
Nicolas Calas, surrealist war-horse; sweet Franze Schulze
and sour Dennis Adrian—Chicago Taste; Sam Hunter of the
   dollar;
Jeremy Gilbert-Rolfe, totally crackers; Lawrence Alloway,
sanitation engineer; Rosalind Krauss and Annette Michelson,
let me out of here!; John Canaday, ugh; Marcia Tucker,
what does she want?; Jack Burnham, eek!, and David Antin,
yipes!, and Robert Hughes, ho hum, and Douglas Davis, ugh;
Emily Genauer, triple ugh; Max Kozloff,
I'll make up my insignificant mind about you eventually;
Thomas B. Hess, *il miglior fabbro*.

(Anyone inadvertently omitted here
may apply for insult in later editions.)

More charming than a cannibal tribe, this bunch,
and more stimulating than a dentists' convention:
a tidy guild on the fringe of useful human endeavor.
I cannot regret having made their acquaintance.
And I will not regret our years together, Profession;
I neither enriched nor eroded you, as others have,
but I would hope I've done my bit for pleasure,
a fleeting kind that is sweet to the serious.
I intended no harm. May my sins be forgotten.

1976–77

What was the question that Tom Hess asked you?
    He said—this was in 1965 and I called him on a pay phone in the
street, and I was young and I didn't know anything. I had never had
an art course. And I called him up and I told him a lot of lies about
my qualifications. He must have detected it. He said, "Never mind all
that. Just write me a letter telling me what makes you think you are
qualified to walk into a gallery where some poor bastard has his paintings and to tell him they are no good." And I think I wrote him a
letter saying in effect that I would never, ever do that—tell anybody
they were no good. But obviously I have. There is an essential humility.
I suppose everything has its essential humility, but with criticism it is
so easy to get seduced by the illusion of power. Only, one of the things
that you have to keep in mind is the different level of commitment
between you and the artist. The different levels of investment. You
might say the same things but you have to think twice.

July 1983

Edouard Manet

Manet: 1832–1883, Metropolitan Museum of Art,
September 10–November 27, 1983

Art love is attained, or contracted, through a series of epiphanies, or seizures. One of mine, seventeen years ago, was triggered by a small Manet on loan to the Metropolitan, and I do mean small: a tiny muted oil of some asparagus. The perversity of concentrating on anything so minor, amid acres of trumpeting masterpieces, was most of the appeal; that afternoon I was feeling hostile toward masterpieces, which seemed to be ganging up to intimidate and exhaust me. A bite-sized daub by a Great Name struck me as just about my speed. Then something happened. Or, rather, two things happened: paint and asparagus.

Such onsets are never clear, but I know that this one had something to do with the thought that Manet probably ate the asparagus after he painted it. A sense of lived time erupted for me in the little picture, which came to represent one pleasure, in eating, delayed by another pleasure, in painting. The deliciousness of the paint—Manet's racy touch and excruciating tones—became continuous with the deliciousness of food, and the associations, once begun, didn't stop there. I felt sensuously alert to the whole world and in a right and graceful relation to things in time: one paints, one eats, one continues. As conversion experiences go, it was mild—more a sudden adjustment or refinement than a mystical illumination—but it had the requisite effect of persuading me that, at least where art was concerned, I would never be the same again. I was silly with contentment, and with love of Manet.

"My" asparagus was not in the monumental Manet retrospective when I saw it in Paris, but I returned to it in memory as something to hang on to in the face of another concatenation of masterpieces, this time all of them by Manet. Time and the museum build up a carapace of numbing familiarity and daunting piety around any art, and one needs one's tricks to break through. Happily for all of us, it may never have been easier than right now to break through to Manet.

Has any retrospective ever been better timed? The sense we have of living at the end of an epoch—a sense encoded in the bizarre term *postmodern*—brings us into abrupt intimacy with the epoch's beginnings. And in the beginning was Manet. Exactly a century after his death, the carapace around him is thin, more akin to Alice's penetrable looking glass than to the encrustation of old-masterdom. Scholars endlessly probe the riddles of his sources and influence; theorists still use his work to support conflicting ideas of tradition and radicalism, of realism and art-for-art's-sake formalism; and social historians are freshly fascinated by the violent reactions of his contemporaries, the legend of frothing critics and jeering throngs. Without entering into these lively but piecemeal concerns, we may yet share the feeling of urgency that informs them all, the renascent challenge of a creator who announced the dawn of a future whose twilight we inhabit.

In paintings and especially photographs of him, Edouard Manet is unprepossessing, an elegantly turned-out but somewhat withdrawn, wary, nervous man. The remarkably little that is known of his life is mostly dull. He was a proper bourgeois by upbringing and habits. His father grudgingly supported his art career when Manet's lack of fitness for law or the military became clear. For six years, until 1856, he was an often rebellious student of the academic painter Thomas Couture. He married a Dutch woman older than himself. Though hungering for official recognition, he almost helplessly produced one outrageously provocative work after another, fretting miserably over the ensuing snubs and ridicule. He died at the age of fifty-one, probably of syphilis.

Manet was not so much ahead of his tumultuous time as he was one of the few who were not behind it. Even Baudelaire—who had yearned for a "painter of modern life," an artist of transitory beauties who would show "how great and poetic we are in our neckties and patent-leather boots"—seemed not to recognize the fulfillment of his dreams in the work of his young friend Manet. (Perspicaciously, genteel society noted, and vilified, redolences common to Manet's paintings and the unspeakable *Fleurs du mal*.) This was at a time when most sophisticated observers agreed that current salon painting was anemic, but even some who had stomached the brash directness of Courbet regarded Manet's art as poison rather than remedy.

What had Manet wrought, and why the fuss about it? He had

unleashed a terrific richness of subject matter and aesthetic effect by a process of encyclopedic assimilation and inspired reduction. He went to old masters and to popular illustrators for motifs, took cues from photography and Japanese prints, and carried the spontaneity of the oil sketch over to the largest scale. His contemporaries were less over-whelmed by this richness than insensible to it, obsessed by what wasn't there—conventional finish, consistent technique, extractable mean-ing—and repelled by the nakedly personal impulse, the raw avidity, which he offered as a sole and sufficient basis for major art.

At the heart of Manet's work is an unalloyed erotic sensitivity—similar to Baudelaire's but without the poet's rhetoric of torment. Ma-net responded to the sensuous charge in things and in paint and to the sexual charge in people, not as anything hidden and shadowy but as the very flavor of a civilized existence. His contemporaries, bemused by their changing world, could not relax enough to appreciate his life-affirming joke: that in rendering the animal in the bonnet or frock coat, he conferred an integrity on living men and women that made them proof against whatever dehumanizing forces the world could inflict. (Except death, treated in his still harrowing *Execution of the Emperor Maximilian* as a mere stupid animal cessation.) Like his Amer-ican near contemporary Walt Whitman, he celebrated modernity as the apotheosis of individual flesh and blood.

The key image is, of course, *Olympia*. To say that *Olympia* is an erotic picture is too tame; *Olympia* is a dirty picture. The pose and all the accoutrements—neckband and high heels, black maid, black cat, rumpled bedclothes—are pornographic effects. Glories of light and color aside, the difference from pornography is wholly in the attitude of the young woman, who is not a passive sex object but a subject, secure in her power. Her level gaze sizes up life and pronounces it good, unsurprising, and perfectly manageable. Refusing to idealize or moralize about the modern courtesan, Manet nevertheless does ro-manticize her—by assimilating her into the deeper romance of the real and the true, the bedrock values of all his work. In a sense, this cool-eyed woman *is* Manet.

Manet is a master of eyes, a genius of gazes. Typically, the eyes look straight out of the picture, but not at the viewer. One of the stronger scintillations of "getting" Manet occurs in the moment when it dawns on you that his people are looking at the painter. Like tinted mirrors, the eyes, colored by the mood of the moment, return the matter-of-fact scrutiny of the artist. The ineluctably sexy situation of painting from life—a situation convention enjoins us to regard as "professionally" defused, like the doctor's examination room—effloresces in Manet's paintings, even and perhaps especially in those where any possibility of impropriety is out of the question.

Not far short of *Olympia* in its eroticism is *Repose*, the portrait of Berthe Morisot reclining with decided unreposefulness on a couch. This impeccable young lady is clad to the wrists, but beneath the petticoats, twisting athwart their arrangement, her body is wild. Wild not with desire, unless the understandable one to have done with this eternal posing, but with the thoughtless animal energy that both desires and induces desire. Morisot's discomfort gives rise to a tension, as do her beauty and fashionable dress, with the humble, rapt attentiveness of the painter—who says with his brush, "There she is. I see her." This picture without a whisper of doting is a lesson in how to love.

That Manet loved Morisot—though chastely, it seems (she married his brother)—is hard to miss. In a way, perhaps, he loved everyone whom he painted with any success: love, as an egoless erotic response (Whitman spoke of "adhesiveness"), may be a very condition of his art's success, even when he paints a man or a child. But such affinity becomes positively delirious in the pictures of Morisot. The portrait with a (barely visible) bouquet of violets—with its brutal tone changes and dark hues (perhaps only Goya achieves blacks so lyrical)—has a quality of intimate violence that might once have been conveyed by the phrase "a broken heart." The experience of beauty and charm here is roughly equivalent to being hit by a train.

Manet generally starts with a subject of charm or piquancy and exacerbates its sensation—roughening the friction, turning up the heat. He does this mainly with the stimulating abrasion of abrupt tonal contrasts, eliminating intermediate gradations of light. He also employs strong, often acid, local colors in clashing or biting juxtaposition. Another of his tactics is the equal emphasis, frequently the exaggeration, of widely separated details, which keep the eye jumping in search of a unity that remains elusive. All these devices are orchestrated in *Baudelaire's Mistress*, one of Manet's most astonishing and least-known paintings (it resides in Budapest). It became my own particular enthusiasm and touchstone in Paris.

Jeanne Duval, a Creole, was in her forties, ill, and partly crippled when Manet painted her in 1862. Her fading exoticism and the dark aura of a stormy twenty-year affair with the author of *Les Fleurs du mal* were not lost on the painter, who made the painting an adventure in strangeness. The tiny homely face drifting above the vastness of skirt sardonically hints at the motif of a baroque angel on a cloud, but nothing angelic clings to this apparition. Isolated details go off like bombs: hand! foot! hair! fan! The unnerving effect of white fabric against green couch may be due to a subliminal vibration of green's absent complementary: red. (Similarly spicy uses of green with white occur in *Olympia* and *The Balcony*.) Summary brushwork knits up the surface, giving the entire picture the luminous unreality of an image projected onto an undulating veil.

Manet's stylistics in *Baudelaire's Mistress* provoke and manipulate an emotional involvement with his subject matter: a woman both pathetic and disquieting, an outcast invested with mysteries of private romance and public notoriety. Can one read too much into such a picture? I don't think so. The vivid ambiguity of Manet's portrayals— ambiguity beyond ambivalence, approaching a Shakespearean fullness of connotation—can sustain endless fantasy and speculation. It is not vulgar to seek the meanings of Manet's pictures, only vulgar to suppose that one has found them.

It seems necessary to insist on Manet's subject matter in order to correct the modern critical tendency to see him as the father of formalism, the starting point for an inexorable march through impressionism and cubism to abstraction. This tendency has had the effect of blurring important differences between Manet and his impressionist followers, who did move a long way in the direction of making subject matter the merest pretext for painting—thus becoming, beyond modern, modern*ist*. The association is a procrustean half-truth that lops off much of what makes Manet uniquely significant in his own time as well as uniquely relevant to the art and sensibility of today.

More young artists are going to look harder at this retrospective than at any other (Picasso's included) in recent memory. The "postmodernist" revaluation of values has revised Manet's pictures without altering a molecule of their pigment. What used to seem old-fashioned about them, such as the borrowings from various pictorial sources and the ad hoc shifts in style from subject to subject, is the present's cup of tea. Like ends meeting, the old optimistic urbanity of Manet links up with the thorny new urbanity of young artists who regard images— any and all images—as a virtual category of nature. Manet's creative traits read like a checklist of current sensibilities: icy aloofness balancing secret romanticism, use of quotation, flat contradiction (or ironic rehabilitation) of convention, high-strung self-consciousness, all-pervading eroticism.

But, as yet, no artist in our time can match the reach and grasp, the sheer power of organization, with which Manet gathered up the loose ends of his day. His problem was, as ours is, how to construct a vision of the world without a hierarchy of values, an order of importance. If your eye falls impartially on all that confronts it—and any other way of looking at the world seems false—how can you compose other than blandly or arbitrarily?

The bland and the arbitrary held no terrors for Manet, who recognized them as qualities of the absolutely modern: the emotional leveling of democracy, the attention-shredding disarray of the city. In every picture, whether imposing stylized conceits or pointedly stripping them away, he registered a sense that what was there could just as easily be different—could, in fact, be something else altogether. But this is not the same as saying, with the formalists, that the subject doesn't count. It means simply that the question of selection is getting a new answer.

Criteria of classical appropriateness and romantic assertion were out for Manet. In their place came the frail antennae of whim and curiosity and erotic velleity, the casual impulses of a walker in the city. In a zone of subtle overlap between the personal and the social, the artist's passing mood became the crossroads of the world and time. The images that emerged were impersonal enough to be shared wholly with others, personal enough so that they danced in time with the artist's inner life.

Amid a glorious shatter of light and incident in the Folies-Bergère, a barmaid is singled out. No one there could be less "important," as the young woman herself might readily agree. She is worn out, oblivious to the spectacle and to her role in it. But a tender, perverse fancy has discovered her; a wandering glance has cast her as the center, the pivot, the vortex of a cyclone of ostentation and pleasure. That glance—quick and secret, amused and touched—is the real hero of the picture. It is a potential seducer's glance assimilated to the more complex passion of an artist—assimilated without, however, losing its specific celerity, its fixation on this woman on this night.

Manet will never be equaled in the particularity of his response to the visible world. If, formally, he generalized matter and light into thoroughly artificial schema of brushstroke and color patch, it was to express a sense of reality livelier and far more profound than that of Courbet or the impressionists. Reality, for Manet, is what is seen by an interested (attracted, implicated, "adhesive") individual. The sentient eyes that gaze from his canvases, the bunch of asparagus that absorbs and radiates an undivided love of art and of living, all the subjects of this artist preserve a contingent aspect and aura of belonging to an unrepeatable moment in a fleeting life, which is the seal of their timelessness.

We may only be starting to understand Manet—that is, to comprehend his wholeness. It is still common to encounter the critical opinion that great as he is, Manet lacks something in the way of consistency, that his work is flawed by a certain overall raggedness and sense of incompletion. This is an opinion of minds offended by contradiction and disorder—the truest, most fundamental conditions of modern experience. Manet intuited that such experience could be both goal and guide for the artist, or for any sensibility courageous enough to cultivate its own vulnerabilities and delights. It may be that in the very fissures and discontinuities, the wrenching entrancements and erotic surges of his work, we can meet the genuine and, for us, the revelatory, the useful, the contemporary Manet.

October 1983

Balthus

A bad man is the sort of man who admires innocence.
Oscar Wilde

A well-known mystery man, famous for being infamous, the seventy-six-year-old Balthus—or to use his full name and self-conferred title, Count Balthasar Klossowski de Rola—has long been as enshrouded in confusion and controversy as an alp in snow. What is this painter of young girls in equivocal poses? Hero of tradition or villain of re-action, poet of childhood or furtive libertine, master or elegant fake? Is he, perhaps, all of the above?

Traveling to see the current Balthus retrospective (Metropolitan Museum of Art, February 29–May 13, 1984), I had an unusually open mind. Normally I maintain a full set of opinions—subject to change—on notable artists, but when I introspected on my preconceptions about Balthus, I found that I didn't have any. I wasn't alone in this. Friends I talked to drew similar blanks on the artist, nearly all of whose best works are in American museums and thus are at least passingly familiar.

Now that I have formed an opinion of Balthus—negative, with qualifications—I see that just such absence of memorable effect is an important point about, and against, him. I see also that it is not really a vacancy, but a stalemate: sensational subject matter in a no-decision bout with genteel style. I'm talking about the general run of his paint-ing. Sometimes subject matter gains an edge, and the art sputters into life. His drawings, for example, are consistently good. At other times—in the work he's done since about 1955, certainly—style triumphs, and the art goes out like a light. What fascinates me about this stalemate, and makes it seem worth reflecting on, is the way it has become a cultural sign: a token for aristocratic, disdainful, naughty sensibility, a shrine of the antimodern in the modern temple of fame.

One tip-off that any art is functioning as a sign, rather than as a subject/object of genuine experience, is a robotic quality in criticism of it. Invariable points, made in unvarying ways, divert us from a direct encounter with the work into comfortable ruts of alibi. After reading a lot of Balthus criticism, both older examples and pieces occasioned by the current show, I have identified three characteristic tacks the painter's enthusiasts take.

The first is old-master invocation. Piero della Francesca, Nicolas Poussin, and Gustave Courbet keep being trooped in to confer legitimacy on their latter-day disciple. It is true enough that Balthus studied these masters and adapted features of their work. But only a numbed mind could juxtapose their names with his and think it a compliment to Balthus, who on his best day didn't attain the height of their shoe-laces. (Though rarely cited, Georges de La Tour is both more Balthus's speed and a more apt precedent for the experience, as opposed to the denatured art historical glamour, of his strongest work.) What we see in such writing about the artist is a pretentious appeal to authority, without any critical illumination of influences.

Then there is lineage mavenry. Balthus's affectation of nobility—he is no more a count than he is Miss America—has long embarrassed even his well-wishers, but many are willing to indulge him in other preenings. The early interest of Rainer Maria Rilke, a devotee of Balthus's painter mother, in the drawings of the precocious youngster is regularly tapped for its quotient of stardust. His friendships with Alberto Giacometti and Antonin Artaud—relations with zero significance for his art, as far as I can see—likewise are treated as affirmations, perhaps of some angelic fraternity of the unspeakably great. The delirious flavor of this sort of thing can be caught in the book on Balthus by Jean Leymarie, the artist's most feckless celebrant: "Some artists are providentially singled out as bearers of the Golden Bough. They abide, pilgrims of eternity, keepers of the spirit, servants of beauty."

A third tack of Balthus's hagiographers is to trigger the romance of initiation. The image of Balthus as an artist "about whom nothing is known" (as he once admonished the critic John Russell to describe him) has been a public-relations coup right up there with Salvador Dalí's mustache. It conjures mysterious figures in cowled robes doing weird things in castle keeps at midnight. Its redolence of the forbidden is powerfully nostalgic in an age like our own, when no one seems up to forbidding anybody anything. By simultaneously arousing and frustrating curiosity, it forestalls the saner thought that, all things considered, one actually does not give a damn.

Note the symmetry of old-master invocation, lineage mavenry, and initiation. They form a tripod with historical, social, and psychological legs to support the myth of a timeless, asocial, and transpersonal Balthus. But if not the "King of Cats," as he styled himself in his youth, Balthus is certainly a prince of foxes. The proof is that so many writers who should know better have fallen for, and into, the same line of mystification about him, displaying the same protective urge to hoist him from the ranks of ordinary humanity into the inviolable firmament of myth. What necessitates this line is, of course, the breath of scandal: Balthus's pedophilia.

It is not completely true that I approached the Balthus retrospective with no opinions. I have a settled opinion against pedophilia. Unripe fruit may have an aesthetic piquancy, but when the fruit is a human personality it is not to be plucked. Children are to be cared for, not used, by adults. To deflect or evade such judgments—for instance, by using the clever shifter *nymphet*, a word, like *mark*, that blames the victim—is the constant study of pedophiles and their apologists. Such tactics have been tried in Balthus's case. For sheer maybe-they'll-believe-anything chutzpah, the prize must go to Balthus's elder son, Stanislas Klossowski de Rola, who wrote that his father's "fabled theme of the young adolescent girl . . . has nothing whatsoever to do with sexual obsession except perhaps in the eye of the beholder." Very nice, Stanislas.

I was prepared, however, to keep my feelings about pedophilia out of my judgment of Balthus as an artist, because his painting, not his character, was at issue. The irony I then discovered, with surprise, is that to view Balthus from the angle of his sexual obsession is not to bury but, to the extent that such is possible, to praise him. The best of his pictures reveal the human heart in a way that may not redeem them but is at least proportionate to the darkness from which they arose. It is precisely in his perversity that Balthus achieves artistic authenticity, and perhaps only there that he does.

Very little, certainly, commands our awe in Balthus's style, about which I agree with the contemporary French critic Philippe Sollers (in words requiring no translation): "Quel ennui! Quelle étroitesse! Quel caoutchouc neo-classique! . . . Quel crincrin!" The main technical characteristic of Balthus's paintings—which makes them look better in reproduction than at first hand—is that their surfaces are dead. Clotted and chalky, the surfaces are made up of layer upon layer of oil-starved pigment. (Their chiaroscuro effects rely on scumbling— underlayers peeking through feathered overlayers.) The labored en- crustations are fussy and ugly, however lovely their colors may be— especially in everything Balthus has painted since the mid-1950s, when, disastrously, he stopped creating strong spatial illusions and put full emphasis on the frescolike light of the surface. Before that time, Bal- thus's work realized numerous glories by setting surface light in ten- sion with the realist fiction of light in three dimensions—light that excavates the space around and behind his typically sculptural figures. This tension became the basis for a resonant erotic metaphor.

Three paintings that seem to me completely successful on these terms are *The Children*, 1937; *Patience*, 1943; and *The Golden Days*, 1945–46. In such relatively modest pictures—rather than in his stren- uously "masterful" billboard ads for his genius, *The Street*, 1930–33, and *The Mountain*, 1937—Balthus attained a concentrated subtlety and intensity of feeling. In each of these three works, the subject is raked by light coming from the side—from both sides in *The Golden Days*, where sunlight and firelight bracket the self-adoring girl. In *Patience*, sunlight blazes with pale acidic fire on the wall behind the shadowy, tranquilly preoccupied girl and caresses the back of her body from her ankle to her shoulder. In *The Children*, wan sunlight leaks into a gloomy room (whose atmosphere seems like vaporized charcoal) and fritters on the girl's legs, clothes, and face with scintillant white high- lights and avid red- and green-toned flesh harmonies.

The classical myth suggested in these and in other of Balthus's best paintings is always the same: that of Danaë, the maiden impregnated by Zeus disguised as a golden rain. The story, being obsessive, never changes. Sunlight enters a room that is occupied by an aroused or submissive or at least vulnerable young girl. I am tempted to say, following the logic of the myth, that the light symbolizes the desire of Zeus/Balthus, but that would be out of key with the passivity, the static or relaxed quality, of most of the pictures. The truth seems both less dramatic and more chilling. Considered as pieces of a narrative, the paintings displace sexual desire not into the future but into the im- mediate or recent past. We are shown a revisit of the god, calm in his intimacy because he has already possessed Danaë. Balthus's girls dis- play not the naked edge of erotic anticipation but, in William Blake's

phrase, "the lineaments of gratified desire." Seduced rather than seductive, few of them would appeal to *Lolita*'s Humbert Humbert as
precociously sluttish nymphets—one exception being the *Thérèse* of
1938, a hard case if ever there was one.

Balthus's most explicitly postcoital picture is also one of his most
histrionically perverse: *The Victim*, 1939–46. This large horizontal
painting of a nude sprawled on a rumpled sheet, with a knife lying
on the floor beside her, rhymes orgasm with death. Balthus took great
care to maintain an ambiguity in the young woman's expression: extinction or sexual exhaustion? I hardly know what to make of *The
Victim* emotionally, other than not to like it very much. The green
tints and grayed reds of the flesh, against the creamy sheet and the
glowing ocher wall, are rather beautiful, and the painting has an animation—as in the flurry of bravura brushwork at the far left end of
the sheet—rare for Balthus and likewise pleasing. But the suggestion
of the scene is too grotesque for me to do much more than stare at it.
It seems to me just possible that *The Victim* is meant to be funny. Did
Balthus, at some point in his life of ritualistic devotions, have a sense
of humor?

Certainly, Balthus's single most scandalous painting, *The Guitar
Lesson*, 1934—which has been consistently withheld from public view
and which I have seen only in black-and-white reproduction—seems
to be, besides extremely shocking, an invitation to hilarity. Called "one
of the great classics of the twentieth century" by the Centre Pompidou's Dominique Bozo, who expresses deep regret for its forced absence from the retrospective (of which he is the curator), this improbable picture shows a woman holding a prepubescent girl—whose skirt
is hitched up to her waist—across her lap. The woman strums the
girl's genitals.

Great classic or no, there is nothing quite like *The Guitar Lesson*
in the art of the twentieth or any other century, and not to show it is
both prudish and hypocritical—as if anyone doubted the erotic subtext
of Balthus's work! *The Guitar Lesson* is also an expression of flat-out
demonic audacity of a kind that, for all my own compunctions, I came
to yearn for from Balthus while viewing his retrospective. In comparison with this painting, most of his work is one long solemn tease.
Not that any comparison is necessary to point up his cynical muffling
of perverse content—with pretentious, old-masterish conceits—to
make a fusty sign of "good taste."

Balthus's other subjects need not detain us for long. His landscapes and still lifes are, to be brief about it, terrible. They communicate not a whisper of feeling for the life in nature or in objects, which they positively entomb in the airless sepulcher of his technique. To the extent that they possess any feeling at all, it is sentimental—a failing that, to his credit, Balthus generally avoided until the mid-fifties. The fertility theme in *The Cherry Tree*, 1940—a golden girl picking cherries in an all too golden landscape—is pure kitsch. Balthus's two great portraits of men, *André Derain*, 1936, and *Joan Miró and His Daughter Dolores*, 1937–38, constitute nearly, but not quite, a separate category. One must record that both also feature girls and project a steamy suggestiveness—very disturbingly in the Miró, which is my own favorite among all Balthus's paintings.

As an extreme test case of the perverse in art, Balthus suggests the need for a standard of discrimination in such matters. At what point does the authentically twisted give way to the merely sordid? I think this may be roughly conceived as a question of personal responsibility: the artist's responsibility to his or her own particular demon. When the artist's responsibility is stinted, the dynamic of the art is muddied with extrinsic appeals—attempts to cajole indulgence or to enlist complicity. When the responsibility is met, the result is a galvanic shock of recognition—recognition of a live possibility of feeling that the viewer, not being asked to excuse, cannot evade. Balthus at his best provides us with some highly special and explosive data on what it means to be human.

The quotation from Oscar Wilde with which I began offers us a way of thinking about Balthus at his more frequent worst. I've discovered another in Nabokov's *Lolita*: "You can always count on a murderer for a fancy prose style." If only Balthus had some of the fictional Humbert Humbert's ironic consciousness, his own fancy painting style might have been turned to more interesting, really sulfurous, account. As it is, that style and its aristocratic mystique offer, in sum, only a vulgar self-satisfaction, a snobbishness so secure in the entitled status of its feelings that it needn't bother—and at last is no longer able—to feel them.

March 1984

In Defense of Artistic Fashion

Once upon a time in the world of art, there was a conservative position that held out for supposedly timeless values and a radical position that stood up for the supposedly new. That time lasted from roughly the middle of the nineteenth century until roughly a decade ago, when the "death" of the avant-garde as the cutting edge of art culture was widely noted. Less remarked was the simultaneous symbiotic "death" (we are so melodramatic about these things!) of coherent artistic conservatism, principled foot-dragging in the face of change.

What had happened was a vast absorption of art culture into a culture of bureaucratic, corporate, and academic institutions. Conservatives and radicals did not disappear—from the neo-conservative journal *The New Criterion* to the poststructuralist *October*, we retain a full spectrum—but in many formerly divisive respects, conservatives and radicals began to resemble one another. On both the Right and the Left today there is substantial agreement about the issue, for instance, of "fashion."

The current art fashion, loosely termed neo-expressionism, is international in scope, with strong German, Italian, and American contingents. It has attained stunning success with almost no help from the institutional culture, being largely a phenomenon of the market and of journalism. Its few critical supporters, like the movement itself, cannot be neatly classed as either conservative or radical. In institutional and ideological circles, the neo-expressionist wave is uniformly disdained for its dependence on commerce and publicity, its fashionability. Is "fashion" art's new cutting edge? I think so.

What, exactly, is objectionable about fashion in art? (I will define such fashion as the widespread temporary popularity of a style, idea, artist, or group of artists.) For conservatives, who idealize good breeding in all things (code word, *quality*), fashion represents the ungrounded vulgar presumption of the arriviste. For radicals, categorically opposed to existing structures (the satanic status quo), it is an engineered illusion of change, an opiate of the people. In common usage, *fashion* is a uniquely powerful pejorative because it piggybacks negative connotations from both ideological tendencies. Contempt for the fashionable is such a united front of our day that a phrase like "Artist X defies the dictates of fashion" will register universally as high praise.

Enmity to artistic and intellectual fashion actually requires no rationale, because it is fueled by potent fears: fears of freedom and of the future. The freest of all our arenas for styles and ideas, fashion is a realm of seriously playful competition that scorns certainty and security in favor of whim, infatuation, wit, and fantasy—all the most volatile forms of imagination and desire. So much liberty intimidates us by shaming our limitations. Fashion also celebrates, by bracketing, the continuous arrival of the future—in an era when thoughts of the future fill most of the human race with dread. The sensation of our momentum in time reminds us of death's encroachment.

Fashion spotlights the characteristic, unprecedented, unrepeatable aspects and attitudes of an age. It is the sphere of immediate evanescent meanings. It is also the essential frame of civilized discourse. Without it we could not agree on what to talk about. Happily, we are never without it, whatever we may imagine. Antifashion rhetoric is itself a contemporary fashion—an unusually vehement and important one. It is important because it resurrects, at least briefly, the broadly based resistance to change, the reflexive antagonism to the new, that is prerequisite for an avant-garde.

April 1984

Minimalism

As a naive newcomer to New York and also to art in the mid-1960s, I was a pushover for the shocks and delights, the puzzlements and sensations, of that liveliest of eras. Among cognoscenti with whom I yearned, despairingly, to be numbered, Andy Warhol and Frank Stella were already established masters, Jasper Johns and Robert Rauschenberg were old masters, and Jackson Pollock and Willem de Kooning occupied the farthest, mistiest reaches of the classical past. The one earlier modernist with a dispensation of awe was Marcel Duchamp, because no way had been found to outsmart or outflank his skepticism. In those days, skepticism was rapture.

The lightning of the movement called minimalism—in retrospect, the dominant aesthetic of the last two decades and one of the most important renovations of the art idea in modern history—struck me in March 1966, when I entered the Tibor de Nagy Gallery and saw some bricks on the floor: eight neat low-lying arrangements of them. Construction in progress, I thought, and I turned to leave. Then another thought halted me: what if it's art? Scarcely daring to hope for anything so wonderful (I may have held my breath), I asked a person in the gallery and was assured that, yes, this was a show of sculpture by Carl Andre. I was ecstatic. I perused the bricks with a feeling of triumph.

Why?

I could not have explained at the time. It seems to me now that my response to Andre's bricks, like the appearance of the work itself, had been long and well prepared, partaking in one of those moments of zeitgeist when unruly threads of history are suddenly, tightly knotted. What elates then is the illumination, in a flash, of much that has been inchoate and strange in the world and, most of all, in one's own sensibility. An instinct for the radical, a hunger for irreducible fact, a disgust with cultural piety, an aesthetic alertness to the commonplace—all these predispositions were galvanized for me, in a form that embodied and extended them. At the root of such an epiphany is the youthful need to be acknowledged, to know that one is not utterly negligible or crazy, and here was an art (was it art?) that existed in relation to me and that I, in a sense, created.

The main art-historical precedent for Andre's bricks, I was immediately aware, had been Duchamp, with his readymades and his theory that the art work is a collaboration of artist and viewer. But the difference was enormous—the difference between the idea of something and the thing itself. Duchamp's readymades gestured. The brick works *were*. With them at my feet as I walked around the gallery, accumulating views, I felt my awkward self-consciousness, physical and psychological, being valorized, being made the focus and even the point of an experience. I had had intimations of this from artists other than Duchamp, mainly Johns and Warhol. By contrast, though, Johns's moody emblems seemed "too personal" and Warhol's iconizations of mass culture "too social." Here, at last, was the purely and cleanly existing heart of the matter.

For a long time this innocent revelation of the bricks remained the high-water mark in my appreciation of minimal art. Like many another mere art lover then, I was dismayed by the arcane criticism that swarmed, rather comically, around the mute simplicities of the work— much of it written by the minimalists themselves, whose often overbearing and scornful personalities daunted and antagonized me. As time passed, I was particularly appalled by the celerity with which minimal art was embraced by art-world institutions, to the point where it became practically emblematic of the certifying authority of those institutions. This seemed a betrayal of the feeling of liberation I had gotten from Andre's bricks, though thinking back, I recognize one ominous sign that afternoon in 1966: before enjoying the bricks as art, *I had to ask*.

Today minimalism is deeply lodged in the blind spot of an art culture bedazzled by a revival of paint and images. There is a tendency to regard it, if at all, as a defunct episode of sensibility, even a period style—which in several ways it is. But it is also the legacy—the living legacy, in the continuing productions of some major artists—of an aesthetic high adventure roughly comparable to that of cubism. Like cubism, it didn't end as much as insinuate itself so thoroughly as a philosophical model that it governs even the reactions of styles hostile to it (neo-expressionism being today's aesthetically conservative, psychologically rebellious equivalent of surrealism in the 1920s). To sort out the ideas and contradictions, successes and failures, of minimalism seems both newly possible and imperative in this moment. For me, there is the added motive of recovering the mystery of another moment, eighteen years ago, when the future was on the floor.

Where did minimalism come from? As attentive a critic as Lucy Lippard, writing in 1967 (of what she then proposed to call "postgeometric structure"), despairingly pronounced the movement "a virgin birth," and the art-historical record still offers scant rebuttal of that improbable judgment. Minimalism at heart was less a style than a critique of styles, less a new look than the imposition on art of modes of thought and feeling previously marginal or downright alien to it. Russian constructivism—particularly its early-1920s phase, when artists including Tatlin and Rodchenko strove to merge art with industrial production—presents certain analogies, striking but almost certainly adventitious. As for earlier geometric abstraction, even the most astringent of it—from Malevich and Mondrian to Ad Reinhardt—appears almost hopelessly fussy from a minimalist viewpoint.

Even Duchamp, the godfather of all anti-art, seems a bit beside the point of minimalism, in a way that is instructive. Duchamp was a wit, a gadfly within the philosophical structures of Western art. He required them for his fun, which was the production of little pun-shaped double binds revealing the rational incoherence of cultural conventions. His was an innocent sort of fun, finally, since he advanced no vision of an alternative, superior convention (except maybe chess). He aimed to sting, not destroy, and to pique rather than demoralize (though to think too long on the implications of Duchamp's work is to have an abyss yawn at one's feet). Committed not to tease but to revolutionize convention, the minimalists were far deadlier. Their works often had the thought structures of Duchampian jokes, but, except now and then, they weren't kidding.

Minimalism was a fiesta of subversion, what with Andre's literal flattening of sculpture (internal space "squeezed out," in Rosalind Krauss's phrase), Robert Morris's gaily cynical manipulation of styles, Sol LeWitt's subordination of the visual to arbitrary mathematical logics, Richard Serra's pitiless physicality, and Bruce Nauman's methodical unpacking of the idea of the artist. (For reasons I will explore, Donald Judd must be kept to one side in such generalizing.) All these activities had the effect of bracketing and freezing—reifying—certain structures and expectations formerly enveloped in the golden haze of the word *art*. In the resulting petrified forest of tropes, the one traditional element that remained alive was artistic intention: not the Mephistophelian intention of a Duchamp, but a Faustian intention like that of the abstract expressionists.

Abstract expressionism was the real sire of minimalism, though in ways that will not register in an art historian's slide lecture. To appreciate the connection visually, one must determinedly—and perversely—view Pollock and Barnett Newman, say, through a filter that will admit the paint-as-paint literalism of the former and the reductive formats of the latter while blocking out their content. Actually, such perversity is something of a modern habit, as when we dutifully inspect the eccentric surfaces of late Cézanne through the scientific eyes of Picasso and Braque; but never before minimalism was creative "misreading" so radically pursued. The explication of minimalist sensibility—the minimalist filter—must ultimately be sought outside of art, I believe, though it has a major anticipator within art: Jasper Johns.

One of several pedagogical coups in the recent rehanging of the Museum of Modern Art's permanent collection comes right after the singing grandeurs of Pollock and Rothko. Entering the next space, one is confronted—with a sensation like that of being hit in the face with a bucket of ice—by one of Johns's Flags of the late 1950s. The conjunction is incredibly rich and, in terms of a sea change in American culture at that time, dead accurate. What we notice right off about Johns's elegant icon, in context, is what it leaves out: self. Subjectivity is reduced to a wandering, empty signature: sensitive waxen brush strokes that, like the bleats of lambs without a shepherd, call feebly after the missing figure of the artist. At MOMA, this painting acts as an Ur-form, and common denominator, of the American pop and minimal works that shortly follow it.

Tentatively in Johns and decisively in minimalism (as also in Warhol), there was a reversal in the polarity of artistic intention: from the expressed, expressive self of the artist to the effected, effective entity of the art work. Rosalind Krauss traces directly to Johns the "rejection of an ideal space that exists prior to experience, waiting to be filled." Anything a priori was out. The production of a work was to be the beginning, not the fulfillment, of its meaning. These reflections help me to understand my feelings about Andre's bricks in 1966: precisely a sense of beginning—a new world, a tabula rasa—fueled my afflatus.

As with many revolutions, what was confidently begun would end in confusion. Today minimalism is more obviously the finish of modernist idealism than the commencement of a new era. But without some imaginative recuperation of its initial ambitions, we will not comprehend the conviction of the best works in its canon.

The destructive threat posed to the modernist tradition by minimalism was not lost on Clement Greenberg and his formalist followers—Kantian idealists all—in the 1960s. Greenberg's own waspish sniping at the movement, like the bland abstract painting he upheld as the legitimate art of the day, was ineffectual, but one Greenbergian, Michael Fried, got off a memorable blast: "Art and Objecthood" (1967). Sometimes hatred can sharpen perception. In his detestation of what he termed "literalist" art—as a species of "theater," the "negation" of all self-sufficing modernist arts—Fried gave an account of minimalist aesthetics that, with adjustments of tone, could serve as a signal appreciation. As it is, his counter-attack on what he saw as a barbarian onslaught is a classic of conservative criticism.

By "theater," Fried meant the essential quality of *"a situation"* that *"includes the beholder,"* who is confronted by minimal works "placed not just in his space but in his *way*." (All italics Fried's.) The viewer

> knows himself to stand in an indeterminate, open-ended—and unexacting—relationship *as subject* to the impassive object on the wall or floor. In fact, being distanced by such objects is not, I suggest, entirely unlike being distanced, or crowded, by the silent presence of another *person*; the experience of coming upon literalist objects unexpectedly—for example, in somewhat darkened rooms—can be strongly, if momentarily, disquieting in just that way.

Fried then pushed this simile too far, asserting that the hollowness of much minimal sculpture, its "quality of having an *inside*," made it "almost blatantly anthropomorphic"—forgetting that people are not hollow. But his basic sense of the way minimal art addresses its viewers is definitive.

As a modernist, Fried wants art to leave him alone, and to do so *explicitly*. In his view, art should emphasize and reinforce—celebrate—autonomy. His is an aristocratic cast of mind that cherishes quiet cultivation and loathes crowds. One can sense in his denunciation of minimalism a tacit protest against the militantly democratic culture of the 1960s, a culture of liberating candor and humane values, on the one hand, and of narcissism and spectacle, on the other. Had he acknowledged this subtext of his theme, Fried might have dropped the "anthropomorphic" red herring and seen minimalism in its full historical lineaments, as the paradigm of a cultural reality in which self-conscious spectatorship—like being "crowded"—is a universal fact of life. He wouldn't have liked it any better, but his sense of what made minimalism "strongly disquieting" would have been illuminated.

Minimalism was substantially determined by American social changes that were felt with special drama in the formerly hermetic precincts of art, where around 1960 a large new audience for avant-garde work suddenly appeared. Owing in part to what might be called the de-Europeanization of the avant-garde by abstract expressionism, the arrival of this new audience (upwardly mobile professionals, mostly) was given a gala welcome by the pop art boom, then registered in more complex and equivocal ways by minimalism. (The apparent sequence of pop and minimal—the former going public around 1962, the latter around 1965—was a happenstance of exhibition; definitively pop and minimal work had first been produced almost simultaneously.) On the simplest level, minimalism was art created with the absolute certainty that it would be exhibited and seen—"stuff you wouldn't make unless you had a place to show it," as Nauman once remarked.

But nothing was simple about minimalist responses to the changed estate of art in the world. If in one way minimal works were virtual symbols of the new order—aggressively outer-directed presences, spraying their surroundings with aesthetic vibrations (inducing in viewers a delirious sensitivity that invested nearby elevator buttons and fire-alarm boxes with vicarious sublimity)—they were also chastisements of too-ready and complacent enjoyment. Inevitable attention being discomfiting—threatening the professional integrity and rectitude of the artist—measures were taken to frustrate, attenuate, or otherwise challenge it. Always obdurate, minimalism in its later stages became overtly hostile to an audience that appeared willing to tolerate any degree at all of enigma, boredom, and even cruelty. Ultimately, limits were reached.

The death of minimalism as a movement was as ineluctable as its birth had been, a process of murder by institutional smothering and suicide by what Greenberg accurately enough termed "hypertrophy."

Having keenly resisted the commodity culture of publicity and commerce, minimalism failed to gain a comparable critical edge on the burgeoning new culture of "support structures"—often publicly funded museums, universities, "site-specific" outdoor shows, sculptural commissions, and "alternative spaces"—which in a sense bureaucratized the movement's principles. And no one who was paying attention to New York in the late 1960s will ever forget the fantastic pace of "dialectical" proliferation, the nightmarish speed with which minimalistic styles (or, really, styloids) succeeded one another, in a torrent of two-noun designations: process art, earth art, body art, performance art, on and on. Conceptualism, the terminal stage, was less the last development in a series than a receiving bin for aesthetic entities too frail to stand on their own.

The disintegration of the American avant-garde in the early 1970s, abetted by political traumas of the day, had long-range consequences that have included the gravitation of young talent to traditional mediums, a revived interest in ideas of "expression," the recommercialization of the art world, and a shift of artistic initiative to Europe. American minimalism itself was more or less expatriated to Europe, where curators and collectors remained hospitable and where native artists have never ceased to extrapolate and to play variations on minimalist themes. (We badly need a full account of minimalism from a European perspective.) In America, meanwhile, minimalist critical consciousness has proved itself capable of surviving with only slight nurturance from actual art. It persists in the robust "anti-aesthetic" stance of numerous poststructuralist, Marxist writers, allied with a few minor conceptualistic artists.

Yet minimalism is still the essential backdrop of all important art since the mid-1960s. What is called postmodernism in culture might as well, within the art culture, be termed the Age of Minimalism. Cardinal features of minimalist thinking—phenomenology, a sense of contexts, criticality—remain aesthetic common sense on both sides of the Atlantic, exerting pressure on and through all but the most determinedly backward-looking new art. Artists may have retreated from the confrontation with non-art that minimalism enacted, but what was learned from the confrontation continues to inform and even haunt. Minimalism lives on in the collective mind as a region of austere rigor and skeptical probity—a troubled, troubling conscience. Its history cannot yet be written because it is not over.

As I write, I have before me a photograph of Carl Andre's *Equivalent VI*. It is one of the arrangements of bricks from the show I saw in 1966. (Does it matter whether these are the same or different bricks? No.) The work comprises a hundred and twenty bricks—firebricks, the color of dirty sugar—in a two-tiered rectangle, five bricks wide by twelve long. (In the 1960s, geometry was poetry.) My mind recognizes it as an "Andre," but the work still fails to awaken an automatic "art" response. If I didn't know, I would still have to ask. I find this oddly reassuring, as perhaps anything permanently intransigent can be in our world of change: in this case, a dour emblem of change itself, an ineffaceable provocation. Though far upstream, now, from the present, those bricks continue to baffle the current.

An art collection is a work of criticism. The occasion for this essay being the presentation of the Saatchi collection of minimal and minimalistic art, I am engaged in adding a text of words to a text of objects, and I am obliged to start with a clear sense of the latter. Though extraordinarily comprehensive, this part of the Saatchi collection has the peculiarity of embodying a connoisseuring approach to a highly theoretical movement. It seizes on intrinsically excellent sculptural objects and paintings instead of trying to document environmental and conceptual works that from other points of view (and in other collections) might appear fulfillments of the minimalist enterprise. It offers and invites traditional judgments: good, better, best. Ironically, this conservative cast, with its effect of questioning the relation of minimalism to the traditions of Western painting and sculpture, highlights the radicalism of the movement, the jagged edge of its break with the past.

As a topographical map of minimalism, the collection emphasizes, by its relative proportions, four of the six major sculptors of the movement's mid-1960s heyday: Andre, Flavin, Judd, and LeWitt. Morris, a supple didact and magician of styles, whose sculpture of the period was a course in three-dimensional art criticism, is properly less well represented, given the collection's character. The late Robert Smithson, whose major contribution (two or three earthworks aside) was his brilliant critical writing, is not represented at all. Around this core, the collection includes some variants of minimal sculpture in the work of Larry Bell, John McCracken, and Fred Sandback. It forms another core around four major figures of what Robert Pincus-Witten has dubbed postminimalism: Eva Hesse, Nauman, Serra, and Richard Tuttle.

The paintings of Jo Baer, Robert Mangold, Brice Marden, Agnes Martin, and Robert Ryman are both a special strength of the collection and a separate category within it. Strictly construed, minimalism was a sculptural movement, and it is misleading to speak of "minimal painting" except within the broad terms of a sensibility that had effects in all areas of culture (notably music and dance). These painters (Ryman perhaps excepted) did not so much advance minimalism as register, and even strategically resist, its impact on their medium. The real-space, real-time phenomenology of minimalist aesthetics, with its anti-illusion, antipictorial bias, tended to question the validity of painting altogether. There was little likelihood that any painting, no matter how simplified, would fail to be perceived as art, and it was an imperative of mainstream minimalism (Judd, as usual, excluded) to risk not only the look but the felt possibility of non-art.

I will offer no definition of minimalism. In a way, the mere use of the word *minimalism* constitutes more definition than is warranted for a movement that relentlessly undermined previous definitions of art. But all style names are no more than gross conveniences ("cubism," if you please), and I will continue to employ this one, which usage has sanctified.

Donald Judd

If Andre is the echt minimalist, Donald Judd—the first name most people associate with the movement and widely deemed its best artist—may scarcely be a minimalist at all. An obstreperous enemy of generalization, he has always renounced the label. At one time, he even eschewed the designation sculptor, preferring to speak of himself as a maker of "specific objects." Whatever his work may be, there is no mistaking it for anything besides art. It is unfailingly elegant—even lapidary, in a grandiose sort of way. To the extent that it is minimalist, Judd's work is definitive of minimalism not as a set of ideas but as a style, the typical expression of a particular visual sensibility—a sensibility itself typical of America in the 1960s and shared by all the artists under consideration here, the painters included.

Michael Fried's position in "Art and Objecthood" would have been more formidable had he been able to claim Judd for the modernist side in his war on minimalism; he had already commandeered Stella, much to Greenberg's disapproval. (The art politics of the 1960s might inspire a nice musical comedy.) Judd and Stella have marked similarities, for example in their uses of materials. Judd's various sheet metals and industrial finishes, like Stella's shaped supports and unconventional paints, are palpably extensions, not disruptions, of the conventional aesthetic field: they are things of beauty. Both artists are essentially formalist, aiming to refresh rather than revolutionize modern art—heirs of Matisse rather than Duchamp. Their initial rationalizations of form were radical, but in ways purely in the service of their common, quite traditional, intent to produce objects at once powerfully engaging and decoratively satisfying.

Already in the earliest and most severe Judd here, a wall-mounted, galvanized-iron box of 1965, one senses not a philosophical gesture but the straightforward operations of an acute eye. The effect of the piece may be analyzed in terms of opposed qualities: aggressive projection/light-softening material, geometric regularity/arbitrary proportions, relief configuration ("pictorialness")/truculent shape ("thingness"). The extreme economy of the piece works to discipline, but not to deny, the pleasure of the viewer, who is simply discouraged from indulging in any partial or tangential thoughts or feelings. The box will be looked at in its own way—for what it is—or not at all. It is tough, bracing, and, without being in the least sensuous, quite lovely.

Loveliness, often of a racy, expensive-looking kind, has been a recurrent tone of Judd's work, as it was not of more doctrinaire minimalism. Judd has been criticized on this score for producing elitist corporate-style decor, a charge to which his only defense is the autonomous value of his determinedly uningratiating rigor. At the least, the rigor distinguishes Judd's objects from the mass of similarly bright and shiny art of the 1960s—art that complacently reflected the bluff pragmatism, faith in technology, and can-do arrogance of pre-Vietnam America. If Judd's style is inconceivable without the background of those values, it is also independent of their survival.

The rigor of Judd's objects is both cause and effect of the emphasis given each decision in their making. Often these decisions are systemic and instrumental, as when Judd used mathematical progressions to determine unit intervals in, for instance, the wall pieces of 1978 and

1981. It is unimportant for viewers to know Judd's systems. (From time to time, I have taken pains to learn them, only to have them slip my memory almost immediately.) They are there to stabilize one's experience by foreclosing the normal "expressive" associations of composition. Judd's work provides satisfactions analogous to those of machinery, architecture, decoration, and the pure structure of poetry and music. It does so by functioning in time with the viewer's movements. This is especially the case with Judd's huge magnificent plywood piece of 1981. Walking along its eighty-foot length is like physically traversing—and, by one's speed, determining the tempo of—a great fugue.

In the nether realm between painting and sculpture that characterizes minimalist sensibility, Judd is the master orchestrator of visual/physical tensions. A fine example is the open copper box with red lacquered bottom of 1973. Three feet high, it has the obtrusiveness and the proportions of a thoroughly impractical piece of furniture; it is, indeed, "in one's way." As one approaches, however, all awkwardness dissolves in sheer optical ravishment, the glow of some spectral substance at once molten and cold. There is no way of reconciling, in an orderly gestalt, one's impressions of the piece from near and far, outside and inside. Rational in conception, the work is irrational in effect, an endlessly and agreeably exacerbating presence.

Dan Flavin

In scale of achievement, Dan Flavin's work might seem in peril of being classed with lesser variants of minimalism, as the limited extension of a single schematic idea. However, he belongs by biographical right with the first generation of the movement, and he is important as a bridge between the minimalist sensibility of Judd and the more conceptual or ideological minimalism of LeWitt, Morris, and Andre. At one extreme the most coldly geometrical and technological of these artists, at the other extreme Flavin is the most romantic, even sentimental; and his contradictory position, though never fully resolved in his art, makes him an intriguing test case of contradictions that beset the movement as a whole.

If Judd's work is minimalism as style, Flavin's is minimalism as period look and period romance, a spectacular and poetic apostrophe of the movement's decorative taste and spiritual cast. All the main points are present, amazingly, in the earliest and simplest work represented here, the *Diagonal of May 25, 1963*, a lone fluorescent tube: the nonart look of the ready-made commercial fixture; the obvious, clean beauty of the light; the art-historical nostalgia of the diagonal (definitive trope of constructivism); and the urbane, diaristic glamour of the title. Flavin has always let tender and exalted feelings, squeezed by the impersonality of his style, leak out in titles and allusive configurations—as in *"Monument" for V. Tatlin*. Recently he has become quite shameless, for instance in a large work of 1984 (not in the collection) dedicated to his pet dog: a sloping series of green and blue tubes evoking the line of a grassy hillside against a summer sky.

In narrowly aesthetic terms, meanwhile, Flavin's work belongs with the purest minimalism, meaning the most explicitly phenomenological: he creates "not so much an art object as the phenomenon of the piece's existence in a particular location, at a particular moment in time," as Gregoire Muller neatly put it. His pieces are art only when installed and electrified; between times, they are just hardware. By being literally illuminated (almost, one may feel, looked at) by the work, the viewer is made even more sharply self-conscious than in the case of Andre's bricks. On a theoretical checklist, then, Flavin emerges as a crack minimalist, the peccadillo of his poetic enthusiasms aside. But such perfection has its costs.

Flavin's art is a hothouse flower, abjectly reliant for its basic meanings on an institutional setting—a place where its nonart qualities can have piquancy and bite as tacit assaults on conventions by which, for instance, lights on the ceiling illuminate art on the walls rather than the other way around. Outside such a setting, Flavin is merely bizarre and merely beautiful, far too ingratiating to generate much aesthetic or critical friction. We do not despise hothouse flowers, of course. We like them for their poignancy as signs of nature unnaturally intensified, and for their dependence on us. By being imprisoned, they are glorified. This being so of Flavin's work, his rhetorical gestures and lurking metaphors are not simply idiosyncratic frills but—by referring to life and history beyond the hothouse—the one level on which Flavin escapes the fate of theory realized not wisely but too well.

Sol LeWitt

If Sol LeWitt, my own favorite minimalist, had never created anything but his wall-drawing ideas—sets of written instructions capable of being executed by anyone almost anywhere—his eminence would be assured. When performed, these exercises in drafting by proxy are works of grace and of a peculiar mystery: the mystery of art (or really of anything at all) as something that people do. In one way, the drawings are no less period pieces than Flavin's light works. Distant relatives of happenings—the partylike performances of the early 1960s—they belong to a moment when getting people involved in gratuitous toil seemed an answer to the problem of an expanded, largely naive, audience. (Christo, with his monumental swaddlings, engaging hordes of volunteer helpers, is the road-show Barnum of this idea.) However, LeWitt's wall drawings differ in that they issue in experiences superior both aesthetically and philosophically. Their executions are as entrancing to the eye as their concept is elegant in the mind.

The equivocal relation between art in the eye and art in the mind is LeWitt's playground. He is the most elusive major figure—the Ariel—of minimalism, with a way of making any perception of him seem almost, but never quite, the right one. This baffling quality is physically palpable in LeWitt's many sculptures of cubic and latticelike forms, works that, like the wall drawings, are relentlessly faithful renderings of arbitrary mathematical formulations. ("Irrational thoughts should be followed absolutely and logically," he has said.) Clear and shapely as prior ideas, the sculptures have been more or less abandoned into actuality. There is a delicate awkwardness, an excruciatingly "off" quality, about them that seems symbolic of the fate of all well-laid plans when they encounter the happenstance of realization. The difference between LeWitt and other planners is that he makes no adjustments to contingency in the fabricating process, because a mismatch of thing and idea is of the essence for him.

There is, besides Ariel, a bit of the social-democratic Pied Piper about LeWitt, who in the high-anxiety art world of the late 1960s was a memorably encouraging and reassuring influence on younger artists—none of the standard swagger and snarl for him. His strangely denatured friendliness, coming across in works of the utmost austerity, is surely one of the unique artistic flavors of modern times, and fascinating for its redolence of a social vision. Minimalism abounded with fragmentary schemes and yearnings for community, for a creative anticapitalist phalanx similar to that of the revolutionary-era Russian avant-garde. Most versions of this aspiration appear foolish or tyrannical in retrospect, but LeWitt's retains appeal because a matter less of fantasy or ideology than of tone: a hint of what a better world would feel like. It would feel, in a word, better.

The symbolic genius of LeWitt's wall drawings, in the broadest terms of our civilization's discontents, is their reconciliation of "scientific" mentality and the frailty of the human machine. They engineer an enjoyment of our waywardness. As Kenneth Baker has written, LeWitt's work "lets us approach and contemplate without anxiety the aspect of aimless energy that belongs to our own spontaneity, and the meaninglessness that characterizes human activity." Given the vagaries of various hands, the drawings will never turn out the same in different executions. No particular execution—one in the Museum of Modern Art, say, when compared with one in somebody's apartment—has more authenticity as art than any other, and no number of executions of a drawing can begin to exhaust its potential—because the drawing, in common with human nature, is a mental inscription of potential, pure and simple.

LeWitt's understanding of art as activity, as an unreasonable course of action reasonably pursued, is the very soul, as opposed to the theory, of mainstream minimalism. Like a soul, it is invisible and only provisionally inhabits material form—as the principle of the form's animation and the idea of its transcendence. If this sounds objectionably theological, there's no remedy for it: minimalism always carried religious as well as political charges, though the positivist sensibility of the 1960s held them in check. (Lucy Lippard's book *Overlay* documents the wide expression of minimalism's mystical side during the 1970s in much pantheistic and otherwise primitivist art.) In LeWitt's case, positivist skepticism is reinforced by a sunlit civic virtue, a determinedly secular, sociable timbre. His is a practical Platonism, a supernaturalism free of spooks.

Robert Morris

Having dubbed Sol LeWitt minimalism's Ariel, I am tempted to call Robert Morris its Caliban—but this would become complicated since it would entail a Caliban in masquerade as Prospero, philosopher king of art's enchanted isle. Morris's presence in the 1960s art world, as artist and theorist, was prodigious. He anticipated, invented, or quickly put his stamp on every twist and turn of minimalist dialectics from geometric structures to earthworks, not disdaining to lift an idea from any younger artist who nipped in ahead of him. Like no one else, he had mastered the subtleties of Duchamp and Johns, and he was sure-footed in the dizzying spirals of irony that for a while were art's sport and passion. There has never been a consistent look to Morris's art, only a consistent cleverness—the distinctive tattoo of an idea faired, trued, and hammered home. That was literally the noise of an early work that Carter Ratcliff has pointed to as the touchstone of Morris's art: *Box with Sound of Its Own Making*, 1961, a wooden box containing a working tape recorder.

Caliban, it will be remembered, is the "natural man" considered as a creature of brute necessity. At a time when step-by-step tactical reductivism seemed the nature of art, Morris, for all his nimbleness, was exactly that. In contrast to Duchamp and Johns—and LeWitt— Morris gives off no fume of liberation in his ironies, but rather the opposite. As Ratcliff has also suggested, *In the Realm of the Carceral*— a series of drawings of imaginary prisons done in the late 1970s— might serve as an apt summary of Morris's entire career (nowadays involved in one-upping the expressionist trend with icons of death and apocalypse). A perverse enjoyment of deprivation and a savoring of entropy (the latter shared by minimalism's greatest critic-artist, Robert Smithson) make Morris a *poète maudit* far more powerfully interesting than can be guessed from his sculptural works alone. He must be sought, if at all, on the mazy island of esoteric discourse he long ruled and terrorized.

Carl Andre

Having made extravagant use of my first encounter with Carl Andre's art, I ought to acknowledge that never again have I had an experience with any Andre of even remotely comparable intensity. Though far from being a one-note artist, Andre definitely packs only one big surprise, which, having once been registered, does not recur. In a sense, all his works are simply reminders and confirmations of a state of affairs: the world according to minimalism. Though monotonous at times, Andre's endlessly repeating formats, all of them making essentially the same point, indicate a faith in the overarching importance of his initial insight. Monotony may even be a matter of honor in such a faith: the monotony of ritual observance or (as Andre has said in punning reference to his metal-plate pieces) of a "great bass," the harmonic drone of a scale's lowest perceptible chord. (Also, of course, a "great base" on which to stand.) And one thinks of Albert Einstein's mild remark that, after all, in his whole life he had had only one or two ideas.

Every now and then I do get a little jolt from an Andre, as I realize something I had forgotten: that his work is, by and large, beautiful. Almost sacrificially, Andre brings to the draconian discipline of his style some fine sculptural gifts, most apparently a sense of the poetry of materials and an acute feeling for scale. These qualities become lyrical in his deployments of wooden blocks or beams, and I daresay that art lovers of the last two decades have, on account of Andre, a vastly increased sensitivity to the color and texture of industrially rolled metals. Not that Andre's work has aesthetic appeal sufficient to justify its importunity: that importunity—insistent, dumb, impassively challenging—still comes first, as the ongoing fanfare of minimalist revolution.

As I have suggested repeatedly, the minimalist revolution turned out to be a palace coup, confined to art's certifying institutions. However, it demands credit for being a real and consequential coup—like cubism, now a fundamental element of aesthetic literacy. The cliché that radical impulses are defeated by acceptance does not always hold true. Andre's work has changed our sense of the museum a lot more than the museum has changed our sense of his work, and anyone who fails to grasp this is doomed to being bewildered by new art today and to the end of time.

John McCracken, Larry Bell, Fred Sandback

My history with Andre repeated itself (as farce) when in 1967 or so I first saw one of the Los Angeles artist John McCracken's lacquered planks—a staggeringly correct painting/sculpture hybrid whose combination of sleek geometry and vernacular disposition (it leaned!) was ineffably racy. Thus was I introduced to the "L.A. Look": feel-good minimalism, minimalism without tears. The L.A. Look favored plastics and dreamy color and was attuned to the intense radiance of the Southern California sun. (It tended to look a bit off-key in New York's weaker and moister Atlantic light.) Besides McCracken's planks, its most iconic expressions were Larry Bell's ubiquitous coated-glass boxes on Plexiglas bases: ultrasubtle inflectors of space and light and, with their stainless-steel fittings, muted paeans to the high-tech sublime.

Regional variants of minimalism were few in America—in Europe they were legion—and this gives the L.A. Look, short-lived as its heyday was, a lasting curiosity. It had something of a counterpart in New York, actually: an unnamed but virtual "N.Y. Look" that emerged in last-ditch opposition to the art object's vanishing in conceptualism. Such art soberly exploited minimalist aesthetic discoveries in an unironic spirit of Less-is-More. Much as the L.A. Look celebrated Southern California beach weather, the N.Y. Look indexed a phenomenon peculiarly congenial to Manhattan: the immaculate "white cube" of the contemporary gallery. Fred Sandback's spare elastic-cord geometries are perfect examples—dependent on a proper setting to the point of being its mascots, but agreeable as environmental grace notes and as tokens of urban refinement.

Bruce Nauman, Richard Serra, Eva Hesse, Richard Tuttle

In a way perhaps unprecedented in any other art movement, much of the best of minimalism was saved for last: a "second generation" that includes two artists, Bruce Nauman and Richard Serra, every bit as important as any of the pioneers—plus a third, Eva Hesse, who might well be on their level but for her death in 1970 at the age of thirty-four. Along with Richard Tuttle (a maverick who is a case unto himself), these artists not only realized a host of possibilities latent in earlier minimal art but retroactively deepened and clarified the movement's premises. They did not do it by theorizing. On the contrary, they created works which, though difficult, were self-explanatory, and in so doing they acted to close the disturbing gap between tight-lipped object and teeming verbiage that at times gave the 1960s art world an air of Alice's Wonderland. The gap had been produced by an all too successful strategy of suppressing artistic personality.

There was always something out of whack about the minimalist first generation's cult of impersonality: a shiftiness on an issue—artistic ego—that forms a subterranean competitive link between the minimalists and their forebears, the abstract expressionists. Deflating myths of "self" was all very well, but the denial of art's subjective dimension reached absurd extremes. Minimal works were made by *somebody*, after all—somebody with motives and attitudes livelier than that shriveled theoretical residue, "intention." (Judd, in his more conventional ambition as a stylist, escapes this objection.) The work of Andre, Morris, Flavin, and even LeWitt often had an eerie, remote-control quality—as of the Wizard of Oz enjoining Dorothy through a fiery apparition, "Pay no attention to that man behind the curtain!"

While no less chary of the "expressive" fallacy, Nauman, Serra, and Hesse found ways of being psychologically present in their art, thereby entitling viewers to a fuller range of response. (Rather than be similarly forthcoming, Tuttle turned the tables in works practically symbolic of evasion: disappearing acts of the artist.) Which is not to say that they cozied up to the public. As often as not, the tones of their work varied between creepy and threatening—and probably contributed to the flight of general viewers from the new art, an exodus well under way by the late 1960s. But to those still paying attention they brought a new dispensation of seriousness (mingled with extraordinary wit, in Nauman's case). Their achievements of the time remain exemplary, and the last has not been heard of their influence.

In January 1968, at the Leo Castelli Gallery, Nauman had one of the most phenomenal of first one-man shows, not the least of its astonishments being that it occasioned the artist's first visit to New York. Seemingly from nowhere (from San Francisco, as it happened), he had arrived with an enormous variety of sculptural objects strange in form and material and bristling with intelligence. Some were loaf-shaped fiberglass casts that produced standard effects of minimalist "presence" with disquieting overtones of organic life. Others involved body casts, neon signs, and such wild congeries of stuffs as aluminum foil, plastic sheet, foam rubber, felt, and grease (*Collection of Various Materials Separated by Layers of Grease with Holes the Size of My Waist and Wrists*, 1966). Many made sly reference to the idea of the artist, perhaps as someone who makes an impression (knee prints in wax) or "helps the world by revealing mystic truths" (as a spiral neon sign surmised). In such works as *Henry Moore Bound to Fail*, many-leveled facetiousness attained heights of poetry.

Nauman reversed a valence of previous minimalism, replacing stark certainty with a process of endlessly ramifying questions about the sources and uses of art. Like the hero-scientist who tests a new serum on himself, Nauman used self-reference to explore notions of what an artist is and does. What kept this innately disintegrative project integral was—beneath the anxious, fencing humor—a conscientious bet that, whatever its contradictions, art somehow truly matters. In myriad forms since 1968, Nauman's conflict of belief and skepticism has remained constant. Lately it has taken on an added weight of moral implication—playfully, in neon amplifications of judgmentally loaded words, and earnestly, in such haunted sculptures for meditating on political torture as *South America Triangle*, 1981: a suspended, eye-level (masking) triangle of I beams framing the mute catastrophe of an upended cast-iron chair.

Without a whisper of irony, Serra observes none of Nauman's equivocating distance from the idea of the artist. *Being* his own idea of the artist, Serra has dramatically forced certain issues of art's role in the world—as an assertion of creative will, a purposeful manipulation of viewers, and a thing distinct from other things. Serra's feat has been to clarify all these relations physically, by sheerly sculptural means. His ambition far surpasses the creation of imposing objects. Part of his work's scale is social, involving a sense of art's capacity to affect an unprepared audience. (This part of Serra's enterprise has encountered the withering contradictions of all "public art" today, but his approach is at least cogent.) In cynical times, the purity and absoluteness of Serra's conviction are exotic.

Serra derived his style through experiments with the fundamental properties of materials, such as the weight of metal. *House of Cards (One Ton Prop)*, 1968–69, was the definitive statement of Serra's decision to let gravity determine the structure of his work. He thereby eliminated the last remnant of illusionism in minimalist aesthetics and came to psychological close quarters with the viewer. The piece's perceived element of danger gives it a cobralike fascination, even as its self-evident logic and blunt beauty satisfy mind and sense. We see exactly what the artist has done and, consulting our own response, why: we are to have a violently heightened sense of the reality of matter, which includes our bodies. Since *House of Cards*, Serra has cautiously expanded his repertoire to include uses for pictorial means and effects and for less clear-cut compositional procedures; but the jolting directness of his prop pieces remains the major characteristic of his art.

Hesse's way of restoring psychological content to sculpture was similar to that of Nauman's loaf-shaped pieces, but she was even less reticent about exploiting the metaphorical charge of organic-looking materials. Self-conscious sexuality, explicit in the ovarian imagery of *Ingeminate* (1965), was progressively suppressed in her later work, but even her most abstract pieces awaken an excruciatingly intimate, under-the-skin sensation. What lends her work authority, and makes her an important figure in the later development of minimalism, is her foregrounding of process. By making perceptible the decisions and manual operations involved in fashioning her work, Hesse realized a deft and theatrical lyricism of the studio.

Tuttle's is an antilyricism of the exhibition space, a series of understated passive-aggressive responses to the demand that an artist do something. After making some remarkably prescient odd-shaped wall pieces in the early 1960s—acknowledged by Nauman as an important influence—Tuttle pursued courses of work parsimonious to the verge of negligibility. The lovely and witty *Tan Octagon*, 1967, proposes a species of painting that can be (and looks as if it had been) transported by being stuffed in a pocket.

The Painters

The 1960s played some dirty tricks on abstract painting. After the Golden Age of Pollock and de Kooning there had come the Brazen Age of Johns and Rauschenberg, and abstract painting thus began the 1960s with a sense of having fallen from a great height and been kicked in the teeth en route. (Intimidating Fathers, mocking Pops.) Then things got worse. The possibility of serious abstraction was increasingly threatened by the Scylla of Greenbergian color-field painting—a sterile formula, but championed by a mighty array of critics, curators, and dealers—and the truly disheartening Charybdis of minimalism, which held all painting in contempt. Frank Stella won through, but only by

purging the subjective dimension—the symbolization of consciousness—that is a raison d'être of Western painting. Stella left in his wake
less a new path than scorched earth.

The minimalists rejected the "illusion" of painting for what
seemed more than enough reasons: its signification of a "self," its
ineradicable fiction of visual depth (even a blank canvas has this), its
finicky dependence on "composition," its tacit acceptance of art's economic status as a portable commodity, and, in general, its entanglement
in archaic, bourgeois, "humanist," individualistic, and "elitist" patterns
of conventionality. (I can still feel, in the pit of my stomach, the ter-
rorizing authority such polemics once carried—before minimalism
was humbled by its own contradictions.) To roll with all those punches
and come up with brush in hand took a special breed of artist, and
the few who did so with force and conviction—notably Agnes Martin,
Robert Ryman, and Brice Marden—are a tough, heroic lot.

Martin and Ryman had a head start on minimalist sensibility. Already a veteran painter by 1960, Martin had been obeying a simplifying
and essentializing impulse for many years without satisfactory result.
Her perfect solution of a symmetrical grid on a monochrome ground
is one of those conjunctions of personal development and zeitgeist that
seem at once implausible and as inevitable as water running downhill.
With it, she had a rational and sturdy form—disarming to the most
positivist eye—that liberated a rich vein of feeling. It wasn't a matter
of "less" being "more," but of "just enough" being the basis for a
sustained spiritual adventure. Her abnegations bespeak not denial but
tact: the tact one would display by refraining from making noise
around a sleepwalker on a precipice.

In Martin's words, "My paintings have neither objects, nor space,
nor time, not anything—no forms. They are light, lightness, about
merging, about formlessness, breaking down forms." It is a lovely thing
to see how Martin's "formlessness" is achieved by exact formal means.
First come her grids, which iron out all possible figure-to-ground relations and forbid any part of a picture more emphasis than another.
Then there is her decision to employ square canvases but to make the
grid units rectangular: if the grids were of squares, too, the work
would be a unitary, semaphoric object, not a picture. The result of
these calculations is like a visual equivalent of silence, in which the
least inflection—a pale hue or the bump of a penciled line over the

tooth of the canvas—sings. Far from formless, the work is indeed "about formlessness": the oceanic feeling it stirs in us.

If Martin is reductivism's mystic, Ryman is its philosopher. (And Marden its poet.) Ryman tests what an analytical inquiry can do to that category of our perception called painting. In a way, his art, no less than Sol LeWitt's, is about activity: the spreading of paint on a delimited surface. His approach is anti-"expressive" in the extreme, and yet, mysteriously, in his work something does get expressed: painting's deeply rooted hold on us, its concordance with the grammar of our imaginations.

The two aesthetically "hot" zones of any painting are its surface and its edge. In most of his work throughout the 1960s, Ryman gave primary attention to the surface, really a coefficient of two surfaces: paint and support. More recently, his interest has shifted to the edge, painting's at once physical and metaphysical frontier. He dramatizes it by highlighting the canvas's attachment to the wall, employing aluminum brackets to make visible this commonly invisible protocol. With a sober, oddly sweet playfulness, Ryman makes all necessary decisions for a painting in advance, methodically carries them out, and then, in effect, stands back to see what has happened. Something rather compelling always has.

Mangold and Baer differently reflect a variation of minimalist sensibility that with reference to Fred Sandback I called the N.Y. Look. Celebrating the contemporary gallery's virtual erotics of austerity, their paintings do not so much satisfy sensibility as signify its satisfaction. Mangold's designs that both suggest and distort geometric regularity can be very pleasurable in this way, delicately stimulating opposed responses and flavoring them with the dry lyricism of his color. Baer's bordered blanknesses hint at astringency but actually use reductivism to realize a special beauty: whiteness for whiteness' sake. (Contrarily, Ryman uses white—the all-color color—as a control element, to allow undistracted registration of texture, transparency, viscosity, and other features of the paint medium.) The works of Baer and Mangold are engines of taste.

I have saved Brice Marden for last because I believe he is the most important abstract painter to emerge during the minimalist era and also because he is the one of all the artists under discussion here who most effectively bridges that era—keeping alive, under severe pressure, artistic traditions that today are flourishing anew. In one way, he is the last of the abstract expressionists, maker of lyrical paint fields that hint at elevated subjective states. In another way, Marden was the first American to anticipate a "return to the figure," not in the form of a drawn image but through recognizing painting itself—its scale and its skin—as a metaphor of the human body.

Marden hardly invented monochrome—like the grid, an anticompositional tactic very much in the air for painters in the 1960s. He owed the idea for his fleshy oil-wax medium to Jasper Johns; and his use of diptych and triptych formats to get lateral extension without losing straight-on address was precedented by Ellsworth Kelly. But his miraculous scale and color are his own, as is his device of hanging his paintings low on the wall so that they confront the viewer body-to-body—with their own subliminal version of the "anthropomorphic" dynamic that Michael Fried deplored in minimal sculpture. Of course, all of this would be only a bag of tricks were it not in the service of a reason for painting, which in Marden's case seems an almost Keatsian ache for erotic connection. Moodily seductive and hypersensitive, his paintings have a vulnerable beauty and a quality of keen wanting. Their formal reductions come to symbolize not what one can do without but precisely what one cannot do without, though one lacks it all the same.

Minimalism was a world event in a special sense. It was an experiment, a great reality-testing *what if,* by which artists—riding the crest of unprecedented public interest in art for its own sake—attempted to locate art's significance in a world beyond art, in the world of things and people and ideas. The experiment had a way of blowing up—for instance, by making the practice of art more hermetic than ever—but that, too, was a datum, and an important contribution to knowledge. Never again will informed people be as naively idealistic about art as in what now seem the innocent, prelapsarian days before minimalism. If you doubt it, spend some time in the company of the works I have been discussing. They are waiting for you, in permanent ambush.

1984

Philip Guston

When in 1968 Philip Guston abruptly abandoned the most restrained and elegant of all abstract expressionist painting styles for a mode of raucous figuration, I hated it. It seemed a rank indecency, a profanation, a joke in the worst conceivable taste. Gradually, over more than a decade, I was brought around to late Guston by the better opinion of others, mainly artists I respected; at some point that I cannot specify—maybe in my sleep—my resistance disintegrated, and the very paintings I had abhorred started giving me surges of pleasure. In itself, this story is only mildly embarrassing. Anyone who has a mind changes it now and then. But the tale seems worth telling, and for me is the token of an atonement, because my own experience coincided so closely with that of the art culture's reaction not just to Guston but to an epochal shift in sensibility of which he was a prophet and a pioneer. Realizing that my "personal" feelings were *typical* was a jolt that I hope has taught me something.

The truly personal component of my animus against late Guston was probably fright. I was scared of the abject psychic content he had unclenched, and I was scared *for* an idealistic sense of art as a refuge from life's disorder that I had absorbed without examining. I didn't require classical elevation of all artists. On the contrary, it was enough that a very few, Philip Guston prominently among them, maintain it—as the existence of saintly monks is spiritual money in the bank for a certain kind of fecklessly sinning believer. Defrocking himself in 1968, Guston declared the faith bankrupt. No more saintliness, no more sin; only mortified humanity and, if one could manage it somehow, painting. This was the courageous message for which many of us blamed the messenger. And today it is our new scripture, to which many artists have added gospels: late Picasso, Malcolm Morley, Susan Rothenberg, others. None had a rougher time of it than Guston, because none sacrificed a greater stake in the previous scheme of things.

Actually, Guston's art always had a skeptical, anxious, potentially sardonic edge, palpable as a materialistic matter-of-factness in his great abstractions of the 1950s and 1960s. There was a closely watched quality to his fantastically sensitive brushstrokes (only de Kooning has better touch), as if they had been deployed in the teeth of powerful misgivings, as if the painter, while avid for aesthetic glory, had been hounded by a suspicion that the whole enterprise was a crock. Precisely this air of haunted compunction made Guston a hero. He appeared to deal with a level of doubt that would paralyze anyone else, and in so doing he provided vicarious reassurance. The paradigm of high formal abstract painting, so severely tested, was seen to hold, to be a fitting vessel for transcendent meanings even amid the contrary insinuations of pop and minimalism and the failing convictions of one abstractionist after another. Had Guston simply failed, there would have been no scandal. His offense was to jettison principles that seemed still sound—though obviously, in hindsight, they were sick unto death.

Looking today at the first late Gustons—for instance, *Head, Bottle, Light*—I must squint to see them in the pejorative way I used to. That is, I must blur my recognition of the images in order to behold an incoherent abstraction, one in which "arbitrary" (as I put it then) cartoonish contours generate no formal tension with the framing edge and in which a still ravishing brushwork is demoted to the busy work of filling in. I could not take seriously Guston's reversal of the modernist priority—the subordination of every element to an aesthetic unity—so I got his work backward, failing to see the purposes of its disunity. Now my eye surrenders to the fierce particularity of the images within the generalized container of the picture: *this* head, *this* bottle, *this* light—but only *that* painting (just another painting). The clunkiness of the composition jars the images loose and dumps them into the viewer's lap. The apparent crudity of the drawing authenticates each image as literally drawn—extruded by imagination from the shambling contingency of the painting process.

Painting's loss, then, is imagination's gain. (And there is a revived, if humbler, role in the world for painting.) One is to bother not at all with how the work was done and only in a casual way with how it looks, or even what it is. One is to witness the emergence—the emergency!—of images that have demanded to be made visible. The head: hood shaped but flesh colored and, it appears, surgically sutured, so not a mask but a naked creature. The bottle: bloody red, lit by the light and watched by the head, so no mere still life but the talisman of an alarmed scrutiny. The light: green like nature and shedding tiny gray bullet rays, no neutral fixture but a funnel or megaphone or eye of intensity. The paint handling is beautiful, with a beauty that in the comfortless context is heartbreaking. Think of it: to be so sensuously alert, so tender, so favored, and yet to be subject to the damned head, the damned bottle, and the goddamned light! And what use is painting that refuses—declines emphatically—to transcend any of this? But where would we be without painting, after all? Poor smelly, indispensable painting.

The unraisably ponderous head of the *Painter in Bed* regards with single eye a vision of shoes—maybe all the shoes he has ever worn and worn out, all those intimate casualities of distance and soil. Painting equipment and some ambiguous other objects weigh on or tumble off his chest, or does he have a chest? The bedcovers are an upright, striated slab of tremulous paint and line, an abstraction complete with mandala-like red circle in the lower right corner and signed "Philip Guston" (the famous painter) in the lower center. What else? A dainty pink light and a bulbous red one dangle from above—the red one with a very pullable-looking pullchain, perhaps for use when one has had enough of this flayed, blood-suffused, liverish, irremediable apparition of things that don't add up. Again, given what it comes to, what rotten luck it seems to be so marvelously sensitive! And still there is painting, for all the good it does: some slight, some provisional good.

Social and political themes have been adduced from Guston's use of hooded figures (Ku Klux Klan?) and heaps of legs (Holocaust?), and the connections are supported by his known left-liberalism. But this class of his imagery evokes a concern both more and less general than politics. On the one hand, it fits into a swing-barreled sense of emergency, a cosmic distress that can be exuded at full strength by anything at all—in *The Magnet*, by a compass that seems to have started life as a clock, a fat light bulb, a painting of open water on a lumpish support, and a "questionable" book. (The picture suggests a rebus communicating an urgent message, completely undecodable.) On the other hand, Guston's political nightmares have a strictly subjective, intimate particularity. Affected by the world but unable to affect it in return, the artist is stuck with his visions, which assume ambivalent roles in the tragicomedy of his inner life. Identification flows to the hooded specters, and the vernacular rug in *Rug III* hints that mass murder, if that's what it is, has moved in and taken up domestic residence. In *Edge*, the dismembered limbs are seen in a killing-ground ambience of red and black, but they are also made to form an insouciant ghoulish chorus line.

The historic significance of Guston's late style has nothing directly to do with issues of abstraction versus figuration, still less with any "return to the figure" (that unslayable journalistic chimera). The fundamental question that Guston addressed was not how or what to paint, but *why*: the need for a reason sufficient to each painting and inescapably evident in each painting. Nothing less could recover conviction for an art gutted by the burnout of modernist ideals. Guston did not reach for a solution but surrendered to content near at hand, abolishing the priesthood of modern art by declaring that the painter is the same person when he is painting and when he is not painting. The same guilts, doubts, and obsessions afflict him inside the studio and out. Painting is one of his obsessions, one that he has privileged above the others but can no longer justify so privileging. Only by introducing it into the flow of his obsessions—incidentally foregrounding the continuum of his life and woes with the life and woes of a culture that has uses for painting—can he gain confidence in the activity as something seriously thinkable, leaving open the question whether it is worth doing.

Only culture, over time, can decide whether an art has been worth doing. Culture has cast a vote for Guston, not simply by noting the resemblance of his late work to present fashions in painting but also by registering, however dimly, its radical truth. This is a truth about the artist as a victim of imagination. When all the heady theories, pretty stories, and other circumlocutions about art are done, we come down to a lone suffering consciousness in aroused communion with its own suffering. For instance, we come down to *Friend—To M.F.*, Guston's great portrait of his close friend Morton Feldman, the composer (his big ear presumably for music). The similarity of this head to those in Guston's many self-portrayals suggests a projected or symbiotic self-portrait. The head is turned away from the viewer—a rarity, to say the least, in portraiture. Nothing sinister seems implied by this disconcerting gesture. The massive head, heavily benign in its tobacco reverie, is simply preoccupied, looking at or into something with bloodshot eye. That something is painting. The head regards the mysterious sky blue field in which it is embedded: the painting field that is always full face to painter and viewer alike. We are used to looking at this field. Guston here gives a demonstration of how to *watch* it: with reverent fear and helpless love.

1984

Eric Fischl

Eric Fischl is an outrageous artist in a time of outrageous artists. He is one of several whose spectacular successes, of esteem and/or scandal, are making today's art world the liveliest and most contentious in twenty years. At the age of thirty-six, he is something of a late bloomer as these things have been going. He is three years older than Julian Schnabel and four years older than David Salle, two more-established art stars whom he has recently joined in the lightning-rod Mary Boone Gallery (October 6–27, 1984). But a good realist style takes time to evolve, as does the maturity required to handle emotional high explosives without doing oneself some injury.

On the verge now of widespread fame, Fischl is in possession of artistic means that seem to promise him a long career. At the same time, his themes of sexual, familial, racial, and social delirium ensure that his career will never be uncontroversial. Make no mistake about Fischl. He is an artist hostile by temperament and principle to norms of propriety. His vocation is painting, but his mission is to blow the lid off messy and painful truths.

Fischl's first picture to rivet the art world's attention—and my own—was the shocking *Bad Boy* of 1981. Writhing seductively on a bed is a voluptuous naked woman, watched by a boy of eleven or twelve who reaches behind him into her purse. It is not a great painting—Fischl's technique was still tentative—but its psychological punch and plain audacity galvanized a range of public response from numbness to furious rejection to ribald hilarity. (The critic Robert Pincus-Witten titled an article on it "Snatch and Snatching.") Suddenly there was a new voice in American art, and what it was saying—or stammering, freighted with dark, congested emotions—beggared the capacity of the art audience to respond.

A recent painting, *Cargo Cults*, shows how far Fischl has come in skill and subtlety, without losing any voltage, in the three years since *Bad Boy*. This scene of sybaritic leisure in the vacation tropics is a constellation of mysteries. Who are these people? What is the naked white man yelling at the two striding, oblivious women? What is in the flight bag, so placed in the composition as to exude a Hitchcockian menace? And the black man, the shaman with upraised knife, where did he come from? Will he attack? Is he real or a hallucination?

What's going on here?

A lot is going on, including lush, slathery paint handling, tonically vigorous color, and some intensely satisfying realist passages. (The flesh tones of the shouting man are a knockout.) These bravura elements fit in oddly but pleasingly with the painting's stolidly narrative and illustrational presentation. The picture has an unironic foursquareness practically unknown in sophisticated art since Edward Hopper.

To deal with Fischl's art is to deal directly with his meanings: in *Cargo Cults* with feelings of outrage, in the sense of hurtful violation, grossness, indecency—and dread. This forced encounter, not some antimodern revival of conservative aesthetics, is the burden of his style, into which he is led by the logic of a compulsion to communicate. His work allows plenty of options for interpretation, but one cannot savor it in a formalist, connoisseuring spirit. Fischl belongs solidly to his avant-garde generation, which is in broad rebellion against modernist ideals of abstract purity. He also opens a new chapter in an intermittent modern tradition (the tradition of Edvard Munch and Max Beckmann) of seeking to put art on intimate speaking terms with life.

Fischl found his first subject matter and the emotional wavelength for his art in memories of his suburban childhood in a home made chaotic by an alcoholic parent. (He denies, however, that any of his painted scenes are specifically autobiographical.) His initial theme was the bewildered shame and rage of a child exposed prematurely to adult sexuality and sorrow. He has since gone far beyond this theme, explicit in *Bad Boy*, to orchestrate, as in *Cargo Cults*, confrontations with the primitive in a grandly fictional vein. But the figure of the hurt, sullen child remains central to his vision.

A boy sulking amid raucous adults at a nude beach or furiously masturbating in a dinky plastic pool or firing at a sunbathing woman with a squirt gun: Fischl's puny heroes register indelible traumas that nonetheless retain an edge of guilty excitement. A scene in Proust comes to mind: the young protagonist's confused, nameless pleasure in the smells of a public lavatory. Fischl likewise conjures memory by sensory association, restoring keen immediacy to the past and at the same time redeeming it—drawing the past into art's timelessness. It is significant that every increment of Fischl's skill—each new command of color and line—has introduced a new depth and sharpness of meaning.

Storytelling is the method, not just the manner, of Fischl's art. He starts with the general conception of a scene, then assembles photographs—his own or from magazines and other sources—which seem to fit that conception. From the photos he casts his characters and selects his settings and props. The picture may evolve through many stages. Characters may appear or disappear, change race or gender, and gain or lose clothing. The setting may slip from one kind of room into another. Such mutability in Fischl's process leaves a distinct residue, accounting for the apparitional presence of each detail within compositions that seem fortuitous, "discovered." At once like the teller of a fairy tale and the wide-eyed listening child, Fischl constitutes, in each picture, a closed circuit of rapture.

The disturbing and tantalizing aspects of Fischl's narrative situations might be paraphrased as a question: Can this really be happening? The strangeness has nothing to do with surrealism—or with any art that imitates dreams. We rarely question events in our dreams, accepting even the most preposterous elements matter-of-factly. Fischl's is a waking strangeness, the kind we experience in moments of shock—the shock either of great joy or of horror. In both cases we feel: "I don't deserve this. This can't be happening to me." Our egos, our whole beings, dissolve in an unwilled act of simply beholding.

Fischl's *The Old Man's Boat and the Old Man's Dog* is a beautiful painting, with its eloquent play of warm flesh tones against cold blue-green water. Here Fischl transposes his favorite theme of the nude beach—where complex tensions underlie supposedly uninhibited relaxation—to the isolated environment of a boat. There is emphatic cause for tension among these lolling pleasure lovers: a snarling, vicious dog. The proximity of fangs and flesh suggests an imminent emergency, but the mood of the painting is more quizzical than panicky.

Simply, no one on the boat is paying the savage cur any attention. Why not? The title offers a vernacular answer, the words of a casual explainer (who?): "Because it's the old man's boat and the old man's dog, and you don't mess with the old man." But no old man is visible— unless it's the beer drinker on the deck and "old man" is his sobriquet. The effect of partial explanation is to render the remaining mystery all the more excruciating. Like an unreachable itch, the picture both compels and frustrates reaction, signaling a meaning that remains elusive. What makes the work more than a teasing game is the way it generates associations, becoming symbolic of all threats we are helpless to defuse, from the bad character of a lover or the arbitrariness of a boss to nuclear war.

Fischl is a moralist. He is driven by the idea of reconciling private experience with public expression, in a culture where the former is typically a realm of inarticulate suffering and the latter a repertoire of glittering falseness. This is a very American type of moral intention, though less familiar in our visual art than in our literature—a recurring motif from the New England transcendentalists to the Beats, a periodic revolt of the individual and the subjective against a relentlessly leveling and repressing body politic. Fischl's bold imagery is a deliberate, even angry, affront, but an affront in the service of compassion for everything in us that is damaged, frightened, and unfulfilled.

Ever since the jolt of my first look at *Bad Boy*, I have followed Fischl's progress with mounting excitement as both the quality and the wider implication of his work have grown. Fischl is attempting to bridge the modern gap between the world of art and the world at large. So are many of his contemporaries, but none with such a potent combination of conservative means and radical ends. His art takes up a previously unoccupied central position in the culture, speaking secrets of the soul in the language of the tribe.

Fischl Talking

Eric Fischl is big-boned and boyish, a slightly lumbering, comfortable presence. Perhaps self-protectively, he is a natural comic, given to one-liners and a tone of light self-mockery. I spoke with Fischl in TriBeCa, where he lives with April Gornik, a talented painter of big, mysterious landscapes.

I found out from my father recently that I was an unwanted child. I always knew I was unexpected. I always felt, I shouldn't be here. It turns out that my mother was severely depressed after I was born.

She was from an old St. Louis WASP family. She died in 1970 when she crashed her car. My father is second-generation Austrian, a retired salesman. Fischl sounds like a Jewish name, but we were Congregational—a really banal religion. I'm sorry I wasn't born into something more dramatic, preferably Catholicism. As it is, I'm always taken for Jewish. I even feel Jewish! We lived in Port Washington, on Long Island, in an upwardly mobile white neighborhood.

I remember enjoying art classes in elementary school, but I didn't do any art from fifth grade until I flunked out of college in my freshman year in 1966. I went to San Francisco to be a hippie. I remember being in a crash pad with thirty people and realizing I didn't like any of them. I thought there must be something wrong with me and maybe I should take more drugs to straighten myself out. So pretty soon I ended up at my parents' new home in Phoenix, unbelievably depressed.

My first painting was an abstract smear that looked like salad going down a drain. I was affected by pop and process art, by those kinds of irony and whimsy. At Arizona State University I resumed school and took a course from Bill Swaim, the kind of teacher everyone needs who is going to amount to anything, the kind who ignites your being. He was into metaphysical abstraction, like Kandinsky and Gorky. The sense of metaphysical mission I got from him ran head-on into the professionalism of CalArts, where I went in 1970. I had a lot of trouble with that. Everybody at CalArts knew that painting was dead. Nothing was good enough. I remember we'd have critiques where people would tear each other to shreds simply out of boredom.

In the middle seventies, in Chicago and Nova Scotia, I was trying to develop an iconography, because absract painting had lost the ability to carry content. In Nova Scotia I wanted to be regionalist, to get into the fishing culture. I made up a general narrative about a fishing family. One idea was that the wife performed sympathetic magic to help her husband fish. She would get in the bathtub when he was out in his boat. And their son participated by playing with the toys they had given him. My first illusionistic painting was of the son's toy boat. About the time I moved to New York in 1978 a friend, Gerry Ferguson, told me, "Quit kidding yourself about myth. This family is really white, middle-class, suburban American." That made me mad, but he was right.

Doing some of my images scared me, like when I painted the boy masturbating in the pool. Then I realized that the world hadn't ended. I am constantly surprised at how well my pictures are taken—

even by radicals, though my presentation is so conservative. I like that my work makes certain kinds of emotions seem okay to have. Other people seem to like that, too.

A lot of artists in my generation have had to confront an incredible disappointment. We were really sucked in by the American Dream, which is based on images and product promises. A big part of the American Dream is visual. That's the seduction: things looking just perfect. I was walking through my father's neighborhood in Phoenix a few years ago. It was quiet—*real* quiet—with cars in driveways, lawns of colored gravel and cactus, ranch-style houses. I walked along looking at how *perfect* it all was, and it was obvious that the feelings going on inside me could not possibly be appropriate in this environment.

I like nude beaches—especially the ones in France, which have very developed social orders—because you can watch people being naked but still acting in a social way. Nudity energizes and dramatizes a tension already existing in social interchange, the tension of sexual repression. You really *feel* the operation of taboo when people have their clothes off.

I would like to think sex is "clean," joyous. One of my fantasies whenever I start a beach painting is to paint a bacchanal, a real celebration. Then, sure enough, the distrust and the horror set in.

My mother was alcoholic. When I was growing up, my family was very united around the problem of her drinking. The tragedy of her death blew us apart. The thing about having a sick parent is that you think it's your problem. You feel like a failure because you can't save her. None of my paintings are strictly autobiographical, but the tone of the work has everything to do with my childhood. Somebody asked me if having a bigger audience changes my work. I had to answer that *my* audience is in the past.

I work hardest at being a likable guy. I can't stand not being liked. I think of it as earning my keep. What else? I don't have any sense of privacy. I assume people can see everything I'm thinking, so when I'm asked anything I can't lie. Painting may be about being asked.

I think most about Max Beckmann, about his incredible theatricality and double and triple meanings and mythic content. But I'm closer to Edward Hopper than Beckmann. And I don't like Hopper. His paintings fail because he was so wrapped up in American Puritanism. With a lot of figures he makes you aware of the wrong part of the body, usually breasts. But Hopper is a real symbolist painter, trying to turn daily American life into metaphors. Like him, I'm making banal scenes and hoping they'll transcend. There is really something tragic about America in the idea that we have *only* daily life to tell us what life is about.

Is my work "confessional"? No. If I'm confessing anything, it's that I have a certain range of nasty thoughts.

May 1984

Ed Ruscha: Traffic and Laughter

To know the art of Ed Ruscha, you should know something about Los Angeles, and the reverse: knowing something about Ruscha's art will help you with Los Angeles. He is the artist of that city as Manet was the artist of Paris, as integral to it as sense organs are to a body. He conveys the flavor of consciousness in Southern California like no one else since Raymond Chandler, the prose poet of American detective fiction. I do not mean by this that Ruscha is a "regional artist," let alone a provincial one. He is the artist of Los Angeles in precisely and only these aspects in which it is world-central. Through his art, as in no other way, Los Angeles announces itself as having and being a civilization.

"The city of the future." That cliché harbors a truth: Los Angeles is the city of the future and always will be. It has been the city of the future at least since World War II, piling up more and more futurity in place of a present. Its "past" is a category of obsolete futures, defeated longings still faintly alive like the tinglings in an amputated limb. Time is impalpable there, where one day and one night endlessly recur. Time drowns in space and light (sun alternating with neon), a brilliant ocean into which one plunges, behind the wheel of a car, several times daily.

There are two sounds in Los Angeles: traffic and laughter. Los Angeles laughter is the most extreme form of American laughter, which bemuses most Europeans and many New Yorkers as well. Such laughter is apparently uncaused, childlike, irresponsible, gratuitous. It is a chuckle in the throat, a constant eddy of mirth that is the opposite of irony: rather than penetrate and expose incongruities, it heals and elides them, homogenizing all differences in the emulsion of a positive attitude. It is the valence, the specific gravity, of American consciousness, and it attains maximum pitch in Los Angeles (whence, via movies and television, it is broadcast to the world).

The sound of Los Angeles laughter interpenetrates with the sound of Los Angeles traffic, the background hum of a rushing future that, always arriving, never arrives. Ruscha's art is a distillate of both these sounds and of what they mean, what strange mutations they propose for the forms of human life.

Ruscha's biography is archetypal for Southern California. He was born and grew up in Oklahoma, source of the epic westward trek of dispossessed farmers in jalopies during the 1930s that permanently marked the population and demotic culture. (Among other waves of newcomers, the only one as decisive has been from Mexico.) In 1956, at the age of eighteen, Ruscha retraced that well-worn migration route—Route 66—across a thousand miles of desert to the coast's sudden irrigated lushness, but he did it with a friend in a hopped-up car. Planning to enter commercial art, he attended the Chouinard Art Institute, known as a school for Walt Disney illustrators but at that moment, quite by chance, a center of advanced art. He immediately became a member of the only generation of Los Angeles artists to achieve international resonance, a generation including Robert Irwin and Larry Bell (later augmented by the presence of Bruce Nauman and John Baldessari). The surge of creative intensity in Los Angeles during the 1960s was determined by several factors, of which I will list three.

1. The de-Europeanization of modern art by abstract expressionism, then its fairly complete Americanization in emerging pop and minimal art. From having been a conduit for modernism, New York temporarily became its source, and what was beamed from the East Coast caused a sharp echo, in the form of a major variant, when it hit the West. Young Americans had a sense of entitlement and adventure.

2. The valuing of mediated imagery and industrial techniques. This was largely an intellectual gesture in New York pop and minimalism, a classically modernist, ironic, strategic trope. Transposed to Southern California, it became straightforward and hedonistic, energizing that region's world-leading sophistication in media technology and vernacular forms of industrial design (customized cars, plastics, etc.). Los Angeles had the tools and skills, ready to hand, for a stylistic apotheosis.

3. The aestheticizing of everyday life. The 1960s were an era of conflations: fantasy with reality, dream with politics, art with life. None of this was the least bit surprising from the viewpoint of South-

ern California, where existence had always been aesthetically mediated. It is a region of instinctive surrealists, matter-of-fact dandies, and cheerful nihilists. Suddenly its local predilection accorded with an international vanguard sensibility.

The period of Los Angeles's artistic eminence was brief, a few years before the city's entropic sprawl and discontinuity dissipated the energy of the moment. (F. Scott Fitzgerald said that there are no second acts in American lives; just so, there are no second generations in California.) However, it lasted long enough to give crucial orientation to Ruscha. He had the advantage of being situated to receive the best artistic information from elsewhere, as the art director of *Artforum* when that magazine was based in Los Angeles from 1964 to 1967. He became simultaneously an informed internationalist and a quintessential Los Angeleno.

Ruscha is personally modest, soft-spoken, and handsome. He is one of the least disliked men I know, though also one of the most envied. He is known as a companion of Hollywood beauties. (Recently a Beverly Hills newspaper ran a photograph of one such beauty in company, the breathless and succinct caption read, "with *him*.") Why this gossip? Because Ruscha's personality, no less than his art, is emblematic of his culture, in a way that makes him enlivening to a historical imagination. (Think again of Manet, the painter in a frock coat.) Ruscha's work emits a subtle emotion from within culture. The emotion is an abstraction of Los Angeles laughter shaded by an austere, slightly disquieting irony—the dandy's irony, a whiff of loss.

In Los Angeles, one laughs to survive, enjoys oneself not to enhance life but to live at all. That society is so tenuous that the only alternative to a spiral of loneliness is a self-contained, steady, pleasurably focused attitude. The L.A. cogito: I laugh, therefore I am. The laughter is ramified and refined. Only with time and effort does a visitor learn its language. It is the absolute form of civility in a civilization that enables nobody to mature beyond adolescence. It can be erotic and quite beautiful when one hears its undertone of sadness. It can be disturbing when one catches its overtone of anger. It is the sound of grown-up children determined not to be afraid.

Los Angeles is a West that lies between two Easts. Across the mountains and desert there is the eastern U.S., and across the Pacific there is the Far East, the Orient. If, as I believe, Ruscha and Robert

Irwin (who is best known for light-filled, nearly empty environments partly inspired by sensory-deprivation research) are the two most important Los Angeles artists of the 1960s, it may be because they made an even division of the two Easts: Irwin took the Pacific route to Zen-like satori, and Ruscha took Route 66. In so doing, they bisected Los Angeles laughter. Irwin isolated the element of bliss—the chortle of infantile well-being—and Ruscha laid bare the reflex of antic irrationality—the child's rapture in absurdity. Irwin is mystical. Ruscha is witty.

In the early sixties Irwin and Ruscha both developed meticulously crafted, medium-scaled versions of New York field painting, the enveloping vehicle of Pollock and Rothko. Irwin inflected his version with a few thin lines of barely contrasting color, nudging the viewer toward oceanic reverie. Ruscha invaded his with signs—commercial labels and logos, pictures of common objects, words—from popular culture, triggering a keen sense of violation. To violate is the fundamental gesture of Ruscha's art as to be inviolable is that of Irwin's.

Ruscha's important insight at the time, akin to Andy Warhol's (Warhol, incidentally, was first shown not in New York but in Los Angeles, in 1962), was that the newly opened field of popular imagery offered far more than a vein of satiric subject matter. He understood that it was potentially a whole structure—subject matter, form, and content in one—capable not merely of being used in painting but of displacing the traditional function of painting altogether. Unlike Warhol, Ruscha had no interest in actually performing this revolutionary dislocation. He was, and has remained, content to work on the verge of the radical break, retaining enough artistic conventions to register the delicate spasms of numberless violations.

Ruscha traces his vocation as an artist to a day in 1957 when he saw the magazine reproduction of a Target painting by Jasper Johns. To be inspired by a reproduction is usually the mark and the debilitating fate of a provincial sensibility, but here it is prophetically in key with Ruscha's later achievement. The moment is delectable: young Ruscha sees the glossy reproduction of a painting that is already a reproduction (in paint, of a mechanical emblem). A mental process of fantastic sophistication commences, and in the sunstruck, sign-filled vacancy of Los Angeles it finds an instantaneous universe of material.

The mode of Ruscha's art is a naturalism of signs, a quizzical and amused investigation of the behavior of signs not in systems but in specific instances, caught red-handed in the act of signifying. He is the artist as semiotic hard-boiled detective. When he traveled around Europe for seven months in 1961 (two months in Paris), Ruscha took little interest in the art he saw. He was attracted instead by street life and street iconography, which he photographed voluminously, and by such iconological curiosities as the famous R. A. Bertelli *Head of Mussolini* in London's Imperial War Museum, a uniformly rounded black ceramic bust that to every viewpoint presents two perfect profiles of Il Duce. Ruscha absorbed the immanence of Los Angeles even in the Old World.

Ruscha's instinct for the penetrating oddness—the laughter—of signs is apparent in the drawings he made during his European sojourn, including *Bicycle Sign* and *Boulangerie*. The semaphoric use of graphic images, such as that of a bicycle to denote a bicycle route, was still rare in America in 1961, and it excited Ruscha. And already his poetic ear was being piqued by words and expressions that, for one contingent reason or another, rupture meaning, causing thought to stumble. The word *boulangerie*, pronounced with an American accent, is ineffably clumsy, a disjointedly lurching clump of syllables that epitomizes the humiliation—well known to me, alas—of an American's struggle to speak French. It has the poignant aura of a remote, unobtainable Frenchness, an aura amusingly at odds with the word's humble referent. Introduced into the formal and seductive medium of oil paint in the manner pioneered by Johns, such linguistic units sit for portraits that expose their secret lives.

Since I am writing for a European audience, I should acknowledge a difficulty that Ruscha's work is bound to pose for non-Americans. Ruscha's use of language, idiomatic in the extreme, is as translation-proof as lyric poetry. Each phrase triggers inchoate associations and a sensation of being engulfed in the very soul of American language making, that intersection of mind and tongue where meaning and laughter blend. The effect is uncanny. One has no sense of Ruscha himself speaking. Such verbal talent is rare among artists. To get a literary equivalent, one might imagine a cross between William Burroughs and John Ashbery, two other American masters of impersonal but intimately explosive colloquial voices.

Fortunately, Ruscha's art speaks in languages other than vernacular American, and one of them is the most universal: photography. He uses photographs in very much the way he uses words, with a flat, apparently mindless, tone that becomes more mysterious the more one tries to grasp it. His photographic style is straightforwardly documentary, but what is being documented? What are we being told about Los Angeles parking lots and condominiums? The questions turn back on themselves like snakes biting their tails.

Ruscha's main use of photography has taken place in counterpoint with another medium: the book. He abolishes the usual relation of pictures and books, by which pictures illustrate a narrative or serve as objects of a discourse. In a Ruscha book, pictures expel narrative and discourse. Every habitual way we have of reading a book, and of looking at photographs, is halted dead in its tracks. Thus described, Ruscha's process may sound like a deconstructive game, but, in fact, it serves a realist function. There is a syntax to the images in a book by Ruscha that comes direct from the phenomenal world. It comes from Los Angeles.

The Rosetta stone of Ruscha's books, the one that most plainly collates the languages of Los Angeles, the book, and photography, is the foldout *Every Building on the Sunset Strip*. Sunset Strip is a gaudy but not terribly exciting mile-long stretch of clubs, restaurants, and hotels on Sunset Boulevard in Hollywood. As a legendary site, Sunset Strip meets a common definition of celebrity, "famous for being famous"; but in reality, suffering from Los Angeles's endemic disjunctures and elastic distances, it is incoherent and bland. There can be no integral experience of Sunset Strip to match the seductive density of its name.

Ruscha's treatment of the Strip has the elegant clarity of a scientific theorem, and it engenders a practically Buddhistic lightness of spirit. The end-to-end photographs of, yes, every building, palm tree, and empty lot on the Sunset Strip convey both the droning incessantness that is Los Angeles and the all-embracing, diffuse alertness that is Los Angeles sanity. Done in 1966, this is a pivotal, prophetic work. The ramifications of *Every Building on the Sunset Strip* (say the title to yourself several times, slowly) amount to a quiet revolution in urban consciousness, an essential prediction of the architectural thinking of, among others, Robert Venturi and Frank Gehry. This work brings a barbarous reality within the ambit of civilized mind.

Every Building has to do with present time; it gives a missing present-ness, a simultaneity, to an entity that otherwise can exist only through time, the time it takes a car to traverse the Strip. (You wouldn't walk it; like most Los Angeles boulevards it lacks continuous side-walks.) *Thirtyfour Parking Lots in Los Angeles* (1967) is, surprisingly, about the past: photographing from the air, Ruscha chose parking lots not for their geometries but for their patterns of oil stains. *Real Estate Opportunities* (1970) is about the future, Los Angeles's metaphysical mainspring, its ever-beckoning promise and lure—here mocked by a selection of obviously atrocious places to live.

Ruscha's presentations of the language of photography and the photographic qualities of language add up to the vision of a totally mediated world: a world of traffic on every level. By accepting this world, Ruscha shows it to be habitable, oddly enjoyable, and even touched by a strange grace. The world of traffic is also the world of laughter. This is not to say (though some critics are bound to say it) that Ruscha is a propagandist for the society of consumption and spectacle. His art maintains an ascetic edge against the trivializing and demoralizing effects of consumerism, its reduction of all value to the economic. Ruscha is not a cynic. He is even, in a way, religious.

Ruscha had a devout Catholic boyhood, uncommon in mostly Prot-estant Oklahoma and also, among non-Hispanics, in Los Angeles. I think this background illuminates something about the ritualistic qualities of his art and about his preoccupation with purity and vio-lation. Los Angeles, as a culture, gives no one any structure of values or, correlatively, any sense of possible transgression. If present at all, these spiritual mechanisms are imported luxuries. Ruscha in 1956, an emigrant teenager wild for sunshine, girls, and fun, brought them along as unsuspected cargo in his customized 1950 Ford.

All the gas stations in Ruscha's first book, *Twentysix Gas Stations* (1963), were found on Route 66, which Ruscha often traveled back and forth between California and Oklahoma City in those days. It seems to me faintly possible that the number twenty-six alludes to the stations of the cross, minus the fourteenth (Calvary) and doubled. In any case, I believe that a liturgical association will help us to grasp the uncan-niness of Ruscha's unprecedented use in drawings of an incredible variety of mineral and organic substances, including gunpowder, egg yolk, spinach, blood, ketchup, shellac, fruit juices, lettuce, and zinc oxide. Besides realizing a range of piquant visual beauties, these tran-substantiations of humble stuff into the communion of art (ironic, to be sure, and sarcastically debased by banal verbal messages) draw a magic circle around consciousness. The comedy, too deep and elusive for hilarity, consists in an imitation of religion. The drawings do God's work: they give meaning to Creation.

The many large oil paintings that Ruscha has made since the middle 1970s are his most disconcerting works. Why would an artist with a genius for graphic and photographic mediums leave them for one in which his proficiency is unremarkable? And what about the incongruity of employing monumental physical means to deliver slight verbal whimsies? Has Ruscha succumbed to a fatuous cultural piety in favor of the more "serious" medium? I don't think so. The culture has scarcely rewarded him, for one thing: these paintings have been the least publicly and commercially successful of his works, and yet he produces them with stubborn persistence.

I think the large paintings are calculated assaults on thought, including the form of thought that is Ruscha's own verbal gift. The aim, I believe, is an ecstatic deracination, laughter mingled with awe.

If the painting *Industrial Village and Its Hill*, 1982, were a drawing (seen only in reproduction, it amounts to one), it would be an effective joke. Using exact geographical terms to particularize the uninflected abstraction of a landscape (a Route 66 landscape par excellence) is witty. A graphic format would permit one to savor the delicate absurdity of it in one's mind. (Drawing is the medium that models thought.) Performed on a three-meter expanse of buttery oil paint, however, the exercise is brutalized, self-destroyed as a witticism. Not the idea of landscape but something like the experience of an actual landscape is induced in the viewer, who seizes on the internal captions "industrial village" and "hill" to stave off vertigo. What is the word for an urgent reliance on verbal formulas? The word is *prayer*.

Ruscha's large paintings do indeed activate the reflex of prayer, or at least of that childlike state in which one stands open to the self-evidence of nature. They enact the mind's swoon in the face of cosmic perspectives. Ever skeptical, Ruscha takes pains to forestall specifically religious conclusions. To evoke a mystery of love, for instance, he appropriates the technical phrase "friction and wear on mating surfaces" from the jargon of mechanical engineers. And his hymn of praise for natural glory is couched in self-deflating colloquial understatement: "Not a bad world is it." Still, he is clearly fascinated by the fact of emotional sublimity, and he schemes to capture it on canvas.

In his large paintings, Ruscha augments the laughter of Route 66 with a laughter of the Orient: the soul of Los Angeles synthesized, complete. Think of it if you visit that city. It will help you. In that basin of bright haze on the Pacific rim, there may seem to be nothing for your mind to grasp—until you realize the palpability of the nothing, the glittering vacancy, itself. Take a drive in it. Cruise past every building on the Sunset Strip. Check on the availability of tacky condominiums. Later, park in the hills near the HOLLYWOOD sign as the sun dips abruptly beneath the horizon and watch ten thousand lighted signs assert sudden, clamorous desires. If the charm has worked, you will have an excited urge to phone Ed Ruscha and tell him about your day. But, of course, he already knows.

1985

To Pico

Guacamole Airlines and Other Drawings by Edward Ruscha
(New York: Harry N. Abrams, 1978)

You are one of the shadowless east-west routes
You start or end, or neither, in breezy Santa Monica
You are one off-ramp on the Santa Monica Freeway
(You cede all long-distance traffic to the Santa Monica Freeway)
You are the back door of Century City, ass-end of the Avenue of the
    Stars
You point at Beverly Hills, then bend unconcerned away
You skulk past Hillcrest Country Club fences and high foliage,
    offended and offending
You dawdle through the endless blurry unnamed reaches of central
    L.A.
You duck under the Harbor Freeway into so-called Downtown, to
    which you lend your irrepressible shabbiness
You consist of asphalt, cement, and largely cheapish small buildings
You have a dustily marginal air
You seem immunized against the showy
You favor the gross wholesaler and the odd small business
You look unphotographed
You are unthronged
You are a familiar address for stop-and-go business
You are unlike swift Olympic, purposeful Santa Monica, wishful
    Wilshire, nerve-racking Sunset
You are the back of the turned back of the city
You are broad and dry
You are blessedly unfoliaged
You jerk through the city, stoplight to stoplight, like a blunt knife
    through an unfeeling body
You are imperturbable and dumb, abstracted in the sun

You abstractly acknowledge the sun
You do not care
You are Los Angeles and not Los Angeles
You have unlimited, because unneeded, parking
You make each pedestrian look like a thief
You are a deserted mansion of air
You are honest and without illusions, with no spoiled illusions,
    because no one ever had any illusions concerning you
You are fiercely depressing
You are poetic—obviously
You are the typical address of a chiropractor
You laze in the afternoons like a long flat cat
You are, late afternoons, almost beautiful, light soaked
You are destroyed by twilight
You are dead in the night of your feverish streetlights
You are ruins in the night, post-nuclear, site of mountainous gloom-
    vapors, suicide alley
You are inhuman horizontal monstrous in the night
You feature, in the night, a few beery, low-wattage Mexican joints, a
    few gas stations, some lighted signs
You feature no haven
You inform the visitor that something is wrong here
You inform the restless, nervous, uprooted visitor
You inform him that where he has come to is a joke on him, and
    you're not kidding
You do not care
You look uncared-about
You look unintended, uncalculated, uncontemplated by anyone ever
    until this moment
You look to be the forlorn historical accident you are
You are like a side street with elephantiasis
You are a great place for a murder
You are a great place for the murder of an obscure, transient person
    by another obscure, transient person
You are without remorse, remorseless
You are innocent with the innocence of a homicidal moron
You inform the visitor that sky, light, air, that nature is not worth
    caring about
You inform the visitor that humanity is not worth caring for

You are a self-fulfilling prophecy
You would taste chalky, if you had a taste
You would smell of dry rust, if you had a smell
You would be, if a sound, a faint, distant rattling
You'd be grainy to the touch, of a hardness gradually crumbling
You would be to the inner sense, and are, the paradox of a grandiose
    humility
You are the spirit of littleness lordly in the sun
You are a parade route for entropy
You lie across the city like a UFO runway
You complacently anticipate a horrible future
You are stronger than love, than intelligence, than energy
You are a spiritual Fault that has slipped, toppling the better, flimsier
    constructs of human aspiration
You are the secret of the city, the incision that reveals its heart of
    stone
You inscribe on the map a vast, mean smirk (upside down)
You attract me; I am yours; I return to you
You resonate to a well-known old emptiness
You are intimate
You whisper
You hiss

1978

The Daemon and Sigmar Polke

One of the most fecund artists of the last twenty years, Sigmar Polke may also be the most mysterious. In New York his mystery is partly circumstantial, since only recently have we begun seeing the work of this forty-three-year-old German in quantity and at its best. The present show (Mary Boone Gallery, January 5–26, 1985) of strong paintings is a big step toward alleviating our ignorance. But anyone who expects that simple familiarity with Polke's production will dispel its obscurity has another think coming. To learn more and more about him, I have discovered, is in a way to know less and less. His art is a Wonderland rabbit hole, entrance to a realm of spiraling perplexities, one of which is his uncanny relation to American art, first as a provincial follower and later as a powerful influence.

From East Germany, that seemingly inexhaustible source of gifted émigrés, Polke studied in Düsseldorf in the late 1950s and early 1960s. In 1963, with Gerhard Richter and Konrad Fischer (the dealer, who was then an artist), he helped to found the German variant of pop art, which they called, with characteristic critical finesse, Capitalist Realism. It was a style that embraced the American preoccupation with mediated imagery and added an intellectually advanced sense of the issues of representation: these artists were at once hip to popular culture and well versed in Walter Benjamin. In Polke's case, it was also a style that, while parodying mechanical modes, was far more freely graphic and painterly than its design-y American counterpart. The manual touch Polke maintained in his paintings of halftone-patterned Playboy bunnies, Dufy-esque decorative motifs, and self-mockingly "expressive" brushwork had to seem old-fashioned at the time (more akin to the earliest pop paintings of Warhol and Lichtenstein than to their slicked-up mature styles). But it was, of course, new-fashioned in the extreme. Evading the trap of a "look," Polke stayed open to a hallucinating plenitude of impulses, old and new and high and low, from Francis Picabia to science fiction. He force-fed the practice of spontaneous picture making a diet of paradoxical consciousness, contributing directly to the epochal delirium that reigns in art today.

The fabulous variety of Polke's technical and stylistic tricks—painting on noncanvas fabrics, overlaying images, and mixing a witch's brew of weird paint mediums, to note only the most obvious—has had a highly visible and invigorating influence on other artists. But Polke's true significance lies beyond the antic surfaces of his art, in a philosophical attitude that haunts current artistic theory and practice like a ghost in a machine. It is an attitude of bottomless skepticism that contemplates—"with terror and delight," as Baudelaire recommended to his fellow connoisseurs of hysteria—its own endlessly ramifying contradictions. Polke is heir to a great secret (because practically indescribable) theme of modern art: the theme of the daemon.

For *daemon*, my dictionary offers a "subordinate deity, as the genius of a place or a man's attendant spirit." That will do, though without the religious overtones. Modern daemonism is the secular revelation of impersonal energies, experienced in the intense activity of, apparently, nothing. Given definite shape in the spiritual dandyism of the late nineteenth century, it is empirical and materialistic, even scientific, in outlook. What do you suppose Oscar Wilde was talking about in this passage from "The Critic as Artist"?

> In the subjective sphere, where the soul is at work, it comes to us, this terrible shadow, with many gifts in its hands, gifts of strange temperaments and subtle susceptibilities, gifts of wild ardours and chill moods of indifference, complex multiform gifts of thoughts that are at variance with each other, and passions that war against themselves. And so, it is not our own life that we live, but the lives of the dead, and the soul that dwells within us is no single spiritual entity, making us personal and individual.

The antecedent of Wilde's "terrible shadow" is "the scientific principle of heredity," understood (in 1890) as canceling the illusion of personal subjectivity, of an autonomous "I." That Wilde's "science" is dated does not matter. He had hit on a metaphor still paradigmatic as an account of the dissociation of modern mind as it is revealed to us, in flashes of epiphany, by certain artists.

Polke is one of these artists. In his art, nothing is either quite subjective or quite objective, though everything seems ordered by some inhuman comprehension. It must be said that this comprehension—the Polkean daemon—is unreassuring. It is derisive, impudent, Mephistophelian. It steers close to outright cynicism. It is without apparent pride, a rascally character. It has an affinity for the debased in imagery, materials, and procedures, a debasement it is at no pains to redeem. The dynamic mess of many of Polke's paintings suggests the work of a blind man with good luck. I have a fantasy of him: he enters a pristine studio, full of exquisite materials all in order, and wrecks the place. The wreckage—a series of paintings—is removed. The studio is bulldozed.

The bulldozing of the studio—meaning the conventionality of painting—is a recurrent avant-garde dream, of course. It was a dominant theme of art in the late 1960s, when Polke, besides looking regressive in the context of pop, courted an impression of complete irrelevance in relation to minimalism and its offshoot tendencies by the simple act of continuing to paint and draw. What a difference a decade or so makes! Nowadays the spirit of sixties radicalism survives in the sphere of picture making—Polke's, in particular—far more robustly than in what remains of "poststudio" aesthetics, hopelessly entangled in conventions of their own. Painting's superior ironic capacity is seen in the way Polke's deeds of artistic vandalism, performed *on* painting, nonetheless end up *in* and *as* painting. He shows painting to be like the tar baby in the Southern folk tale, absorbing and trapping the force of every blow against it. And yet he keeps hitting, with an imperious irrationality that begins to feel like a force of nature.

If Polke's perversity is an enigma, his frequent whimsicality is almost an insult. Instances of crude jokiness, decorative fuss, and dubious mysticism abound in his work, sometimes making one feel vaguely humiliated for even looking at it. This is a salutary humiliation. Polke's tastelessness (never bad taste, which is still taste) is an earnest of his daemonic seriousness, his sense of a permanent emergency at the core of all cultural conventions. For him, aesthetic decorum appears to be roughly as important in the present state of civilization as table manners during an air raid, and this includes the surreptitious decorum, the tacit, easy agreement, that makes lugubriousness, frenzy, and apocalypse the unearned small change of current style. Polke's immunity to the self-fulfilling and self-justifying imperatives of any style whatsoever, at a time when we are drowning in styles, qualifies him as an artist's artist of and for our day.

As might be expected, Polke's work beggars standard modes of analysis, whether formal or heuristic. He produces sheer double binds in which each element of a picture preserves a two-way "deniability," glinting with poetic lights when one tries to nail it down formally, and presenting a face of dumb materiality when one tries to interpret it metaphorically. A good example is the painting *Lager* (Camp). Perhaps encouraged by the resolutions of similar themes by Anselm Kiefer, its chilling motif of concentration-camp fences may excite an expectation of catharsis. But what do we get? A cloud of black murk shoved in our faces is what we get. Murk that in its slapdash physicality is less death evoking than just deadening, saying in effect: "Here's some paint. Did you, by chance, expect something else in a painting?" Which is not to say that the provocation of the barbed wire goes away. Finally, what one responds to is a phenomenon of mutual exclusion, a sort of aggressive indifference: the daemon.

In the metaphysical junkyard of Polke's art, everything is broken, then broken again. No received image, in his hands, seems too mean or too destroyed to be beyond further debasement and destruction. The very medium of paint (or whatever evil fluids Polke uses in lieu of paint) is severed from its own properties, notably color (which invariably looks arbitrary, even mistaken), and is viciously at odds with its support. Polke doesn't so much cover a surface as obliterate it, as with *Lager*'s black murk and the bilious stains of *The Computer Moves In*. Jules Olitski once declared a yearning to paint in thin air, without canvas. Polke seems motivated to make simple messes on walls and floors, but canvases keep getting in the way: there is often a sense of material rudely intercepted on its way to somewhere else. The upshot of all this depredation is a rawness beyond *art-brut* primitivism, like the rawness of sandpapered nerve ends.

If popular culture has a form hospitable to the daemon, it is stand-up comedy, the strange ritual by which a man or woman, isolated and exposed, becomes an open spigot of personal and collective dark stuff, a convulsive mentioner of the unmentionable. Polke is not alone in realizing, within art, a structural equivalent of the form—today practically the definitive trope of younger American artists, especially. But his is easily the most profound version, for he triggers the effect of comedy while directing it to levels too deep and inchoate for laughter. Polke's is an art of cosmic pratfalls—or rather cosmic pratfreefalls, which never encounter the embarrassing but reassuring reality of a floor. Part of my own typical response to his work is a certain ache, like an ache to laugh, that is without issue, a sensation of blockage in the mechanism of humor, a monkey wrench lodged in the autonomic cycle of tension and release. It is a brief, fitful, and not terribly pleasant feeling, but it is the basis of my conviction about Polke.

The daemonic artist awakens a sense of conviction, of being in the vicinity of things self-evidently true, and, most particularly, puts this sense to violent tests. Oscar Wilde's aestheticism takes on a surprising grandeur, in the passage I quoted, by being used to cope positively with a situation of, one would think, primordial fear, the fear of divorce from oneself that is a dire corollary of scientific imagination. Similarly, Polke's high-handed slovenliness with the means of art— his sarcastic shamanism—becomes charged with dignity in the face of what it both enacts and counteracts, namely the disintegration of the self in a hypertrophic, doom-laden culture. Polke evokes an organic heroism, a heroism without enemies. It may not count for much in the larger scheme of things, but Polkean defiance is a present touchstone of art's always provisional capacity to sustain a hope and an appetite for the future.

1985

Adrian Saxe and the Smart Pot

Adrian Saxe's complicated, erudite, faintly didactic nonfunctioning vessels are ceramics about ceramics. They are beautiful and spectacularly well made, but also intellectually thorny and demanding. They both are and are not what they seem, like a spy agency cloaking its actions in "deniability." I find that I don't look at so much as *watch* them, with alternating admiration and perplexity at what—whatever it is—they are up to, which turns out to be packed with insight about the predicament of decorative handcraft in the late twentieth century. They are philosophical objects—I'm tempted to say dialectical, but who still believes in thesis/antithesis/synthesis, the old optimistic clickety-clack?—which means that they pose rather than answer questions, or else take your questions and hand them back to you in more fundamental, more worrisome terms. They don't seek ways out of current contradictions; they turn current contradictions to direct account. They are period pieces from a period—ours—of multiple fractures.

I don't imagine that many people in the ceramics world take Saxe's work in the heady way I do. Undertaking to write about it, I'm aware of encroaching on a field where suspicion of intellect is a given, anti-intellectualism being the shadow of certain positive values embodied in most modern craft movements. Loyal to feeling and intuition, craft ideology in this century has tended to exert a corrective drag on modernist eagerness to make life conform to abstract thinking. The primordial goodness of handwork, with its deep continuities and life-enhancing domestic uses, has been seen to oppose the spiritual violence of modernization. But this idea, like any other, can have its assumptions yanked out from under it by fickle history. Simply, no one is arguing with it anymore. Today modernist faith in "progress" is disintegrating, and so is, or should, the counter-arrogance of taciturn craft humanism. This is a moment of bizarre perspectives and hybrid forms, a moment when all the old bets are off. One sign of the change is what

I'll call the smart pot, a species of anxious object—anxious because it cannot decide what it is—pioneered by Adrian Saxe.

The smart pot is an academic object positing an imaginary academy, the brains of an imaginary all-embracing civilization. The smart pot is so removed from innocence, so thoroughly implicated in every received notion of nature and culture, so promiscuous in its means and open in its ends, that it's almost innocent all over again—like Magellan leaving by the front door and circumnavigating the globe to come in the back. The smart pot is tantalizing rather than pleasing. It hangs fire. It is not "art." The smart pot X-rays hoary art-versus-craft distinctions to reveal their confusion of values: values of prestige fouling up values of use.

The smart pot accepts the semiotic fate of everything made by human beings, the present wisdom that every such thing is consciously or unconsciously a sign. Given the choice, the smart pot opts to be conscious. It represses no meaning, however disturbing. Is the gallery ceramic now a sign of wealth and taste, a snob-appeal material mascot? Very well, that will be foregrounded. Not by accident are Saxe's pieces flamboyantly expensive looking. The social form many of them activate is that ceremonial fetish, the trophy: materialized congratulations. In a way, a Saxe ceramic congratulates its owner on being able to afford it. But this way is slippery, ironic, reversible; it ridicules even as it flatters. The smart pot escapes the smarmy corruption symptomized by appeals to "quality," a code word of insecure wealth, by plowing straight through it. It is glamorous and untrustworthy, like a pedigreed dog that has been known to bite. The smart pot's attitude to history is similarly double-edged: enraptured and cannibalistic.

Saxe's intensive study of eighteenth-century Sèvres porcelain, touchstone of the rococo, is among the most improbable and inspired of recent creative rediscoveries, paying off on a lot of levels. The rococo is a great dense blind spot in the history of taste. Practically the definition of *old-fashioned* for two centuries, it is marked by the most extreme combinations of strenuous technique and lighthearted effect. (For its essence in English literature, think of Alexander Pope's "Rape of the Lock"—one of the greatest of all poems, and yet intended, like a greeting card, exclusively to charm.) Modern tastes since romanticism have been revolted by so much mastery so trivially, it has seemed, employed: a mode impersonal without being collective, the style of a bloated and irresponsible ancien régime. But don't we feel, today, that we are living in the declining years of something or other, in a soon-to-be-ancien state of affairs? Certainly we have lost faith in the capacity of artistic initiative to better the future in any important way. Thus the suddenly intimate drama of the rococo, expression of another culture that was going nowhere—and made the most of it. And thus the unexpected appeal of Saxe's researches as something more than an academic exercise.

More, but not other. Saxe is as fearless of the pejorative "academic exercise" as he is of the look of conspicuous consumption. His simultaneous firing of incompatible clays, say, is on the immediate level an academic trick comparable to the glossy verisimilitude of Beaux-Arts painting, provoking the shallow astonishment of something merely hard to do (as indeed it is, giving Saxe something like a Guinness record for disasters in the kiln). Saxe's *more* is the edge, at once elevating and debilitating, that our time has over the eighteenth century: irony. We are to know that he knows that we're supposed to know what he's doing, figuratively looking over his shoulder as he does it. In itself, this is not praise. Every eight-year-old watching television today is an ironist. Irony can be a lame alibi, as for the lazy whimsicality and tedious trompe l'oeil of too much recent ceramic "art." But my experience of Saxe's work teaches me that for him irony is just the inescapable climate—the opportunity, the curse—of a dead-serious adventure upriver in the philosophical jungles of pottery aesthetics. He sacrifices sincerity in order to be, to the highest pitch possible, sincerely insincere.

It is crucial not to understand Saxe too quickly. His jarring juxtapositions—abstract pots topped with antelopes or "brass knuckles," rocklike forms and ornate geometries like shotgun weddings of Nature and Culture—are vulnerable to being taken with defensive superficiality, a comfortable sense of getting the joke. They *are* jokes (witticisms, to be exact), but the elements are not neutralized by the release of humor. It took me a while to get this about Saxe. I was disconcerted by the crudity of his non sequiturs, funny in a way that made me forget to laugh. Then gradually I learned to focus on the parts individually, letting the troubled whole take care of itself. My reward was, and is, a sense of inexhaustible complexity. It entails a conviction of the utter specificity of each element—what it specifically is, what specific class of things it signifies—and a visceral sensation of how each fights for its autonomy. A Saxe disjuncture is like a war in which both sides win, which isn't to say it's not violent. Facture and color key up each form, making the balance excruciatingly risky. When it fails even a little, the result isn't a so-so pot; it's a mess.

Saxe's way of handling the figurative versus the abstract is an easy example of how he hefts the different mental weights of things. The rightness of a Saxe composition can prove to an algebraic certainty that, for instance, exactly this much antelope (a little antelope) equals exactly that much lapidary pattern (lots). My point is that proper appreciation of Saxe's combinations follows rather than precedes a contemplative involvement with each part for its own sake. It's like a lesson in how to live in the world: perceive the reality of each thing and, besides becoming anxious, experience the strange exhilaration of a shattered time and begin to master the spiritual art of coping with it. This is a moral dimension, of a kind long familiar in arts and crafts but always fresh and surprising in its particular occurrences: the classic mystery by which the success of a mere artifice can come to matter, somehow, very much.

In Western culture this dynamic—the moral effect of aesthetic decisions—is more typical of fine art than of craft, and more typical within craft of the best folk expressions than of professional work. (The pleasing proportions in Shaker furniture, I am convinced, have less to do with "simplicity" than with a positive terror of being found in wrong relation with the divine: get the slats right as you get your soul right, or else.) Which is not to associate Saxe with the prestige of either "art" or "primitivism." Actually, he stands rather closer to the workaday practice of pottery, both professional and academic, than to the aesthetically ambitious Voulkos-Price tradition of "ceramic sculpture," on the one hand, and to craftworkers' penchant for cabin-feverish myth and mysticism, on the other. But no one else in the sadly wised-up present moment pushes the boundary of honest possibility farther. The honesty consists in an almost aggressive modesty about the worldly limitations specific to pots.

Besides its itchy social status as an upper-middle-class trophy, the nonfunctioning contemporary ceramic is forced to admit, under torture by analysis, these among other limitations: ornamental (pedestaled or shelved), fragmentary (unintegrated in any William Morrisish or Bernard Leachian gestalt), self-conscious. The probity of a Saxe ceramic is to plead guilty on all counts before it can be accused. Then it goes on from there, not to subvert the limitations, exactly, but to show by its own exaggerated artifice their artificiality. Saxe communicates the liberation not of escape from constraint but, failing that, of knowing clearly that one is constrained—and that a certain order of aesthetic delight is inconceivable otherwise. I get the same relaxing feeling from his work that I have from the very best work in any field: of being in good hands, and of those hands being entirely visible, all cards on the table. The feeling can be labored and edgy in Saxe's case, lacking sweetness and spontaneity; but it is real and clear, which are the main things. Other ceramists are more ingratiating, but their lack of fundamental clarity—they lean on tastes and notions that are not made manifest—dooms them to an inferior level.

What I love most about Saxe's work is its way of maintaining a gravity, a mood of utmost seriousness, that is governed entirely by rules of play. Which may be a pretty good thumbnail description of civilization as we can imagine it in our moments of brightest vision. Lately Saxe has been working on some mind-boggling functional vessels that are right to the point: funerary urns for cremated human remains. The intention seems problematic, to put it mildly: attempting to find a line (which may not exist) between an intolerable depressiveness and the black hilarity of Evelyn Waugh's *The Loved One*. But whose problem is this if not that of our whole death-denying and spiritually miserable culture? Recent scholarship about ancient Egypt, which we know mainly from its fantastic elaboration of death rituals, has concluded that the land of the sphinx, far from being morbidly haunted, was the most lively and playful of societies. The funerary crafts of Egypt were the work of happy people. I have no hope that Saxe's urns will effect any cultural reform—their use can only be private—but their gesture is profound. It shows the essential pattern of all civilized agreements, which is to embrace—to celebrate!—that which cannot be evaded. It redreams the mystery by which craft, the pure labor of human hands, can embody such agreements, solemnizing an ideal marriage of necessity and freedom, culture and nature, death and life.

I've been trying in this essay to adduce some general significance for Adrian Saxe's work. Being an amateur in the craft field, I have not attempted any detailed critique. Nor have I felt the need to advance a biographical or otherwise developmental story of Saxe's achievement. Clearly and quite remarkably, there is a lot to be said about him without recourse to the standard approaches, a lot that could not be said about most other potters; and this suggests a final point. The cultural change I began by noting—change signaled by the smart pot, an eloquent stammer in craft's language of conventions—may have its most positive effect in the opening of a new domain of ideas outside the hothouses of specialization. In this domain, the appearance of anything at all, of any embodied sign, can be an occasion for intelligence and passion, for speaking together of what most concerns us: our fate, in the understanding of which we are all amateurs. The primary test of the object will be its hospitality to an analysis by which it is not consumed. Precisely by being deprived of certainties, might we not be entering a great era of mutual questioning, of conversation? Certainly Saxe's pots are wonderful conversation pieces, appropriately pedestaled not only in elegant living rooms but in freely possessing, aroused minds.

1986

The Immigrant Strain

The United States is properly called a nation of immigrants, and not just because of our foreign ancestries. Americans immigrate all the time. To be American is to leave where you come from and go somewhere else. Americans emigrate from Michigan to Texas or from Illinois to California or, as in my case, from North Dakota to New York. A person hardly counts as American until he or she has abandoned one life for another.

Americans are continually, and simultaneously, leaving and discovering their country. That's our strength. It makes us great modernizers. It's also our weakness. It's why we are eternal adolescents. It's why our being is so light and insubstantial, so thin when compared with the density of persons in other cultures.

Americans are a bit ghostly. We don't live in places so much as haunt them. Another way of saying this is that the U.S. really is a free country, and freedom has a dark side. Still, I am devoted to the habit of freedom, and I accept the condition of immigration, of life led always somewhere between departing and arriving.

Nearly all the best American art and literature is about departing, setting off, getting rid of entanglements, breaking loyalties, killing the father. Once the father was Europe, but culturally we got rid of Europe a long time ago. (When we visit Europe, it is with twinges of shame, feeling like the lost and ungrateful children we are.)

What American creativity departs from now must itself be American. To become less American without becoming anything else has become the basic drive of American serious culture. By "serious culture" I do not mean institutional or academic or otherwise foreordained culture. I mean the culture generated by individuals responding to the pressure of their own needs. Without that, the U.S. or any country is just another vote in the General Assembly.

In relation to Europe today, this current stage of American serious culture is attended by one irony and one agony. The irony is a new openness of American artists and intellectuals to European influence. German painters, say, and French critics are embraced, though in a spirit not exactly respectful, not the spirit of emulation that pertained until after World War II.

The spirit is high-handed and cannibalistic. Americans sense that our culture of constant departing, of continuous disposal and self-emptying, needs a steady supply of new spiritual inventories. Thus European culture, and to some extent Asian and South American and even Soviet culture, is scavenged to feed American manufacture. The motive of this scavenging is to go on: not to progress, but, like a shark, to keep swimming in order not to drown.

I think this irony is widely misunderstood in Europe, with its highly institutionalized cultures. Institutions, which assume a fundamental preference for reason and contentment, do not understand the desperate determination to go on at any cost. I remember the traumatic experience of Parisian art people a few years ago when a big government-sponsored presentation of contemporary French art, through cooperating private galleries, fell flat in New York. They were scandalized by what they took to be a chauvinistic rejection.

The simpler truth is that the French art had nothing in it that Americans found useful. If it had, the useful part would have been seized on and plowed into production. And the effect would scarcely have been more flattering to France. Even when serious, American attention to other cultures is not gracious. It's just another raid on the pantry of workable ideas.

The irony I've been talking about is a small one, pertaining to the small shifting sphere of serious culture. The agony of present European-American relations is an extremely big one, pertaining to the global crisis of American power. World politics seem increasingly arranged in magnetic repulsion to that power, a blundering imperial anachronism. Americans are starting to accept that their nation is hated, and many are happy to hate right back.

Thus the thick-skinned right wing gains power in foreign policy, and the heartbroken liberal center, which still dominates cultural institutions, retreats into the concerns of local and special-interest domestic politics. This development reverses the old American pattern according to which liberals are outward looking and the right wing is regional and isolationist.

In serious culture, the agony sharpens the irony. The innate contrariness of American serious culture, the very soul of American freedom, makes it more and more international as real politics become more and more nationalist or local. I am not talking about a political opposition, but about an antipolitical reflex to spurn whatever the prevailing trend happens to be and by that act to be American. Suddenly American immigrant restlessness is a snake biting its own tail, spinning in a dizzy circle back toward everything it has escaped.

The new tenor of American serious culture, especially apparent in the visual arts, is either classicist—timeless and placeless, outside geography and history—or radically popular—throwing itself away in and for the moment of its consumption. This is a strange momentum, and it confuses me. But I feel in my bones its iron logic, continuous with the momentum of my own ancestors when they left Norway a century ago, not knowing what awaited them across the wide sea.

August 1986

Welcome to Helgaland

Summertime's normal torpor on the art front got interrupted this year by a Helgasm. The "discovery" of many Andrew Wyeth portraits of a "mystery woman" called Helga—certain of the story's elements are safely handled only with the tongs of inverted commas—triggered media coverage unprecedented for any other art topic, ever. Pending an exhibition slated for next May at the National Gallery, Helga is already in the King Tut class of instantly ubiquitous icons. The chain reaction of hype—by which a story sufficiently hotted up becomes a story in itself that (as in this writing) spawns a fallout of commentary—remains at meltdown, a demonstration of publicity power that should humble an art world quick to deplore the occasional mild boosting of a Schnabel, Salle, Clemente, or Kiefer. What we have here is the real thing, full of portent about the real disposition of art in American society.

Media views of this disposition intrigue. Helga has "set the art world aflame," *Newsweek* averred, referring to an art world few would recognize. Aside from career crowd pleasers like Thomas Hoving and the National Gallery's J. Carter Brown, art professionals, including those on media payrolls, have been catatonically cool to Helgamania. None of the national publications that ran with the story used its staff art critic for the job. Feature writers pumped the requisite molasses. From *Time* to the *New York Times*, the primary voice of authority turned out to be that of Wyeth's business-manager wife Betsy, upon whose word that she knew nothing of Helga the whole putative "mystery" rests. Is the work good, Mrs. Wyeth? "Oh God!" she remarked. "The paintings are remarkable. I practically dropped dead because of the quality." Add the crowing of the collector (now Helgarch) Leonard E. B. Andrews, publisher of *The Swine Flu Claim and Litigation Reporter*—e.g., Wyeth is "*the* incredibly finest artist to come out of America in the twentieth century"—and you have a splendid chorus of disinterested expertise.

Expert opinion has never counted for much in Wyeth's reputation, of course, and this argues against a reflex inclination to dismiss the whole affair as a stunt. Though conspicuously manipulated by Betsy Wyeth, and by *Art & Antiques*'s executive editor Jeffrey Schaire and publisher Wick Allison—whose press release in July, fortuitously timed for journalism's slow season, touched off the explosion—the phenomenon could hardly be manufactured from scratch. Public-relations wizards hit the craze button daily, and ninety-nine times out of a hundred nothing happens. A ready susceptibility, involving wide and deep affection for Wyeth and his work, had to precede the ex-ploitive claptrap. Some clarity about this affection will help us learn the lessons that Helgology has to teach.

What attracts people to Wyeth has to be largely extrinsic to the work, which is formulaic stuff not very effective even as illustrational "realism." Whether Wyeth's world is believably contemporary—lacking wristwatches and vapor trails, as Henry Geldzahler has noted—seems less important than whether it is believably presented on its own terms. Wyeth does have a flair for textures, as in getting pale sunlight to lie just so on weathered wood—a "sense of place" convincing in expanses of a few square inches. Bump it up the scale to rooms and fields, however, and Wyeth's space becomes generalized, flat, and un-persuasive. It works only when he can give it a specific narrative func-tion, as in reinforcing the depressiveness of *Christina's World*—a tour de force, illustrating an unknown story, that towers over the rest of his work as *American Gothic* does over Grant Wood's.

Good stories do not occur to Wyeth very often, but a certain nar-rative glamour envelops him as a public figure. I think his fans get satisfaction from the simple fact of his existence. The idea *of* Wyeth, not Wyeth's pictorial ideas, seems the operative appeal. In a culture where the mystery of fine art makes people both defensive and solemn, he manages the hard trick of allaying the defensiveness while retaining the solemnity (as opposed to, say, Norman Rockwell, who cheerfully dispensed with both). To be at once a mass reassurer and an avatar of the Art myth is not nothing, though it is apt to prove as sterile as anything hybrid. Beyond that, the taste for Wyeth's visually and emo-tionally starved art suggests a self-enjoying puritanical rectitude, the flip side of American consumer gluttony.

The possibility that people respond to a positive denial of meaning and pleasure in Wyeth is raised most strongly by his strange nudes, pictures numb to the poetics and erotics of painted flesh. *Time* observed that the sensationalism of the Helga tale (artist and model, tee hee) cast "a lurid glow that was not in the paintings," which is a gem of understatement. Judging from reproductions, all the new nudes taken together haven't the sensuality to ignite a firefly. The lack of psychological tension extends to Helga's face, typically stolid and tired (when she is not asleep). In general, these pictures appear minor even for Wyeth, being essentially story-less studies.

To judge Wyeth's work from reproduction is defensible on the grounds that that is precisely where his talent shines brightest. This peculiarity points to what type of artist—intensely modern, nostalgic themes notwithstanding—he truly is. Brian O'Doherty has termed him a maker of "master images," a phrase perfect for its suggestion of, among other things, handmade prototypes of mechanical mass production. Reproduction doesn't represent Wyeth's art so much as complete it, for instance by lending the sumptuousness of clay-coated paper to surfaces deadly dry in the original. That Leonard Andrews spent millions not only for the Helgas but also for their copyright seems to bemuse commentators, but it shouldn't. Ownership of the crabby little pictures is just gravy on the right to their gorgeous dissemination, in which we are going to be awash for a long time.

As for the saga of a classic hype, that will continue too—muttering along until it hits a second crescendo on the occasion of the Washington show. Its future tack will be interesting now that what *Time* incautiously called "Andrew Wyeth's Stunning Secret" (*Newsweek* weighed in with "Secret Obsession") is developing a distinctive odor. As the *Washington Post* reported after a little digging, the Helga works never were "hidden," many of them having been sold and reproduced since 1979. Nor is there anything the least bit shadowy about Helga Testorf, a housekeeper for Wyeth's sister Carolyn (who succinctly termed intimations of a Helga-Wyeth romance "a bunch of crap"). Some Wyeth fans may take the evident hoax in stride, perhaps as a hot one pulled by country folk on the city slickers. (That would be the bold way for Andrew and Betsy to play it.) But the media tend to feel that it's not nice to fool the media. Will their embarrassment dictate silence or bring a backlash? Will their fling with Helga become Helgagate? Can a culture hero be impeached?

October 1986

A Visit to the Salon of Autumn 1986

The Salon of Autumn 1986 was held in rooms off the corridors that are the streets of New York. The rooms were private galleries, and no central authority decided what would be shown; but the fact that a kind of jury system was in operation should have been lost on no one. We sensed as we walked the open-air corridors of palace Manhattan that we were seeing what has long been promised, or threatened: a sampler of the quasi-official, a stabilization of taste and style, the academy of the future opening its doors. Bright and impressive and tinged with nausea, it was a moment of newness to end newness. Nearly everything in the Salon of Autumn 1986 was new and fresh and confident, even if not very good. Much of it wasn't very good at all, but it all belonged somehow; and the good things were correspondingly gratified, not disdaining to be elevated relative to their inferiors. Top-of-the-heap was a common status: innumerable tiny heaps.

Famous tensions have collapsed. Politics and aesthetics have fallen into each other to yield this strange new topography: hierarchy everywhere, a democracy of aristocrats. Any informed subversion is obviated. For the moment, the only revolution going is the permanent one of fools. Baudelaire began the greatest of Salon reviews, that of 1846, with an address "To the Bourgeois," announcing the place of art in the spiritual economy of the newly dominant class. His tone burned with misgiving, but he was thrilled by the possibility of a new criticism that would be, he said, "partial, passionate, political." One hundred and forty years later, a new class born of the bourgeoisie and occupying the same economic level, but different from it, is ascendant. With it comes a new art, reminiscent of the modern but likewise different, and the opportunity for criticism that will engage a changed world.

The new class is that of managers. It is large. Most jobs created in recent decades entail managing something or other, however humble: a democracy of operators, and, since everyone is managed by someone else, of flunkies. Less and less do workers labor for capitalists. From hamburger flipper to executive, people work not for someone but for something, some system or mechanism that must be kept in tune with greater and still greater systems and mechanisms.

What this has to do with art is nothing and everything—in that order. Art is timeless and placeless before it is absolutely bound to place and time. Its particular meanings and uses orbit the belief that art conquers death and contingency. "You can live three days without food; without poetry, never," Baudelaire wrote, and no one does live without the self-pleasing modulations that are the basis of the aesthetic in consciousness. Our nerves resonate to the aesthetic, though relatively few have the leisure and inclination—free of deprivation, anger, and fear—to heed or cultivate, let alone transcribe, its music. It is in any case an endless performance where we arrive late, at birth, and, dying, leave early. The cultural forms of art—even the identification of the aesthetic with something called art—are sheerly incidental, variations of light and costume.

But only in the pursuit and understanding of those variations does the aesthetic enter into the actual conduct of life. A passion for art is a decision to develop one's aesthetic capacity to ever higher levels of differentiation, and to do so in and for the company of like-minded others (including people who may be dead, unborn, or otherwise imaginary). It conduces to a vision of civilization in its ideal state: maximum variety within maximum unity. This ideal is a recurrent feverish aspiration throughout history. Very rarely are its articulations clear in the moment of their conjuring. The present may be one such rare moment. Attending the Salon of Autumn 1986, we sensed agreements falling into place like tumblers of a turning lock.

Decadence? Positively. The new situation of art in New York is implosive, developing nuance and velleity and irony at the cost of energy and conviction and rigor. A frictionless absence of resistance, not an increase of force, makes things seem speedy. And there is dread, spilling in on us through daily headlines from sites of the Unmanageable, of no middle ground. Marginalized by the new orderliness, old chaos gains power like a tropical low-pressure zone breeding a storm. But at the Salon of Autumn 1986 such intimations were scarcely palpable, or were just palpable enough to give a shiver that could pass for excitement. It made no sense not to enjoy oneself, seeing what there was to see.

There was a movement, for one thing.

What Is Simulationism?

Simulationism, the new ironically chilled abstract painting and mechanically appropriative object sculpture, is heady, flimsy, and so cynical it almost redefines innocence, wearing a seraphic "what-me-worry?" countenance even as it rattles off poststructuralist critical jargon to an upscale clientele. Simulationism (my choice among labels of which the catchiest is neo-geo) was ubiquitous in the Salon of Autumn 1986, mainly in Ileana Sonnabend's aggressive launching of a core group—Peter Halley, Jeff Koons, Ashley Bickerton, Meyer Vaisman—but also in a Koons solo at International with Monument and numerous cameo appearances in group shows at Tony Shafrazi, Wolff, Bess Cutler, Craig Cornelius, and elsewhere. The group shows afforded us the fun of guessing who is and who isn't a simulationist. Philip Taaffe is one somehow, though Peter Schuyff somehow isn't. Allan McCollum is one and so is Jack Goldstein, both in a retroactive or honorary way. Sherrie Levine is one if she wants to be. The Swiss painter John Armleder is so good that the movement would be foolish not to claim him. And so on.

The most striking item of the "so on," incidentally, is the return in force of Richard Artschwager, seen in a mini-retrospective of sixties work at Mary Boone and in group shows hither and yon. At the Harm Bouckaert Gallery his work looked cozy in a selection of seventies-type *informel* (e.g., Pat Steir and Alan Saret), and at Kent it bristled portentously in a politically tinged show (with, e.g., Leon Golub and Jerry Kearns). At Wolff and at Cutler, meanwhile, Artschwager came off as simulationist *avant la lettre*, at least to my own febrile first glance. (A painting at Cutler by Julie Wachtel titled *Overstimulated*, showing a happily frazzled cartoon character, made me laugh because it was such an apt mirror of my mental state as I prowled the Salon.) Actually, I was experiencing the addled perspective that always accompanies a genuine shift in sensibility, by which strange things become familiar and familiar things—in this case, Artschwager's furniturelike/artlike objects, which once struck me as mainly clunky and eccentric—become glamorously estranged.

I'm going to sidestep here simulationism's intellectual merits, which seem pretty trashy on the whole—Baudrillard boiled down to the scale of gallery press releases, with hints of medium-as-message Marshall McLuhanism redux. As a proper Salon-goer, I am primarily concerned with the phenomenal level of perception and sensation. On this level, simulationism delivers an unmistakable but remarkably gentle tang of novelty. It gives the moment a flavor without really changing anything. Nothing in its vicinity looks abruptly outdated or invalidated (except the idealism that is always old hat and takes defiant pride in being so). It is less a new wave than a sheen of light that shows a wave's shape. It is a movement for a time without faith in the capacity of art to change anything except the ways of art, and only within limits to change those. It has a distinctive double affect: excitement, discouragement. One's mind quickens as one's heart sinks.

Simulationism is managerial, to the hilt. It meets, plainly and cleanly, the practical artistic needs of the elite of the newly dominant class. In a nutshell: art shall be a beautiful object that shall not insult the intelligence. It is state-of-the-art art, in every way including the critical. It assimilates end-of-originality and antiexpressionist deconstructions, then zaps them by turning their own skeptical ray against their lurking political sentimentality. It straightforwardly undertakes the management of aesthetic engineering—color and line, mass and contour, symbol and sign—and leaves other problems to the proper authorities. As for management of the burgeoning simulationist canon, that is conducted with out-in-the-open candor. Collectors—the Saatchis in London, Michael Schwartz and others in New York—collect it in critical mass, creating simultaneous demand and scarcity; the dealers deal; the magazines and museums either do or do not play along, imparting a certain spin to it in either case. Never in this century have art and money been so finely harmonized. The harmony is ironic (that's the finesse), though one would not exactly characterize the irony as "biting."

Simulationism is so insubstantial, so much a fleeting edge of hipness, that it will bloom and die with the celerity of a jungle orchid. Its crimes, if any, will prove to be of the self-punishing variety. There seems no point in attacking it. And I do like its freshness. I like the self-abnegating generosity with which it anticipates the viewer, whose bracketed responses—summarized in the idea of "seduction"—are the point of it all. Simulationist works take pains to be beautiful, an effort in itself pleasing. The beauty is self-consciously generic—applied professional know-how in proportion, color, facture, and so forth—and has the piquance of the generic, the down-to-earth virtue of no-brand aspirin. It is frankly what modern art dreaded to be and usually ended up being anyway: something to hang over the sofa. That had better be a perfect sofa, though, with enough sofa-ness to stand up to the art-ness of the art. Simulationism is housebroken minimalism, resolving minimalism's sullen standoff with the world in a state of elegant détente. It is probably not what Donald Judd has in mind when in his favorite illustration of aesthetic probity he praises unblended scotch, but it might as well be.

Speaking of Judd, he too was in the Salon of Autumn 1986, opening at Paula Cooper with some standard-variant wall and floor boxes (aluminum or sanded plywood or Cor-Ten and colored Plexiglas). The simulationist vibrations that blew in the door when one entered from Wooster Street surrounded the objects with a positive aureole of ravishment. This moment does for Judd's type of beauty what it does for Artschwager's type of perversity: gives it an august grandfatherliness. There was something a trifle off, still out of fashion, about the Judds. They seemed to take up more space than was necessary and to be too loudly declarative, like someone yelling in the mistaken belief that you are hard-of-hearing. But their decorative gist felt right on the money.

On Furniture

Speaking of sofas, furniture is art's paradigm right now, compulsive as reference and model and insistent as subtext. Scott Burton's clever camouflaging of the many dilemmas of public sculpture—with functional amenities that are ingratiating to the naive while backloaded with winks and nudges for the sophisticated—are only the most explicit examples. (Some Burtons are always available to Salon-goers in rooms of the Max Protetch Gallery.) Of course, Judd has made actual furniture, of a severity and pitiless uncomfortableness beyond the dreams even of his hero Gerrit Rietveld. And as many chairs and light fixtures as nudes appear in the work of David Salle, constituting by now an encyclopedia of circa-1950s largely Italian design. The theoretical point suggested by both Judd and Salle is that the chair is a royal road to the most intimate nexus of nature and culture: where decorative artifice literally embraces the human body. As befits painting, Salle's light fixtures, depicted or actual, similarly apostrophize vision: a lamp is the-visible-that-makes-visible. (Be it noted in passing that Salle in many ways loomed over this Salon much as Delacroix did over that of 1846). What accounts for the furniture fascination?

My answer is that the bourgeoisie, failing as a class, has entered upon a new life as subject matter. Increasingly unplugged from social life, the aesthetics and erotics of the bourgeois domestic interior—the family castle—are free-floating and infinitely adaptable. Just as nineteenth-century Parisian Salons entertained the new bourgeois with the subject matter (including palatial scale and expensiveness) of the waning aristocracy, so today's new managerials (who live in electronic wombs) are beguiled with the look and feel of the defunct middle-class home. The preoccupation with furniture in art and as art feeds a hunger for spiritual continuity—at once distancing and preserving, in aesthetic brackets, what can never again be a norm.

The irony of the chair is this: you can't use it and look at it at the same time. There is something drastic in the notion of "chairs to look at," as about tables literally turned: two by John Armleder, their tops painted with geometric forms and facing each other across the room, were attached high on walls at Bess Cutler. The use of a table as a painting support hints at the fact that, in eighties-style interiors, works of art are often the initial and prime furnishings, lording it over all the rest. The main exceptions prove the rule: interiors where art is obviated by an architect's megalomania or by an antiques-happy historicism that museumifies everything. The result in any case is the frisson of an environment that one remains outside of even as one occupies it.

There is a term for that kind of space: public. In the age of collectivist corporatism and businesslike socialism, the public space has become the template for all spaces, including the domestic. This was foretold by the lobby scale of 1960s formalism and minimalism (Frank Stella the champion), and it helps to explain today's museum-building frenzy. (A museum may be defined as a building that is all lobby.) Like streets, offices, theaters, and plazas, the museum is a traditional type of public space being revived and revamped as it converges with newer types, of which the most majestic are the freeway, the airport, and the shopping mall. Artists are responding with work for and about this aggrandizement of public space, which some of the work goes on to question profoundly: can we live humanly and sanely in this new world? The best art does not answer the question too quickly. It may even suggest that the answer is no. We may be obliged henceforth to be inhuman and insane, if we aren't already.

That's a thing that is there to be said—and criticism is largely the saying of things that are there to be said—but I don't believe it. I like freeways and most shopping malls and, after years of fighting back anxiety, some airports. And I like them all the more when I reflect on how their rise lends a corresponding poetic glamour, a sharpened edge, to the spaces I truly love, notably the streets and galleries and museums of New York. Do you want the height of managerial-era bliss? Try the Frick Collection! Since your last visit, it has been totally transformed into a perfect simulacrum of itself. And the secret is out: Rembrandt is the most up-to-date painter in town.

"Even Rembrandt Had Monday Mornings"

That was said recently by a curator cautioning against deauthenticating "Rembrandts" on the sole account of their inferior quality. The remark is apt for a situation in which many people (too many of them critics) are pleased to look the gift horse of contemporary art in the mouth and reject it on the basis of some cavities and yellowing. Even Western civilization has Monday mornings. Consider the imponderableness of the word *bad* in the phrase "a bad Rembrandt painting." Rembrandt could falter, but as an instrument for the revelation of painting—and of history, in his prophecy of bourgeois pathos—he couldn't not be Rembrandt, who is always interesting. The development of a culture always interests its members, unless they are waylaid by despair or vanity. Self-protective incuriosity about new cultural ways only contributes to the indiscriminateness we might rightly dislike in them, much as dismissing Rembrandt's lesser works will feed, rather than starve, a feverish penchant to deify the guy. The best proof of intelligence is not in recognizing big, glorious values, which anyone can do; it is in doing exact justice to small, fugitive values in the world's adulterated flow.

Morris Louis Was No Rembrandt

The poignant Morris Louis retrospective at the Museum of Modern Art was nicely timed for the Salon of Autumn 1986. It was poignant because hopelessly square, in the way unique to past styles that in their heyday too confidently held themselves to be transcendent. (The halcyon "nonobjectivism" of Mondrian's and Kandinsky's more bubble-headed epigones is an earlier case.) The show was nicely timed as a revisit to the last great stab at a contemporary Beaux-Arts orthodoxy, an art stamped with "quality" (like prime meat) for consumption by an ambitious class: the retro-bourgeois sector of sixties wealth and power, appalled by Andy Warholian cultural democracy and craving a parental style. It produced an intricately evasive criticism with a power to seduce sheltered minds. The formalist project was whammied at birth by the plainly superior aesthetic integrations of early Rauschenberg and Johns, but it proved able to ignore the obvious.

Morris Louis's stain paintings were instant relics of the true faith laid down by the Reverend Moon of art criticism, Clement Greenberg. We had Greenberg's assurance that Louis was a mainstream distillation of Jackson Pollock via Helen Frankenthaler. Wrong. Louis was a provincial synthesis of Frankenthaler and Franz Kline, a maker of kinesthetic "lyrical" images lacking the grace of the former and the latter's kick. His historical importance is limited, as far as I can see, to his having popularized some technical possibilities of acrylic paint. He reconventionalized old-fashioned "beautiful effects"—effects *of* beauty (without beauty's bite). Louis did seem to be getting somewhere with his late stripe paintings, where chromatic charges intensify to the point of rupturing the tyranny of tasteful format. But the legacy of that experiment was perhaps best left in the hands of Gene Davis, a better because less pretentious artist (whose still refreshing sixties stripe paintings augmented the Salon in a retrospective at the Charles Cowles Gallery). You can like Davis, or not, without self-induced hysteria.

Louis's relevance to the new academicism is cautionary, warning against our human tendency to overvalue what we have on the mere grounds that it's ours. (This is an imperial susceptibility, opposite to the glum provincial conviction that whatever is ours must be second-rate.) Presuming to the prestige of abstract expressionism, color-field formalism required a major artist, and since Louis looked like the best available, he was automatically granted that status. This formalist afflatus typified an era of American arrogance, when we coasted into disasters on the delusion that American power must be right and invincible because it felt so good. The notion of self-evident "quality" was crazy in the same way, and I can still feel the mad inevitability it projected in the sixties. Now the impulse to hold self-flattering beliefs of all sorts, long chastened, is stirring again, and something of its squawky, cocksure, overbearing tone is being heard again in the culture. I hope it is not politically ominous—that the worst we'll see is an equivalent of tragic history repeating itself as farce—but the pattern bears watching.

The Little Masters

Happy the lot of the artist's artist, the petit maître whose special virtue is conveyed to the world indirectly via the esteem in which he or she is held by peers and followers. Perhaps partly because of the sheer number of artists now, all needing intimate heroes, this is a good epoch for little masters—whose charm is to have some debility, some lack of "what it takes" to be a public hit, that is more than compensated by an extreme realization of values shared by all who aspire to art. Even great and successful artists can have this appeal, strangely. I've heard Willem de Kooning discussed in studios in tones that suggest he is a well-kept secret. And Jasper Johns is an artist's artist endlessly. But the true little master is famous for not being famous enough, in the opinion of enough people to remove the taint of cultishness. There may be an element of condescension involved. But who would not want the devoted Eros that is the little master's estate?

The paragon of the type in the Salon of Autumn 1986 was Ross Bleckner, hands down. It wasn't just his work in this or that group show—though his large oval canvas at Shafrazi, picturing a chandelier in a rotunda, was impressive. It was his tangible influence and intangible presence as an anticipator of styles and roles, an exemplary denizen of the current order of things. Since the late 1970s Bleckner has been at or near the inception of such painting fashions as neo-abstraction, op effects, chiaroscuro glazing, and light-through-fog luminous illusion, without ever becoming fashionable. The reason is a certain earnestness, heroic or excessive—a tormented seriousness about painting itself, as distinct from any particular reason for doing it. His work is bitterly self-conscious, as if he had been tricked into looking straight at areas where luckier artists have well-tended blind spots.

To put it another way, Bleckner's paintings are honest, to a fault, about their own condition, which is the condition of painting without trust. A product of the seventies avant-garde, he bears the scar of a time when painting was supposedly, and apparently, dead. His optical and theatrical effects, never cheap or lazy, seem produced by an anxious need to see something literal happening on the canvas while he works, something to maintain an endangered confidence. This can be extremely moving, especially in some recent pictures that can only be called nocturnes—night images with night moods of longing and fear. These pictures have layered, hazy surfaces, punished into songfulness. The best of them could make you weep without knowing quite why. They are about something important, sorrowful, and all but impossible. If you love painting, you will have a tender feeling for the person who made them.

The disposition of fashion now, running hard against traditional types of both abstraction and realism, nominates almost any practitioner of those modes for little-masterdom. An abstractionist as good as Elizabeth Murray and a realist as good as Rackstraw Downes, both with deservedly secure markets and reputations, have positions that feel quietly embattled. (It's so easy to feel embattled in this paranoiac culture!) In the Salon of Autumn 1986, Sean Scully at David McKee, Gary Stephan at Diane Brown, Louise Fishman at Baskerville + Watson, and David Reed at Protetch had shows of serious (unsimulated) abstraction, each good and each touched with the glamour of the resolutely out-of-step. Meanwhile, the archconceptualist Joseph Kosuth, with neon-and-text works at Shafrazi and Jay Gorney, continued his surprising reemergence on the downtown scene as an avuncular little master.

Kosuth notwithstanding, little masters are almost never artists with ideas, because ideas promote efficiency and it is of the essence for a little master to do everything the hard way. Ideas also make people nervous—they insult the precious complexity of our feelings—and the little master must reassure. What little masters have are notions of how to do a thing, notions perhaps a little too demanding and unforgiving, all but guaranteeing a certain margin of failure. Such artists are probably priests of failure. This is no mean or unnecessary thing in a world, and not just an art world, where failure is the rule, and "success" is a glittering but dubious and temporary condition. The little master gives animation and honor to a realm of chronic and painful uncertainty, which would otherwise be a howling waste. The little master teaches disappointment how to dance.

Words

Gallery catalogues, press releases, and artists' statements made lively reading at the Salon of Autumn 1986, showing repeatedly that recent critical jargon is well suited to promotion once you comb the politics out of it. Jeff Koons's very fine tough show of liquor-advertising posters printed in oil colors on linen and drinking paraphernalia cast in stainless steel, both without any other alteration, featured a gallery handout no less staggering than the contents of his Jim Beam decanters. A sample sentence: "The work and the theme of intoxication reveal the trauma and the social disappointment and investment of the emptying of desire into the simulacra, the counterfeit, as the hyperreal and as a legislated dystopia." Reading that splendid torture rack for unsuspecting English words, I reflect, first, that I need a drink and, second, how true! Displaced into an aesthetic context, ideas become inarguable. The fairly unremarkable idea here about desire—that it gets twisted by advertising—is given in terms as gaga and glitzy as Koons's work itself. The convergence of thing and idea, look and rhetoric, is very satisfying.

I wonder if a teetotaler would agree. I meant it about needing a drink. Koons's reifying of alcohol fetishes (so to speak) made me conscious of my own physiological habitual yen—a hollow sensation around the solar plexus—for alcohol, a yen that constitutes my small share in the management problems created by demon rum. Koons shows me how liquor advertising aims to weaken the inner voice that advises me not to be a drunk, thus elating the part of me that would just as soon. I was both stimulated and deflated—the simulationist double affect—to see this intimate conflict powerfully distanced. Not that the therapeutic interlude left me full of gratitude to Dr. Koons. He is playing his own game, part of which is to render the viewer's experience as objectively predictable as possible. (Strange shades of Russian constructivism!) If I cling to my personal (unmanageable) thoughts about Koons's work, it is to fight off the overbearingness of his game while staying in its vicinity.

Another text that helped me take bearings in mid-Salon was a nugget of theory in the catalogue of Tony Shafrazi's group show entitled What It Is (curated by Wilfred Dickhoff). The essay, by Mayo Thompson, was keyed to a conversation overheard at an opening:

> *Artist 1:* Your work is shit.
> *Artist 2:* It is what it is.

Thompson hazards that Artist 2's riposte is up-to-the-minute in bespeaking "the hegemony of laissez-faire, pluralist ideology—here expressed in the form of a classic zen-historicism—in the productive sphere." If what's being said is that contemporary art is a haven of individualism—where to have a style that's specific, no matter what else it is, is to be irreproachable—I almost agree. In large part, the Salon of Autumn 1986 was a herd of individualists, showing that art's appeal as an existential story (about how the artist is someone in particular) still has punch. The story has gotten threadbare, though, to the point of being an adolescent tease—like saying, "That's for me to know and for you to find out." Maybe every painting, like every person, says that simply by existing—in which case, a crisis is afoot when people feel driven to insist on it.

The Shafrazi show was an anthology of such insistences, with mostly strong work by (besides the uninsistent Armleder, Taaffe, Keith Haring, and Kenny Scharf) Bleckner, Donald Baechler, George Condo, Francesco Clemente, Jiri Georg Dokoupil, Walter Dahn, Jean Michel Basquiat, Peter Schuyff, Andreas Schulze, Jonathan Lasker, and several others, grouped around a cryptic painting on tarpaulin by the Grand Insister, Julian Schnabel: a Star of David bearing the letters *FF* surrounded by a ring of what looked like frankfurters. It is impossible not to start guessing what, besides frankfurters, "FF" might signify, a game lately given high solemnity by Anselm Kiefer's use of inscriptions. (At Shafrazi when I visited, giddy viewers were making guesses decidedly unsolemn.) Asked about it, Schnabel has said that the "FF" signifies nothing at all—a denial that in the context of the show only intensifies an air of "me-to-know-and-you-to-find-out"-ness, a claim to shamanistic license.

The assertion of such license, by Schnabel among others, immensely altered and rejuvenated the art culture a few years ago, retrieving for the artist an authority that had been lost to institutions. The anarchic vitality of that new art incidentally strengthened the gallery system, which was the only structure flexible enough to manage it. But now the signifying of individualism is becoming a predictable gesture, and the galleries grow restless for less ponderous fare. The figure of the life-giving meaning-producing artist is shriveling again, as its juices are drawn off by the apparatus that purports to serve it. A spell of hard bewilderment seems in the offing for the several mid-career artists who have ridden to fame on the myth of heroic subjectivity. For the best of them the crisis may be a crucible. Those who come out of it intact might get to be heroes all over again, but they will be diminished, chastened heroes.

Returning to Mayo Thompson's smart remarks, "the hegemony of laissez-faire, pluralist ideology" is overrated. It does accord with an aspect of the new academicism, which on a crude level may be characterized by a young artist's prospect of having an actual real-world career. Without it—without careerism's instinctive balancing of security and competition, fairness of reward and the shrewd move—I couldn't be narrating the 1986 art world as a Salon. But worldliness, no less than idealism, can make fools of us. We are talking here about the aesthetic—eternal and fickle principle of human vivacity, which soon enough humiliates anyone who would direct or predict it. If, at the moment, the situation of art is one of no important change—simulationism being a fiesta of unchanges—that means only that large stresses are getting a chance to build in darkness. Meanwhile, the peculiarity of this moment must not be despised.

The Heroism of Managerial Life

"It is true that the great tradition is lost and that the new one is as yet unformed," Baudelaire wrote toward the end of his "Salon of 1846." Such is the case again today, though today's artistic situation is surely better than that of 1846, when, aside from the middle-aged Delacroix, Baudelaire found little to revere and, aside from Daumier and a few little masters, little to excite him. A century and a half of bourgeois evolution and antibourgeois insurgency have left us with an art culture never so rich and various as right now, in the time of its phosphorescent decay. But a root feeling of ebb, of emptying, is unmistakable. At such a moment, the aesthetic sense is valorized. It is an indispensable feeler and lifeline for those who would brave reality without the dull armor of habit.

Baudelaire reveled in the sudden poetry of streets thronged with citizens in black frock coats, "an immense procession of undertakers' mourners, political mourners, mourners in love, bourgeois mourners. All of us are attending some funeral or other." Today the throngs are apt to be motorized, and dressed in today's hysterically varied but uniformly strenuous notions of proper attire (much of which, again, is black). All of us are attending some emergency or other. All of us are trying to get something right.

The typical joy of our age of management is the sigh of relief when something works. Our comedy and tragedy both concern things going haywire. Our philosophy and even our science are transfixed by the delicate mechanics of breakdown. Seldom in history has human imagination had so ramified and subtle an appreciation of disaster.

Our lives are governed by material and immaterial things that break. We are experts in triage, deciding on the spot which things will mend themselves, which must be seen to, and which are hopeless. In a word, we manage. We are heroes of management.

I saw Corazon Aquino interviewed by Ted Koppel on the ABC news show "Nightline." He posed probing questions, which she calmly deflected. "I will not conduct Philippine politics through the media," she said very mildly, and her dignity in that moment was massive, crushing. Koppel became uncharacteristically flustered, because, I like to think, he caught a naked glimpse of the relative triviality of what he was doing. Here was a plain woman with important things on her mind. Her simple lucidity was the very ideal of the new managerial heroism, upon which we now rely for political hope—and for beauty.

In the teeth of things that threaten, in the face of routine disaster, the poetic blossoms. Even, or especially, in the reality of poverty and disorder that build toward political reckoning, there are new tones and new colors. Anyone insensitive to them will deserve taking history by the medicinal spoonful from Ted Koppel on television. Likewise, those blind to the gorgeous hues in corruption's rainbow—the perfume in flowers of evil—will never overcome corruption.

To manage a thing well you must know what it is. To ask what things are, ready to take in stride the least welcome answer, is the heroism of today. It may get you called cynical by those who want only to hear their favorite fairy tale. But they know nothing.

The Salon of Autumn 1986 had a distinguished Russian visitor, on loan to the Metropolitan: Matisse's great bourgeois icon *The Conver-*

sation, 1911. If ever a work supported Baudelaire's 1846 definition of beauty as the combination of "an absolute and a particular element," that blazing anecdote of mild monsieur and formidable madame by a window in the morning is it. It is a religious ecstasy and a situation comedy. (My wife and I decided that he's saying, "What's for breakfast, honey?" and she's replying, "Get your own damned breakfast.") There will never be another painting like that one, the fantastic image of a lost world. But we will aspire to an analogous beauty.

We will ransack the Salon of our day for hints of it. If none of our artists can manage the level of *The Conversation*, we won't begrudge them, because we are gathering hints—not of some Edenic past or utopian future but of something so near and enveloping that we fail to see it.

Like sleepers who dream of being awake, we consider waking up.

December 1986

Our Kiefer

"Wouldn't it be amazing if he turned out to be *really* great?" someone blurted at me recently apropos of Anselm Kiefer. I understood the speaker's mixed emotions, which I share: joy in being the contemporary of an extraordinary artist—it's a lucky feeling, a vicarious redemption—shadowed by suspicions of eventual disappointment. Thus the note of wistfulness. (The speaker, like me, had been drinking.) Hedged awe is the generous variant of a mental distress—call it Anselm Angst—widespread in art circles this winter, as Kiefer's long-awaited American retrospective (Art Institute of Chicago, December 5, 1987–January 31, 1988) begins what promises to be a triumphal march through these States. The mean variant is the somewhat comical grumpiness of purists and hipsters betrayed by fascination with the German's work into unaccustomed agreement with a middlebrow market-and-publicity-driven majority. They would be only too happy if Kiefer proved not to be *"really* great," especially if they were the first to target his Achilles heel. Lacking that bull's eye, they may be expected to level shotguns at the excesses of Kiefer's following, with its sententious journalists and salivating millionaire collectors.

Why is Kiefer so popular in the United States? The often-asked question would be more interesting were Kiefer not popular in a lot of places. His shows have drawn crowds and praise throughout Western Europe and in Israel. Even some of the English and the French—testy and disdainful, respectively, toward most contemporary art—have permitted themselves to melt a little. Young painters everywhere flatter him with imitation. Only in his own land, at least until recently, has the prophet lacked honor. I've heard Germans denounce him with a vehemence I don't entirely understand, though it seems to entail bitterness at being represented, internationally, by an artist somehow inauthentically German, unlike their beloved, *echt-Deutsch* Georg Baselitz. Bizarre suggestions, once rife there, that Kiefer is some kind of neo-Nazi seem to have abated, however; and an issue of *Der Spiegel* last year reported a tidal shift of German opinion in Kiefer's favor, maybe because he's become a world-beating export right up there with the BMW. Still, there is a particular flavor, as well as an eerie unanimity, to Kiefer's welcome in the U.S. It may owe to the mixture of aesthetic, historical, and emotional susceptibilities that I find, making a specimen of one American, in myself—with the consequent misgivings that symptomize Anselm Angst.

Kiefer hits the spot with us in at least four main ways, none readily separable from his talent but each giving its appeal a peculiar spin. In no special order: (1) he roils our very complicated feelings about World War II, an event that apotheosized American pride; (2) he reawakens the glamour of European pastness, a half-forgotten American ache for lost roots; (3) he is a public individualist of a sort, pledging unallegiance to both custom and fashion, that we may still idealize but seem increasingly helpless to produce; and (4) he is an "American-type" painter. In saying the last, I am aware that Kiefer's sensibility has been a virtual Rorschach test for national narcissisms: some French see a reviver of nineteenth-century French romanticism (Victor Hugo laced with Baudelaire), some Scandinavians an heir of Munch and Strindberg (citing the latter's little-known but quite apposite paintings), and some English a Turner avatar (an affinity anyone with eyes must note). All foreign claims will have to wait, however; this is an American essay. Simply, in forty years no other European artist—not one!—had so thoroughly assimilated and advanced the aesthetic lessons of Jackson Pollock, specifically Pollock's doubleness of spatial illusion and material literalness on a scale not just big but exploded, enveloping, discomposed.

Contrary to an inexplicably persistent critical shibboleth, Pollock's aesthetic has nothing to do with emphasizing the picture plane. Rather, it renders "surface" unlocatable, replacing it simultaneously with optical depth and tactile fact—infinity and *stuff*—defying us to know what, exactly, we are looking at. Omnipresence of this tension throughout the (big) picture makes the scale. Pollock's own uniformity of marking is not required, but only an overall energetic contradiction of the frontal and the recessive, evoking at once a wall and a veil. Is this practically an academic convention in painting by now? It is (and is treated as such, to sardonic effect, by Kiefer's older countrymen Gerhard Richter and Sigmar Polke), but Kiefer cranks up its tension to an unprecedented pitch with receding architectural and landscape images that amplify illusion and encrustrations that maximize literalness. He resensitizes us to the convention, making it new somewhat in the way the young Manet renewed past Spanish masters. For Americans, the resulting formal idiom is as clear as a midwestern newscaster, as big as all outdoors, and straightforwardly stunning.

What's unclear is why so many of us experience Kiefer's works— even in the first split second of a first encounter (I saw an acquaintance, catching her initial glimpse of one, almost fall down)—as so much more than gratifying aesthetic presences. His big paintings instill a feeling of conviction bordering on religious faith, an intuition of knowledge that proves remarkably inarticulate when you try to debrief people about it. It can't be a function of Kiefer's narrative and poetic themes, of which many American Kiefer fans remain complacently ignorant (with no excuse now that we have an accessible, all but definitive, exegesis in Mark Rosenthal's introduction to the retrospective's catalogue). The feeling is mysterious even to the intellectually prideful who, finding it regressive, might love to analyze it away—the problem being that to analyze it you have to feel it, and doing that puts your analytical faculties in traction. Listening to word of mouth and reading reviews of the Chicago show, you get the sense that American emotional responses to Kiefer, matched against what I think is actually there in the art, are largely distorted and probably irresistible, a reflux of collective psychic material that says more about us than about him— while saying much *for* him, as an artist on the nerve of his world and time.

The immediately recognizable master metaphor of Kiefer's art is the Wasteland, the modernist trope par excellence for this century's characteristic experiences of fragmentation and chaos. An Englishman, Charles Harrison, has observed: "The 'wasteland' space functions in [Kiefer's] pictures much as the pastoral landscape functioned in the art of the seventeenth century: as an ahistorical terrain upon which diverse material may be assembled into allegorical form, and thus absorbed." That seems correct, but it doesn't begin to account for the impact of an image that even as a metacliché has nothing neutral about it. The Wasteland idea has taken on a lot of contradictory freight since a distraught young expatriate from St. Louis, T. S. Eliot, gave it supreme literary expression nearly seventy years ago. For many Americans, it retains the special aura it had for Eliot, one not apt to be shared by a German born in 1945: an emanation of deep, unkillable yearnings toward the "heap of broken images" that remains of a lost European heritage. Eliot surely couldn't have disagreed more with his colleague James Joyce's sentiment, palpably seconded by Kiefer: "History is a nightmare from which I am trying to awake." For many of us, on the contrary, history is a dream we'd be thrilled to sink into if only the racket of modernization, blasted at us through media that have already forgotten what happened last week, would shut up for a second.

Kiefer's Pollockian machines—with their heart-grabbing yellows, blacks, and browns that affect like tastes, sounds, and smells and their incorporation of photographs that drench the mind in tones of memory—evoke a quasi-religious feeling of delicious, melancholy, slightly masochistic abasement before sheer ancientness. Such seems the gist of an eloquent, extremely American, take on Kiefer by Sanford Schwartz:

> Enthralling and bleak at the same time, [Kiefer's paintings] are like a visit to a great cathedral on a winter's afternoon, when the light is sunless and white, snow is in the air, and you have the place to yourself. As you go away, you may believe that you have taken the sacred and sad drama into yourself, and that it has ennobled and elevated you: later, though, you may be left with a feeling that your experience can't be made part of the rest of your life, and that it sucks out of you more than it gives.

For "a great cathedral" read "Europe," or the "idea of Europe," or whatever signifies for you a civilized spiritual nourishment you crave and, if you were unfortunate enough to get it, couldn't possibly digest. The trouble with this response to Kiefer's art is that it may well be the opposite of what he intends. It is humorless, for one thing. Kiefer is usually funny.

Broaching Kiefer's humor can stop a conversation, I've found. People blink, and I start thinking I must be wrong. Only patient looking, staring down "the sacred and sad drama" for which I, too, am a pushover, convinces me that it's true: even the most plangent or anguished of Kiefer's works, when he is obviously fired with sincerity or gripped by some unresolved hysteria, display joke structures: antic stuff with palettes and angels, slaphappy incongruities of scale like "Operation Sea Lion" battleships in bathtubs in plowed fields, "books" in which absolutely nothing happens (except that at a certain point, as the pages turn, your hair may suddenly stand on end), and in case we didn't get it—Kiefer may wonder at times if anyone in the land of industrialized comedy has a funny bone—cast-iron skis attached to an eighteen-foot-long picture called *Jerusalem*, violating the delicately haunting associations of the layered and punished surface with the suggestion of a Middle Eastern Aspen. The provocation is so blatant that one might want to make excuses for it, as in retrieving a friend's social gaffe; but Kiefer is incorrigible. He affixes a lead propeller to another grand painting (*The Order of the Angels*, not in the show) to hammer home an awful bookish pun on the name of an early Christian theologian, Dionysius the Areopagite—"Aeropagite," maybe because Dionysius's obsession with angels suggested flyboy proclivities. With such things, Kiefer makes rude noises amid his own painstakingly induced reveries, and if viewers persist in genuflecting, they're on their own.

The art student who began his career two decades ago by having himself photographed giving the Nazi salute in various European locales was a prankster, though a serious as well as a staggeringly audacious one—getting at something that needed to be gotten at, the repressed emotions of the Third Reich, as a means to the end of a comprehensive, untrammeled art. "How could it happen?" he was asking, partly as a young German disgusted with the evasiveness of his elders but most pointedly as an ambitious, rebellious artist, defiantly asserting, right from the start, an absolute license for his imagination. Faustian pride may underlie the defiance, but its operative mode is Mephistophelian irony: self-satirizing in the Nazi-salute images (see the related watercolor *Every Human Being Stands beneath His Own Dome of Heaven*, 1970) and in such subsequent things as drawings of fiery aeries or sullen bunkers all titled *The Artist's Studio* and a hilarious lead sculpture of a winged palette as bird of prey. Kiefer's recent preoccupation with alchemy is likewise double-edged, evoking at once a mystic metaphor of creativity and the folly of mumbling crackpots who, in stinking laboratories, tried to make matter imitate an idea. Kiefer directly mocks most of his thematic material, historical and mythic, theatricalizing it into absurdity. In the process, some very serious, barely sane, perhaps poisonous meanings are released as an intoxicating poetic vapor.

I know a woman who when excited or moved, in ways that would make me exclaim or get a lump in my throat, invariably laughs—

"because it's *wonderful*," she says. I think Kiefer is like that. Even his darkest work has a warmth, if not of humor then of the eroticism that probably underlies the polymorphous, "wonderful" type of laughter. I'm thinking of his *Margarete/Shulamite* series of works about the Holocaust, which do the supposedly impossible—make successful art of the ultimate horror—by elaborating Paul Celan's tragic erotic projections, the "golden-haired" Aryan and the "ashen-haired" Jew. No humor there, but an emotional nexus of desire and loss, love and death, that may be related physiologically to the release of laughter (the sudden restoration of subjectivity that has been threatened). The feeling-saturated terrain of this and other themes from Kiefer's Wasteland—a realm of stories with which he keeps himself engaged and interested, scared and entertained—has nothing in common with the American way of revering things historical, thereby to fantasize ourselves into a past we never had. Oppressed by history, Kiefer uses fantasy to spring the locks on one dungeon of pastness after another. When he succeeds, there is a buoyancy, a glee. I think we may sense this even as we cling to the projection of our own nostalgias. No wonder Kiefer is so confusing to us.

The single most beclouding element in American responses to Kiefer is our complex of feelings about World War II, Nazism, and the Holocaust, subjects really addressed only in some of his work and never so directly as imputations of "mourning," "catharsis," and "exorcism" (the obligatory terms in Kiefer criticism) would suggest. Even indirect reference more or less ended five years ago, when the masterpiece *Shulamite* (menorahlike flames in a war-hero memorial) climaxed both the *Margarete/Shulamite* series and another protracted series based on motifs of Nazi architecture. Kiefer has since been off into regions ahistorically mythical, theological, alchemical, and otherwise self-referential, making art largely about the mental and physical processes of making art. Kiefer's involvement with Third Reich themes needs to be confronted—it remains the most riveting aspect of his career—but with reference to pertinent works rather than to everything from the artist's hand. The ingenuity of a Jack Kroll, writing in *Newsweek*, shows what Kiefer is up against in his efforts to change the subject: "[*Jerusalem*] is a touchingly surreal image of transcendence, as if Germany, crazy with remorse, were saying to Israel: 'Here, take our skis. They take us through our mountains. Maybe they'll take you through yours.'"

Crazy is right, though Kroll's heuristic high jump is so terrific I'm half-convinced. Kroll's conceit fails the test of Kiefer's established artistic temperament, however, in having "Germany" talk to Israel, or to anybody. Kiefer may cultivate imaginative territory cleared by Joseph Beuys, but he is no Beuys-like holy fool or shaman, ritualizing collective hopes, guilts, and fears. He has always operated strictly on his own, a lone artist bent on becoming ever more alone and free through acting out, then having done with, the determining myth and history of "a German." As an artist, he speaks neither for nor to Germany, nor even for himself as a German citizen—a subtle point, given his massive use of highly charged stuff from his German heritage, but also the crux of his meaning. An Israeli critic, Meri Ronnen, writing in the *Jerusalem Post Magazine* in 1984, got it succinctly: "While Kiefer the German acknowledges his past in a way that suggests exorcism as well as a search for cathartic understanding, Kiefer the painter rejects it." That is, what he feels as a citizen belongs to the material, not the motivation, of his art. The motive is an aggrandizement of art's critical as well as aesthetic powers.

The major critical project pursued by Kiefer from his first Nazi salutes to the 1983 *Shulamite* seems precisely a reclamation of certain aesthetic modes (neoclassical, Wagnerian, nature-romantic) from the death grip of their political uses in the Third Reich: comprehension of the real beauty of an Albert Speer interior, say, simultaneous with comprehension of its sinister historic significance. The procedure might be compared to a vaccine that by mimicking the action of a virus to produce antibodies forestalls the virus. Of course, vaccines can be contaminated, and Kiefer's—his absolutist conception of the artist—is scarcely hygienic. Kiefer's heroizing of the artist (never exactly himself, never exactly not himself) is subject to a volatility apparent in the adventures of his signature symbol, the palette: associated with the megalomania of a Nero (*Nero Paints*) or a Hitler (*Operation Barbarossa*), imposed on scenes of nature like an angry cancellation mark, or identified with a missing, mysterious "Unknown Painter," tropes that bespeak the vicissitudes—arrogance, hysteria, depression—of piloting an archetype. The palette is straightforwardly ironic in its archaism (as a posteasel painter, Kiefer doesn't use that item of professional equipment), but he leaves himself and us no choice but to regard it as a serious declaration of his willfulness. It is the badge he flashes to go wherever his imagination tends, most particularly to places marked

"Off Limits." In Germany, that would seem to be anywhere it is possible to experience emotions even remotely associated with Nazism.

Embarrassment is a frequent theme of German journalistic attacks on Kiefer (translated for me by writer Ulrike Henn): "Painfully embarrassing nationalist motifs," complained a 1982 issue of *Der Spiegel*, and a Frankfurt critic in 1984 saw a German past "dark, whispering, embarrassingly remembered ('How grand we were!')." Petra Kipphoff (*Die Zeit*, April 1984) specifically ruled out "the freedom of art" as an excuse for a painting titled *Poland Is Not Yet Lost*, because "this song title [that of a Polish anthem], misused by German aggressors, cannot be used lightly by any German." Taking another tack, a critic of the *Kölner Stadtanzeiger* (February 1981) decried Kiefer's wholesale implication of Germanic history and culture in the Nazi disaster (as in his *Ways of Worldly Wisdom* roundups of the good, the bad, and the ugly from two millennia of German artistic, military, and political worthies): "It is not only failed but dangerous historic consciousness to link wars to demonic powers of fate." The common thread in all these journalistic scoldings is an implied demand for civic rectitude, obedient to the compunctions of postwar German political culture. Such censorious reactions to an artist who has vastly enhanced the prestige of contemporary German art in American eyes gives rise to a sense of cognitive dissonance between our countries that makes the head swim.

Americans will have to get used to such things. The Kiefer phenomenon only contributes to a virtual reprovincialization of the U.S. as regards renascent cultural energies in Europe. How the mighty have fallen. "Think of it!" yet another wistful friend said to me the other day, with references to art and tennis. "Germany has Kiefer and Boris Becker. We've got Schnabel and John McEnroe." He might have added Fassbinder versus Spielberg and Peter Handke (okay, an Austrian) versus Raymond Carver—it's a game you can play. At any rate, we are put in the unaccustomed position of spectators trying to figure out such dramas on distant stages as the one apparently being enacted between Kiefer and his country's cultivated happy-face image as a hardworking, social-democratic, loyal international good guy with a sideline in smoky, sexy, *Cabaret* wildness. (Might Kiefer propitiate his country by engaging in spectacular self-destruction à la Fassbinder?) This particular spectacle, casting Kiefer as a foe of repression, may appeal strongly to our individualist mythos. The nature of the repression—German war neurosis, say, which is not our problem—matters less than the way it activates values of our own, with which we may have lost touch. Anselm Kiefer is not Ralph Waldo Emerson, and he is not Davy Crockett. But he is self-reliant, and he's got guts. Attending to him, we may seem to remember something good about ourselves.

I propose, finally, to set all such projections aside: the sick excitement of historical associations, the afternoon-in-a-cathedral afflatus, the flattery of recycled American aesthetics, and the appeal of Kiefer as a good old Black Forest country boy. What's left? I think it is the figure of an artist in a studio, tinkering interestingly with interesting ideas and materials. He is exemplary. His work conveys the texture, the feel, of making something substantial out of nothing much. He is the maker, deciding what he'd like to do and doing it. Each thing retains the rough evidence of his decisions about it. It has no style other than the manner of its making, which looks simple and self-evident, like something anyone could do. I've had such thoughts and feelings about Marcel Duchamp, Jasper Johns, Bruce Nauman, Ed Ruscha, and other artists, not very many. (People are surprised to hear that Ruscha is a favorite of Kiefer's, but they shouldn't be: the books, the uses of language and photography, the odd materials, the playfulness with scale, the putting of words in landscapes, and an individualism expressed in geographical isolation all make the affinity a natural one.) Like those artists, and also like Beuys and Andy Warhol, Kiefer rattles the received wisdom about what an artist is and does, letting us know that the world has changed even as art has found a new way to go on.

Our Kiefer? One among many (mine, yours, theirs). Kiefer is product, catalyst, and test case of a new internationalism in culture, which will seek to build a unity of reference, of conversation. In other words, Kiefer is a prime conversation piece of this era—a difficult position, even a crisis, for any artist. Out of the frying pan of "Germanness," how will he exorcise the fire of international stardom? Maybe it can't be done. And what about the paintings? They're good, but how good? Kiefer is uneven, as I'm reminded when I see the relatively lifeless *Red Sea* in the Museum of Modern Art—MOMA's inept selection from a 1985 gallery show that included the wonderful *Departure from Egypt* (now in the Museum of Contemporary Art in Los Angeles). Even his misfired pictures can feel contingently valuable, however, as pieces of a puzzle, a creative sum, that one would like to grasp whole. Is Kiefer *"really* great"? If the phrase is kept in quotes then the answer must be "absolutely"—that is, tautologically, since his entire activity parades an idea of greatness. That may be neither here nor there in judging the quality of the work, but if our excursion through American responses to Kiefer proves anything, it is that bringing a judicious eye to the work is not so simple. We may have to wear out the idea of Kiefer in good, heady talk before we can see Kiefer plain. What's the hurry?

March 1988

Hopperesque

Edward Hopper: Light Years,
Hirschl & Adler Gallery, October 1–November 12, 1988

Edward Hopper had first-rate artistic skills which in his mature work, after 1924 or so, he seemed to regard with familiar contempt. In his best pictures—each one-of-a-kind and started from scratch, as if it were the first painting in the world—he regularly pushed his talents to the breaking point. You can sense their creaks and groans in Hopper's often tortured surfaces and "awkward" figures at the same time that you feel the force of driven genius that made him the best American artist to emerge after Homer and Eakins and before the abstract expressionists: better than Hartley, Marin, and Davis, though not as compelling in pictorial invention, and better than Demuth, Dove, and O'Keeffe, though not nearly as refined. Hopper was better because his ambition for art was larger—too large to permit him a moment of feeling successful—and because he submitted himself to it with a passion rivaled only in Hartley's most eloquent late paintings. His contemporaries pursued the necessary task of getting the U.S. up to speed with European modernism. Hopper's job was the self-assigned, quite uncalled-for one of combining formal rudiments of postimpressionism with a meager American store of pictorial authenticities—from Eakins and Homer, from unnoticed aesthetics of demotic architecture and popular culture, from folk art and commercial illustration—to tell the truth and, if not the whole truth, nothing but the truth about the human soul in a hard country.

The next time you are in any museum's room of American "early modernism," perform this test: run your eyes passively along the walls. When you're jarred, like a car hitting a rock in the road, stop. Nearly always, you will be gazing at a Hopper. The reason won't be the picture's subject matter—if you've done the test fairly, you won't be aware of subjects—but the way it is put together and how the construction grips you. A Hopper has no style, properly speaking, unless sheer effort, straining against the limits of technique, can be called a style. Each element feels ad hoc, an emergency measure. The emergency is a moment in narrative time, the breathless midpoint of an unknown story. There are oddly angled vertiginous spaces and dramatic light, and color that sneaks up on you; but time is the key. The length of your contemplation—literally, how long you pay attention—is time spent outside yourself, in the suspended moment of the scene. (How does Hopper do it? We'll get to that.) You rarely feel that some actual place or person or event is being represented. Simply, you are not given the leisure to wonder about the subject, because you are plunged directly into an apprehension of its meaning. Hopper is more a naturalist than a realist, and a symbolist above all.

Hopper's nonrealism is clinched by the sketches and studies for his paintings. These are the work not of an observer of the visible world but of an imagination-powered *metteur en scène*, a stage or film director blocking in the vision of a final effect to be reached through cunning labor. Each drawing considers one or more of the decisions that will accumulate to dictate the picture. Even the simple selection of format makes meaning. I find something ineffably racy about the rectangle Hopper draws to start a sketch. It is like a blank movie screen when I'm in the mood for a movie: a silver terrain teeming with memory and anticipation, rife with spiritual possibility. Hopper understood the metaphysic of film like no other artist until, perhaps, Andy Warhol, and better than all but the greatest filmmakers. He had an instinct for the definitive, unarguable mythic construction of great film images, all the more potent when their subjects are humble and "typical." He understood that afternoon or early morning in a successful picture must evoke every afternoon or all early mornings, just as each featured man must be Man and each woman Woman. You can see it coming together—and being concentrated, edited down to irreducibles—in the drawing: set making, lighting, casting.

The figure study for *Cape Cod Morning* is a fine drawing, architectonic and sculptural (it seems to me a waste that Hopper didn't make sculpture). Though covered by a skirt, the woman's legs palpably rise like a solid column to the pelvis, which hinges sharply forward. The torso falls heavily, caught and supported on powerful arms. Note the detail drawings of the hands, subtly distorted to suggest strong pressure. The head and neck strain away from the body, as if to pull free of it. In the painting, the finesse of the draftsmanly conception is literally covered up with paint. (The mature Hopper ruthlessly expunges any "admirable" passage; he forbids us to admire him.) In swift, lovely studies of the bay-windowed house, meanwhile, we see to-be-abolished architectural detail and, on one sheet, a change in the picture's rectangular proportions that reorients it from squarish to horizontal. Brought together on the canvas, raked at a slight forward angle from the right by pale morning sun, the staring woman and the house generate a lateral force like that of a ship plowing into swells. *Yearning*, the automatic word for the mood suggested, is pathetically inadequate to the frozen violence of the scene, which tells us that whatever we think we know of disconsolateness and desire isn't even the half of it.

Hopper's paintings (portraits, in a real sense) of buildings seem his most conventional, most nearly realist works, making especially instructive their Hopperesque qualities, the narrow margin by which they transcend visual description for psychological symbolism. As always, it is an affair of decisions, strange emphases and abnegations, too pronounced for either realist comfort or aesthetic savor. Some of the decisions may be unconscious. A psychoanalyst might adduce a neurotic pattern from the unenterableness of most Hopper buildings: we rarely see a door clearly, and when we do it rarely looks operable, let alone inviting. All the life of the buildings is in their glaring windows. However, such a lot of life is there, such a visionary intensity (an intensity *of* vision, of purely seeing), that any glib analysis is confounded. Whatever may have been stymied in Hopper's psyche did not fail or fester but simply went elsewhere with the ornery vitality of a tree growing sideways to come up around a boulder. Any sense of isolation in Hopper is always defiantly upbeat: not loneliness, but solitude. Regard deserted, apparently forlorn *Gloucester Street*. See how the windows of the banal house *look* in more ways than one, so many rectangular eyes. The doors of the houses may be impassable, but you just know somebody's home. And note the fiercely red priapic chimneys: there is heat in the cellars equal to a new Ice Age. Waste no pity on those houses.

Waste no pity, either, on any of Hopper's figures, whose meaning is too often marred by sentimental, patronizing interpretations. They are heroes and heroines of American survival, every one of them unkillably resilient. What they are up against in their lives could make you cry, but only to imagine yourself in their places. They are dry-eyed and doing fine. Like Hopper's houses, his people are invariably caught in the act of seeing. They look outward, like the Cape Cod woman, or abstractedly gaze inward upon thoughts no less real for being invisible to us. In the latter cases, Hopper always provides ambient clues to the character of the person and to the occasion and nature of his or her thoughts. In my own favorite Hopper painting, *New York Movie*, an orchestration of ferociously sensual effects pivots in the reverie of the tired usherette. (She overwhelms me: sister, daughter, lover, victim, goddess all in one, caught in the movie palace that is a modern philosophical realization of Plato's Cave.) You attain Hopper's wavelength when you register how the subjectivity of his places and people is subsumed to the whole picture. A Hopper painting is a window turned inside out. You don't look into it. It looks out at you, a cyclopean glance that rivets and penetrates. To see and to be seen are the terms of the deal Hopper strikes with us. It is a spirit-enhancing bargain in which some gaucherie, some forced quality of form or execution, is about as onerous as a crooked halo on an angel who has appeared to us, offering to share state secrets of Heaven.

Hopper's crooked halo—formal abruptness, technical rawness— is basic to his profound modernity: not as a self-conscious reflection on a medium (modernist) and still less as an expressive mannerism ("modernistic"), but as an objective correlative of what lived modern experience is like. Fragmentary, distracted, moment-to-moment, phenomenological, existential, empirical: every useful term for the character of modern life is also a straightforward characterization of Hopper's paintings. It has taken American art culture, transfixed by superficial distinctions of style, a long time fully to catch up to Hopper's advanced truth, his news that stays news. (Like "Kafkaesque," "Hopperesque" names not a style but a particular face of reality— which we would feel even if Hopper had never lived, though more obscurely.) Along with Manet, Munch, and other past masters whose "heroism of modern life" (in Baudelaire's clairvoyant phrase) had been depreciated by blinkered attention to signs of the modern (modernist, modernistic), Hopper has gained a freshly honed edge from the sensibility of the 1980s. Hopper's keynote—images of life presented with tough-minded candor about the artificial, theatrical nature of images—is also that of some of our most impressive contemporaries, notably Eric Fischl and Cindy Sherman. Like him, they obtrude technique as a democratic site of complicity with the viewer, of dead-level, intimate communication in which aesthetic value must play a subordinate (though scarcely negligible) role.

Tellingly, few of us could say of a Hopper painting that it is "beautiful" without feeling that we had said, thereby, both too much and too little. A supreme masterpiece like the Whitney Museum's *Early Sunday Morning*, with its light-transfigured row of dumpy storefronts, may ravish us, but not in a way apt to remind us of Raphael. A poignance of imperfection unites the painting with its subject, producing a naked factuality as lethal to idealism as DDT is to gnats. Nor is a sentimental formula like "beauty in the ordinary" called for. What Hopper does in paintings of the mundane is far more devastating: he annihilates "the ordinary" along with "the beautiful" and every other conceivable category of aesthetic experience. The effect is "striking," shall we say, keeping in mind that so is being hit by a truck. I think the effect is this: the arousal of more emotion than can be explained or contained by its evident cause. It is a lonely sensation, a congestion of feeling incapable of articulation, like being tongue-tied with love. The parallel is pretty close: the aspect of the buildings in *Early Sunday Morning* is like that of an unremarkable person of whom you are suddenly, hopelessly enamored. You can no more describe the aspect than you can breathe under water. You may feel terror unless the person breaks your isolation by speaking to you, if only with a look— as Hopper does with his plainspoken brushwork, showing his hand.

The Hopperesque pertains to a glimpse that burns into memory like a branding iron. Anyone who has done much living knows situations in which mood and moment produce a spark, and some utterly neutral thing is permanently charged. I remember being emotionally distressed once in a restaurant in a country town. A distant window in the shadowy room framed an aspen tree against summer sky. I will never forget it. More to the point, I knew immediately, in that instant, that I would never forget the look of that tree, which seemed to me sacred. (I've since forgotten exactly what I was upset about.) I try, and fail, to fantasize how Hopper might have rendered this experience of mine, and my failure instructs me. To lose one's soul to a vision is no more communicable than any other neurological glitch: it might make a needle jump on some brain-monitoring device. To reel one's soul back in with the vision attached, preserving both in a formal order, is genius. It is what W. B. Yeats called poetry: "a raid on the inarticulate." It is also hard, complicated, equivocal work with a frequent air of rough, even shocking, presumption, as Hopper never took pains to conceal.

What is most equivocal in Hopper's practice—shady and potentially embarrassing, an open secret that critics mention evasively if at all—is the kinship of such psychological vision to voyeurism: you can get a quick, cheap equivalent—an automatic "burning glimpse"—by peeping at someone who is oblivious of you. (If properly brought up, you will also feel sick; but that's your business.) Hopper plainly was comfortable with the voyeurist impulse, which informs so much of his art directly and just about all of it indirectly—along a Platonic sliding scale from the grossest to the most transcendent knowledge, from the intrusive glance of *Night Windows* to the metaphysical mystery of *Light in an Empty Room*. (No one has ever seen, with their own eyes, the inside of an empty room.) Genius may rely as much on a lack of something normal as on possession of something exceptional: in Hopper's case, a lack of shame. Though distinctly puritan in his detachment, his proud spiritual isolation, he wasn't at all inhibited about his sexual interest, notoriously explicit in his characteristic exaggerations of the female body. Only squeamishness might make us see those distortions differently from the distortions Hopper visits on trees, lighthouses, gas stations, and everything else he responds to. I submit that a polymorphous sexual alertness—"adhesiveness," in Walt Whitman's wonderful term—informed Hopper's perception of the whole world. In the lowest is the highest. A mystic is a voyeur who peeps at God.

Tension between voyeurism and detachment, an aroused fascination and a reticent distance, is the moral engine of Hopper's mature art, giving rise at times to an almost Buddhistic, compassionate equilibrium. He is excited by the unguarded moment, the exposed innocence, of a person, a building, a place—anything at all, though certain things and situations (generally involving windows) pique him more than others. At the same time, he is devoted to the inviolability of the innocence he surveys. You may feel in his work the tug of sex, and often a tug toward satire; but they are always checked. (That's my ideal of morality, founded not in repression and shame but in respect—the function of self-respect called character.) The "coming egghead," as Hopper wryly termed the primly seated incongruously muscular woman in the late painting *Intermission*, need fear no humiliation from the gazing artist, who claims, however, a corresponding liberty to gaze without qualm. We know such gazes from the work of Hopper's French heroes: the meltingly sensual gaze of Manet, the urbanely cool one of Degas. It is the way civilized eyes behave in the modern city. To have transposed this protocol of gazing from molten Paris to stony America was not the least of Hopper's feats.

If, as I've said, Hopper has won special, heightened appreciation in the 1980s, that does not mean he has been fully and finally understood. On the contrary, we have become wise precisely to the limitations, the premature closure, of all previous interpretations of his achievement. Our uncertainty was usefully complicated, perhaps, by the rather grueling retrospective that opened in 1980 at the Whitney. That show flooded us with unfamiliar early and otherwise minor pictures, many excellent in their way and valuable for, among other things, showing the virtuosity that Hopper's strongest work suppresses. We learned that Hopper was artistically equipped to develop in any number of ways other than the way he did, which thus took on more dramatic definition as a conscious, even arbitrary, quest—an action of the spirit with historic and moral resonance. The task now is to winnow from the lovely chaff of Hoppers the obdurate kernel of the Hopperesque, the narrow canon of his works primary to an American intuition of modernity. It is not a task reserved for specialists, though they will play their roles in it. Only individual human hearts can ultimately assess the diagnoses of this doctor of democracy, who asked if the soul—and art, which is its mirror—could survive an inclement century. His answer: yes, *in a way*. I have given my views about the nature and meaning of that way, on the occasion of a discriminating show in which minor work combines with major to explore the threshold of the Hopperesque. I am pleased to believe that in this matter there can be no end of views while there are viewers with courage to think and feel.

1988

Mike Kelley ✓

The reputation of Los Angeles artist Mike Kelley has been simmering in the downtown art world for years, and this could be the season when it boils over to a larger public. At thirty-three, Kelley may be the most significant artist of his generation. You wouldn't call him the best, because his performance-derived work shrugs off, when not insulting, conventional notions of "quality." That's part of his significance, and one of the things a lot of people will hate about him.

Attending Kelley's show at Metro Pictures (September 10–October 1, 1988), some viewers may have a sincere inclination to flee the grotesque banners, assemblages, and paintings, with their themes of sticky sentimentality and bodily disgust. I can sympathize, because I gave Kelley's work a certain berth for a long time, vaguely hoping it would go away. But I've become convinced that he bears important news, at once socially dire and poetically fecund. He is an artist's artist for those artists—now in the making—who will matter to us in the nineties.

Kelley, a self-described "blue-collar anarchist," is from Detroit. He studied at the California Institute of the Arts, a major think tank of American art since the early seventies, and lives in Los Angeles. That's significant, too. There is a westward drift in art's concerns now, reflecting an ever more total identification of American culture with pop forms and mass media. In still-Europeanized old New York, the attitudes of our neo-geo and neo-conceptual artists toward masscult tend to be ironic and either romantic (it's exotic!) or paranoid (it's a plot!)— provincial, in other words.

In Southern California, wellhead of the commodity culture that is oozing around the globe, the facts of the matter are plain enough to be taken for granted. Kelley starts from a point well beyond fret or infatuation with the U.S. dream machine. In so doing, he awakens and updates an old American myth of the candid and resourceful pariah: Huck Finn on the lam, rafting past golden arches.

Kelley's art is about how to be a person—and, taking ambition into account, how to "be somebody"—in a culture of manufactured fictions that numb our capacity to believe in anything. He makes do with whatever is left out of the fictions: shame, impotence, cruelty, hysteria, rage, failure, and all-around abjection. His work is funny, but the laughter it suggests is a sputtering kind that accompanies embarrassment and isn't far from a sob.

PANTS SHITTER & PROUD reads the lettering on one of fourteen big felt banners loosely inspired by the work of Sister Mary Corita, the nun who in the sixties served a hapless movement to make Christianity groovy with modernistic, feel-good graphics. Each of Kelley's banners spells out a different malaise in the language of Sister Mary's idealist kitsch. I liked a Matissean blue-and-white one in which a St. Francis figure ministering to animals stirs a thrill of revulsion when you notice the frog clinging to his foot, the dog humping his leg, and the snake about to bite him. In another, a sunny UNICEF-type dove motif and the word JOY are reversed in clashing colors, like euphoria flipping over into anxiety attack.

Most of the work at Metro was shown recently in Chicago with a huge controversial installation that incorporated portraits of Western thinkers who have spoken in apparent praise of criminality ("I want to sing murder, for I love murderers"—Jean Genet) and an amateurish clown painting made in prison by mass killer John Wayne Gacy. (Kelley wanted to include collection boxes for victims' rights organizations, but these groups balked at the Gacy picture.) It sounds like a scrappy American version of the works in which Anselm Kiefer convenes German cultural heroes to confront the Holocaust.

A piece that does appear here, an assemblage of thrift-shop stuffed animals paired with a table bearing "novelty" candles, is tellingly described in the current *Artforum* by a Chicago critic named Laurie Palmer, in tones that speak to me of an emerging generational sensibility:

> The wall-hanging *More Love Hours Than Can Ever Be Repaid*, 1987, is made from hand-knitted, tatted, and crocheted effluvia (which resale shops have a constantly rotting supply of) in burnt oranges, limey yellows, and sour purples; it is accompanied by a pyramid of shaped and colored candles, melted into one obnoxious, perfumed mass. Redolent with the sickly-sweet sentiment of gifts that are less about giving than about incurring a bottomless debt in the receiver,

the horror in these pieces comes in part from a recognition of the child's impossible position, forced to welcome even these treacly substitutes for love in exchange for a lifetime of feeling guilty.

Palmer's heartfelt sarcasm expresses a widespread and potentially dynamic pissed-offness with our culture of "treacly substitutes," though it doesn't convey the depth of Kelley's sorrow. You get that the degradation of religion, the awful glibness of cultural fathers, and the neuroses of popular handicraft are bleeding wounds for him. With obsessive fascination, he opens the wounds wider and wider, releasing a tremendous energy of unassuageable feeling. If you resist it, that's understandable, but if you try to argue with it, you have dealt yourself a losing hand.

Kelley has jokingly termed his frieze of stuffed animals "my homage to Jackson Pollock." The joke seems to me at least half-serious. Like Pollock and the other postwar abstract expressionists, Kelley struggles for selfhood as an artist in the teeth of frightening historical discontinuities. Forty years ago, the crisis was a disintegration of European tradition. Today it's the disintegration of practically everything, or so it can seem after an evening of television in which horrible facts mingle with idiotic "values" and you may catch yourself smiling at cute beer commercials tailored for children.

At the heart of Kelley's fiesta of morbidity and derision—harshest in schematic paintings of eyeballs, brains, and intestines—there is an odd sad tenderness, apparent in an assemblage that evokes the romantic life of a young girl: an "antiqued" pink chest of drawers standing on a mirror that reveals, in a net beneath the chest, copies of *Sex and Girls* and *How to Make Love to a Man* and a package of birth-control pills. Under the chest's glass top are photos of Kelley (a skinny, pleasantly homely guy), in "moody teenager" poses. It's easy to miss one tiny picture, from a performance piece, of the artist in drag.

Is a furtive girl in love with Mike Kelley? Or is she Mike Kelley in love with himself? Whom or what is anyone in love with, when anyone falls in love? This visual poem curls back on itself, becoming another link in a chain of meaning that Kelley is extending into a big commonly shared darkness.

October 5, 1988

302

Paintings by Aborigines

Dreamings: The Art of Aboriginal Australia
Asia Society, October 6–December 31, 1988

A couple of years ago in Australia I visited Alice Springs, an unpre-possessing burg at dead center in the vast, hot, hallucinatory bush. I remember aborigines. I remember how strange it was, shaking hands with an aborigine for the first time. His hand in mine was inert, like an object given by its owner on the understanding that he would get it back when I was through with it. I felt slighted for a moment, but he was perfectly benign. Handshaking simply didn't mean much to him, evidently.

Another aborigine scared me by the way he stood inside a general store in the bush. Small and dusty, he had an unfocused gaze and a rangy posture bespeaking the immensity outdoors, as if the walls of the store did not exist for him. But for the floorboards, he was in fact standing on the bush—and so was I, suddenly conscious of the store as something fragile and temporary in the bush's eternity. I felt a flare of hatred against him for his insulting attitude toward the reality of a building. Yet he was a mild man, only standing at his ease.

Between one thing and another, my equanimity was already in trouble by the morning, in an apartment on the edge of Alice Springs, when I was awakened by a terrific din. It seemed some aborigines disliked a policeman who lived next door. Stones flung by children were hitting the steel roofs and the steel stockadelike fence of the apartment complex. The kids didn't break anything and, according to my host, who knew them well, probably weren't so much angry as gleeful, making percussive wake-up music with their stones. But it was a dreadful noise. What if the cop started shooting?

That the ritual of the handshake, the substantiality of walls, the prudence not to arouse armed enemies—"universal" verities that I never leave home without—were not being honored in the outback toyed with my mind. I was shaken by the alienness of the place—and disgusted by what was familiar, by prosaic Alice Springs with its tacky shopping center, scorched golf course, and stockadelike fences. I became obsessed with the bottoms of fences, the straight lines where they jammed down into the reddish bush of otherworldly plants and lizards. The straight lines struck me as violent.

Drifting through Alice Springs, the aborigines made the stolid middle-class town, with its imported shade trees and World War I memorial, seem a temporary illusion, a heat mirage. I knew they were a decimated people, ravaged by alcohol and reduced to welfare dependency. But with the eternal bush at hand, their small, dusty, lithe demeanor had a power that made big, scrubbed, blundering whites seem flimsy. In the differences between "them" and "us," almost incredibly extreme within one species, I sensed the roots of racism in intimidation. I got a sickening hint of why white settlers had wanted to annihilate the aborigines: for their mocking grace.

Don't go looking for that power of strangeness at the Asia Society. It's not there, except faintly in a few old carvings and paintings on bark. Instead there is the violence of fences, unconsciously erected by people wanting only good things for aborigines. The show is an American boost for an Australian project to market symbols of the aboriginal religion, which has long been known by such pretty names: "songlines," "dreaming." The violence lurks in the straight lines of stretched canvases that aborigines are painting with acrylics, using motifs proper to the ephemeral sand- and body-painting employed in their rituals. Promoted internationally, the paintings are seen as a means to build independent wealth and self-esteem for a people gravely lacking both.

In problem-solving terms, the idea is impeccable. But the paintings are no good. They are turgid and nerveless, with their doggedly completed designs in plastic paint. They look like a type of abstraction briefly fashionable in the 1970s, when this project was born. Wall labels and a maudlin video accompanying the show assure us that the pictures are full of religious meaning, but what is religious meaning when divorced from religious practice and churned out in synthetic materials for export to nonbelievers? It is a symbol eclipsed by another symbol, to which it submits: here, the almighty white rectangle.

In its innocence, the Western mind fancies that the rectangle, divine form of the Parthenon, is purely neutral ground, rather than a template for mastering the world. Our way of looking at a rectangle is itself rectangular, congruent to it—so that the rectangle disappears. We see it not as a form but as a "universal" condition of form. Was there a true right angle anywhere on the Australian continent before the Europeans arrived? Those who innocently give an aborigine rectangles to decorate jam down fences they can't even see.

Aborigine painters don't know what to do with the edges and corners of rectangles, and why should they? Their bark paintings— already suspect because the earliest surviving ones date from a century after the first whites—may be roughly rectangular, but in the roughness is the life: a slightly off angle carries throughout the composition as a compression or torque, making the picture squirm like an organic thing. On the crisp oblongs now in use, patterns burgeon absentmindedly to the edges and just stop there. The bush stops that way at the bottoms of Alice Springs's stockadelike fences—on the other side of which lawns and pavement happen to it.

White (and nonwhite) Americans should readily grasp a dilemma here. Our efforts to "help" American Indians, since genocide went out of style, have been similarly clumsy, to say the least. When we think of ameliorating ills, we seek progress and innovation, which are death to the absolute conservatism of tribal cultures. The helping hand brings only softer varieties of ruin. We ought to leave native peoples alone, but it would be too late for that even if, for once in a tradition of tampering older than the Acropolis, Western minds could tolerate such un-Western passivity.

One thing we have gotten good at, in our rectangular way, is preserving the legacy of what we haplessly destroy. I am thinking of a Plexiglas case at the Asia Society that contains a carved and painted wallaby, "attributed to George Ngallametta" (a delectably insane pedantry in context), that is the loveliest thing imaginable. The wallaby (a type of small kangaroo) stretches up and up in a series of vertical exaggerations that sing of horizontality: the creature is straining for a distant view across a vastness in which the Mojave Desert could nestle like a sandbox. It is also, perhaps, making itself visible to aboriginal hunters, who are elated by the sight.

Most of us imagine "primitive" people, though we no longer feel free to admit it, in terms of animals or children—for the excellent reason that only in sensations of our own animal selves and memories of our childhoods can we draw near to them. Their maturity and sophistication branch differently from ours and are inaccessible. In the wonderful carving of the wallaby, I understand the visceral insouciance of an animal and the childlike joy of a hunter. It is a tiny communion, like a flicker of light in darkness, but I want to remember it, in all its frailty, for the little seed of respect it nurtures. The carving was made for actual use in a ritual, which accounts for its dignity.

There is no such dignity in the aborigines' acrylics, whose pristine rectangles are semaphores of the rectangular mind congratulating itself. It's excruciatingly sad. I was struck, in Australia, by the depth of guilty sensitivity felt by many whites toward the aborigines, in contrast to an old American callousness to the ongoing devastation of American Indians. It is an awful thing to confront crimes on which your culture is founded, and it is almost unbearable to think that you can make no amends to the victims without committing fresh offenses. As usual in our culture, which is not without resources, the answer is simply more and more consciousness, because only in the most painful knowledge does the idea of justice rise.

November 16, 1988

Jeff Koons

Jeff Koons makes me sick. He may be the definitive artist of this moment, and that makes me sickest. I'm interested in my response, which includes excitement and helpless pleasure along with alienation and disgust. As a professional critic, I'm thrilled. Koons's accurate blend of aesthetic perfect pitch and blazing sociological significance gives critical sensibility the equivalent of a new freeway system that will take it anywhere fast. But the critic in me must drive with irrational penchants—old ideals and new discontents—grabbing his arm and complaining in his ear.

As luck would have it, you don't need a wholehearted guide to help you understand Koons's new work (Sonnabend Gallery, November 19–December 23, 1988), which is as self-explanatory as a kick in the stomach: staggeringly vulgar statues of stuffed animals and smutty-joke tableaux in painted wood or glazed porcelain, and some grotesquely ornamented mirrors, all executed (largely by Italian and German craftsmen under the artist's direction) with staggeringly exquisite finesse.

The pieces faithfully reproduce the detail, while blowing up the size and infinitely amplifying the allure, of various grades of kitsch commonly found in living rooms with vinyl slipcovers, Toys R Us–stocked nurseries, and knotty-pine-paneled dens. They represent genres that educated folk tend to regard generically, with blanket disdain. But in Koons's hands, each tchotchke sings a specific and riveting aria.

To stroll into the Sonnabend Gallery today is to be gang-banged by a crew of inanimate demons. A simpering love-me bear sinks icy talons in the heart, and a nude grabbing her breasts in alarm at the surfacing of a snorkel in her bathtub stirs a brute laughter reflex that could drive you straight to a monastery. I defy anybody to shrug off this stuff. As a phenomenon, furthermore, it is somehow obviously a bell—or a carillon—tolling for thee, thee, and thee. Go look. Be your own critic.

When I first encountered a work by Koons in 1981—two vacuum cleaners encased in spotless flourescent-lighted Plexiglas—I was amazed that someone had taken so much trouble to make a unique but surely unnecessary pop-minimalist hybrid. Later I was only slightly more detained by his aquariumlike tanks in which basketballs disconcertingly floated underwater (something to do with liquid chemistry): vaguely nasty things with a metaphysical pizzazz that still seemed mainly eccentric.

I became a Koons konvert suddenly, in 1986, at a show of drinking paraphernalia cast in stainless steel and of liquor advertising posters reprinted in oil inks on linen. My physiological reaction to the kicked-up visual appeal was overwhelming: I wanted a drink! I got in a flash what Koons was after—what a lot of artists were then after, a concrescence of the "commodity fetishism" concept much in the air—and saw that he had nailed it with his intoxicatingly beautiful works about intoxication (some of which, as sealed decanters, held actual booze). In a time given to heavy theorizing about "desire" (by critics seemingly immune to wanting so much as a chocolate-chip cookie themselves), here was the living article: desire objectified, in objects wildly desirable.

This was, and is, the ticky-tum-tum part: the way Koons feeds off, and exacerbates, our culture's hysterical telescoping of all values into the seductiveness of things for sale, symptomized lately by a psychotic art market. Koons, thirty-three, is a former Wall Street broker and an unabashed self-promoter who comes on with the sunny narcissism of a bubblegum rock star. He would like to be Michael Jackson, he has said, and he sort of is. He has the Gloved One's aura of naive decadence down cold, and he gives hints of similar don't-touch-me phobias about germs, dirt, and other sorts of imperfection, such as poverty and sex.

"The trick is to be outrageous, but not offensive," Koons has said. For the record, I am offended by that sentiment, which reduces the artist, in my ideal a figure of freedom, to the slavishness of a court jester. It's a twerp's ethos, though I don't doubt that Koons is a one-in-a-million twerp.

The court is duly appreciative. Koons has positioned himself for wholesale production of multiples presold to today's insatiable collectors, who will crave one of each thing he issues. He is going to be rich beyond the dreams of his contemporaries, who, be they ever so glamorous, retain difficult, audience-limiting edges. You can love him or hate him. Either way, remember this: it doesn't matter. That's the awesomeness of Koons's success. He is like the greenhouse effect—toxic, unstoppable, and here. Get used to him.

The last time an artist had an analogous impact (though hedged by a more high-art quality), it was probably David Salle, seven or so years ago: imposing a paradigm on the art culture that seemed to preempt the most important new creative matters and manners. The paradigm of paradigms, in this connection, will always be Andy Warhol in 1962, ratifying Copernican shifts on all levels of art and society. Artists don't change the world. But any big historic development makes room for a creative individual who, understanding it sooner and better than others, will come to symbolize it. The appearance of such a personality is never guaranteed, and it always rightly feels auspicious, like it or not.

Koons symbolizes the apotheosis of corporate culture, the increasingly sacrosanct authority of money, the eroticizing of social status, and other emergent diseases not yet diagnosed. He does so with fierce poise and an irony so large that no single analysis can encompass it. In social terms, the loop of Koons's irony delivers, to an ever bolder upper-class hegemony, elixirs of repressed and debased content from working-class, petit-bourgeois, nouveau-riche, Disneylandish, Las Vegas-ite, and other compost-heap American sensibilities. With perfectly balanced condescension and celebration—a noblesse oblige so deft that none of his sources seems actually mocked—he concocts talismans of class-structural harmony that (lots of) money can buy.

So is Koons playing the fool for his audience or making fools of them? It's useless to ask, because his irony isn't a vector but a spiral, showing a special smirk to every available point of view. Only the incurably self-righteous, standing on quicksand and fancying that it is solid ground, will fail to see that Koons has their number, too. I love it, and pardon me while I throw up. It's not that Koons promulgates any great truth. But he brackets a cultural ground zero whose very emptiness is faithful to current sensations of dizzying velocity in time, as day after day we encroach on unprecedented historical terrain.

Okay, how do I get all of this from the dumbest-looking sculpture you ever saw? I must assume that you have already seen the show, because there is no future in trying to reproduce Koons's diabolical magic in either photographs or words. The effect hits simultaneously above and below any reasonable expectation one brings to sculpture. The work's technical perfection and flat-out beauty are like divine redemptions of every luxury ever rejected by modern art in the name of authenticity. Meanwhile, the treacly subject matter, which would insult the intelligence of a relatively sophisticated eight-year-old, embraces emotions so hapless as to seem to obviate "art" altogether.

Between soaring ravishment and bottomless gross-out in the contemporary temple of the art gallery, you may feel possessed of a solve-it-yourself Delphic oracle on the present state and imminent fate of Western civilization. (I like a last-days-of-Versailles scenario, in which pseudo-shepherdesses traipse amid rococo bric-a-brac while an odd, troubling noise starts to filter in from distant streets; but that's just silly old offended me again.) What you won't feel is the pressure of an individual mind or the existence of any heart or soul at all. You will feel your own individuality being degraded and dismissed and your consciousness at once hypercharged and trivialized, like an interchangeable node of some collective megabrain.

Koons's impersonality is stunning and refreshing. It is a slate wiped clean, a future that commences now. The future pertains to a new oligarchy that after years of throwing money at art of all sorts, at last has in Koons a major artist specifically attuned to its finer feelings: lust for possessions and anxiety about the lower classes. This oligarchy has at least four more years to develop a really big-time style, the last I checked. It may well be a feast for the eyes, if you can stand the indigestion.

December 14, 1988

Courbet

Courbet Reconsidered, Brooklyn Museum
November 4, 1988–January 16, 1989

The Courbet show is right on time for us, but then when wouldn't it be? We are always in the mood, whether we know it or not, for a brash, authentic arriver who is wild for our approval and, cheerfully absorbing all sorts of abuse, keeps on coming. Gustave Courbet was like that in mid–nineteenth-century Paris—a swaggering fanatic importuning the public with paintings that Edgar Degas said made him feel he was being nuzzled by the wet nose of a calf—and Courbet is the same today in Brooklyn, which is a good place for him. He is to great art what a "dem"-and-"dose" accent is to American speech, and in Brooklyn, as in all else, he is off-center in a way that makes the center feel colorless and effete.

The show is a curatorial gem (by Sarah Faunce and Linda Nochlin), a neatly crafted container for Courbet's big, sloppy talent—necessarily minus the Musée d'Orsay's unbudgeable *A Burial at Ornans* and *The Painter's Studio*, two stupefying masterpieces which, by failing to terminate art history, proved conclusively that no painting can do that. The show is also very racy, giving pride of place to Courbet's, shall we say, erotic or, well, pornographic—or, not to put too fine a point on it, filthy—pictures *The Origin of the World* and *The Sleepers*.

Seeing this show, I feel that I've finally met someone I had heard about for so long that I felt I knew him, but I didn't. Not that I really know him now, or ever will. Courbet was one of those blustering self-revealers who, maintaining a stubbornly childlike lack of self-consciousness, hide in plain sight. I think it's a shame that Courbet never met his exact contemporary Walt Whitman (they were born eleven days apart in 1819), who was like that, too, with an ego that embraced the world. The half-dozen most robust people of today, standing on each other's shoulders, wouldn't reach the kneecaps of those two.

Courbet billed himself a "realist"—he promulgated the first, most naive, most often revived, and still most elusive of the "isms" that have jazzed and befuddled modern culture—and I went to the show with questions in my mind about what that meant and might still mean. I got that it was, and is, an antiartistic reflex, asserting—against art's constant tendency to grow precious and detached—the superior claims on us of actual, breathing life. I got this from the way Courbet's pictures are painted, which at best is thrilling and inculcates a restless disgust with the merely aesthetic. You want to run out and start a riot, milk a cow, have sex, eat an apple, die—do anything rather than stand around abrading your nerves with the angel-grit of "fine" art.

Technically and formally, Courbet pioneered nothing much in modern art except negatively, trashing conventional ideals of finish and finesse. Some of his pet stylistic tricks, such as making fast smudges with a palette knife to render highlights of "sea," "rock," and so on, predict nothing so much as the stuff of stores that advertise "1,001 Original Oil Paintings, Half-Price." To go for facts in his way is to seek effects that convince the imagination instantly, and when you see them operating before they grab you, the painting turns stone dead. Courbet's results are sometimes bizarre: you haven't the slightest idea what you're supposed to be experiencing, even as the vastly self-confident effects swarm out at you.

Maybe largely because their colors have darkened with age, nearly all of Courbet's landscapes, which comprise about two-thirds of his total production but little of what we esteem about him now, have that sort of dumb, futile feeling for me. To succeed, his paintings have to be like sudden reminders of something you know already, such as what makes people interesting. Most of his portraits are fantastic, in exactly the way other people are when you're crazy about them. And his sexy stuff—the early fully clothed *Young Ladies on the Banks of the Seine* somehow even more than the later lascivious nudes—might just about make your knees buckle, remembering your desires.

Courbet made few drawings, going straight to work with paint. This was his sharpest break with drawing-based norms of painting that Ingres had taken as far as they could go. It wasn't a clean break. Nothing about Courbet was clean. (He wasn't the kind of man who takes a lot of baths, for instance.) As it was, he could fake up a very reasonable facsimile of traditional figure-study modeling right off the palette, delivering figures with a panache that is like the word *Master* in blinking neon. But there's no delectation in it. He treated tradition like a powdered aristocrat on the day after a revolution, handing it a shovel and telling it to start digging.

Looking at the paintings, you can plainly see Courbet disdaining chances to realize art-for-art's-sake exquisitenesses—all tantalizingly within easy reach—on his way to colliding head-on with some messy truth. His intractable matter-of-factness excites me. We can use that now. We have a culture today suffocating under heaped technologies of fiction, and even to speak of truth is to arch people's eyebrows. Courbet suggests that the trick to being true is no trick. Just do it. Julian Schnabel has that quality sometimes, though without much savor of a world anybody actually lives in.

Charles Baudelaire, who is my hero, evidently didn't like the portrait Courbet painted of him, and I think I see why. It's like a caricature of genius, in a way. The poet is perched uncomfortably on the edge of a seat, supporting himself with a clawlike hand as he reads a book with an intensity that could burn holes in it. I love the portrait, and I believe it. It doesn't even try to empathize with Baudelaire, whose loneliness must have throbbed painfully when he saw it. All it does is revel in this incredibly intelligent guy's eerie energy, as you would in a thunderstorm or a spectacular sunset.

Sex is the key to Courbet. Like Whitman, Courbet kept the business of life simple: possess everything that possesses you. When he painted *The Origin of the World*, a nude view for which the up-to-date term is the name of a clever animal that builds dams in country streams, he made an all-time philosophers' stone for transmuting the lead of lust into the gold of awe—and vice versa, in a continual flicker. It is indefensible as art. Somebody should probably have punched Courbet in the jaw for it. It is a gesture of contempt for art. It is an idea indistinguishable from reality.

Courbet, whose public triumphs may have made him creatively lazy but didn't mellow him a bit, became an actual revolutionary in 1871, as arts commissioner of the Commune. He was associated with the famous toppling of the Napoleon column in the Place Vendôme, and the restored government, faced with the problem of punishing a certified genius of France, sardonically opted to bill him for putting it back up: 323,091.68 francs. Taking refuge from the debt in Switzerland, he may have more or less drunk himself to death. It was a Falstaffian end, in disgrace on a scale that befitted him.

Now he's in Brooklyn, inviting the public. He has a number of things there that he knows you are going to like.

December 21, 1988

De Kooning Alone

Around 1960, Willem de Kooning dropped from the charts of public sensation in contemporary art. This wouldn't be worth mentioning if he were a private artist, tending his own garden, but he never was. "There is perhaps more Luciferian pride behind de Kooning's ambition than there is behind Picasso's," Clement Greenberg wrote with mixed feelings in 1953. De Kooning remained the best painter of this half-century, in the opinion of anyone with eyes in a head. He has been the best at any kind of painting, but his particular kind, based in the old European way on mastery of drawing, became uninteresting for people keen to experience the world changing and art changing with it. It was already old-fashioned for Pollock and Rothko. Johns and Rauschenberg didn't even have to think about it if they didn't want to. There is something still drastic, something hurtful, about de Kooning's ceasing to matter, unless you don't care about history.

Ever since, there has been a haunting lonesomeness about the way de Kooning's hand moves in his pictures, like a C. B. deMille pharaonic gesture at horizon-to-horizon synthetic multitudes. The gesture is so assured of sovereignty it can even be sweet about it. It has a quirk so specific and extreme that you want to call it something, but there's no word for it, just the man's name. Then you want to bracket it with the quirks of other great artists, great composers or poets, great greats; but that's gush and takes you away from the meaning, which never simply resides in a work but resides always between the work and everything else. The meaning for me is the imagined possession of a perfect instrument with no proper function. I think that state is partly saintly and mostly awful. Instead of describing a nude or a landscape, maybe it describes what becomes of us, of what we're "the best" at, in society. I can understand the urge to make a virtue of art's being private, but that throws the baby of ambition out with the bathwater of cold shoulders and is way too cozy, if we're talking about de Kooning.

"Willem de Kooning is the outstanding painter of the ideological epoch in American art": this is how Harold Rosenberg began his big book on de Kooning. It sounds like praise, but for me it's a label on this terrible headache, a battle of ideas which, once you're in it, you have to say you've won and, once you've said that, you're a fool. Rosenberg was great, but his "action painting" (i.e., whatever de Kooning was up to) was an evasive maneuver to get art into his head so he wouldn't have to look at it so much. I figure that Greenberg, meanwhile, conned painters into eliminating drawing so he could look at their nice colors and stop thinking about how much better de Kooning was. The two critics were like different kinds of unhappy lover: embarrassed and disappointed, respectively. I feel both ways, and then some. It's humiliating how overqualified de Kooning is for the uses of this half-century and hemisphere. It's like badly needing a screwdriver and going to the toolbox only to find it—damn!—filled with the crown jewels. De Kooning is unplugged from art of the last three decades as the soul is unplugged from the self is unplugged from the body is unplugged from paradise, and the parts lie around where anyone can ignore them.

1989

Treason of Clerks

The recent public outcries against art works by Robert Mapplethorpe and Andres Serrano, the ongoing flag furor (including outcries against an art work by Dread Scott Tyler), and the distinct possibility of a nationwide wave of anticosmopolitan populism remind us that political controversy is like a speeding train. It has one aspect when passing by (vicariously stimulating on "Nightline," say) and quite another when it is coming directly at you.

Long comfortably marginal to public debate, the sector of the art world reliant on government funding has had particular reason lately to feel tied to the tracks in front of a political runaway freight. But anyone living the American life of art is apt to glimpse in a general uglification of attitudes toward artistic license the mesmerizing glare of an approaching headlight.

We are in for something. What it will be and how bad it will be are shrouded, but we are in for something. And we—meaning those of us committed to art as not only a refined pleasure but also an oracle of worldly change, a redeemer of things debased, and a cosmopolitan communion—are going to make whatever badness there is worse, because we can't help it.

Two weeks ago the House of Representatives nibbled $45,000 from the $171.4-million budget of the National Endowment for the Arts for next year, withholding only the pittance spent last year toward the offending shows of Mapplethorpe and Serrano. It was a chilling but elegantly understated threat, engineered by liberals to finesse conservatives who were out to gut the agency, that as much as said (or pleaded): "Do not come to our attention again." How do you think my kind of art person, who identifies with art's ambition to make a difference in the world, will receive that message?

My kind of art person will be happy that art has had such an impact. To come to people's attention is what all artists always try to do, and what almost no artist ever does on a substantial scale in this country. We have had nearly three decades now of a liberal dispensation that abides almost any expression so long as it stays within its proper little red-light district of the culture.

Those of us who have chafed at this, grumbling about "repressive tolerance," may soon have our chance to put up or shut up in the face of conservative intolerance that rejects the notion of any sanctuary for sinners.

Nothing so terrible has happened yet. By themselves, the scandals of Serrano's urine-immersed crucifix in North Carolina and Tyler's flag-on-the-floor provocation in Chicago might be isolated rages of a sort that can happen in the U.S. when normally separate cultural spheres accidentally jostle. And Congress has signaled the preference of its majority for simply shoving the spheres back apart and stuffing insulation in the restored gap. In this context, the demagogueries of redneck-as-art-critic Dick ("morally reprehensible trash") Armey of Texas and art-critic-as-redneck Hilton (protector of children from homo-propaganda) Kramer of Connecticut might seem passing squalls.

The single event so far that makes a fading away of the stink improbable is the decision by the Corcoran Gallery of Art in Washington, D.C., on June 13, to cancel a Mapplethorpe show for fear of upsetting a Congress on the verge of considering the NEA budget. On one level, this grotesque act succeeded mainly in letting blood into waters crowded with right-wing sharks who seem to find artistic turpitude even more delightfully frenzying than the tasty but lean meat of flag desecration. But the Corcoran's display of weakness is ominous on another, subtler, and deadlier level: its save-the-NEA rationale.

Precisely that rationale has galvanized initial responses to the crisis by art institutions and even political activists. "Don't Take Away My NEA!" was a slogan emerging from a rally I attended at Artists Space on July 12. Thus is an issue of artistic freedom turned into one of a special interest group's claim on federal largesse.

The question of the NEA's fate (involving as it does the agency's mighty influence on state, local, and corporate funding policies) is serious for art people much as the possible closing of an auto plant is serious for auto workers, but it is beside the point of art's role and prerogative in American society. Just you watch. That point is going to split the art world between grant-protective Corcoranists—or more likely crypto-Corcoranists, who will mouth a liberal line while pursuing conservative agendas (never mounting a show that anyone could object to, for starters)—and my kind of art people, who will borrow trouble to pay dues as believers in actual liberty.

Though heretofore nameless, Corcoranism is not new. It is a tacit doctrine that preserving the means of cultural support justifies suppressing the ends of culture. Under Corcoranism, bureaucratic insularity and institutionalized self-censorship are good, and art's spontaneous fermentation of ideas and passions is bad. Corcoranism is a treason of clerks. It is a formerly obscure treason whose exposure in the present emergency makes this an occasion not for defensiveness in the cause of art but for attack.

Let's keep a sharp eye on our institutions now. Do demand that they pledge anti-Corcoranist allegiance to artistic freedom, but don't heed what they say so much as look at what they do. In an era of conservative hostility, artists may be counted on to put new edges on their own disaffection. Keep tabs on the responsiveness of the institutions to those edges as also to specifically controversial artists—Mapplethorpe, Serrano, Tyler, and the many more to come—whose cases can no longer be regarded as peripheral.

Things may get dramatic presently here in our cosmopolis. Forces of brain and brawn on the American right—the stuffy but powerfully aggrieved Kramers and the stupid but powerfully numerous Armeys—seem to be getting in rare sync, no doubt pooling enemies lists that toll for thee and me. So what? You don't abandon your principles just because some louts are in a mood to resent them. We aren't going anywhere. And a fight for the soul of American art culture may be just what is needed to clear a lot of lingering cobwebs, immediately including the uncertainty of who, in the culture's ranks, is or isn't artistic freedom's friend.

August 2, 1989

Velázquez

Diego Velázquez (1599–1660) was as good at oil painting as anyone has been at anything. When Edouard Manet, seeing Velázquez's paintings at the Prado in Madrid in 1865, said he wondered why others including himself bothered trying to paint, he expressed an enduring thought: painting has been done, and Velázquez did it.

The feeling of Velázquez is light, sparkling, swift, and easy. He is never "intense." Unprolific, he worked and reworked his pictures at length, as is attested by many pentimenti; but you rarely catch him sweating. He is profound, but in ways that seem to say, "Isn't everybody?" His truth has a self-evidence, as if you always knew it. It isn't a matter of "knowing about" something—the kingliness of Philip IV, say. You just know. Or, because this is painting, you just see.

Velázquez is Mr. Cool. If he were a rock singer, he would be Roy Orbison. He respects all possible sentiments but is never sentimental; he is alert to every manner of charm without being charmed himself. He is somehow detached in the very act of being engaged, staying out of the way of what he avidly fixes on. Compared with him, all other painters "seem completely like fakers," as Manet said, too.

The toughest thing about getting Velázquez is believing your eyes, accepting that such lucidity is really happening. That's why it's necessary to see many Velázquez paintings, so the easy, gliding truth of him can break down the suspicion that when you look at art, you're bound to miss something. The only way to miss Velázquez is to be blind.

Those of us who know the Prado have an unfair edge at the Met's Velázquez show (October 3, 1989–January 7, 1990), because we can view it in light of what's lacking: *Las Meninas*, of course, but also a long list of the artist's greatest works (including London's *Rokeby Venus* and Rome's portrait of Pope Innocent X). Maybe a dozen of the thirty-eight pictures in this startlingly brief compendium ("When did they start putting the gift shop in the middle of the show?" an unprepared friend said as she reached the end) are top drawer. The rest are early, odd, in bad shape, or quite grand but gloomed by the constrictions of their commissions (not that Velázquez couldn't handle them, but you sense his oppression). I'm ready to believe Met director Philippe de Montebello when he crows in the catalogue that this show realizes what seemed "an unrealizable dream"—but when I have unrealizable dreams they tend to be, you know, fabulous.

The idea of "reviewing" Velázquez is silly. What follows are notes toward an opinionated user's manual for this show.

Remember in the first room that you are seeing a very young provincial show-off from Seville out to make it at court in Madrid (where painters had roughly the social standing of carpenters). The coups of verisimilitude in *Old Woman Cooking Eggs* and *The Water Seller* are staggering, but space in the pictures is hopelessly tortured. Already there is philosophical and poetic, self-delighting brilliance. If you want to tell yourself intricate stories about the meaning of the old-woman picture, do. Velázquez approves.

There is something painful in the second room about the big Philip IV portraits and even the terrific *Forge of Vulcan*, because Velázquez was laboring to prove himself as a reliable propagandist, in the first case, and as an artist up to speed with Italian academic fashion, in the second. High status seems to have been his main goal, leading him to all but quit painting in his later, best, years for the more prestigious jobs of court decorator, art advisor, and household manager.

The show's first clean hit is *Prince Baltasar Carlos with a Dwarf*: the sixteen-month-old prince posed regally in military garb (poor kid) while a little person shuffles past with a rattle and an apple (parody of scepter and orb). Taking sides in an art historian's argument, I believe (with Julian Gallego in the catalogue) that this is a "picture-within-a-picture": the dwarf is painted in front of a painting of the royal tot. The textures are an express elevator to heaven.

As you move along, zero in on the snapshot-modern *Riding School* picture, which narrates the dynastic hopes, power relations (centering on unsavory Count-Duke Olivares), moral values, and lifestyle of Philip IV's reign as they pertained one crisp, cool morning. This isn't an art work, it's a world. Note also the easily missed, small, unfinished *Needlewoman*, a great poem about work: she is caught in skilled action and a concentration so transfiguring it's scary.

I think the show's two perfect works are the Met's own *Juan de Pareja* and the portrait of the dwarf Francisco Lezcano. The slackly arrogant Lezcano is often described as "witless," but ask yourself this: what if he's intelligent? The answer is that he is then the most dangerous little creep you ever saw—Velázquez gazing calmly into the attitude of a killer.

In the last room, with things from the period of *Las Meninas*, there is supreme artistry (brushwork in dizzying interplay with color) but no supreme art. The Met's poster child *Infanta Margarita* is gorgeous (salmon pink dress, blue-green drapes) but feels like a rushed job. (In *Las Meninas*, the same infanta tosses out a frank little-girl gaze that knocks two eye-shaped holes in your heart.)

Overall, in the mature work, register the theatricality that includes you in its dynamic. The baroque space is basically cylindrical, swooping around behind figures and out into your space. Time lives in the cylinder, as everything turns. When the eyes of a subject meet yours, they will just have done so: turning toward you, click. (A half-dozen sets of eyes do it in *Las Meninas*, and, jet-lagged my first time in Madrid, I became obsessed with catching the figures turning—looking at them faster than they looked at me. I hallucinated, hearing the rustle of a *menina*'s crinolines. I suppose I should be glad I didn't see her move.)

As with hallucinations, you know that what you see in a great Velázquez isn't real because it is too real—in terms not only of optical illusion but of virtual feel and smell, and the tingle when someone you can imagine being in love with looks at you. He knew how to keep his distance, did the courtly Velázquez, and the keeping of distance is excruciatingly palpable in his official portraits, but when it was okay to home in, the doors of any soul were going to spring open, no problem.

Almost nothing is known of his personal life. He did well in court for his family, nepotistically. He fathered an illegitimate child in Rome (living there in middle age for nearly three years on an art-collecting mission, fending off the king's demands that he come home). He performed in women's clothes in a court burlesque. Aside from the sensual *Rokeby Venus*, done for a patron who was a notorious libertine, he painted at least three other female nudes, now lost. I figure that his talent for decorum was an expedient check on a major wild streak.

He got away with the feat, rare in Spain, of painting very little religious art—unlike his exact contemporary Zurbarán. (Imagine being as great a painter as Zurbarán and knowing you'll always be the second-best painter in town.) Why do the many masteries in the huge *Saint Anthony Abbot and Saint Paul the Hermit* add up to less than the sum of their parts? I think Velázquez did the picture sullenly, not necessarily because he was unreligious but because he was bound to nurse a grudge against any reality that insisted on being invisible.

My favorite explanation of nearly naked, crestfallen *Mars* (proposed in Jonathan Brown's 1986 book on Velázquez) is that it pictures the god as an adulterer, caught with Venus by Vulcan. Be alert in all Velázquez's art for a strain of down and dirty, slightly cruel, also strangely redemptive comedy that he projects forward from Cervantes to Goya. Velázquez as archetypal Spaniard: you can count on his humanity, but if you take his sympathy for granted you're in danger.

We can use Velázquez for remembering how to love life: directly, with an attentiveness and a responsiveness that drive thoughts of "love" and "life" out of our heads and consume us like a clear flame. How to make inanimate matter, such as paint, dance attendance—as if the flame painted the pictures—is a secret probably lost forever, but we won't be wrong in taking it as a compliment. One of our kind did that.

October 18, 1989

Baselitz and Kippenberger

Germany charges toward reunification like a rhinoceros with pinwheel eyes, and people wonder nervously what it portends. I don't wonder so much. As an art critic during the past decade, when German art did to American art what the Mercedes did to the Cadillac—outclassed it—I've experienced regularly in symbolic ways what the world may presently be up against for real: a culture marked by obdurate will-power, an affinity for extremes, and a tendency to be fantastically good at what it does.

By my own and many other people's lights, the four best artists to have emerged internationally since the 1970s—Sigmar Polke, Gerhard Richter, and Anselm Kiefer, along with the late Joseph Beuys—are German, and German talents teem at every more modest level. The art culture that has incubated so much creativity breaks the traditional mold for art-intensive nations in being wildly decentralized, with no capital like New York but instead a practically medieval array of competing city-states. What will it be like when, pretty soon, German money, power, and culture convene in the coming new Berlin?

Pending the testimony of events, German art may yield insights into the present character of a country many of whose past characteristics have been, shall we say, nerve-racking. Using art for national stereotyping is rightly deplored, of course, but present fascination makes it irresistible in the case of Germany, especially since one upshot is bound to be admiration. And it often does pay off in crude but fairly apt rules of thumb—not so much with major artists, who transform categories, as with relatively limited ones like Georg Baselitz and Martin Kippenberger.

How German are the old gladiator Baselitz, he of the upside-down figures and growling painterly panache, and the youngish Kippenberger, a Cologne multimedia rascal? Oh boy, very. Like unblended scotch, each concentrates a particular essence of the complicated national elixir. The Red Baron of art, Baselitz displays a strain of stunningly arrogant self-assertion, wielding his brush like a combination scepter and club. Kippenberger's is an arrogance devolved to a pitch of anarchic brattiness. They share the abetting benefit of a culture that, radically unlike its anti-intellectual and antipoetic U.S. counterpart, tends to vest the role of the artist with priestly prestige and jesterlike license.

The eleven *Hero Paintings* from the mid-1960s by Baselitz in his present show (Michael Werner Gallery, March 1990) are masterpieces, actually: the finest things he has done, in my view, and Ur-works in the formation of a self-confident, daredevil West German art from ruins of the war and banalities of the "economic miracle." From a series of twenty-some paintings and many etchings on the same theme, they have a cumulative force amplified by our knowledge of what went before them and of what has come since. In an ideal museum of contemporary German art, they would merit a primary room of their own.

Baselitz's hero figures are hulking and virile but also vulnerable and wounded young men wandering or standing transfixed in blasted landscapes (blessedly right side up, from a time before the artist decided to advertise his own heroism by literally overturning his subjects). In browns, liverish reds, and hospital greens, painted with urgent, pawing strokes on canvases about five feet high, they practically sweat hypermasculinity. Their shameless fusion of power and innocence is like Rambo *avant la lettre*: poor big bullyboys, suffering Siegfrieds. What's astounding is that so much sensitivity can be wedded to subjects so inherently brutal, with a rhapsodic, sharply disquieting final fillip of rendered gazes that, as noted in the show's catalogue by Günther Gercken, are "ecstatic, prophetic, faraway, into the future."

If Baselitz's heroes could foresee in that future the likes of Martin Kippenberger, they'd be grumpy. An artistic Beastie Boy, Kippenberger makes a fetish of bad jokes and bad behavior with gracelessness so thoroughgoing it's almost, but not really, another kind of elegance. He is no Sigmar Polke, whose high-handed mockeries of painting, with trashy materials and content, were basic to painting's reinvigoration throughout Europe and the U.S. in the 1980s. He is even no Walter Dahn or Jiri Georg Dokoupil, predecessors in a Cologne tradition of art as adult delinquency who seem genteel compared with him. Is there anything an artist can't get away with over there? Not, it seems, if the artist is sufficiently wholehearted in embodying some archetypal pattern: in this case, the snotty nihilist.

Kippenberger's show (Metro Pictures, April 1990) of sculptural objects and drawings is a geyser of ideas, most of them dumb. The cartoony drawings on various hotel stationeries, in a show-off variety of styles, tacitly brag of a touring-rock-star lifestyle. (With over forty one-man shows in the last five years, according to his gallery bio, this artist does get around). The objects unite dozens of found and formed materials to deliver a similarly self-absorbed message: roughly, "I'm-Martin-Kippenberger-and-you're-not." They are internationally hip in their neo-conceptual, neo-postminimalist aesthetics—tipped off by deliberate mismatches of ideas and appearances—while strictly German in their clunking effrontery.

The fun, if that's what it is, starts at the door, framed by the blue curtain that demarcates business class on European airliners. (The gallery is "business class." Get it?) Among the twelve assembled pieces that ensue is a life-size jerry-built gondola supporting huge crates labeled "SOZIAL" and "PASTA." (You don't get it? Me neither.) *Love Affair without Racism* confronts a six-foot column of inflated black rubber with another of pink cinder blocks on wheels. (I think I'd rather not get this one.) Then, just when you're thinking "Martin, stand in the corner and shame on you," there's a piece so named: a clothed wooden figure with a plastic head standing downcast in a corner.

The simple existence, never mind the quality, of Baselitz and Kippenberger makes me aware of the relative pinched narrowness of American art culture, whose professional-mindedness would pretty much rule out of serious consideration both the loftiness of the older artist and the insolence of the younger. Any art fan must envy a country that actively nurtures such extremes of creative possibility (with the payoff of occasional synthesizing geniuses on the order of Polke, Richter, and Kiefer). However, any citizen might also reflect, remembering Plato, that a republic in which the poetic carries so much authority may be asking for trouble.

Keep an eye on Germany.

April 11, 1990

BIBLIOGRAPHY OF PETER SCHJELDAHL'S WRITINGS ON ART

Newspapers

Village Voice

"A New Domain" (June 30, 1966): 11.
  Reuben Nakian retrospective, Museum of Modern Art.
"Summering" (July 21, 1966): 11–12.
  Gauguin and the Decorative Style exhibition, Solomon R. Guggenheim Museum; The Heritage of French Poster Art exhibition, IBM Gallery of Science and Art; Graham Gallery; Marlborough-Gerson Gallery; Noah Goldowsky Gallery; Cliff Joseph, Aspects Gallery.
"Frank O'Hara: 'He Made Things & People Sacred'" (August 11, 1966): 11–12, 24.
"Another Season" (September 15, 1966): 13.
"Starting Over" (September 22, 1966): 14–15.
  Howard Kanowitz, Jewish Museum.
"Unfashionable and Unfettered" (October 6, 1966): 13.
  Tenth Street Now exhibition.
"Erotic And/Or Art" (October 13, 1966): 13.
  Erotic Art '66 exhibition, Sidney Janis Gallery; new Whitney Museum of American Art building.
"Riffing Out on Art's Grave" (November 3, 1966): 16.
  Les Levine, Fischbach Gallery.
"Taking Up the Slack" (November 10, 1966): 14.
  Michael Steiner, Dwan Gallery; Donald Kaufman, Richard L. Feigen and Co.; Darby Bannard, Tibor de Nagy Gallery; Jules Olitski, Andre Emmerich Gallery; Lucas Samaras, Pace Gallery; Robert Nelson, Banfer Gallery.
"Appraising Passions" (January 7, 1981): 67.
"Different Strokes" (January 21–27, 1981): 70.
  George McNeil, Gruenebaum Gallery; 1981 Painting Invitational exhibition, Oscarsson Hood Gallery; Gary Stephan, Mary Boone Gallery.

"An Inclement Critic" (February 4, 1981): 77.
> Clement Greenberg.

"Stock Options" (February 18–24, 1981): 73.
> Nineteen Artists—Emergent Americans: 1981 Exxon National Exhibition, Solomon R. Guggenheim Museum.

"New Wave, No Fun" (March 4–10, 1981): 69.
> New York/New Wave exhibition, P.S. 1, Long Island City, New York.

"Hallelujah Trail" (March 18–24, 1981): 77.
> 1981 Biennial exhibition, Whitney Museum of American Art.

"Drawing Conclusions" (April 1–7, 1981): 83–84.
> Old master drawings, Pierpont Morgan Library; Leonardo da Vinci drawings, Metropolitan Museum of Art; New Works on Paper exhibition, Museum of Modern Art.

"Opposites Attract" (April 15–21, 1981): 83.
> Nancy Spero, A.I.R. Gallery; Robert Bechtle, O.K. Harris Works of Art.

"Bravery in Action" (April 29–May 5, 1981): 81.
> Julian Schnabel, Leo Castelli Gallery and Mary Boone Gallery; Susan Rothenberg, Willard Gallery.

"The Great Gorky" (May 13–19, 1981): 101.
> Arshile Gorky retrospective, Solomon R. Guggenheim Museum.

"Is There Life before Photography?" (May 27–June 2, 1981): 83.
> Before Photography exhibition, Museum of Modern Art.

"L.A. Demystified! Art and Life in the Eternal Present" (June 3–9, 1981): 1, 32–38.

"A Russian Revolution" (June 17–23, 1981): 75.
> New Trends in Russian Unofficial Art, 1970–1980 exhibition, Museum of Soviet Unofficial Art, Jersey City, New Jersey.

"Affairs of the Heat" (July 1–7, 1981): 77.
> The Frick Collection; Lovers of Manhattan Summers (LOMS) contest.

"American Nightmares" (August 5–11, 1981): 68.
> Disney Animation and Animators exhibition, Whitney Museum of American Art.

"Endless Love" (August 12–16, 1981): 66.
> LOMS winner.

"Anxiety as a Rallying Cry" (September 16–22, 1981): 86.
> Represent/Representation/Representative exhibition, Brooke Alexander; The Anxious Figure exhibition, Semaphore Gallery.

"The Culture Brokers" (September 30–October 6, 1981): 78.
> For Love and Money: Dealers Choose exhibition, Pratt Manhattan Center Gallery.

"Artistic Control" (October 14–20, 1981): 100.

Richard Serra's *Tilted Arc*, Javits Federal Building.

"Notes for Eight Columns I'm Not Writing This Week" (October 28–November 3, 1981): 80.

Miscellanea.

"Realism on the Comeback Trail" (November 11–17, 1981): 77.

Contemporary American Realism since 1960 exhibition, Pennsylvania Academy of the Fine Arts, Philadelphia.

"Crimes of the Heartland" (November 25–December 1, 1981): 88.

H. C. Westermann memorial exhibition, Xavier Fourcade Gallery.

"But Seriously, Folks" (December 9–15, 1981): 102.

Not Just for Laughs: The Art of Subversion exhibition, New Museum of Contemporary Art.

"California Goes to Pot" (December 23–29, 1981): 85.

Ceramic Sculpture: Six Artists exhibition, Whitney Museum of American Art.

"Second Thoughts" (January 6–12, 1982): 70.

Re: previous articles on Serra's *Tilted Arc* and "The Culture Brokers."

"Only Connect" (January 20–26, 1982): 72.

Bruce Nauman exhibitions, Leo Castelli Gallery and Sperone Westwater Fischer.

" 'Les Drippings' in Paris: The Jackson Pollock Retrospective" (February 10–16, 1982): 94.

Jackson Pollock retrospective, Musée national d'art moderne, Centre Georges Pompidou, Paris.

"The Ardor of Ambition" (February 23, 1982): 79.

Julian Schnabel retrospective, Stedelijk Museum, Amsterdam.

"Mind over Matter" (March 9, 1982): 79.

Critical Perspectives exhibition, P.S. 1, Long Island City, New York.

"David Salle's Objects of Disaffection" (March 23, 1982): 84.

David Salle, Mary Boone I Gallery, Mary Boone II Gallery, and Leo Castelli Gallery.

"Why New French Art Is Lousy" (April 6, 1982): 37–39.

"Delights by de Kooning" (April 13, 1982): 79.

Willem de Kooning, Xavier Fourcade Gallery.

"Treachery on the High Cs" (April 27, 1982): 96.

Italian Art Now. An American Perspective: 1982 Exxon International exhibition, Solomon R. Guggenheim Museum.

"Curator Cure Thyself" (May 18, 1982): 87.

Focus on the Figure: Twenty Years exhibition, Whitney Museum of American Art; The Anxious Edge exhibition, Walker Art Center, Minneapolis.

"A Nose for the Abyss" (June 1982): 1, 7–8, Literary Supplement. Review of

The Writings of Robert Smithson, edited by Nancy Holt. New York: New York University Press, 1979.

"Scott Burton Chairs the Discussion" (June 1, 1982): 86.
   Vintage Modern and Recent Burton exhibition, Max Protetch Gallery.

"Situations" (June 22, 1984): 105.
   Site-specific sculpture at Wave Hill, Bronx.

"King Curator" (July 20, 1982): 73.
   Re: Rudi Fuchs's curatorial biases, Documenta 7 exhibition, Kassel, West Germany.

"The Germans' Marshall Arts" (August 3, 1982): 66.
   Documenta 7 exhibition, Kassel, West Germany.

"About Reverence" (August 31, 1982): 73.
   The Reverend Howard Finster, New Museum of Contemporary Art.

"Space Invaders" (September 14, 1982): 74.
   The UFO Show, Queens Museum.

"Northern Cross" (September 28, 1982): 100.
   Scandinavia Today multiple exhibitions; Asger Jorn and Oyvind Fahlstrom retrospectives and Sleeping Beauty and Art Now exhibitions, Solomon R. Guggenheim Museum.

"Clemente to Marden to Kiefer" (October 12, 1982): 83.
   Re: Art and baseball.

"Red Planet" (October 26, 1982): 96.
   Leon Golub, Susan Caldwell Gallery.

"So Long, Friends" (October 26, 1982): 97.

New York Times

"Survival on Tenth Street" (November 19, 1967): D33.
   Re: Decline of small galleries on Tenth Street.

"Marilyn: Still Being Exploited?" (December 17, 1967): D40.
   Homage to Marilyn Monroe exhibition, Sidney Janis Gallery.

"By Lonely, Difficult Evolutions . . ." (February 18, 1968): D27.
   Larry Zox, Kornblee Gallery; Sol LeWitt, Dwan Gallery; Lowell Nesbitt, Stable Gallery.

"Simplifications, Complications, Mystifications" (April 7, 1968): D23.
   Robert Goodnough, Tibor de Nagy Gallery; Howard Mehring, Sachs Gallery; Ray Johnson, Richard L. Feigen and Co.

"Stripes, Paper Bags, and TV" (May 5, 1968): D29.
   Morris Louis, Andre Emmerich Gallery; Alex Hay, Kornblee Gallery; Nam June Paik, Galeria Bonino.

"Stylistic Somersaults" (November 17, 1968): D41.
  Larry Poons, Leo Castelli Gallery; Edward Avedesian, Elkon Gallery.
"The Vicissitudes of Sculpture" (February 9, 1969): D33.
  John Chamberlain, Leo Castelli Gallery; Anne Truitt, Andre Emmerich
  Gallery; Duayne Hatchett, Royal Marks Gallery.
"For Thompson, a Trimuph Too Late" (February 23, 1969): D31–32.
  Bob Thompson retrospective, New School for Social Research.
"The Flowering of the Super-Real" (March 2, 1969): D31, 33.
  Howard Kanowitz, Waddell Gallery; Malcolm Morley, Kornblee Gal-
  lery; Richard Estes, Alan Stone Gallery.
"Enter Demons and Angels" (March 23, 1969): D27, 30.
  Willem de Kooning, Museum of Modern Art and M. Knoedler & Co.;
  Frederick Kiesler, Howard Wise Gallery.
"A Triumph Rather Than a Threat" (April 27, 1969): D33, 35.
  Afro-American Artists: Since 1950 exhibition, Museum of the Borough
  of Brooklyn at Brooklyn College.
"Red Grooms: He Dares to Make Art That Is Fun" (June 15, 1969): D25.
"'Boxie Was a Cutie Was a Sweetie Was a Blondie Was a Pootsy'" (August
  24, 1969): D23.
  Lucas Samaras, Museum of Modern Art and Pace Gallery.
"Alive with the Strength and Variety of Its Passions" (August 31, 1969): D10.
  Harlem Artists '69, Studio Museum in Harlem.
"Dubuffet: Still Doing Work That Ranks among His Best" (November 30,
  1969): D23.
  Jean Dubuffet, Richard L. Feigen and Co. and Pace Gallery.
"To Experience Art As It Is Evolving" (December 28, 1969): D29.
  Paula Cooper Gallery; O. K. Harris Works of Art; Richard L. Feigen
  and Co.
"Can the How Become the What?" (January 11, 1970): D25.
  Hans Hoffmann, Andre Emmerich Gallery.
"The Audacity of Rafael Ferrer" (January 25, 1970): D27.
  Rafael Ferrer, Leo Castelli Warehouse; Tony DeLap, Elkon Gallery.
"After Nothing Less Than Emotional Profundity" (February 8, 1970): D23.
  Theodore Stamos, Andre Emmerich Gallery.
"Breadworks as Earthworks" (February 22, 1970): D27.
  Peter Hutchinson, John Gibson; Brice Marden and Bob Duran, Bykert
  Gallery.
"Moholy-Nagy: Champion of a Doomed Heroic Cause" (March 8, 1970):
  D21.
  László Moholy-Nagy retrospective, Solomon R. Guggenheim Museum.
"A World of Raucous, Challenging Images" (March 22, 1970): D29.

Rhino Horn exhibition, New School for Social Research.

"Designed for Use Rather Than Delectation" (April 5, 1970): D19.

Tantric drawings and stone "lingams" from the Alexandra Marc collection, Jewish Museum and Richard L. Feigen and Co.

"Pop Goes the Playmate's Sister" (April 19, 1970): D21.

Tom Wesselmann, Sidney Janis Gallery.

"A Dead Style? Bluhm Seems Not to Have Heard" (May 3, 1970): D22.

Norman Bluhm, Martha Jackson Gallery.

"Art: Anything the Artist Says It Is?" (May 17, 1970): D21.

Bill Bollinger environment, 601 West Twenty-sixth Street.

"A Trip with Rosenquist" (May 31, 1970): D17.

James Rosenquist's Horizon, Home Sweet Home exhibition, Leo Castelli Gallery.

"An Unabashedly Joyful Eroticism" (June 14, 1970): D19, 20.

Reuben Nakian, Egan Gallery; H. C. Westermann, Allan Frumkin Gallery.

"Three for the Mini-Show" (July 19, 1970): D17.

Pop Art Prints, Drawings & Multiples; Popular Mechanics in Printmaking; and Preliminary Drawings exhibitions, Museum of Modern Art.

"Don't Just Stand There—Read!" (August 19, 1970): D17.

Conceptual Art and Conceptual Aspects exhibition, New York Cultural Center.

"Is the Art World Heading for a Nervous Breakdown?" (August 23, 1970): D22, 24.

"Barnett Newman: 'Aspiration toward the Sublime'" (September 6, 1970): D21.

Barnett Newman memorial exhibition, Museum of Modern Art.

"From Creative Plumbing to Lyrical Abstraction" (September 20, 1970): D29.

John Seery, Andre Emmerich Gallery; Victor Huggins, Bertha Schaefer Gallery.

"A Sculpture to Command Public Places" (October 4, 1970): D23.

James Rosati, Marlborough-Gerson Gallery; Lila Katzen, Max Hutchinson Gallery; John Freeman, Reese Palley Gallery.

"High Priest of Minimal" (October 18, 1970): D23.

Carl Andre, Solomon R. Guggenheim Museum.

"Sculpture Found in a Rag Factory" (November 1, 1970): D23.

Alan Saret, Rafael Ferrer, Barry Le Va, Richard Van Buren, Gordon Matta, George Tracas, Jeffrey Lew, and Bill Beckly, 112 Greene Street.

"What's for an Encore?" (November 15, 1970): D25.

Claes Oldenburg retrospective, Museum of Modern Art.

"Like Nudes Reflected in a Funhouse Mirror" (November 29, 1970): D25.

Enrique Castro-Cid, Richard L. Feigen and Co.; Gary Wojcik, Kornblee Gallery; Larry Bennet, French & Company.

"Ernst: Brainstorms of Wit and Fantasy" (December 13, 1970): D25.

Max Ernst, Byron Gallery; Man Ray, Goldowsky Gallery.

"Larry Rivers: 'Achingly Erratic'" (December 27, 1970): D25.

Larry Rivers, Marlborough-Gerson Gallery.

"'An Artist Who Can Make a Corkscrew His Own'" (January 24, 1971): D21.

William Copley, Iolas Gallery.

"The Ice Palace That Robert Ryman Built" (February 7, 1971): D21.

Robert Ryman, Fischbach Gallery and Dwan Gallery.

"William Baziotes: On the Way to Obscurity?" (February 21, 1971): D19–20.

William Baziotes and Adolph Gottlieb, Marlborough-Gerson Gallery.

"Artist with an Excess of Elegance?" (March 7, 1971): D21.

Richard Smith, Richard L. Feigen and Co.; Harvey Quaytman, Paula Cooper Gallery.

"The Artist for Whom 'Style' Is All" (March 21, 1971): D21.

Roy Lichtenstein, Leo Castelli Gallery.

"Fahlstrom's 'Games'" (April 4, 1971): 21.

Oyvind Fahlstrom, Sidney Janis Gallery.

"Well, It's a Heck of a Long Way from 'Marcus Welby'" (April 11, 1971): D21.

National Center for Experimental Television, San Francisco.

"The New Painting: Return to the Sublime?" (April 18, 1971): D23.

Phillip Wofford, David Whitney Gallery; Herbert Schiffrin, Paley & Lowe Gallery; Natvar Bhavsar, Max Hutchinson Gallery.

"Finding Alex Hay: 'Gentle Maverick'" (May 2, 1971): D21.

Alex Hay, New York Cultural Center.

"The Italian Way: It's Beautiful, but Is It Likable?" (May 16, 1971): D19.

Gio Pomodoro, Martha Jackson Gallery.

"The 'Lost Generation' of the Avant-Garde" (May 30, 1971): D19.

Younger Abstract Expressionists of the Fifties exhibition, Museum of Modern Art.

"A Coming of Age in Africa" (June 13, 1971): D23.

Contemporary Art of Oshogbo, Nigeria, exhibition, Loeb Student Center, New York University.

"It's Quirky, It's Literal, It's Literate" (June 27, 1971): D23.

The British Avant-Garde exhibition, New York Cultural Center.

"Still a Man's World—for the Woman Artist" (June 8, 1971): D17.

Pride and Prejudice: A Woman's Show, Brooklyn Museum.

"What Artists' Models Cause Traffic Jams?" (August 22, 1971): D12.

Art around the Automobile exhibition, Emily Lowe Gallery, Hofstra University.

"An Artist Who Was Wild about Art" (September 5, 1971): D17.
Manfred Schwartz, Whitney Museum of American Art.

"My Children Don't Want a New Father, They Want a Pizza" (September 19, 1971): D23.
Mini shows, Westbeth.

"Sculptors Make It Big down in Soho" (October 3, 1971): D23.
Sol LeWitt, John Weber Gallery; Lynda Benglis, Paula Cooper Gallery; Salvatore Romano, Max Hutchinson Gallery; Mike Bakaty, Paley & Lowe Gallery.

"And Now a 'Teddy' for the Artist" (October 17, 1971): D25.
Theodoron Awards exhibition, Solomon R. Guggenheim Museum.

"Rauschenberg Just Won't Be Boxed In" (October 31, 1971): D21.
Robert Rauschenberg, Leo Castelli Gallery.

"The Subject Is His Own Uneasiness" (November 14, 1971): D23.
Allan D'Arcangelo, Marlborough Gallery.

"Art That Owes Nothing to 'Nature,' but Everything to Man Himself" (November 28, 1971): D21.
Josef Albers retrospective, Metropolitan Museum of Art; Piet Mondrian, and Robert Mangold retrospectives, Solomon R. Guggenheim Museum.

"Through the Window and into the Woods" (December 12, 1971): D27.
Lois Dodd, Green Mountain Gallery; Gary Hudson, Reese Palley Gallery.

"From Stuffed Camels to Clam Shells" (December 26, 1971): D25.
Nancy Graves, Museum of Modern Art.

"If Not Timeless, It's at Least Open-Ended" (January 23, 1972): D21.
Ronald Bladen, Fischbach Gallery.

"Down Memory Lane to the Fifties" (February 6, 1972): D23.
Abstract Expressionism: The First and Second Generations exhibition, Albright-Knox Art Gallery, Buffalo, New York.

"Surrealist Fernando Botero Deflates the Effete and the Elite" (February 20, 1972): D19.
Fernando Botero, Marlborough Gallery.

"Two on the Move in a 'Movement-Less' Time" (March 19, 1972): D21.
David Dao, Reese Palley Gallery; Michael Goldberg, Paley & Lowe Gallery.

"Nostalgia for a Native Past" (March 26, 1972): D23.
Stewart F. Gregory Collection exhibition, Museum of American Folk Art.

"There's No Touchdown, but Chalk Up Plenty of Yardage" (April 2, 1972): D19.

Susan Crile, Kornblee Gallery; Wayne Thiebaud, Alan Stone Gallery.
"Blake: A Publicist for the Apocalypse" (April 16, 1972): D19.
William Blake, Yale University Art Gallery, New Haven, Connecticut.
"Joan Mitchell: To Obscurity and Back" (April 30, 1972): D23.
Joan Mitchell, Everson Museum of Art, Syracuse, New York.
"Robert Morris: Maxi of the Minimals" (May 7, 1972): D23.
Robert Morris, Leo Castelli Galleries.
"Jo Baer: Playing on the Senses" (May 14, 1972): D23.
Jo Baer, LoGiudice Gallery; Alma W. Thomas, Whitney Museum of American Art.
"L.A. Art? 'Interesting—but Painful'" (May 21, 1972): D25.
Los Angeles '72 exhibition, Sidney Janis Gallery; Ed Ruscha, Multiples.
"Ever Intimidated by a Painting?" (May 28, 1972): D17.
Alfred Jensen, Pace Gallery.
"The Malaise That Afflicts SoHo's Avant-Garde Galleries" (June 11, 1972): D21.
420 West Broadway: Leo Castelli Gallery, John Weber Gallery, Andre Emmerich Gallery, and Sonnabend Gallery.
"Two 'Projects' That Project" (June 25, 1972): D19.
David Novros, Richard Tuttle "Projects" exhibitions, Museum of Modern Art.
"The Return of the 'Native'" (July 9, 1972): D15.
Native North American Art exhibition, Brooklyn Museum.
"The Games M. C. Escher Plays" (July 23, 1972): D15.
M. C. Escher, La Boetie, Inc., and National Gallery of Art, Washington, D.C.
"Schwitters: The Man behind the 'Merz'" (August 6, 1972): D17.
Kurt Schwitters, Museum of Modern Art.
"Now and Then It's Nice Just to Look at Things" (August 20, 1972): D19.
Outsized Drawings and Multiples exhibition, Loeb Student Center, New York University.
"New Art: We May Dislike It, but Can We Reject It?" (September 10, 1972): D33.
Gilbert & George, Sonnabend Gallery.
"The Changing Gallery Scene: Return of the Co-Op" (September 17, 1972): D23.
Rosemary Wright and Janet Alling, 55 Mercer.
"Take Wheels and Feathers and Fishing Lines . . ." (October 1, 1972): D25.
Keith Hollingworth, Paula Cooper Gallery; Richard Calabro, Max Hutchinson Gallery.
"Larry Poons—'A Sort of Soap Opera Career'" (October 15, 1972): D23.
Larry Poons, Lawrence Rubin Gallery.

"When Modern Art Was Alien—and Shocking" (October 29, 1972): 25.
Philadelphia in New York exhibition, Museum of Modern Art.

"From Outdoor Nudes to Just Outdoors" (November 12, 1972): D25.
Neil Welliver, John Bernard Myers Gallery.

"Very Well Done—and Very Boring" (November 19, 1972): 21.
James Brooks, Martha Jackson Gallery; Wolf Kahn, Grace Borgenicht Gallery.

"The Content? Information" (November 26, 1972): D17.
Michael Snow, Center for International Relations.

"Dubuffet: Upholding Alone the Honor of French Art?" (December 10, 1972): D27.
Jean Dubuffet retrospective, Museum of Modern Art.

"Something Funny's Going On" (January 7, 1973): D23.
William King, Terry Dintenfass; Jon Wesley, Elkon Gallery.

"Frank Stella: The Best—and Last—of His Breed?" (January 21, 1973): D23.
Frank Stella, Leo Castelli Gallery.

"A Shot in the Arm for Realism?" (February 18, 1973): D25.
Jack Beal, Allan Frumkin Gallery.

"They Please—but Do They Satisfy?" (March 4, 1973): D25.
Jim Dine, Sonnabend Gallery.

"How to Explain the Flood of Realist Art?" (March 18, 1973): D23.
John Salt, O. K. Harris Works of Art; Joseph Fiore, Green Mountain Gallery.

"Let's Be Flexible, but Let's Not Be Flabby" (April 1, 1973): D23.
Soft as Art exhibition, New York Cultural Center.

"Time to Return to Roots We Disowned Long Ago?" (April 15, 1973): D21.
Winslow Homer retrospective, Whitney Museum of American Art.

"One Takes Away, the Other Piles It On" (April 29, 1973): D21.
Carl Andre and Robert Whitman "Projects" series exhibitions, Museum of Modern Art.

"Joan Snyder—the Energy and Surprise Have Gone" (May 13, 1973): D23.
Joan Snyder, Paley & Lowe, Inc.

"Marisol: A Humorist in Three Dimensions" (May 27, 1973): D19.
Marisol Escobar, Sidney Janis Gallery.

"The Diffident Avant-Garde Has an Outpost in the Sky" (June 10, 1973): D23.
James Bishop, Clocktower building, Institute for Art and Urban Resources.

"Still on the Side of the Boy Scouts—but Why Not?" (June 24, 1973): D23.
Norman Rockwell retrospective, Bernard Danenberg Gallery.

"Beyond Those Giddy Sixties" (July 8, 1973): D21.

Robert Fried, Brooklyn Museum; group show, O. K. Harris Works of Art.

"Poe—with a French Accent" (July 22, 1973): D15.

Homage to Edgar Allen Poe exhibition, Metropolitan Museum of Art.

"Surprise from Puerto Rico" (August 5, 1973): D25.

The Art Heritage of Puerto Rico exhibition, Metropolitan Museum of Art.

"Robert Smithson: He Made Fantasies as Real as Mountains" (August 12, 1973): D21.

Robert Smithson memorial.

"At Fifty-one, He's London's Official Enfant Terrible" (September 30, 1973): D23.

Richard Hamilton, Solomon R. Guggenheim Museum.

"What Others Call Junk, He Transforms into Art" (October 28, 1973): D25.

Arman, John Gibson Gallery.

"The Flowering of Haiti" (November 25, 1973): D23.

Haitian Painting: The Naive Tradition exhibition, New York Cultural Center.

"Early Success: Can It Be Lived Down?" (December 9, 1973): D27.

John Chamberlain, Leo Castelli Gallery and Dag Hammarskjöld Plaza.

"Utterly Lifelike, Yes, but Is It Anything More?" (December 23, 1973): D23.

John DeAndrea, O. K. Harris Works of Art.

"She's Everybody's Favorite Grandma" (January 6, 1974): D21.

Grandma [Anna Mary Robertson] Moses, Hammer Galleries.

"A Journey Well Worth Making" (January 20, 1974): D23.

Alice Adams, Julius Tobias, and Susan Smith, 55 Mercer.

"Just This Side of Non-Existence" (February 3, 1974): D25.

Barry Flanagan, Museum of Modern Art.

"What the Flesh on Real Humans Looks Like" (February 11, 1974): D27.

Philip Pearlstein, Finch College Museum and Allan Frumkin Gallery.

"Of Primitive and Enigmatic Mysteries" (April 14, 1974): D23.

Ree Morton, Whitney Museum of American Art; Stephen Porter, Betty Parsons Gallery.

"Nicholson Has Turned 80, and Is Better Than Ever" (April 28, 1974): D19.

Ben Nicholson, Andre Emmerich Gallery.

"Too Easy to Be Art?" (May 12, 1974): D23.

Robert Cottingham and Robert Bechtle, O. K. Harris Works of Art.

"Updated Data on the Adventure of Being Human" (May 26, 1974): D17.

Lynda Benglis, Paula Cooper Gallery.

"The Playful Improvisation of West Coast Ceramic Art" (June 9, 1974): D19.

Clay exhibition, Whitney Museum Downtown Branch.

337

"Picture Postcards since the 1880's: Rich and Potent Folk Art" (July 7, 1974): D19.
  Wish You Were Here exhibition, New York Cultural Center.
"Non-Event at the Museum of Modern Art: Graphics Show on a Specious Theme" (July 21, 1974): D19.
  Printed in Germany, 1923; and Printed, Cut, Folded, and Torn exhibitions, Museum of Modern Art.
"Drawings of Georges Lacombe: The Inward Vision of a 'Minor' Artist" (August 4, 1974): D19.
  Georges Lacombe, Shepherd Gallery.
"A Dog Days' View of Last Season's Sensations" (September 1, 1974): D17.
"Whimsical Amalgam of Pop Art and Surrealism" (September 15, 1974): D29.
  Jim Nutt, Whitney Museum of American Art.
"Bolotowsky—'A Triumph As Much of a Personality As for a Talent'" (October 6, 1974): D29.
  Ilya Bolotowsky, Solomon R. Guggenheim Museum.
"New Abstract Painting: A Variety of Feelings" (October 13, 1974): D29.
  Continuing Abstraction in American Art exhibition, Whitney Museum Downtown Branch.
"Recasting Rodin's Reputation in Sculpture" (November 24, 1974): D29.
  Rodin and Balzac exhibition, New York Cultural Center.
"Let's Not Read Narrative Art Too Seriously" (December 8, 1974): D35.
  Bill Beckley, John Gibson Gallery.
"Les Levine, from Chewing Gum to Chou En-Lai" (December 22, 1974): D37.
  The Les Levine Group Show, Stefanotty Gallery.
"Public Art Should Be Art for the Public" (January 5, 1975): D29.
"Fragments of an Awesome Whole" (January 19, 1975): D24.
  Robert Motherwell, M. Knoedler & Co.
"The Mysterious Images of Henry Michaux" (February 23, 1975): D35.
  Henri Michaux, Lefebre Gallery.
"Surrealist Films: A Mixture of Fun and Terror" (March 2, 1975): D17.
  Surrealist films, Solomon R. Guggenheim Museum.
Reviews of Art as Art: The Selected Writings of Ad Reinhardt, edited by Barbara Rose. New York: The Viking Press, 1976; and The Art Comics and Satires of Ad Reinhardt, by Thomas B. Hess. Rome: Marlborough Gallery, 1976. Book Review (February 15, 1976): 7.
"An unpredictable maverick of baffling predictions . . . Yes, but . . ." Review of A Critical Study of Philip Guston, by Dore Ashton. New York: The Viking Press, 1976. Book Review (July 4, 1976): 4.
"The Scene." Review of The Scene: Reports on Post-Modern Art, by Calvin

Tompkins. New York: The Viking Press, 1976. *Book Review* (July 25, 1976): 2–3.

"At the Mad Fringes of Art." Review of *Drawings and Digressions*, by Larry Rivers with Carol Brightman. New York: Clarkson N. Potter, 1979. *Book Review* (November 18, 1979): 7, 38.

"Improvising in Art and Life." Review of *Seeing Is Forgetting the Name of the Thing One Sees: A Life of Contemporary Artist Robert Irwin*, by Lawrence Weschler. Berkeley: University of California Press, 1982. *Book Review* (April 18, 1982): 3, 30.

"Reflections of a Dialectical Lover." Review of *And Our Faces, My Heart, Brief as Photos*, by John Berger. New York: Pantheon Books, 1984. *Book Review* (May 13, 1984): 18.

7 Days

"Is New York Necessary?" (March 30, 1988): 56.

"The New Dumb Artists" (April 6, 1988): 47.

George Condo, Pace Gallery.

"Glasnostalgia" (April 13, 1988): 51.

Dutch and Flemish Paintings from the Hermitage exhibition, Metropolitan Museum of Art.

"Magnificent Weirdness" (April 20, 1988): 51.

Jonathan Borofsky, Paula Cooper Gallery.

"Artist as Watchdog" (April 27, 1988): 52.

Hans Haacke, John Weber Gallery.

"Bound and Disciplined" (May 11, 1988): 51, 52.

Altered States group exhibition, Kent Fine Art; Elizabeth Murray exhibition, Whitney Museum of American Art.

"Seeing Things" (May 18, 1988): 50.

Forrest Bess exhibition, Hirschl & Adler Modern Gallery.

"Loving It to Death" (May 25, 1988): 50.

Visions/Revisions group exhibition, Marlborough Gallery.

"Home Wrecker" (June 1, 1988): 50.

Gordon Matta-Clark retrospective, Brooklyn Museum.

"Art *as* Money" (June 8, 1988): 44.

"Space Invaders: Does Sculpture Know Its Place?" (June 22, 1988): 52.

Contemporary Sculpture exhibition, Marian Goodman Gallery.

"A Dance on the Shore: Love, Anxiety, and Edvard Munch" (July 6, 1988): 69.

Modern Treasures from the National Gallery in Prague exhibition, Solomon R. Guggenheim Museum.

339

"David Hockney Minds His Manners, Alas . . ." (July 13, 1988): 46.

David Hockney retrospective, Metropolitan Museum of Art.

"Bang for Bang's Sake: Do-It-Yourself Fireworks" (July 20, 1988): 47–48.

"Life Equals Noise: Can Political Art Be Real Art?" (August 3, 1988): 48.

ACT UP at White Columns AIDS exhibition, White Columns.

"Taste and Hunger: The Mainstreaming of Mapplethorpe" (August 10, 1988): 48.

Robert Mapplethorpe retrospective, Whitney Museum of American Art.

"Hemlines for Skylines" (August 24, 1988): 48.

Deconstructivist Architecture exhibition, Museum of Modern Art.

"Future Ruins" (August 31, 1988): 53.

Battery Park City landfill development art works, New York City.

"Hope and Malice: The Early Word on the Fall Season" (September 7, 1988): 49–50.

"Game Theory" (September 14, 1988): 50.

Baseball and art.

"Martyr without a Cause" (September 21, 1988): 52–54.

Jean Michel Basquiat (1961–1988).

"Daddy Dearest." Review of *Night Studio: A Memoir of Philip Guston*, by Musa Mayer. New York: Alfred A. Knopf, 1988 (September 28, 1988): 51–52.

"Technical Whoop-De-Doo" (September 28, 1988): 18.

Re: New York "architecture."

"New Blue Collar" (October 5, 1988): 59–60.

Mike Kelley, Metro Pictures.

"The Great Gallery Swindle" (October 12, 1988): 60.

Impresario: Malcolm McLaren and the British New Wave exhibition, New Museum of Contemporary Art.

"Losing Face" (October 19, 1988): 59–60.

Edgar Degas, Metropolitan Museum of Art.

"Starnstruck" (October 26, 1988): 58.

Starn Twins, Stux Gallery.

"Kieferville" (November 2, 1988): 60.

Anselm Kiefer, Museum of Modern Art.

"Patronizing Primitives" and "Group Show" (November 16, 1988): 67–68.

Dreamings: The Art of Aboriginal Australia exhibition, Asia Society Galleries; Jasper Johns, Bruce Nauman, and David Salle, Leo Castelli Gallery.

"The Painted Word" (November 23, 1988): 65–66.

Edward Ruscha, Tony Shafrazi Gallery.

"Artsburgh" (November 30, 1988): 62.

Carnegie International exhibition, Carnegie Museum of Art, Pittsburgh, Pennsylvania.

"Looney Koons" (December 14, 1988): 66.

Jeff Koons, Sonnabend Gallery.

"Peep Show" (December 21, 1988): 69–70.

[Gustave] Courbet Reconsidered exhibition, Brooklyn Museum.

"Thok!" (January 4, 1989): 49–52.

Re: November art auctions.

"Up the Damn Ramp" and "Christian Boltanski" (January 11, 1989): 53, 54.

Viewpoints: Postwar Painting and Sculpture exhibition, Solomon R. Guggenheim Museum; Christian Boltanski, New Museum of Contemporary Art.

"She Would Not Yield" (January 18, 1989): 51.

Georgia O'Keeffe, 1887–1986, exhibition, Metropolitan Museum of Art.

"Wild and Crazy Guys" (February 1, 1989): 52–53. Review of *Komar and Melamid*, by Carter Ratcliff. New York: Abbeville Press, 1988.

"Agnes Martin" (February 8, 1989): 55.

Agnes Martin, Pace Gallery.

"White-Out" and "Frederick Kiesler" (February 15, 1989): 55, 56.

Robert Ryman, Dia Art Foundation; Frederick Kiesler, Whitney Museum of American Art.

"Poptimism" (February 22, 1989): 57–58.

Andy Warhol retrospective, Museum of Modern Art.

"Goya Fishing" and "Refigured Painting: The German Image, 1960–88" (March 8, 1989): 54, 55.

A visit to Madrid; The German Images, 1960–88 exhibition, Solomon R. Guggenheim Museum.

"How the West Was Lost" (March 15, 1989): 71.

Frederic Remington: The Masterworks exhibition, Metropolitan Museum of Art.

"La Dolce Vito" (March 22, 1989): 71.

Vito Acconci, Barbara Gladstone Gallery and Sonnabend Gallery.

"Arc Brevis" and "The Great Unknown" (March 29, 1989): 9, 83.

Removal of Serra sculpture; Susan Hiller, Pat Hearn Gallery.

"Little Show of Horrors" (April 12, 1989): 62.

Cindy Sherman, Metro Pictures.

"Earthy but Housebroken" (April 19, 1989): 64–65.

Alison Wilding, Hirschl & Adler Modern Gallery; Anish Kapoor, Barbara Gladstone Gallery.

"The Beuys Stratagem" (April 26, 1989): 66–67.

Sigmar Polke, Mary Boone Gallery.

"A Biennial of Our Own" (May 3, 1989): 23–31.

A fantasy biennial curated by Rosetta Brooks, Dennis Cooper, Manuel Gonzalez, Walter Robinson, and Ingrid Sischy.

"Burton on Brancusi" (May 3, 1989): 64.

Burton on Brancusi exhibition, Museum of Modern Art.

"The Muses on Strike" (May 17, 1989): 67.

1989 Biennial exhibition, Whitney Museum of American Art.

"Prissy Wall Labels" (May 31, 1989): 62.

Goya and the Spirit of Enlightenment exhibition, Metropolitan Museum of Art.

"Flavin of the Week" (June 7, 1989): 62.

Dan Flavin, Leo Castelli Gallery.

"Arnulf Rainer" (June 14, 1989): 62.

Arnulf Rainer retrospective, Solomon R. Guggenheim Museum.

"Big Blobs of Color" (June 21, 1989): 60.

Helen Frankenthaler retrospective, Museum of Modern Art.

"Jeff Koons: Can His Silver Bunny Hold All That Hot Air?" (July 12, 1989): 14.

"Pawn Shop" (July 26, 1989): 54.

Lafayette, Hero of Two Worlds: The Art and Pageantry of His Farewell Tour of America, 1824–1825, exhibition, Queens Museum.

"A Treason of Clerks" (August 2, 1989): 53.

Controversy surrounding the work of Robert Mapplethorpe, Andres Serrano, and Dread Scott Tyler; and the self-censorship of the Corcoran Gallery of Art.

"Gallery-phobia" (August 16, 1989): 51.

Intimidation by art galleries.

"Theory-itis" (August 23, 1989): 51.

The Desire of the Museum exhibition, Whitney Museum of American Art, Wall Street area branch.

"Exhibit A" (September 6, 1989): 47.

Portrait of Joseph Roulin by Vincent van Gogh, a new acquisition, Museum of Modern Art.

"Poor Helga" (September 20, 1989): 67.

Mughal Paintings and Andrew Wyeth: The Helga Pictures exhibitions, Brooklyn Museum.

"Now Voyeur" (September 27, 1989): 67.

Edward Hopper: Selections from the Permanent Collection exhibition, Whitney Museum of American Art.

"Paperweight" (October 4, 1989): 67.

Sherrie Levine, Mary Boone Gallery.

"Icy Cubism" (October 11, 1989): 68.
Picasso and Braque: Pioneering Cubism exhibition, Museum of Modern Art.
"Mr. Cool" (October 18, 1989): 72.
Diego Velázquez retrospective, Metropolitan Museum of Art.
"Dancing on the Flag" (October 25, 1989): 67.
To Push & to Probe exhibition, Wessel O'Connor Gallery; Jules Olitski, Andre Emmerich Gallery.
"Brainy Bliss" (November 1, 1989): 68.
Chris Burden, Kent Fine Art.
"Greenpieces" (November 8, 1989): 69–70.
Ashley Bickerton, Sonnabend Gallery.
"Tomorrowland" (November 29, 1989): 63–64.
Image World: Art and Media Culture exhibition, Whitney Museum of American Art.
"Red Apple" (December 13, 1989): 70.
Erik Bulatov, Phyllis Kind Gallery.
"Love Conquers Wall" (December 27, 1989): 66.
Three days in Berlin.
"In Your Eye" (January 10, 1990): 70–71.
New Year's "Toasts" to New York museums and artists.
"Says Who?" (January 17, 1990): 50–51.
Jenny Holzer, Solomon R. Guggenheim Museum.
"Save the Whitney" (January 24, 1990): 52.
"Painter's Painter" (February 7, 1990): 50–51.
Bob Thompson, Vanderwoude / Tananbaum.
"Painted Words" (February 21, 1990): 53–54.
Robert Yarber, Sonnabend Gallery; Storyline exhibition, Edward Thorp Gallery; Gary Stephan, Mary Boone Gallery.
"Neo-Smut" (March 7, 1990): 63–64.
Territory of Desire exhibition, Louver Gallery; Odalisque exhibition, Jane H. Baum Gallery.
"Photo Synthesis" (March 14, 1990): 50–51.
Photography until Now exhibition, Museum of Modern Art; Moving Pictures: Films by Photographers series, Public Theater.
"Daredevil" (March 28, 1990): 52–53.
Bruce Nauman, Leo Castelli Gallery and Sperone Westwater.
"Toontown" (April 4, 1990): 60–61.
John Wesley, Fiction/Nonfiction Gallery; Steven Gianakos, Barbara Toll Gallery.
"Bully Boys" (April 11, 1990): 63–64.

Georg Baselitz, Michael Werner Gallery; Martin Kippenberger, Metro Pictures.

Magazines

Art News

Reviews and Previews. 64 (December 1965): 12–20.
  Unsigned short notices.
Reviews and Previews. 64 (January 1966): 10–16.
  Armando Baldinelli and Graham Redgrave-Rust, Jason Gallery; Barbara Bisgyer, Environment Gallery; Chen Chi, Ken Davies, Henry Gasser, and Joseph Sheppard, Grand Central Gallery; Don Gottschalk, Art Collector's Place; Martin Maloney, Sieglaub Gallery; Roy Medders, Selected Artists Gallery; Jane Orcutt-Blatter and Dorothy Rawles, Duncan Gallery; Ed Randel, Spectrum Gallery; Joan Lam Schwartz, Barzansky Gallery; Ladislas Segy, White Gallery; Gene Smith (da Lamoureux), Lerner Gallery.
Reviews and Previews. 64 (February 1966): 12–19, 52–54.
  Marion Bellod, Midge Karr, and Blanche Mayer, Barzansky Gallery; Ojars Bisenicks and Margareta Hylten-Cavallius, Duncan Gallery; Frank Pietrantonio, Pietrantonio Gallery; Margaret Harvey Shotwell, Shuster Gallery; Dora Simonyi, Crespi Gallery; Edward Whiteman, Sieglaub Gallery; prints at Wittenborn's.
Reviews and Previews. 65 (March 1966): 10–19, 64.
  Claude Assian and Zoltan Hecht, Galerie Internationale; Ariane Berman, Salpeter Gallery; Mary Bohan and Robert Newman, One Eleven Gallery; Jules Engel, White Gallery; Robert Ludwig, Phoenix Gallery; Salpi Mavian, AGBU Gallery; Edward Meneeley, Teuscher Gallery; Franco Minei, Selected Artists Gallery; Helen Seasonwein, Barzansky Gallery.
Reviews and Previews. 65 (April 1966): 15, 55.
  Drachler, Brata Gallery; Florence Weinstein, Phoenix Gallery.
Reviews and Previews. 65 (May 1966): 16–20, 54–55.
  Sanford Fraser, Spectrum Gallery; Kusama and Clara Skinner, Castallane Gallery; Heinz Mack, Wise Gallery; William McCartin, Nash Gallery; Tamara Melcher, Park Place Gallery; Jack Moore, John Perreault, Regina Snyder, and Ted Wester, One Eleven Gallery; Kenneth Snelson, Dwan Gallery; Margery Soroka, Studio Workshop; Lars Spark, Duncan Gallery.

Reviews and Previews. 65 (Summer 1966): 10–18.

Francis Celentano and Minoru Niizuma, Wise Gallery; Peter Forakis and Edwin Ruda, Park Place Gallery; Alfred Jensen, Marks Gallery; Edna Schmerler and Earl Zehner, Insel Gallery.

Reviews and Previews. 65 (September 1966): 14–15.

Christo, Leo Castelli Gallery; Miles R. Hodson, Jason Gallery.

Reviews and Previews. 65 (October 1966): 10–15, 64.

Will Barnet and George Mueller, Waddell Gallery; Zevi Blum, Peter Takal, and Elizabeth Mamorsky, Contemporaries Gallery; Silvana Cenci, Wataru Fuki, and James Kroeplin, Capricorn Gallery; Ira Kaufman, Brata Gallery; Ivan Tabakovic, Dorsky Gallery.

Reviews and Previews. 65 (November 1966): 12–13, 62, 66.

Peter Forakis, Park Place Gallery; Frederic Hobbs and Jay Robinson, XXth Century West Gallery; David Millstone, Alonzo Gallery.

Reviews and Previews. 65 (December 1966): 8, 11–14, 59.

Roy Adzak, Sachs Gallery; James Gill, Landau-Alan Gallery; Be'van der Heide, New Masters Gallery; Sinan A. Korle and Edis Tezel, Sawdust Gallery; Frank Metz, Roko Gallery; Richard Smith, Richard L. Feigen and Co.

"Urban Pastorals: The Manhattan Scene." 69 (February 1971): 32–33, 60, 62.

Jane Freilicher, John B. Meyers Gallery.

"De Kooning: Subtle Renewals." 71 (November 1972): 21–23.

Willem de Kooning, Sidney Janis Gallery.

Art International

New York Letter. 13 (April 20, 1969): 62–67.

Les Levine, Fischbach Gallery plus sited work; Robert Smithson, Dwan Gallery; Lester Johnson, Martha Jackson Gallery; Allan D'Arcangelo, Fischbach Gallery; Giorgio Cavallon, A. M. Sachs Gallery; Takis, Howard Wise Gallery; Ronald Mallory, Galeria Bonino; Craig Kauffman, Pace Gallery; Ralph Humphrey, Bykert Gallery; Konrad Klapneck, Sidney Janis Gallery; Varujan Boghosian, Cordier-Ekstrom Gallery; Group, Lawrence Rubin Gallery; Larry Rivers, Gotham Book Mart.

New York Letter. 13 (May 20, 1969): 34–39.

Willem de Kooning retrospective, Museum of Modern Art; Jackson Pollock, Marlborough-Gerson Gallery; Joe Brainard, Landau-Alan Gallery; Oyvind Fahlstrom, Sidney Janis Gallery; Paul Thek, Stable Gallery; Charles Ross, Dwan Gallery; Peter Alexander, Elkon Gallery; David Carr, Bertha Schaefer Gallery; Fernando Botero, Center for Inter-American Relations; Peter Agostino, Radich Gallery; Kenzo Okada,

Betty Parsons Gallery; Jason Seley, Kornblee Gallery; Paul Morgensen, Bykert Gallery; Doug Ohlson, Fischbach Gallery; Darby Bannard, Tibor de Nagy Gallery.

New York Letter. 13 (Summer 1969): 65–69.
Barnett Newman, M. Knoedler & Co.; Stella, Noland, and Olitski exhibition, Lawrence Rubin Gallery; James Rosenquist, Leo Castelli Gallery; Lyonel Feininger, Marlborough-Gerson Gallery; Herbert Ferber, Andre Emmerich Gallery; Frederick Kiesler, Howard Wise Gallery; Harvey Quaytman and Robert Huot, Paula Cooper Gallery; Sylvia Stone, Tibor de Nagy Gallery; George Sugarman, Fischbach Gallery; Walter De Maria, Dwan Gallery; Edgar Negret, Galeria Bonino; Arthur Kern, Ruth White Gallery; Richard Anuszkiewicz, Sidney Janis Gallery; Ben Cunningham, A. M. Sachs Gallery; Nicolas Krushenick, Pace Gallery; Morteza Sazegar, Poindexter Gallery; John Healey, Waddell Gallery.

New York Letter. 13 (September 1969): 70–73.
Anti-Illusion: Procedure/Materials exhibition, Whitney Museum of American Art; Nine Young Artists exhibition, Solomon R. Guggenheim Museum; Bruce Nauman, Leo Castelli Gallery; Richard Serra; Robert Ryman, Fischbach Gallery; Carl Andre, Dwan Gallery; Lynda Benglis and Richard Van Buren, Bykert Gallery; Etienne Hadju, M. Knoedler & Co.; Robert Motherwell, Marlborough-Gerson Gallery; Leon Berkowitz and Alice Barber, A. M. Sachs Gallery.

New York Letter. 13 (October 1969): 74–79.
The New American Painting and Sculpture: The First Generation exhibition, Museum of Modern Art; de Kooning, Newman, and Gorky, M. Knoedler & Co.; Language III exhibition, Dwan Gallery; Afro-American Artists: Since 1950 exhibition and Bob Thompson, Brooklyn Museum Gallery; Harlem Artists 69 exhibition, Studio Museum in Harlem; Inflatable Sculpture exhibition, Jewish Museum; Alexander Calder, Perls Galleries; Lucas Samaras, Museum of Modern Art.

New York Letter. 13 (November 1969): 69–73.
Claes Oldenburg retrospective, Museum of Modern Art; Direct Representation exhibition curated by Scott Burton at Fischbach Gallery; Abstract Illusionism exhibition, Tibor de Nagy Gallery; Peter Gourfain, Bykert Gallery; Barry Flanagan, Fischbach Gallery; Lynda Benglis, Alan Shields, and Gary Dobosen, Paul Cooper Gallery; Esteban Vicente, Andre Emmerich Gallery; Ecologic Art exhibition, John Gibson's "Projects for Commissions"; Therese Schwartz, A. M. Sachs Gallery; David Chapin and Allan Robinson, Hemingway Galleries; Amilcar De Castro,

Kornblee Gallery; Tibor Freund and Aaronel de Gruber, Bertha Schaefer Gallery.
"Bluhm's Progress." 18 (May 1974): 35, 38.
Norman Bluhm.

Art in America

"Movies: *Carnal Knowledge*." 60 (January 1972): 100–101.
"James Sullivan at Paley & Lowe, New York." 60 (January 1972): 35–36.
"Rosenquist Synthesis." 60 (March 1972): 56–61.
Preview of James Rosenquist retrospective, Whitney Museum of American Art.
"Vito Acconci at Sonnabend." 60 (March 1972): 119.
"Robert Ryman at the Guggenheim." 60 (May 1972): 33–34.
"Robert Duran at Bykert." 61 (January 1973): 114.
"De Kooning's Sculpture: Amplified Touch." 62 (March 1974): 59–63.
Willem de Kooning, Walker Art Center, Minneapolis.
"Letter from Chicago." 64 (July 1976): 52–58.
"Late Cézanne: A Symposium." 66 (March 1978): 93.
"Rothko and Belief." 67 (March–April 1979): 78–85.
Mark Rothko retrospective, Solomon R. Guggenheim Museum.
"Munch: The Missing Master." 67 (May–June 1979): 80–95.
Edvard Munch retrospective, National Gallery of Art, Washington, D.C.
"Warhol and Class Content." 68 (May 1980): 111–119.
Andy Warhol's Portraits of the 70s exhibition, Whitney Museum of American Art.
"Anxieties of Eminence: Recent Exhibitions and Catalogs Devoted to the Drawings of Four Major Postwar Figures—Pollock, Newman, Louis, and Smith." 68 (September 1980): 106–115.
Jackson Pollock, Museum of Modern Art; Barnett Newman, Metropolitan Museum of Art; David Smith, Whitney Museum of American Art; Morris Louis, Fogg Art Museum, Harvard University.
"Steiner's Confidence: His Recent Frontal Sculpture." 68 (October 1980): 124–126.
Michael Steiner, Andre Emmerich Gallery.
"Picasso: A Symposium." 68 (December 1980): 11–12.
"Eye of the Revolution." 69 (April 1981): 76–91.
The Avant-Garde in Russia, 1910–1930: New Perspectives exhibition, Los Angeles County Museum of Art.
"Shermanettes." 70 (March 1982): 110–111.
Cindy Sherman, Metro Pictures.

"Postcards from Scandinavia." 70 (September 1982): 51–53, 55.
"The Real Salle." 72 (September 1984): 180–187.
    David Salle, Leo Castelli Gallery.
Issues and Commentary: "Welcome to Helgaland." 74 (October 1986): 11, 13.
    Re: Andrew Wyeth's portraits of Helga.
"A Visit to the Salon of Autumn 1986." 74 (December 1986): 15–21.
"Julian Schnabel at Pace." 75 (January 1987): 129–130.
"Andy Warhol, 1928–1987." 75 (May 1987): 137.
    Memorial.
"Our Kiefer." 76 (March 1988): 116–126.
    Anselm Kiefer retrospective, Art Institute of Chicago and Philadelphia
    Museum of Art.

Vanity Fair

"Falling in Style: The New Art and Our Discontents." 46 (March 1983): 115–
    116, 252, 254.
"Up against the Wall: A Berlin Story." 46 (April 1983): 92–97, 162.
    Zeitgeist exhibition, West Berlin.
"Profoundly Practical Jokes: The Art of Bruce Nauman." 46 (May 1983): 88–
    93.
"American Gothic Again: The Grant Wood Revival." 46 (June 1983): 93–99.
    Grant Wood retrospective, Whitney Museum of American Art.
"Putting Painting Back on Its Feet: Susan Rothenberg Talks about Art, An-
    imals, and 'Getting Serious.'" 46 (August 1983): 82–85.
"Love of Manet." 46 (October 1983): 62–68.
    Edouard Manet retrospective, Metropolitan Museum of Art.
"The Anti-Master Now." 46 (January 1984): 66–73.
    Willem de Kooning exhibition, Whitney Museum of American Art.
"Spain: The Structure of Ritual." 47 (March 1984): 61–66.
"In Defense of Artistic Fashion." 47 (April 1984): 97.
"Bad Boy of Brilliance." 47 (May 1984): 66–72.
    Eric Fischl.

Miscellaneous

"The Hydrogen Jukebox: Terror, Narcissism, and Art." *Journal: A Contem-
    porary Art Magazine* 10 (October–November 1978): 44–46. Reprinted with
    update in *The New Common Good* (June 1985): 1, 5–6.
"Painterly Jewelry by Robert Ebendorf." *American Craft* 40 (June–July 1980):
    24–27.
    Robert Ebendorf, Florence Duhl Gallery.

"David Salle Interview." *LAICA Journal Contemporary Art Magazine* 30 (September–October 1981): 15–21.

"Edward Ruscha." *Arts and Architecture* 3 (August 1982): 23, 26–27.

"High-Tact Photojournalism." *Camera Arts* 2 (September 1982): 8, 10–12. James Hamilton.

"Rembrandt's Lucretia." *ARTS* of the Minneapolis Society of Fine Arts (November 1983): 16–17.

"Pretty Babies." *Art & Antiques* 5 (March 1984): 91–96. Balthus retrospective, Metropolitan Museum of Art.

"The Illicit Joy of Dufy." *Vogue* 174 (November 1984): 454–457. Raoul Dufy, Holly Solomon Gallery.

"Un romantisme réaliste et austère," *Art Press* (Paris) 90 (February 1985): 32–33. Scott Burton.

"Post-Innocence: Eric Fischl and the Social Fate of American Painting." *Parkett* 5 (1985): 31–43. Eric Fischl's fall 1984 exhibition, Mary Boone Gallery.

"'Chicagoization': Some Second Thoughts on the Second City." *New Art Examiner* 12 (May 1985): 28–32.

"98A Boundary Road." *House and Garden* 157 (June 1985): 136–139, 210. Architect Max Gordon's Saatchi Collection building.

"Anselm Kiefer and the Exodus of the Jews." *Art & Text* 19 (October–December 1985): 4–11. Anselm Kiefer's Departure from Egypt exhibition, Marian Goodman Gallery.

"Eric Fischl's Vanity." *Art & Text* 20 (June 1986): 57–58.

"The Happy and the Unhappy." *Harpers* 272 (June 1986): 30–31.

"The Uses of Shame." *ICI Newsletter* (Independent Curators Incorporated) 1 (Fall 1986): recto & verso.

"Irony and Agony." *In These Times* (August 20–September 2, 1986): 24, 23.

"Art Lovers and Other Strangers: A Distant View of L.A. Mania." *Los Angeles Herald Examiner*, California Living section (November 16, 1986): 12–13.

"De Kooning Alone." *Art Journal* 48, no. 3 (Fall 1989): 247.

Catalogue and Monograph Essays

"Talking about Larry Zox." *Larry Zox*. Hanover, New Hampshire: Jaffe-Friede Gallery, Hopkins Center, Dartmouth College, 1969, 5–7.

Foreword to *Recent Work by Fairfield Porter*. New York: Hirschl & Adler Galleries, 1972, 3–11.

"Six Painters." *Six Painters of the Seventies: Abstract Painting in New York.* Chapel Hill, North Carolina: William Hayes Ackland Memorial Art Center, 1973, 4–5.

"De Kooning's Sculpture." *De Kooning—Drawings/Sculpture.* New York: Walker Art Center & E. P. Dutton & Company, Inc., 1974, 33–43. Reprinted with changes as "De Kooning's Sculpture So Far." In *De Kooning: Paintings, Drawings, Sculpture, 1967–1975.* West Palm Beach, Florida: Norton Gallery of Art, 1975, 7–22.

"Notes on Studio Graffiti." *United Graffiti Artists, 1975.* New York: Artists Space, United Graffiti Writers Inc., 1975, 10–11.

"Reinhardt's Needle." *Ad Reinhardt: Art Comics and Satires.* New York: Truman Gallery, 1976, portfolio cover sheet, verso and recto.

"East and West and Robert Hudson." *Robert Hudson.* Philadelphia: Moore College of Art Gallery, 1978, 7–10.

"Dubuffet, 1980." *Jean Dubuffet.* New York: The Pace Gallery, 1980, 3–10.

"Lucas Samaras: The Pastels." *Samaras Pastels.* Denver: Denver Art Museum, 1981, 6–16.

"Decade of Wonders." *Abstract Painting: 1960–1969.* Long Island City: P.S. 1, 1982, 12–13.
    1960s abstract painting exhibition, P.S. 1.

"Art at the Gates of Hell." *New Figuration in America.* Milwaukee: Milwaukee Art Center, 1982, 16–18.

"Minimalism." Bk. 1 of *Art of Our Time: The Saatchi Collection.* New York: Rizzoli, 1984, 11–24.

"Andy Warhol." Bk. 2 of *Art of Our Time: The Saatchi Collection.* New York: Rizzoli, 1984, 28–29.

"Philip Guston." Bk. 3 of *Art of Our Time: The Saatchi Collection.* New York: Rizzoli, 1984, 12–14.

"Anselm Kiefer." Bk. 3 of *Art of Our Time: The Saatchi Collection.* New York: Rizzoli, 1984, 15–17.

"The Oracle of Images." *Cindy Sherman.* New York: Pantheon Books, 1984, 7–11.

"Toward a New Miró." *Miró: Sculpture, April 27–June 9, 1984.* New York: The Pace Gallery, 1984, 4–8.

"David Salle." *David Salle: Sieben Bilder.* Cologne: Michael Werner Gallery, 1985, 3–20.

"Ed Ruscha: Traffic and Laughter." *Edward Ruscha.* Lyon, France: Musée Saint Pierre Art Contemporain, 1985, 40–53.

"The Daemon and Sigmar Polke." *Sigmar Polke.* New York: Mary Boone/ Michael Werner Gallery, 1985, 4–5.

"Jensen's Difficulty." *Alfred Jensen: Paintings and Works on Paper.* New York: Solomon R. Guggenheim Museum, 1985, 21–26.

"Leon Golub." *Leon Golub*. New York: Mary Boone/Michael Werner Gallery, 1986, 7–9.

"The Kirkeby Effect." *Per Kirkeby*. New York: Mary Boone Gallery, 1986, 4–5.

"The Smart Pot: Adrian Saxe and Post-Everything Ceramics." *Adrian Saxe*. Kansas City: University of Missouri Gallery of Art, 1986, 13–17.

"An Interview with David Salle." *Salle*. New York: Random House, Inc., Elizabeth Avedon Editions, 1987, 9–75.

"A Park for the Prairie God." *The Nathan Manilow Sculpture Park*. University Park, Illinois: Governor's State University Foundation, 1987, 8–44.

"Marrying Abstraction." *Brice Marden*. New York: Mary Boone Gallery, 1987, 6–11.

"Contemporary American Art." *Contemporary American Art*. Tampere, Finland: Sara Hilden Art Museum, 1988.

"Richard Deacon." *Richard Deacon*. New York: Marian Goodman Gallery, 1988, 3–26.

"The Tone of Labor." *Richard Deacon*. Pittsburgh: The Carnegie Museum of Art, 1988, 59–69.

"The Structure of Who: Jackie Winsor's Sculpture." *Jackie Winsor*. Locamine, France: Centre d'Art Contemporain du Domaine de Kerguehennec, 1988, 4–12.

"Spiritual Materialism: Ross Bleckner's New Paintings." *Ross Bleckner*. London: Waddington Galleries, 1988, 4–7.

"Hopperesque." *Edward Hopper: Light Years*. New York: Hirschl & Adler Gallery, 1988, 5–12.

"Witness." Introduction to *Eric Fischl*. New York: Art in America/Stewart, Tabori & Chang, 1988, 9–30.

"The New Wegman." *William Wegman*. Saint-Etienne, France: Maison de la Culture et de la Communication de Saint-Etienne, 1989, 11–19.

Poetry

"Dear Profession of Art Writing." *Since 1964: New and Selected Poems*. New York: SUN, 1978, 12–20. (Reprinted in "On Art and Artists: Peter Schjeldahl." *Profile* 3, no. 4 [July 1983]: 16–22.)

"I Missed Punk." *The Brute*. Los Angeles: Little Caesar, 1981, 7–8.

"Absent Minded Female Nude on Bed. (For David Salle)." *Artforum* 20 (December 1981): 49.

"The Artist." *Since 1964: New and Selected Poems*. New York: SUN, 1978, 22–23. (Reprinted in "On Art and Artists: Peter Schjeldahl." *Profile* 3, no. 4 [July 1983]: 7–8.)

"To Pico." *Guacamole Airlines and Other Drawings by Edward Ruscha*. New York: Harry N. Abrams, 1978, 6–7.

Interview/Transcribed Lecture

Interview by Robert Storr. Video interview transcribed as "On Art and Artists: Peter Schjeldahl." *Profile* 3, no. 4 (July 1983).

"A Personal Overview." Lecture presented at Adelaide University Union House, Australia, and transcribed in *Adelaide* (June–July 1986): 18–21.

INDEX

Designer:	Sandy Drooker
Compositor:	Wilsted & Taylor
Text:	11/13 Granjon
Display:	Granjon
Printer:	Malloy Lithographing, Inc.
Binder:	John H. Dekker & Sons